Transparency, Society and Subjectivity

"Incessantly invoked as a necessary condition of all aspects of democratic life, transparency is being hailed as a top priority in public management, corporate business, and international relations. But the more we critically examine what transparency actually means, the more it emerges as an opaque, and perhaps even occluding, concept. By offering a bold and comprehensive picture of the new field of Critical Transparency Studies, this collection of essays is certain to become the standard reference for years to come."
—Giovanna Borradori, *Professor of Philosophy at Vassar College, USA*

"This important collection historicizes and criticizes transparency, one of neoliberalism's most ubiquitous norms. As the contributors draw out the normative presumptions of the concept, they alert us to its regulatory effects, its implications for surveillance and subjectivation. Rather than an ideal of democratic freedom, transparency mobilizes distrust and commands exposure. Crucial reading for anyone interested in critical assessment of our present values."
—Jodi Dean, *Hobart and William Smith Colleges, USA, and author of Publicity's Secret: How Technoculture Capitalizes on Democracy (2002)*

Emmanuel Alloa • Dieter Thomä
Editors

Transparency, Society and Subjectivity

Critical Perspectives

palgrave
macmillan

Editors
Emmanuel Alloa
School of Humanities and Social Sciences
University of St. Gallen
St. Gallen, Switzerland

Dieter Thomä
School of Humanities and Social Sciences
University of St. Gallen
St. Gallen, Switzerland

ISBN 978-3-319-77160-1   ISBN 978-3-319-77161-8 (eBook)
https://doi.org/10.1007/978-3-319-77161-8

Library of Congress Control Number: 2018937890

© The Editor(s) (if applicable) and The Author(s) 2018
This work is subject to copyright. All rights are solely and exclusively licensed by the Publisher, whether the whole or part of the material is concerned, specifically the rights of translation, reprinting, reuse of illustrations, recitation, broadcasting, reproduction on microfilms or in any other physical way, and transmission or information storage and retrieval, electronic adaptation, computer software, or by similar or dissimilar methodology now known or hereafter developed.
The use of general descriptive names, registered names, trademarks, service marks, etc. in this publication does not imply, even in the absence of a specific statement, that such names are exempt from the relevant protective laws and regulations and therefore free for general use.
The publisher, the authors and the editors are safe to assume that the advice and information in this book are believed to be true and accurate at the date of publication. Neither the publisher nor the authors or the editors give a warranty, express or implied, with respect to the material contained herein or for any errors or omissions that may have been made. The publisher remains neutral with regard to jurisdictional claims in published maps and institutional affiliations.

Cover illustration: BubbleTree, www.bubbletree.fr, Pierre-Stéphane Dumas

Printed on acid-free paper

This Palgrave Macmillan imprint is published by the registered company Springer International Publishing AG part of Springer Nature.
The registered company address is: Gewerbestrasse 11, 6330 Cham, Switzerland

Contents

Transparency: Thinking Through an Opaque Concept   1
Emmanuel Alloa and Dieter Thomä

Not such Wicked Leaks   15
Umberto Eco

Part I   Transparency in the Making   19

Transparency: A Magic Concept of Modernity   21
Emmanuel Alloa

Seeing It All, Doing It All, Saying It All: Transparency, Subject, and the World   57
Dieter Thomä

The Dream of Transparency: Aquinas, Rousseau, Sartre   85
Manfred Schneider

v

The Unbounded Confession 105
Noreen Khawaja

Seeing It All: Bentham's Panopticon and the Dark Spots
of Enlightenment 133
Miran Božovič

Transparency, Humanism, and the Politics of the Future Before
and After May '68 155
Stefanos Geroulanos

Part II   Under the Crystal Dome 177

The Limits of Transparency 179
Amitai Etzioni

Publicity and Transparency: The Itinerary of a Subtle
Distinction 203
Sandrine Baume

Regulation and Transparency as Rituals of Distrust: Reading
Niklas Luhmann Against the Grain 225
Caspar Hirschi

Not Individuals, Relations: What Transparency Is Really
About. A Theory of Algorithmic Governmentality 243
Thomas Berns

Obfuscated Transparency 259
Dieter Mersch

The Privatization of Human Interests or, How Transparency
Breeds Conformity   283
Thomas Docherty

Part III   From the Panopticon to the Selfie and Back   305

Transparency and Subjectivity: Remembering Jennifer
Ringley   307
Vincent Kaufmann

Putting Oneself Out There: The "Selfie" and the Alter-Rithmic
Transformations of Subjectivity   323
Jörg Metelmann and Thomas Telios

Interrupting Transparency   343
Clare Birchall

Virtual Transparency: From the Panopticon to the Expository
Society and Beyond   369
Bernard E. Harcourt

Author Index   393

Subject Index   403

Notes on Contributors

Emmanuel Alloa is Research Leader in Philosophy at the University of St. Gallen.

Sandrine Baume is Associate Professor at the Centre for Public Law in the Faculty of Law and Criminal Justice at the University of Lausanne.

Thomas Berns is Senior Lecturer in Political Philosophy and Ethics at the Free University of Brussels (ULB).

Clare Birchall is Senior Lecturer in Contemporary Culture in the Department of English at King's College London.

Miran Božovič is Professor of Early modern philosophy at the Faculty of Arts of the University of Ljubljana.

Thomas Docherty is Professor of English and Comparative Literature at the University of Warwick.

Umberto Eco (†) was a novelist, literary critic and professor in semiotics at the University of Bologna.

Amitai Etzioni is Professor of International Affairs at George Washington University.

Stefanos Geroulanos is Associate Professor of European History at New York University, and Director of the Center for International Research in the Humanities and Social Sciences.

Bernard E. Harcourt is Isidor and Seville Sulzbacher Professor of Law at Columbia University and Director of the Columbia Center for Contemporary Critical Thought.

Caspar Hirschi is Professor of History at the University St. Gallen.

Vincent Kaufmann is Professor of French Literature, Media and Culture at the University of St. Gallen.

Noreen Khawaja is Associate Professor of Religious Studies at Yale University.

Dieter Mersch is Philosophy chair and Head of the Institute for Theory at the Zurich University of the Arts.

Jörg Metelmann is Associate Professor of Culture and Media Studies at the University of St. Gallen.

Manfred Schneider is Professor of German Literature at the Ruhr-Universität Bochum.

Thomas Telios is Lecturer in Philosophy at the University of St. Gallen.

Dieter Thomä is Professor of Philosophy at the University of St. Gallen.

List of Figures

Transparency: A Magic Concept of Modernity
Fig. 1 Hajo Rose, *Untitled* [*Self-Portrait with Dessau Façade (double exposure)*], 1930. © Hajo Rose Estate and Artists Rights Society (ARS), New York/VG Bild-Kunst   26
Fig. 2 László Moholy-Nagy, *Space Modulator* [*Transparency Plus!*], 1940, 33.7 × 25.4 cm. *Private Collection*. Photo: Milton Halberstadt   50
Fig. 3 Siegfried Giedion, *Space, Time and Architecture: The growth of the new tradition*, 2nd edition Cambridge: The Harvard University Press, 1949, pp. 426–427   51

Publicity and Transparency: The Itinerary of a Subtle Distinction
Fig. 1 Google Books Ngram Viewer, instances of publicity and transparency, 1800–2008. Source: Ngram/Sandrine Baume   205

Virtual Transparency: From the Panopticon to the Expository Society and Beyond
Fig. 1 Dan Graham, Günther Vogt *Hedge Two-Way Mirror Walkabout*, Installation Metropolitan Museum, New York, (2014). Photographs copyright © Tod Seelie, reproduced by permission   379

xi

Transparency: Thinking Through an Opaque Concept

Emmanuel Alloa and Dieter Thomä

In his novel *The Circle* (2013), acclaimed fiction writer Dave Eggers presents the reader with an almost Orwellian vision of a near future of a totally transparent society. Eggers' vision, later adapted as a Hollywood screenplay and brought to the big screen by Emma Watson and Tom Hanks, is set in Silicon Valley, and revolves around a company—The Circle—which embodies all the promises of a tech-driven society. For The Circle (depicted as decidedly vicious), all behavior can been driven by an algorithm. The trinitarian dogma of Orwell's *1984* echoes unmistakably in Dave Eggers' novel. Whereas in *1984*, the surveillance state had proclaimed that "War is peace, freedom is slavery, ignorance is strength," in the new, libertarian and Web 2.0 version of the surveillance state, the credo is summarized in the following mantra-like principle: "Secrets are Lies, Privacy is Theft, Sharing is Caring."

Even in 1999, Sun Microsystems CEO Scott McNealy had put this straightforwardly: "You have no privacy, get over it." In the past, it was

---

E. Alloa (✉) • D. Thomä
School of Humanities and Social Sciences, University of St. Gallen,
St. Gallen, Switzerland
e-mail: emmanuel.alloa@unisg.ch; dieter.thomae@unisg.ch

© The Author(s) 2018
E. Alloa, D. Thomä (eds.), *Transparency, Society and Subjectivity*,
https://doi.org/10.1007/978-3-319-77161-8_1

part of a certain Puritan ethos to live without curtains, signaling that there was nothing to hide. Today, technology thrusts transparency upon everybody. Resistance to this unauthorized and undesired transparency remains rather marginal, and the reason may be that shedding full light onto subjective conduct and behavior is believed to have a positive effect. Being watched, so the belief goes, automatically leads to more moral action, consistent with the Supreme Court Justice Louis Brandeis's famous statement at the beginning of the twentieth century that "Sunlight is said to be the best of disinfectants." One hundred years later, there is a growing consensus that transparency is one of democracy's best tools and that every citizen has a right to transparency. Demands for more transparency are more widespread than ever, in fields as diverse as corporate and public administration, finance, scientific research, sports, technology, media, and healthcare. Transparency is not restricted to the social or corporate spheres, however, but is also seen as an effective way to increase accountability and responsibility on an individual level: acting under the gaze of the public eye leads to more ethical behavior, or so we're told. As opposed to concepts like regulation or surveillance, transparency doesn't seem to have a negative counterpart that would counter its ambitions. In a certain sense, thus, it could be said that the demands of transparency are unlimited as it lacks a corrective or does not allow for any "Outside."

Perhaps the ultimate consensual value of our time, transparency has been invoked by Barack Obama and whistleblower Edward Snowden alike, by Wikileaks founder Julian Assange but also by Facebook CEO Mark Zuckerberg. Yet nothing is less clear than what exactly is meant when the word "transparency" is used. At a moment when institutions start releasing transparency reports, including national intelligence agencies, one might wonder if this is more than a merely rhetoric exercise: releasing documents and figures alone can hardly count as a guarantee for accountability, and besides, this overflow of data can even be seen as a strategy of opacification. Quite often, transparency is only affected, simulated, through deliberate practices of data-flooding ("drowning in disclosure") no average citizen can make sense of.

At times the power of "transparency" appears to lie in its mere utterance, as if it were a magic formula whose meaning doesn't need to be understood for its effects to be felt. But what *does* "transparency" refer to?

The metaphoric level of the notion seems to strangely mirror its literal meaning: the perfectly transparent window is one which completely diverts the attention from itself. The less we see the windowpane, the more we see through it. But having seeing-through be synonymous with overlooking, makes it easy to understand why transparency—as an operative concept—rarely is an object of reflection in its own right.

Fortunately, these last years have seen the emergence of a yet small, but rapidly growing field dedicated precisely to this kind of reflection: Critical Transparency Studies. Unlike the now virtually infinite scholarly literature about transparency policies, which mainly studies how transparency is implemented in public management, corporate businesses, and other national and transnational contexts, Critical Transparency Studies start with questioning that transparency has a stable semantic core. What they share is the sense that one must ask for the reasons lying behind the sudden rise of this catchword. Their approach to transparency also entails determining what transparency stands for. Undeniably, to think through transparency means to think through an opaque concept.

The book gathers some of the most prominent voices from this emerging field. By combining various approaches to the problem (philosophy, intellectual history, political science, cultural theory, media studies, literary studies), the book offers a preliminary attempt at mapping the problem, interconnecting the various sites at which it went viral and connecting the dots between past and present. The fact that no unified theory has been put forward which would cover all these aspects mustn't be to the disadvantage of the overall project, rather the opposite. In order to better understand this hegemonic term, it is appropriate to take a step back and look at the field in all its diversity. This also entails seeing the current obsession with transparency in a broader perspective of the history of ideas. By linking this leading catchword in today's hyper-mediated economies of information back to its historical roots, the book scrutinizes the various reasons why it has become the new imperative of a supposedly post-ideological age.

This book is organized in three sections: "Transparency in the Making," "Under the Crystal Dome" and "From the Panopticon to the Selfie and Back." The first section, "Transparency in the Making," aims to investigate the historical circumstances which allowed the concept of transparency to emerge in Early Modernity and how it progressively came to occupy such a central place in contemporary discourse.

In his introductory chapter "Transparency: A Magic Concept of Modernity," Emmanuel Alloa gives an overview of the emergent field of Critical Transparency Studies, and traces some genealogical lines of how, from the eighteenth century onwards, what was known in Antiquity as an optical and aesthetic phenomenon—diaphaneity—was transformed and came to stand for central concerns in self-knowledge, morality and politics. It turns out that "transparency" incessantly wavers between a factual requirement and a normative claim, an optical impression and a metaphorical promise. The conceptual clarity transparency heralds is inversely proportional to its factual semantic vagueness. Arguably, it is this very vagueness that allowed it to become a magic concept, which promises to solve problems by the very fact of being uttered. Against tendencies of seeing transparency as a means of achieving self-coincidence, unicity and self-stability, the chapter recalls alternative meanings of the term. When the artistic avant-gardes such as Soviet Constructivism experimented with transparent materials and layers, they were interested in the fact that in one single viewpoint, objects that occupy different, mutually exclusive positions in space can come to coexist and overlap. Seeing the overlaps between what is usually deemed to be apart makes way for a renewed understanding of what coexistence means.

In his chapter "Seeing It All, Doing It All, Saying It All: Transparency, Subject, and the World," Dieter Thomä situates the debate on transparency in a larger context by comparing three epistemological or practical attitudes of the subject towards the world: the ability of "seeing it all" linked to the ideal of transparency, the courage of "saying it all" epitomized in "parrhesia" or free speech, and the power of "doing it all" labeled as "panourgia" in Greek. By analyzing a vast array of sources reaching from Sophocles and Euripides to Descartes, Diderot, and Bentham, Thomä identifies the sharp differences between those three attitudes. They represent competing ways of reading the subject and its outreach to the world. The debate between Rousseau and Diderot is of particular relevance: While Rousseau indulges in the dream of total self-transparency,

Diderot embraces roleplay as part and parcel of social existence: Re-imagining one's own presence and representing different personae serve the purpose of exploring and pondering comprehensive, collective self-images. Transparency loses some of its appeal in this context: As it induces a turn from an active to a perceptive attitude, it tends to reduce citizens to mere onlookers or observers.

In the next chapter of the section, Manfred Schneider argues that the Western imaginary is haunted by a dream of transparency pervading the philosophical, political and moral spheres alike. In "The Dream of Transparency: Aquinas, Rousseau, Sartre," Schneider turns to the first occurrence of this dream in Greek and Latin literature. In the fabulous anecdote of Momus told by Hesiod in his *Theogony*, Zeus is being blamed for his failure of putting a door in man's breast, through which you could see their thoughts and control them. Schneider reconstructs the legacy of the dream of transparency by turning to three pivotal authors from the Middle Ages, the Enlightenment and the twentieth century: Saint Thomas Aquinas, Jean-Jacques Rousseau and Jean-Paul Sartre. In the last part of his chapter, Schneider aims at disentangling the linguistic, political and interpersonal aspects of transparency. He takes issue with the fact that it leads to a curious conflation between the verbal and the visual.

In her contribution to the section—"Unbounded Confession"— Noreen Khawaja explores the shifting status of religious confession in the cultural imaginary of Protestantism. No longer considered a sacrament by most reformers, the rite of confession was detached from its liturgical context to take on an array of civic and political functions. Far from a diminution of the importance of confession, Khawaja shows, the effect of lifting confession's sacramental status meant that one was "free" to make confession at all times—in any company, at any place, under any circumstances. Through such shifts, confession became more than a particular sort of speech act; it became a discursive form, a medium of communication in which the Christian citizen addressed not only God and her conscience, but also the world. Appreciating the dynamic history of Protestant confessional discourse allows to grasp the formation of confession as a political and literary genre in Goethe, Rousseau and others, and allows us to bring contemporary concerns about transparency into historical and theological relief.

In "Seeing It All: Bentham's Panopticon and the Dark Spots of Enlightenment," Miran Božovič returns to Bentham's Panopticon writings he has extensively worked on and draws a line between French Enlightenment and subsequent utilitarianism. A yet underrated source for reflections on transparency is Diderot's anonymously published novel *Les Bijoux indiscrets* (The Indiscreet Jewels). The novel depicts an African empire in which purity of mores is established and maintained by the unseen voice of female sex organs which is aware of all sexual transgressions and impure thoughts of its bearer. As Božovič argues, Diderot's fantasy of a transparent empire is later realized by Jeremy Bentham in his plans for the famous *Panopticon* prison. In the panoptic architecture, Diderot's multitude of unseen voices, each of which knows all actions and thoughts of its bearer is replaced by a single never-seen voice which knows everything about everyone, thus ensuring the smooth functioning of the compact, transparent microcosm of the panopticon.

In the last contribution to this section, Stefanos Geroulanos turns to the French critiques of transparency in the second half of twentieth century which he has been dealing with extensively in the past. His text in this volume "Transparency, Humanism, and the Politics of the Future Before and After May '68," considers the effect of May '68 on French anti-transparency discourses and argues that a significant gap existed between (1) principally epistemological critiques published shortly before 1968, and (2) the rise of a new set of political critiques of transparency in the 1970s. The three years before May '68 saw the publication of Leroi-Gourhan's *Gesture and Speech*, Foucault's *Order of Things*, and Derrida's *Of Grammatology*, which all took for granted that no mind/world transparency was available to the human subject. All three works signaled that a certain transparency might be possible—even imminent—in the near future, provided a certain humanism was jettisoned, and with it the expectation that transparency would be achievable by humans themselves. May '68 completely obviated this line of thinking.

The contributions to the second section, "Under the Crystal Dome," scrutinize the hopes (as well as the concerns) associated with a society that would be ruled entirely by the principle of transparency and a state of thorough permeability of social relationships.

In public discourse, transparency is widely considered a self-evident good on the face of it, similar to privacy and free speech. In his chapter on "The Limits of Transparency," Amitai Etzioni re-examines the theoretical assumptions underlying the claim that transparency can play a major role in holding democratic governments accountable. His analysis reveals that transparency plays a much smaller role than is often assumed in sustaining democratic regimes. In addition, Etzioni indicates that transparency cannot be relied upon to replace regulation, both because it is, itself, a form of regulation and because of the way in which democracies actually function. Etzioni argues that the ideological usages of transparency are off the mark. A social science analysis shows that transparency cannot fulfill the functions its advocates assign to it; at best it can play a limited role in their service. When assessing transparency, one must take into account a continuum composed of the order of disutility and the level of information costs. The higher the score on both variables, the less useful transparency is. Moreover, these scores need not be particularly high to greatly limit the extent to which the public can benefit from transparency.

The next chapter in the section starts where the previous one ends, and looks back at the historical genesis of the discourse on transparency in public affairs. As Sandrine Baume shows in "Publicity and Transparency: The Itinerary of a Subtle Distinction," these two terms are often used interchangeably, as if transparency was just a synonym of the older term publicity. The chapter investigates whether there is a discontinuity of meaning between the principle of publicity, which appears in classical writings, and the call for transparency emerging in parallel as a metaphor in the eighteenth century. By putting together an inventory of both the positive and negative associations of transparency stated by authors such as Rousseau, Kant, Bentham and Constant, it can be shown that transparency may be divided into six dimensions: legality, virtue, veracity, responsibility/accountability, honor and control. Baume addresses the reasons for distinguishing between the concepts of transparency and publicity and builds on suggestions by Tero Erkkilä, Jon Elster, Erin Kelly, and Daniel Naurin. After analyzing the contributions of these authors and their limits, she suggests a different method of distinguishing publicity from transparency by drawing on the polyvalence in the semantics of the latter.

After discussing the relationship between transparency and publicity, the second section moves on to the relationship between transparency and regulation. In his chapter, "Regulation and Transparency as Rituals of Distrust: Reading Niklas Luhmann against the Grain," Caspar Hirschi argues that such principles are presented by their advocates as procedural measures to establish trust in public persons or institutions. Both transparency and regulation claim to reduce the risk of individuals abusing the system, and claim to be impersonal and dispassionate: this is what Niklas Luhmann termed "legitimation through procedure." Instead of believing a decision to be valuable based on a personal assessment of its content, it is considered legitimate by virtue of its immanent procedural standards, regardless of content. As Caspar Hirschi claims, it would be more accurate to describe them as political rituals, which actually do the contrary of what they claim: they raise the level of distrust in public persons and institutions. As a result, just as with regulation, transparency turns out to be a distrust-generating ritual which exacerbates the problems it allegedly solves.

The next chapter makes a point in claiming that transparency has very little to do with critical publicity. According to Thomas Berns, the contemporary call for more transparency marks a very different paradigm. The triviality of a government priding itself on adhering to reality by making it transparent, is accompanied by the ideal of its own invisibility: an efficient norm is one that does not even appear. The less a norm is explicitly made public, the more transparent it will be. This see-through invisibility is the key feature of the new kind of governmentality based on algorithms. In his contribution, "Not Individuals, Relations: What Transparency Is Really About," Berns elaborates on his notion of algorithmic transparency developed with Antoinette Rouvroy. The target of algorithmic governmentality is not the individual subject, as this concept has sometimes been misunderstood, but the relations between them. This new approach of algorithmic governmentality and the specific ontology it implements is based on Gilbert Simondon's ontology of relations. But with this nuance: algorithmic governmentality also leads to an individualization of relations.

In his contribution, "Obfuscated Transparency," Dieter Mersch reflects on the transformation of transparency and opacity in the realm of digital networks. Transparency requirements pose a challenge to well-established conceptions of the "social" and the "political." Mersch argues that transparency is caught in an insufficiently acknowledged dialectic: Complete transparency leads to obfuscation. Today, the designated medium supposedly producing a maximum of transparency is the technological system of digital communication through networks, social platforms and data exchanges. Digital transparency is far from being neutral and generates a social and political sphere subject to its logic. What once pertained to Enlightenment's program of human emancipation boils down to a mathematical form. Ultimately, noble ideas like digital equality or the democracy of seemingly free information flows come down to formal choices based on a binary code. The ideal of a transparent society based on justice and trust reveals itself to be nothing but an empty surface.

In the last contribution to the section, Thomas Docherty ponders on the role of transparency in imposing conformist mindsets. "The Privatization of Human Interests or, How Transparency Breeds Conformity" argues that in a specific version of "modernity," deriving from Arendt, transparency has become a mechanism through which we eviscerate politics of content and substance, replacing it with the policing of behaviors that constitute social conformity as a normative ideal. The argument explores an account of modernity that situates public life (the realm of politics) explicitly in relation to a private sphere (the realm of the personal and of "selfhood"). Such modernity is dedicated to the task of properly regulating the claims of the personal and of the political on human identity. Docherty argues that modernity resolves this dialectical tension by the privatization of ecology: the individual withdraws from the political world in order to "cultiver son jardin" (as in Voltaire's *Candide*). Thus the private realm—and not politics—becomes the space for distinctive human individuality, whereas the public sphere becomes the place for social conformity. The demand for transparency is complicit with the acceptance of a normative surveillance society, where "deviant" behavior must be eradicated.

The third section, "From the Panopticon to the Selfie and Back," focuses on the connection between surveillance and subjectivation, from Early Modern devices of imposed transparency to contemporary practices of voluntary self-exposure.

The section opens with Vincent Kaufmann's chapter "Transparency and Subjectivity: Remembering Jennifer Ringley." Drawing upon media studies as well as psychoanalysis, Kaufmann discusses the double meaning of transparency applied to personality or subjectivity. On the one hand, transparency refers to invisibility, to a lack of subjectivity or even to psychosis: it's the Orwellian Big Brother syndrome. On the other hand, it refers to hypervisibility, to the exhibition of privacy, the horizon of which is indeed exhibitionism and therefore perversion: the *Jennicam* syndrome, named after the first *lifecaster* in the history of the Internet. The two definitions of transparency seem to be contradictory, but they aren't. A twofold transparency is precisely what the contemporary media environment forces us to live in, oscillating between psychotic invisibility and perverse visibility, in which we have no choice but to swing constantly between our submission to Big Brother—as described in Orwell's desubjectivized universe—and our desire to be part of *Big Brother*, one of the first and most successful Reality TV shows. The latter appears as a modern form of *servitude volontaire*. At the end, we might no longer know if Jenni was rather psychotic or perverse.

Contemporary media culture forces us to rethink customary dichotomies, so the authors of the next contribution state. According to Jörg Metelmann and Thomas Telios, two interpretations that are both versions of the transparency dream, seek to come to grips with the recent phenomenon of taking "selfies" of oneself: the first focuses on the process of turning oneself inside out and on the longing for being looked at (narcissism), the second sticks to the task of totally grasping oneself through self-objectivization (quantified self). In their text—"Putting Oneself Out There: The "Selfie" and the Alter-Rithmic Transformations of Subjectivity"—Metelmann and Telios argue that neither version fully matches the "selfie" phenomenon. Instead, so they say, the "selfie" should be seen as an exemplary device for a subjectivation process which already thwarts the aim of full subjectification. The storage, serialization and dissemination of "selfies" points to a "selfing" project that already takes place "out there," under conditions of sociality and sharedness. In this respect, the "selfie" is neither a diminished version of the "I" nor an idealized type, neither merely self-referential nor merely self-quantificational, but a device of an ongoing "selfing" process, which opacifies a given identity all the while it pretends making it transparent.

In "Interrupting Transparency," Clare Birchall asks how we need to rethink transparency issues since Donald Trump's election. Certain aspects of Trump's presidential campaign and the early days of his administration challenged a binary visual code that pits opacity against openness, as well as a teleological narrative that establishes transparency as the logical incarnation of Enlightenment ideals and an administrative norm today. Because of the ideological nature of contemporary transparency tools, an interruption of technocratic transparency in its data-driven form might not in all circumstances be a regressive move. While recognizing the risks inherent in a displacement of technocratic transparency by a figure like Trump, Birchall explores the possibility of utilizing the unsettled conditions of visibility, in which openness and obfuscation merge, to recalibrate and radicalize the politics of transparency. Birchall then makes a plea for "radical transparency" which indicates not more (of the same) transparency, whether moralistic populist transparency or technocratic data driven transparency, but a transparency robust enough to contend with "post-truth" figures, strategies, and politics.

In a previous book, *Exposed: Desire and Disobedience in the Digital Age* (2015), Bernard Harcourt explored our new digital age and its many seductions—the ways in which our own desires to take selfies, post Snapchats, and stream NetFlix unwittingly feed the surveillance machinery of the NSA, Google, Facebook, Twitter, Amazon, Microsoft, and so on. Harcourt argued there that we had entered an "expository society" where we increasingly exhibit ourselves online, and in the process freely give away our most personal and private data. No longer an Orwellian or a panoptic society, ours is now fueled by our own proclivities, joy, and narcissism—posting on Facebook, searching on Google, buying on Amazon, Instagramming selfies. While this remains true, the relation of our new digital exposure to the more violent practices associated with the war on terrorism—to drone strikes and other new digital technologies of warfare—requires more detailed attention. Beyond the original diagnosis in *Exposed*, our expository society must be understood within the larger framework of a new security apparatus, Harcourt states in "Virtual Transparency: From the Panopticon to the Expository Society and Beyond." By starting off again in 1973, when Michel Foucault delivered his Lecture Series on the Punitive Society, the chapter attempts at spelling that out in a detailed engagement with new techniques of surveillance and warfare.

As the title of this book epitomizes, the aim is to explore how two domains which have often been discussed separately (the ideal of a transparent self and the ideal of a transparent society) actually yield to analogous logics. Epistemic and moral discourses about self-transparency and those about the transparency of procedures in social life might have much more in common than just the sharing of a metaphor. In modernity, so the hypothesis, psychogenesis and sociogenesis are intimately intertwined, and analyzing the mutual correspondences is instrumental for understanding the normative transformations put forward in modern and late modern discourses about society and subjectivity.

As an *ouverture* to the volume, we republish an article that the late Umberto Eco wrote in the immediate aftermath of the Wikileaks revelations. In "Not such Wicked Leaks," Umberto Eco argues that the Wikileaks or Cablegate affair not only shows up the hypocrisy that governs relations between states, citizens and the press, but also presages a "crabwise" return to more archaic forms of communication. When skimming through the leaked secret diplomatic cables, the world discovered that their content mainly contained knowledge about facts already widely available in daily news. This shouldn't surprise anyone, in an age where embassies ask the press for an inside story. The real issue, however, is another one, Eco argues. As Georg Simmel once remarked, a real secret is an empty secret, since this is the only condition for making sure that it can't be eventually unearthed. The content of diplomacy itself is an open secret, protected only by hypocrisy. But to actually reveal, as WikiLeaks has done, that politician's secrets were empty secrets amounts to taking away their power. This even holds true for modern governments, which— unlike those of the Ancien Régime that quite openly staged their *arcana imperii*—have a tendency to make a secret of their own dependence on secrets.

In an age of digital transparency, hypocrisy faces an uncertain future. On the other hand, the newly induced transparency is not merely imposed by disciplinary surveillance technologies, but also actively engineered by the subjects themselves. All netizens take part, whether they like it or not, in the huge data assemblage about themselves which will then orient their own future behavior and options. But often this self-transparency is something willfully looked for, through ever-greater forms of self-exposure in the social media. We must interrogate the reasons which led to a situation where what is felt as punishment is no longer being watched by others, but in the absence thereof. The ways in which society thinks about itself and subjects conceive of their existence is currently undergoing decisive changes, which need to be described and conceptualized, not least for elaborating strategies of resistance to this self-induced servitude.

Not such Wicked Leaks

Umberto Eco

The WikiLeaks affair has a twofold value. On the one hand, it turns out to be a bogus scandal, a scandal that only appears to be a scandal against the backdrop of the hypocrisy governing relations between the state, the citizenry and the press. On the other hand, it heralds a sea change in international communication—and prefigures a regressive future of "crabwise" progress.

But let's take it one step at a time. First off, the WikiLeaks confirm the fact that every file put together by a secret service (of any nation you like) is exclusively made up of press clippings. The "extraordinary" American revelations about Berlusconi's sex habits merely relay what could already be read for months in any newspaper (except those owned by Berlusconi himself, needless to say), and the sinister caricature of Gaddafi has long been the stuff of cabaret farce.

U. Eco (✉)
University of Bologna, Bologna, Italy
e-mail: emmanuel.alloa@unisg.ch

Embassies Have Morphed into Espionage Centers

The rule that says secret files must only contain news that is already common knowledge is essential to the dynamic of secret services, and not only in the present century. Go to an esoteric book shop and you'll find that every book on the shelf (on the Holy Grail, the "mystery" of Rennes-le-Château [a hoax theory concocted to draw tourists to a French town], on the Templars or the Rosicrucians) is a point-by-point rehash of what is already written in older books. And it's not just because occult authors are averse to doing original research (or don't know where to look for news about the non-existent), but because those given to the occult only believe what they already know and what corroborates what they've already heard. That happens to be Dan Brown's success formula.

The same goes for secret files. The informant is lazy. So is the head of the secret service (or at least he's limited—otherwise he could be, what do I know, an editor at *Libération*): he only regards as true what he recognizes. The top-secret dope on Berlusconi that the US embassy in Rome beamed to the Department of State was the same story that had come out in *Newsweek* the week before.

So why so much ado about these leaks? For one thing, they say what any savvy observer already knows: that the embassies, at least since the end of World War II, and since heads of state can call each other up or fly over to meet for dinner, have lost their diplomatic function and, but for the occasional ceremonial function, have morphed into espionage centers. Anyone who watches investigative documentaries knows that full well, and it is only out of hypocrisy that we feign ignorance. Still, repeating that in public constitutes a breach of the duty of hypocrisy, and puts American diplomacy in a lousy light.

A Real Secret Is an Empty Secret

Secondly, the very notion that any old hacker can delve into the most secret secrets of the most powerful country in the world has dealt a hefty blow to the State Department's prestige. So the scandal actually hurts the "perpetrators" more than the "victims."

But let's turn to the more profound significance of what has occurred. Formerly, back in the days of Orwell, every power could be conceived of as a Big Brother watching over its subjects' every move. The Orwellian prophecy came completely true once the powers that be could monitor every phone call made by the citizen, every hotel he stayed in, every toll road he took and so on and so forth. The citizen became the total victim of the watchful eye of the state. But when it transpires, as it has now, that even the crypts of state secrets are not beyond the hacker's grasp, the surveillance ceases to work only one-way and becomes circular. The state has its eye on every citizen, but every citizen, or at least every hacker—the citizens' self-appointed avenger—can pry into the state's every secret.

How can a power hold up if it can't even keep its own secrets anymore? It is true, as Georg Simmel once remarked, that a real secret is an empty secret (which can never be unearthed); it is also true that anything known about Berlusconi or Merkel's character is essentially an empty secret, a secret without a secret, because it is public domain. But to actually reveal, as WikiLeaks has done, that Hillary Clinton's secrets were empty secrets amounts to taking away all her power. WikiLeaks didn't do any harm to Sarkozy or Merkel, but did irreparable damage to Clinton and Obama.

Technology Now Advances Crabwise

What will be the consequences of this wound inflicted on a very mighty power? It's obvious that in future, states won't be able to put any restricted information online anymore: that would be tantamount to posting it on a street corner. But it is equally clear that, given today's technologies, it is pointless to hope to have confidential dealings over the phone. Nothing is easier than finding out whether a head of state flew in or out or contacted one of his counterparts. So how can privy matters be conducted in future? Now I know that for the time being, my forecast is still science fiction and therefore fantastic, but I can't help imagining state agents riding discreetly in stagecoaches along untrackable routes, bearing only memorized messages or, at most, the occasional document concealed in the heel of a shoe. Only a single copy thereof will be kept—in locked drawers. Ultimately, the attempted Watergate break-in was less successful than WikiLeaks.

I once had occasion to observe that technology now advances crabwise, that is, backwards. A century after the wireless telegraph revolutionized communications, the Internet has re-established a telegraph that runs on (telephone) wires. (Analog) video cassettes enabled film buffs to peruse a movie frame by frame, by fast-forwarding and rewinding to lay bare all the secrets of the editing process, but (digital) CDs now only allow us quantum leaps from one chapter to another. High-speed trains take us from Rome to Milan in three hours, but flying there, if you include transfers to and from the airports, takes three and a half hours. So it wouldn't be extraordinary if politics and communications technologies were to revert to the horse-drawn carriage.

One last observation: In days of yore, the press would try to figure out what was hatching *sub rosa* inside the embassies. Nowadays, it's the embassies that are asking the press for the inside story.

Translated by Eric Rosencrantz/*VoxEurop*

Part I

Transparency in the Making

Transparency: A Magic Concept of Modernity

Emmanuel Alloa

A New Transparentocene?

The aim of phrasing the latest and definite concept for describing our age has led observers to engage in a race with inflationary outbidding. Among the boldest proposals made, the following deserves special mention. In March 2015, the *Scientific American* published an article titled "Our Transparent Future." In the article, neurophilosopher Daniel C. Dennett and Deb Roy, director of the Massachusetts Institute of Technology (MIT) Laboratory for Social Machines, argue that we are currently witnessing a "transparency explosion" (Dennett and Roy 2015). This explosion, Dennett and Roy suggest, should be understood in its true implications, which means considering it on the scale of geological eons. As it were, transparency would not so much amount to a societal demand currently voiced in public and corporate contexts as to a major threshold in the development of collective life-forms, and as such, the authors

E. Alloa (✉)
School of Humanities and Social Sciences, University of St. Gallen, St. Gallen, Switzerland
e-mail: emmanuel.alloa@unisg.ch

© The Author(s) 2018
E. Alloa, D. Thomä (eds.), *Transparency, Society and Subjectivity*, https://doi.org/10.1007/978-3-319-77161-8_3

claim, it should be compared to the Cambrian revolution. No doubt: one would be hard pressed to make more brazen a claim. As the authors recall, more than half a billion years ago, a major event took place in terms of geological history. The Cambrian age represents a spectacular evolutionary burst, arguably the most important one in the history of life on Earth: within a geological "instant," all the important forms of life emerged, with new physiological structures, bodily organs and predatory strategies. One influential explanation for this evolutionary burst, which transformed the biosphere irrevocably, is that within a relatively short span of time a "transparency explosion" occurred. According to the so-called Parker hypothesis, around 543 million years ago, the chemistry of the oceans and the atmosphere underwent a sudden change with the consequence that they become much more transparent. Lighter carbon isotopes swiftly replaced heavier ones, light flooded the aquatic zones, and vision became possible for the first time. Suddenly, it was immensely beneficial to have sight organs, either to see prey or predators in the offing, and animals equipped with eyes quickly gained the upper hand over other organisms. This newly expanded range of perception privileged distal senses over proximal ones, and a drastic natural selection process solidified this new hierarchy. Consistent with the Parker hypothesis, the oceans' new transparency galvanized the emergence of camera-style retinas, which themselves propelled new defensive body parts, even as nervous systems were evolving in parallel to the development of novel predatory behaviors, all of which led in turn to new methods of evasion, mimicry and camouflage. The old tactics of obtaining information (or misinformation) no longer worked, and organisms that didn't quickly adapt, and evolve, were doomed to extinction, in the new era of fully lit, visible environments.

Dennett and Roy do not restrict themselves to recalling the geochemical hypotheses concerning the Cambrian age, but use it as a foil for a straightforward claim concerning the present. What the authors of "Our Transparent Future" surmise is that on the brink of the twenty-first century, we are witnessing a transparency explosion which might be as important, on the scale of geological life, as the Cambrian one. The old ways no longer suffice in a world of widespread, universalized transparency: individuals and corporate entities are now exposed to the general gaze, for better and for worse, while the transparency of information generated by electronic technology has drastically modified our epistemological environments in which we live, impacting notions such as knowledge, belief, illusion or confidence. Dennett and Roy present a radically Darwinian reading of these changes:

> The tremendous change in our world triggered by this media inundation can be summed up in a word: transparency. We can now see further, faster, and more cheaply and easily than ever before—and we can be seen. And you and I can see that everyone can see what we see, in a recursive hall of mirrors of mutual knowledge that both enables and hobbles. The age-old game of hide-and-seek that has shaped all life on the planet has suddenly shifted its playing field, its equipment and its rules. The players who cannot adjust will not last long. (Dennett and Roy 2015: 66–67)

The two authors don't use that expression themselves, but if a similar claim hadn't already been made for the Cambrian age, one would be persuaded to believe that Dennett and Roy were in fact suggesting renaming our current age in terms of geological *transparentocene*. Suddenly, it seems as if we had leaped forward: rather than seeing it a normative demand for achieving a different future, transparency would now stand for a stage already achieved (or on the verge of being so). According to such a picture, transparency stands for an uncontestable new state of affairs, as the new overarching characteristic of an entire age, the age of reciprocal and unrestricted exposure. As bold as it may sound, Dennett's and Roy's claim is matched by many concurrent descriptions. In such an age, secrets will, if not entirely dissolve, at least dramatically diminish in their half-time value. As a former NSA (National Security Agency) senior counselor, Joel Brenner, eventually declared, "those things which are kept secret won't stay secret very long.... The real goal in security now is to retard the degradation of the half-lives of secrets."

As a matter of fact, the Snowden Papers as well as the ongoing Wikileaks revelation have had the effect of not only divulging the degree of mass surveillance to which citizens are exposed worldwide—the secret PRISM program of the US National Security Agency being just one amongst many—but also to show how the surveillance technology itself has left traces which could be used and disclosed by counter-surveillance actors. *Quis custodiet ipsos custodes* could be the question of our time: who watches the watchmen? Beyond the classical purview of the "right to know," many voices are raised to demand a "right to know about those who know." Transparency initiatives flourish in numerous contexts—public governance, financial transactions, extractive industries, food chains, pharmaceutics, global sports contests, and so on—in order to provide a legal framework for surveillance practices. Significantly, some of them focus on making a certain perceptibility visible, for example, when *Global Witness* reports things "seen" by local informants or when *Transparency International* publishes its annual "corruption perception index": the stress lies not on mortgageable, objective data, which purports to be impervious to corruption, but on its "perception," which in turn is meant to be shared with the international audience. Making perceptions visible (indeed, making them perceptible) and amplifying availability seem to be the internal mechanisms of these initiatives occasionally referred to as "civilizing techniques." By subjecting such things to the glare of the public eye, the aim is to force institutions to practice self-restraint. Still, it would be naïve to confine the transparency initiatives to civil society and non-governmental organizations, as—and so far Roy and Dennett seem to be proven right—governments and corporate entities are now increasingly under pressure to implement transparency standards and to release transparency reports. From comprehensive transparency standards such as the EU Transparency Directive (TD) to individual decisions made by companies that they will publish annual transparency reports for the public, numerous indicators converge to the point of calling secrecy a thing of the past. Such general demand extends even to intelligence agencies: since 2016, the U.S. Freedom Act has required the NSA itself to start publishing a transparency report of its own.

If an agency whose actions by definition must be secretive is suddenly forced to disclose details about its actions, Dennett and Roy have been proven right. Rather than continuing to debate the *normative* contents of the transparency claim, one should accept that it names a *descriptive* situation; we've moved from value judgments to fact. Contesting that the rules of the games have changed would be as futile as to contest the reality of evolutionary biology: that is, in substance, the naturalized standpoint the two authors have adopted. Yet such confidence is misplaced, and it remains to be seen what we are claiming precisely when claiming that modernity has experienced a "transparency explosion." Undoubtedly, this way of narrating the story doesn't do justice to the ambivalence of the concept. Just as some might say that we have never been modern (Latour 1993), it is quite possible to argue that we have never been transparent. Just as the perception of modernity oscillates between an era now firmly in the past and a project that is still ongoing, transparency permanently wavers between a state and a future requirement, an optical impression and a metaphorical promise, which makes it a "thick concept" that cannot be simplified into a purely descriptive or prescriptive concept. As such, it makes little sense to speak of a transparency explosion within modernity; rather, modernity is but a name for this explosion. Consequently, studying the discursive effects of transparency can shed light on the very project inherent to modernity.

A Magic Concept

In the 1920s, during the Weimar Republic, Walter Benjamin used to associate transparency with modern glass architecture. As opposed to the overloaded and highly personalized nineteenth-century bourgeois *intérieur*, Benjamin states, glass is a building material that is fundamentally anonymous, because it can't be personalized. As he explains, the progressive artists resorted to glass in order to create transient spaces, which no one could appropriate for himself. Drawing on Bertolt Brecht's advice *Erase the traces*, which he gave out to the modern city-dwellers, Benjamin believes that glass would be such material which allows for such an erasure of traces. A little less than a century later, transparency has completely transformed and now stands for encompassing, all-comprehensive traceability. Benjamin's prediction *Was kommt steht im Zeichen der Transparenz* ("what is about to come will be dominated by transparency"—Benjamin 1929: 264) was mainly referring to the new architecture, but it resonates differently today. In a sense, history has proven him right, although probably in a sense very different from what he would have imagined (on this Benjaminian prediction, see Alloa 2016). Around the same time that Benjamin made his predictions about the transparency to come, the Bauhaus teacher, designer and photographer Hajo Rose created a self-portrait which has been read as a dark foreshadowing of an age of total exposure and technological surveillance (Fig. 1). In point of fact, with every click, with every keystroke, with every swipe over a tablet,

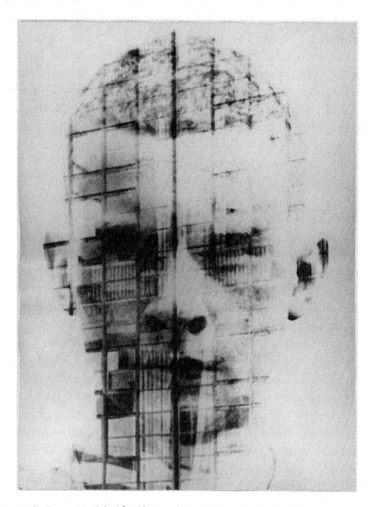

Fig. 1 Hajo Rose, *Untitled [Self-Portrait with Dessau Façade (double exposure)]*, 1930. © Hajo Rose Estate and Artists Rights Society (ARS), New York/VG Bild-Kunst

every card payment, every Google search, supermarket self-scan or Facebook "like," and thanks to the RFID technology (Radio-Frequency IDentification) even with every movement, our lives are being recorded. The most banal, daily routines leave digital traces: answering a phone call, withdrawing cash at the ATM, consulting the Internet, checking out at the supermarket, posting Instagram photos, tweeting, checking out a book with a library card, reading an e-book on a tablet, entering a WiFi-equipped area, a nurse updating a patient's electronic medical records, swiping a gift card, using public transportation, taking an elevator, entering buildings with a security badge, being tagged in photographs taken by friends, and so forth—the profile of our digital selves might, oddly enough, be more detailed now than that of our physical ones, and at this point they are heavily used and commodified by employers, credit rating agencies, and insurance companies, in order to have a better view of whom they interact with. Typing speed, browsing habits, and search patterns become powerful aggregators for predicting, to an astoundingly high degree of precision, our gender, our age, our professional field, our political orientation, and other demographic categories. For sure, as David Lyon stressed, "the codes by which persons and groups are categorized are seldom under public scrutiny [...] and yet they have huge potential and actual consequences for the life chances and the choices of ordinary citizens" (Lyon 2009: 465). Such actions as the way we express ourselves, the concerns we share, and the protest marches we join can be of sensitive interest to governments. Search engines, website cookies, biometric passports, connected devices, online music accounts, heart-rate monitoring apps, cinema passes, and brand loyalty cards all generate data strings about ourselves and, if compiled, make it possible to construct a highly detailed profile of who we are and what we do, of our orientations, preferences and disgusts, adolescent aberrations, subconscious interests and guilty pleasures, political stances or health afflictions. Immense data sets about our selves are stored on remote servers and incessantly fed; over time, they can be of as much interest to governmental agencies as to commercial actors, and inaugurate new regimes of "algorithmic governmentality" (on this concept, see Thomas Berns's chapter in this volume).

    The revelations about the extent to which citizens are spied on around the world has created a sustained uproar. However, the main response to becoming aware of this fact of general exposure has been homeopathic: it has to be made transparent to what extent we are being made transparent, (bad) transparency can only be cured by more transparency—in other words, transparency is still too partial because it is unilateral. Tellingly, very few actors have called for unrestricted opacity, and advocates for strategies of "obfuscation" have mostly aimed for rebalancing a situation of asymmetry in which the surveilled citizens were clearly disfavored. Despite demands for more transparency on both sides, the very concept of transparency has hardly been questioned, and this fact is quite telling. It seems that no one would venture as far as to put the very promise of transparency into question. The consensus is that one might be against bad transparency, but fighting transparency at large looks like an endeavor which will very likely end up costing general support. New technologies such as blockchain payments, devised by net activists, may present themselves as cryptographic at first; in truth, however, they aspire to create truly transparent communication, through end-to-end connections: all users fully look into every piece of the chain, without any need of external authorities or third-party services. With blockchain transactions, trust becomes a value of the past, from now on promising fully transparent peer-to-peer transactions.

Although one might find notable exceptions (the *French theory* of the 60s and 70s would qualify for that, as Stefanos Geroulanos points out in his contribution to this volume, and as already mentioned, one sees today the emergence of new Critical Transparency studies), on the whole, transparency still constitutes a largely consensual norm today, as many observers have highlighted. It has become a "taken-for-granted ideal and explanation of how society and its organizations must function" (Christensen and Cornelissen 2015: 133), or, as Thierry Libaert (2003: 13) has it, transparency has grown into the "inescapable ideology" of our times. It is no coincidence that, amid public discourse obsessed with problem-solving, such ideology foreshadows the overcoming of conflicts through a one-size-fits-all "transparency fix" (Fenster 2017). As a matter of fact, transparency seems to share characteristics with so-called "magic concepts." The political scientists Christopher Pollitt and Peter Hupe (Pollitt and Hupe 2011) have introduced this tag in order to qualify concepts that are imbued with a magic aura which promises to solve major dilemmas encountered by society. Here are some characteristic features defining such "magic concepts": "A high degree of abstraction, a strongly positive normative charge, a seeming ability to dissolve previous dilemmas and a mobility across domains, give them their 'magic' character" (Pollitt and Hupe 2011: 641). What all of these magic concepts have in common is an exceedingly positive connotation, and as a result, it becomes extremely difficult to be "against" them. On the other hand, magic concepts—examples of which would be concepts such as governance, networks, participation, responsibility, creativity or innovation—are as powerful as they play on a certain semantic vagueness, and as such, they are often used glibly, as catchwords that short-circuit real reflection or debate. As Pollitt and Hupe explain, magic concepts are attractive to academics and practitioners alike. Ultimately, they do "*not* reconcile the oppositional proverbs and doctrines which previous generations of public administration scholars painstakingly documented and discussed. Rather, they rise above them—to a higher level of abstraction—or, if one prefers, they avoid them" (2011: 653).

Transparency has undoubtedly achieved the status of such a magic concept, since it meets the following main requirements: it boasts *broadness* (covering large domains and having multiple, overlapping, and sometimes conflicting definitions), *normative attractiveness* (this can be tied back its positive connotation), *implication of consensus* (diluting, obscuring, or even denying traditional social science concerns with conflicting interests and logics), and last but not least *global marketability* (being well known as well as fashionable, among the most diverse audiences). In other words: it is extremely hard to be against transparency. Research in various contexts (politics, finance, social networks, humanities) generally confirms that there is an overall consensus around the values of transparency: transparency has no exact antonym, that is, it has no exact counter-concept which would negatively cover all its meanings. On the contrary, it seems as if transparency, with its malleable form, had pared away any form of negativity and somehow resorbed it entirely.

Today, by and large, transparency stands for optimization and futurity. If the outcry over this drive toward creating "glassy individuals" has remained muted, this is because these same technologies also make possible a public life that the user believes he has control over. States and companies aren't the only ones publishing transparency reports; Sunday-morning joggers with smartwatches broadcasting their heart rates to their Facebook profiles pride themselves on having an online community that essentially acts as their superego. The so-called "quantified self" movement stands for a promise of a more lucid, rational relationship to oneself, for a subject that knows how to make "the best" out of itself. Whereas Kant resisted the need to publicize every decision before it had been presented to the tribunal of reason, now lives are made public in full, and have no choice otherwise. In an era characterized by expressivity, by a constant flow of data on every scale—a liberal equivalent to the *glasnost* that Gorbachev had promised—the digital subject can command attention, and thereby a promise of unconstrained, integral existence. Consequently, transparency has become a guarantee of morality both for institutions and for subjects. The connotations tied to it are almost exclusively positive: transparency is held to be impartial, neutral, democratic and progressive. As such, it promises stability.

An Emergent Field—But No Field Glasses

The momentum and the broad consensus around the concept hides the fact that its meaning is far from being clear. Is transparency a quality? A state? A process? What do we mean when we use this term? Given its omnipresence, it is significant to see how little research has been carried out on this concept, about its historical roots, its actual uses and wider implications. Admittedly, just as policymakers are recognizing the importance of the question, academia is increasingly turned towards transparency issues. Beyond numerous publications touching upon transparency issues in more prominent fields, such as finance, European law, public governance, tax policy or technology, academic research has even started to organize itself, with anthologies (Piotrowski 2010) or the first *Research Handbook on Transparency* (Ala'i and Vaughn 2014). The recent creation of an *International Transparency and Secrecy Research Network* and the yearly held *Global Conferences on Transparency Research* seem to confirm that we are indeed in the presence of an "emergent field" (Götz and Marklund 2015: 242). Still, it has to be noted that except for a group of scholars gathered under the umbrella of *Critical Transparency Studies* (see Birchall 2014 and her contribution to this very volume; Hansen et al. 2015), the academic research scarcely ever critically engages with its unifying concept. Although these publications all feature the notion of "transparency" in the title, they rarely reflect on the specific logic of transparency. Transparency research, as it were, is research *through* transparency and not *about* transparency. Generally speaking, it seems as if "transparency' is more an *operative* concept than a concept that would have been *thematized* in its own right. As Mark Fenster aptly recapitulated the situation, transparency finds itself "in search of a theory" (Fenster 2015: 150).

The lucidity promised by the concept is inversely proportional to its semantic clarity. This perhaps might be explained by the fact that the pursuit of transparency has been "adopted by an extraordinarily broad array of political and policy actors in a remarkably brief period of time" (Fox 2007: 663). Indeed, large-scale semantic analyses confirm that the mention of the notion of transparency in public documents has skyrocketed in the past two decades. This, however, shouldn't preclude any blanked assumptions about the ramified history and adoption of transparency. Christopher Hood has provided a first sketch towards a history of the political concept of transparency, which links back the contemporary notion to its sources in the age of Enlightenment, and even to Greek philosophy (Hood 2006). Such a preliminary overview highlights the extraordinary difficulty of tracing the concept's genealogy, as any attempt at the task immediately diffracts transparency into a variety of competing different meanings, with sometimes irreconcilable implications that oscillate arbitrarily between political and aesthetic meanings (Alloa and Guindani 2011). In actual fact, the stability, clarity and reliability the concept of transparency yields stands in stark contrast to its murky historical grounds.

Transparency has come to be associated with different aspirations in different contexts. In fact, the hopes tied to transparency were multifaceted:

1. Transparency as *accessibility*: Ensuring informational access to all citizens and implementing a "right to know."
2. Transparency as *procedural fairness*: Safeguarding due process to all parties involved.

3. Transparency as *accountability*: By making decisions available to the public, stakeholders are meant to develop a sharpened sense of responsibility and improved accountability.
4. Transparency as *asymmetry reduction*: Against practices of secrecy, which give certain actors an excessive power over certain sectors, disclosure generally is held to re-establish a certain balance of power.
5. Transparency as a *public good*: When actions are placed under public scrutiny, reducing (if not removing altogether) actions driven by self-interest.
6. Transparency as *rationalization*: Forcing actors to give reasons for their actions leads to pervasive bettering of rational behavioral standards.
7. Transparency as *truth-making*: By compelling individuals to speak out, deceit, falseness and duplicity are dispelled.
8. Transparency as *moralization*: Where everything is under permanent exposure, individuals are forced to act virtuously.
9. Transparency as *(self-)knowledge*: Only a subject that *knows* about herself knows what she can rely on and what she can account for.
10. Transparency as *authenticity*: Only where nothing is withheld can things be genuine and subjects true to themselves.

Going further and further down this list means gradually leaving the domain proper of the political and proceeding toward individual morals. Is there a substantial connection between the demand of procedural transparency in the political realm and that of moral or epistemic self-transparency in that of the subject or are we simply faced with a homonymic effect? Is there nothing but a faint family resemblance, as Wittgenstein might put it? What kind of language games are being played via the transparency discourse? The hypothesis guiding this book is that there is indeed more than just a vague family resemblance, and that it is worthwhile to connect those various lines in order to map a discursive and conceptual constellation where so many decisive issues of modernity are negotiated.

From Transparency to Diaphaneity and Back

Today, transparency is often held to be a demand that has to do with the realm of the political. Such a political inflection of transparency, however, is a rather late phenomenon, as the origins of the terms are to be found in optics. Most of the early modern literature about transparency is exclusively concerned with material properties, light transmission, refractive indices and the like. Isaac Newton's *Opticks* from 1704 starts with defining its objects in the following terms: "Refrangibility of the Rays of Light, is their Disposition to be refracted or turned out of their Way in in passing out of one transparent Body or Medium into another" (Newton 1704, Book One: 1) In Newton's optics, transparency is considered to be the minimal state of any material: "*The least parts of almost all natural Bodies are in some measure transparent: And the opacity of those Bodies ariseth from the multitude of reflexions caused in their internal Parts*" (Book 2: 52). However, not all natural scientists believed transparency to be a sign of genuineness, since seeing through also implied the risk of disrespecting the boundaries of things. In his *Micrographia* from 1665, Robert Hooke complained about the sudden transparency of things generated by the microscope. The artificial light under the glass creates a translucency that does not correspond to the natural condition, Hooke complains: "the transparency of most Objects renders much more difficult than if they were opacous" (1665: 23). For a long time, transparency was intended in a strict, literal sense of something through which the gaze could peer freely. However, from the late 1590s on, the earliest occurrences were recorded of a figurative use of "transparency," and consequently not only materials but also situations, schemes, argumentations or personalities could be characterized as "transparent." In the eighteenth century, openness would become a morally laudable character trait, indicating someone who isn't withholding secretive intentions. Yet this metaphorical usage, and the moralization it later allowed, were rather slow to take root in English as well as in other modern European languages.

The English word "transparent," which only later gave rise to the substantivized notion of "transparency," is modeled on the Middle French equivalent ("transparent"/"transparenz"), which is first attested around

1370 in medieval theological and cosmological literature. It is used interchangeably with the word "diaphane," diaphanous, and echoes the semantic array that is to be found in twelfth- and thirteenth-century Latin treatises: *transparens, transparentia, diaphanum, dyaphonum*. The coupling of transparency with diaphaneity happens for good reason: "transparent" constitutes the literal equivalent in Latin of the Greek original word *diaphanês*. The Greek word consists of two parts, *dia* and *phainestai*. While the latter is the middle voice of *phainô*, "to appear," "to shine forth," the former is a preposition corresponding to a wide range of different functions: "through," "on account of," "across," "by" and "over." In light of current scholarly knowledge, the author who coined the term *transparens* is Burgundio of Pisa, in his 1165 translation of *De natura hominis* by Nemesius of Emesa (at the time wrongly held to be a *Treatise on the Soul*; Vasiliu 1997: 90), and this word creation is legitimate in a medieval perspective: "trans"-"parens" is the best possible equivalent of *dia-phanês*, since the Latin prefix "trans" roughly covers most of the functions of the Greek *dia* (in compounds such as *transfiguratio, traductio, transactio, transitus*, and so on, analogously to the notion of perspicuity, which refers to "seeing through," *per-spicere*). Only gradually, the notion of transparency came to alter its semantic valence.

In classical Greek philosophy—and in the medieval commentaries thereof—the first meaning of *diaphanês* is that of a translucid, opalescent quality. In Plato's *Phaedrus*, Socrates and his followers take a walk along the waters of the Ilisos river in the vicinities of Athens, which is described as "*diaphanês*" (229b), and in Near-Eastern Cilicia, Pliny reports details about a river plainly called *Diaphanês*. Rather than transparency, *diaphanês* is probably better rendered by translucidity. In other contexts, it refers to something that "shines through," for example, when a sculptor's talent is said to be measured by his capacity of sculpting a person's bust where the inner personality would "shine through" (*diaphainei*; Xenophon, *Memorabilia* III, 10, 5). Such passages already stress the importance of the "through": the prefix *dia* is meant not alone in a spatial sense, as an obstacle that would be crossed by the gaze, but also in a causal sense, as the instrument of medium "through" which something comes into sight. (Late Antiquity was still very much aware of this causal dimension: in the early sixth century AD, when Boethius had to find an equivalent for the Greek science of optics (*optikê technê*), he minted the expression *perspectiva*, that is, very literally the art of "looking through," where the prefix *per-* both stands for the spatial as well as for the causal aspect.) This twofold aspect of the diaphanous is something that Aristotle will crucially exploit in his theory of perception, turning an everyday expression into a philosophical concept.

In order to understand the complex history of transparency and its premodern sources, it is necessary to focus on the decisive step undertaken by Aristotle. Aristotle is indeed responsible for having transformed, for the purposes of his theory of media perception, an adjective commonly used, up until Plato, into a conceptual idea, by substantivizing what was merely an adjective (*diaphanês*) into a noun (*to diaphanês*). Aristotle's elaborate theory can only be briefly drafted here (for a detailed reconstruction, as well as the reception history of the concept of the diaphanous, see Vasiliu 1997; Alloa 2011). As opposed to preceding accounts of perception, such as the atomist's doctrines, Aristotle does not believe that perception is ever an unmediated process. As the outlines in his *Treatise on the Soul* (*Peri psuchês, De anima*), any sensorial perception occurs in an element such as air or water, and these elements possess certain characteristics that allow them to operate as sensible intermediaries. As such, air may serve as a milieu for hearing, smell and vision, whereas water is solely a medium for vision. Now sensation occurs not so much *in* a milieu as through it, *dia*. Whatever appears (*phainestai*) in sense perception appears *through* (*dia*) something else, which does so much appear *in itself*, rather, it lets something else appear. In the case of vision, any element that yields this quality will be called "diaphanous," inasmuch as on the one hand, it lets the gaze through (*dia*) and on the other, it brings about or generates (*dia*) the visible object for the gaze.

In short, *diaphaneity* encompasses two aspects:

1. *Translucidity*: the permeable quality of a medium that (spatially) lets the vision through
2. *Generativity*: the productive quality of a medium that (causally) lets something come into view.

As it can be easily appreciated, the aspect of generativity is significantly dependent on the aspect of translucidity: in order to let something (else) come to the fore, a diaphanous medium must deflect the attention from itself, anesthetize itself and recede into the background. However, such an inconspicuous, neutralized medium shouldn't be mistaken for an absence of mediation; if the medium is in the remove, it is because from that position, it will fulfill its task all the better. If anything, it occasionally shines through the screen of appearances it helps setting up. In these cases, the medium "appears through," just as one might sense the presence of the wind behind a fluttering flag, although the mass of air is only perceptible through the effects it induces. Following a classical distinction made in phenomenology, one can say that the diaphanous medium is operative though not thematic: the operation consists precisely in setting up a sense of immediacy, in making contact with the thing itself, which thus appears, as it were, in the mode of a "mediated immediacy."

When Burgundio of Pisa translates *to diaphanês* into *transparens* in the twelfth century, both aspects—the translucid and the generative one—are, at least in principle, still preserved. Only over the course of time will the concept of transparency take on the generative, causal sense, and come to signify pure, uncorrupted immediacy. Both the *trans*—the movement, the transfer, the ordeal—and the *parency*—the coming into view—have been ruled out to the benefit of immediate givenness, for a pure *datum*. Yet this means to forget that to establish a transparency between two things and actuate a congruence among them supposes an initial distinction. Instituting a transparent relationship consists, to borrow Nietzsche's expression, in the "identification of what was not identical" (*Gleichsetzen des Nichtgleichen*). Diaphaneity is reminiscent of this fact through its prefix *dia*, which is related to the root *dis*, that is, two-ness or divergence. In other terms, harking back to the historicity of the transparency requirement draws out how transparency is always implying that an instance is made transparent with or for another, that is, transparency always implies that we are in the presence of more than one thing. Where there are transparency effects, we have to do with a situation that is nonidentical, and thus, at odds with itself (for further developments on these points, see Dieter Mersch's contribution to the volume). Consequently, transparency is never given—such would be Aristotle's lesson—but is the result of a specific operation, which comes at a price. Yet, this is precisely what transparency regimes deny: in such regimes, that which is of the order of effects presents itself as unconstrued facts. However, if transparency exists only as manufactured, there can be only transparency where the manufacturing operations are negated or made invisible, just as the windowpane only works if one sees through the glass and not the glass itself. When looking at the windowpane itself, one would learn that it has a frame and that it is meant to offer a view at a particular section of the outside world only. It is unfortunate that framing effects—which are widely discussed in psychology and economics—are not properly addressed in field of transparency studies, even though transparent objects tend to come in certain sizes and to have margins. Transparency symbolizes a medium without qualities, a cultural signifier which stands for the absence of any form of symbolic or non-symbolic intervention. It is synonymous with a *mise-en-scène* whose spectacle consists in staging the absence of any *mise-en-scène*. The "dream of transparency," as Manfred Schneider has poignantly characterized it (see his contribution in this volume), could hence claim many things except one: being a lucid dream; the dreamers dreaming it hardly ever realize the oneiric nature of their aspirations.

Inward and Outward: Psychogenetic and Sociogenetic Transparency

What to make of these observations on the history of the concept? For a better understanding of its implications, we need to return to the present situation. Late modernity is defined by a loosening of grand narratives and a shattering of binding ideologies. After the end of the Cold War, the Western world presents itself as fundamentally post-ideological. It might not be an accident thus, when among all the shining concepts in the pantheon of Enlightenment, transparency has been chosen as the less controversial and most widely acceptable one. Yet, if transparency has become the dominant ideal of an age that considers itself to be post-ideological, it is this very claim that must be interrogated. Faced with the self-asserted neutrality towards ideology of late modernity, it becomes growingly important to analyze transparency for what it purports to be: an ideology of neutrality. What requires attention is how, of all the various leading normative demands modernity inherited from Enlightenment, transparency is the one that survived, almost unscathed, all fundamental self-criticisms of modernity.

What can be observed, in the light of the history of the idea, from a translation of the Greek notion of the diaphanous to early modern theories of vision, is how the metaphorization of the concept has been immediately subject to a self-denial. The metaphorical, derivative use of transparency, which allowed it, mainly from the eighteenth century on, to be used as a normative concept for intervening in the fields of morals and against political authorities, essentially rested on a self-fashioning as literal and non-metaphorical: the *trans-* was reserved to the travesties and charades, while appearances themselves became suspicious. Against the play of masks and roles, transparency progressively came to mark a demand for openness and immediacy. Wherever external actors or forces are likely to intervene, the objectivity of the process is brought into question. Just as the transparent medium had to deny any responsibility to the operating medium, the procedure now presents itself as inherently self-steering, since any hint of a potential intervention would stigmatize the procedure as biased.

No one embodies this paradigm shift better than Jean-Jacques Rousseau, whose obsession for transparency is well known, not least because of Starobinki's influential *Transparency and Obstruction* (Starobinski 1972). His writings are entirely suffused, as Starobinski showed, by the ideal of achieved intrasubjective and intersubjective transparency, of unhindered communication of souls cleared of dissimulation, devised as the paradise of reciprocal, heart-to-heart communication. "In the whole course of my life one has seen that my heart, transparent as crystal, has never been able to hide for an entire minute a slightly lively feeling that has taken refuge in it" (Rousseau 1995: 375). Yet paradoxically, all the while claiming that the subject of enunciation never was but transparent, Rousseau's *Confessions* aim at *making* that very subject transparent: "I would like to be able to render my soul transparent to the eyes of the reader in some fashion, and to do so I seek to show it to him under all points of view, to clarify it by all lights, to act in such a way that no motion occurs in it that he does not perceive so that he might be able to judge by himself about the principle which produces them" (Rousseau 1995: 146). Once again, the tension between transparency as a claimed original state and transparency as a *telos* to be reached is palpable, as if the originary unmasked condition could only be reached by a deliberate operation, by a *confession*, a *confiteor*, that performatively brings about what it bespeaks (on the confessional paradigm, see Noreen Khawaja's contribution to this book). Rousseauism's echoes in modernity have been numerous, perhaps most prominently in existentialism. In a famous interview, Jean-Paul Sartre professed his engagement towards full transparency as the only means for an authentic society:

> I think transparency should always be substituted for what is secret, and I can quite well imagine the day when two men will no longer have secrets from each other, because no one will have any more secrets from anyone, because subjective life, as well as objective life, will be completely offered up, given. It is impossible to accept the fact that we would yield our bodies as we do and keep our thoughts hidden, since for me there is no basic difference between the body and the consciousness. (Sartre 1975: 12)

Beyond this individual thread about transparency as a psychogenetic technique, both inward and outward-directed, we find transparency invoked in political terms, as an instrument for achieving a better, more rational and just society. While it comes up in the eighteenth century, it is mainly in the nineteenth century that transparency is featured as a tool of the oppressed for forcing into the *arcana imperii* and the occult dealings behind closed doors. In close relation to the notion of publicity (*Öffentlichkeit*)—scholarship debates whether they are synonymous or whether they should be set apart—transparency gestures towards a public tribunal of reason, an idea central in Rousseau and in the French Revolution, but also in later philosophers, in authors such as John Stuart Mill, Madison and most sharply in Jeremy Bentham.

The "eye of the public," Bentham states, "makes the statesman virtuous" (Bentham 1843, vol. X: 227) and forces it to provide reasons for each and every one of his acts. Although Bentham is often credited for having formulated the transparency demand for the first time explicitly, and thus the legitimacy of the demand for a "right to know," such a description only grasps half the truth, since Bentham not only upholds the idea of the public of a "superintendent," but also that of a self-moralization of society. The famous "civilizing effect" of publicity (J. Elster) can be seen at work in the pragmatist environment. Bentham, who presented himself as the "Newton of legislation" wants to imagine a conception of law based on nature itself, and transparency, studied extensively by the author of *Opticks*, comes to stand for a powerful instrument for shaping a new commonwealth. In his famed *Panopticon*, transparency is meant to represent an unprecedented "new mode of obtaining power of mind over mind" (Bentham 1995: 31). All traces of punishment should be erased, to the benefit of what Bentham describes as "indirect" legislation. While the old form of punitive, "vulgar" legislation "drags men to its purposes in chains," which will eventually lead to their breakdown, indirect or "transcendental" legislation will guide individuals "by silken threads, entwined round their affections, and makes them its own forever" (*Essays on the Poor Laws*; quoted after Pitkin 1990: 552). No longer should the authority of the law impose itself through coercive power, rather should the laws "infuse themselves, so to speak, into the minds of the people" and "obedience to the laws would be come to be hardly distinguishable from the feeling of liberty" (*Promulgation of the Laws*; quoted after Pitkin 1990: 552). Bentham's soft power (for a more detailed analysis, and its inner ambivalences, see Miran Božovič's contribution to this volume) draws close not only to contemporary practices of "nudging" (also known as liberal paternalism), it also exemplifies the move from external coercion to internalized self-control described by Foucault. When behavior is likely to be judged by others, so the argument, subjects will automatically adapt their conduct. In a conversation with David Collins, who in 1803 planned to implement Bentham's Panopticon model in Australia, Bentham makes clear that transparency must have two sides, an inward and an outward one: an inward transparency, between the inmates and the warden, and an outward transparency, since the panoptic architecture as a whole should be understood in a glance by the external world. Often decried in surveillance studies, the unidirectionality within the Panopticon would thus only represent a first step in this societal model characterized by decompartmentalization and permeability.

Transparency as Openness: A Contradiction?

The ideal of a transparent subject, characterized by self-knowledge, self-rule and ownership, is mirrored in the ideal of a transparent society characterized by openness and self-governance. What is at stake is whether transparency can claim to stand for the openness it purports to bring about. An openness that can take various forms, and in part it overlaps with some of the varieties of transparency listed above: an openness in terms of accessibility of information ("seeing it all"), an openness in terms of sincerity ("saying it all") as well as an openness in terms of potential participation and transformation ("doing it all") (see also the contribution by Dieter Thomä in this volume). These requirements, which emerge in rather different fields (epistemology, moral philosophy, theory of action) are significantly conflated in the single ideal of transparency, although its very metaphor often seems at odds with the openness attached to it: the visual semantics of "seeing-through" cannot be immediately connected to the verbal semantics, not to mention the semantics of action: after all, actions taking place behind a glassy windowpane might be in view of an onlooker, but this visual access might just exacerbate a sense of impotence. Frequently, the rhetoric of transparency masks factual inaccessibility. More importantly, however, transparency as openness faces an ontological contradiction: is transparency constative or transformative? Does it register a fact or does it elicit change?

One of the defining features of publicity as *Öffentlichkeit* (from German *offen*, "open," which is very imperfectly rendered as "public sphere") was its stress on the open-endedness of deliberative processes. From the perspective of Enlightenment, public matters need decisions on the basis of the sole fact that they are not prescribed by any external authority, but should be determined in cooperation with those affected by these decisions. The openness of *Öffentlichkeit* thus not only concerns the external gazes, but the indeterminacy of the procedures, whose outcome must be unpredictable, if the procedure is to be more than just a staged ritual. In other words; openness has to do with contingency: the course of events is inherently undetermined, *things could be otherwise*. Such an understanding is directly tied to an understanding of democracy as an infinite, unresolved process of deliberation as Habermas defined it or as a "democracy to come" in the sense of Derrida, which can have no previous or ultimate foundation other than an unwavering openness to what is yet to come. In any event, such conceptualizations offer a standard by which to evaluate current conceptions of the transparency demand. Can a procedure ever be "fully transparent"? Certainly not if it is still to come, given that the only procedure that can be made fully transparent is a procedure whose outcome has already been decided beforehand. There is an inherent contradiction between the two adjectives within the demand for "open and transparent procedures": both parameters seem to contradict each other. Some authors have then argued that, while there can be no transparency *ex ante* without compromising the open-endedness of the process, what legislations should require is a transparency *ex post*, which retrospectively discloses the reasons leading to a certain decision-making result. Yet what must be borne in mind is that such *ex post* transparency is itself an act of "justification," an *operation*, which itself might modify further processes.

A similar argument can be made for the debate about the improvement of markets and the requirements of market transparency. Long before the financial crisis of 2008, analogous questions were raised right after World War II by the Austrian economist Oskar Morgenstern, who would coauthor the *Theory of Games and Economic Behaviour* with John von Neumann. One of its crucial assumptions, however—that market behavior can never be made fully transparent—had already been put forward in 1935, in a journal article titled "Perfect Foresight and Economic Equilibrium" ("Vollkommene Voraussicht und Wirtschaftliches Gleichgewicht"). In this article, Morgenstern asserted that transparent expectation and the balanced equilibrium are mutually exclusive. In the case of a complete knowledge of all parameters, including that of all future behavior of its participants, the market, rather than following a better rationale, will stall. The reason for this being that in the case of full predictability, the plans and future actions of a market participant would be dependent on the plans and future actions of all the others. Since this condition holds true for all market participants, Morgenstern asserts that we are faced with the following paradox: all actions would have to be determined before they can be determined. Morgenstern illustrated his position by means of the following example, already used in his monograph on *Economic Prognostics* (*Wirtschaftsprognose*, 1928), and which is drawn from a famous episode in Sherlock Holmes.

> Sherlock Holmes, pursued by his opponent, Moriarty, leaves for Dover. The train stops at a station on the way, and he alights there rather than traveling on to Dover. He has seen Moriarty at the railway station, recognizes that he is very clever, and expects that Moriarty will take a special faster train in order to catch him at Dover. Holmes' anticipation turns out to be correct. But what if Moriarty had been still more clever, had estimated Holmes' mental abilities better and had foreseen his actions accordingly? Then obviously he would have traveled to the intermediate station. Holmes, again, would have had to calculate that, and he himself would have decided to go on to Dover. Whereupon Moriarty would have "reacted" differently. Because of so much thinking they might not have been able to act at all or the intellectually weaker of the two would have surrendered to the other in the Victoria Station, since the whole flight would have become unnecessary. (Morgenstern 1928: 173–174)

If one were to radicalize Morgenstern's thesis, this would imply that full market transparency does not lead to more fluid, harmonious and rational behavior, but that it rather tends to immobilize all potential actions and ultimately leads to complete stalemate. In less dramatic terms, the Morgenstern example epitomizes why the hope for a full market transparency is based on false premises, inasmuch as it doesn't take into account what social theory has described as "double contingency."

Double contingency—a concept originally put forth by Talcott Parsons and then generalized by Niklas Luhmann—refers to the fact that whenever communicative interaction takes place, the communicative act must take into account the way it will be received, which adds a further parameter of uncertainty: not only is the success of the communicative act hazardous, as the channel between a sender and a receiver can be disrupted, but also the act's success must be measured according to the receiver's reaction (Luhmann 1995: 103–137). Beyond a first black box, there is a second one, and for a certain number of accidental or non-accidental reasons, these two black boxes have dealings with one another. Such double contingency gestures towards a form of reciprocal dependency, where two behaviors are literally "stapled together." In extreme cases, this leads to a paralytic state, given that with two black boxes each one's behavior becomes dependent upon the other's. Market behavior itself is always based on some asymmetry of information, but this observation could be generalized beyond the realm of the market, since, in a Freudian sense, civilization too is based on self-restraint and concealment, and would break down if people could read each other's minds. As such, even though transparency has now largely replaced the notions of publicity and *Öffentlichkeit* (on this point, see Sandrine Baume's contribution to this book), it seems unlikely that the newer concept could cover all the aspects of the older ones. But, to a great extent, this is precisely what has happened.

Whose Enlightenment?

Davd Pozen (2018) has gathered instructive materials which testify that in the last decades of US legal history, transparency has diverged from broader progressive values such as egalitarianism or social improvement through state action (Pozen describes this as an *ideological drift*). Although transparency is still heralded as an instrument to improve procedures and to root out undesirable conduct, across many policy domains, the ideal of transparency has increasingly been integrated with agendas seeking to reduce the impact of regulations and to increase private choice. Even as notions of participation and public-spiritedness wane, transparency has become an argument for libertarian agendas in order to make government smaller, less intrusive, and less influential. Pozen's evidence for the US American situation can be generalized to other contexts too: uncontestably, in contemporary discourses, transparency risen to the status of a kind of post-ideological norm. As Byung-Chul Han pointed out, transparency could just as easily be seen as an "ideology" which "like all ideologies [...] has a positive core that has been mystified and made absolute" (Han 2015: viii). Enlightenment broadly stood in for epistemic, social and moral progress, for the project of knowing oneself and shedding full light onto one's own deepest motives and drives, but moreover, for the promise of universal accessibility, for clearing up occult wheelings and dealings, and more generally for the fight against all processes that take place behind closed doors and which are therefore under suspicion of serving particular interests. Transparency seems to be the last lingering remnant of the heritage of the European Enlightenment, after its ambivalent questionings in the course of the twentieth century. "Sunlight is the best disinfectant," Justice Louis Brandeis famously said (Brandeis 1913: 10). More recently, Wikileaks founder Julian Assange put this even more plainly: "lights on, rats out."[1] While there would be indeed good reasons to list it among the catalogue of values which form the basic requests formulated by Enlightenment (emancipation, autonomy, universality, tolerance etc.), transparency also occupies a peculiar position: on the one hand, of such demands, transparency is maybe the one most intimately connected with the project of Enlightenment as such (even if only because of its semantic origin, which has to do with optics and clarity); on the other, it is the only one that has probably never undergone any thorough questioning during the twentieth century.

Horkheimer and Adorno famously argued that Enlightenment is characterized by an inherent yet unavowed dialectics in its relationship to myth. In their *Dialectic of Enlightenment* (Horkheimer and Adorno 1947), the two authors described the Enlightenment as a project of a general *Entzauberung* or dis-enchantment, aiming at reverting to plain reality and to things as they are, stripped bare of mythical projections, the ruin of fancy and the substitution of imagination with knowledge. However, all the while trying to extirpate myth, the Enlightenment itself sets up a new myth, that of history as endless progress, which it violently rigidifies. Written under the immediate impression of World War II, *The Dialectic of Enlightenment* bespeaks a profound disillusionment concerning the regulating ideals of Enlightenment. The program of a general pacification through the free use of reason—the *Eternal Peace*, to which Kant dedicated a famous essay—appears, in the historical context of the

---

[1] Julian Assange in Alex Gibney's documentary movie *We Steal Secrets: The Story of WikiLeaks* (USA, 2013).

twentieth century's extremes of violence, as utter naïve: signed in the name of pacifism, the Munich Agreement of 1938 stood not so much for an end of war as for heralding its start. When confronted with the rise of fascism, liberal democracies reach their self-imposed limits in trying to decide whether tolerance should be applicable also to opinions which seek to abolish those democracies' principles. According to a famous phrase posthumously attributed to him, Voltaire allegedly declared that although he might disapprove of (or wholly disagree with) his opponent's position, he would defend to the death the right to say it. However, every democracy touches upon an inner paradox when confronted with the enemies of freedom, insofar as it can't concede such enemies that they abolish democracy as such. The same goes for the claim of universality: this principle so central to the rationality of Enlightenment fell into disrepute in the course of decolonization movements, when it became obvious that universality had functioned as a linchpin in the expansionist discourses of European colonial powers. Last but not least, the idea of self-legislation, inherent in the concept of the autonomous individual, has become far less cut-and-dry in these times of "enterprising selves" (M. Foucault), who manage themselves as resources and as investment assets.

In contrast to these leading principles of Enlightenment that have started to shimmer ambivalently, transparency rides out the past almost intact; it almost seems to have usurped the conceptual space ceded by the other, dwindling principles. It now stands as the ideal that must fulfill the unkept promises of the others. Today, transparency appears as fundamentally *undialectical*, bereft of any negative outside and as such, as unrestrictedly positive. In a society ruled by the paradigm of transparency, transparency itself represents the blind spot; when transparency ended up absorbing other forms of critique, there is no longer any outside left from where transparency could potentially be criticized. Evidence has accumulated that the effects of transparency regimes often generate the opposite of what they proclaim, such as the fact that transparency regimes frequently favor demagogic argumentations in order to please and flatter the audience, while excluding arguments that might be sincerer, but less likely acceptable (Chambers 2004: esp. 393). Moreover, they hardly ever restore trust: transparency as a trust-building measure is hardly ever efficient (on the topic of trust and transparency, see Caspar Hirschi's essay in this volume). Recent research in Western European countries have shown that transparency is first and foremost a "hygiene factor": it does not necessarily contribute towards higher levels of trust. In some cases, it eventually even lowers general trust scores as a result of a general disappointment after the disclosure of the inner proceedings of government (Grimmelikhuijsen and Meijer 2014). As Bismarck allegedly remarked—and this remark is topical in this context too—"Laws, like sausages, cease to inspire respect in proportion as we know how they are made." Most importantly, however, transparency regimes suggest a dubious neutrality where the procedure would have no bearing on the content.

From Univocity to Plurality: A Cubist Outlook

Some preliminary conclusions can be drawn. In an allegedly post-ideological era, it is telling that the highest, uncontroversial value is a principle pretending to regulate only the form, not the content, of social interactions: a principle that purports to be neutral, all the while imposing a morality upon both public and private life. Open-plan offices, reality TV, corporate buildings made of glass, personal computers in translucent casings, online confessions, restaurant kitchens where food is prepared in plain view—much hints indeed at transparency being a major obsession of our time. On the backdrop of a more detailed analysis of transparency's historical semantics, however, the proclamation of a new transparentocene and the kind of "transparency explosion" envisioned by Daniel C. Dennett and Deb Roy appear questionable: the variety of things covered by the catchword hardly mask its polysemy. When both political leaders and dissidents, corporate CEOs as well as hacktivists, find themselves commonly defending the value of transparency, the grounds for this consensual merging begin to founder and those who surmise ongoing practices of "openwashing" might have a reason. As an unrestrictedly positive ideal, it is hard to criticize transparency policies, unless exposing oneself to the suspicion of defending regressive aims. Against those who castigate the "new narcissism" of the social media generation, many of its actors consider it to be a liberating move to be able to unrestrictedly express themselves on their blogs and online profiles (on this self-exposure oscillating between narcissistic hyperindividualization and perverse de-personalization, see Vincent Kaufmann's contribution to this volume). As it were, exposure has moved from a repressive Panopticism to a voluntary form of self-exposure; while few might question that there is something like an *expository power*, many consider that, rather than fighting it, it should be diverted for one's own proper interests (on this aspect, see Bernard Harcourt's chapter in this book). Taking "selfies" becomes a new means for fashioning subjectivity (on the paradoxes of the selfie, see Jörg Metelmann's and Thomas Telios's essay).

The best organized resistance chiefly takes place in the name of "privacy" and the defense of individual rights. Such a perspective, where the "right to be left alone" would derive from an inalienable personal prerogative presupposes, however, that the boundaries between public and private are drawn once and for all, what many political struggles have contested (e.g. feminist claims that 'the private is political' or the fight against marital rape), not to mention the fact that it presumes that identity is a matter of personal ownership, preceding the individual's social interactions. As they fight against surveillance and unwilling exposure, privacy advocates oftentimes fall into the trap of an inverted transparentism, when turning personal identity into a realm fully under the individual's oversight. On the one hand, Facebook's claims that it would be "immoral" to have more than one identity; on the other, the defense of privacy becomes an argument for an immunization against commonality, shared identities and transversal concerns. As a result, transparency regimes often lead to increased segmentation and compartmentalization, where the travesty of full visibility significantly curtails most prospects of action and perspectives of change. Paradoxically, rather than eliciting transformation, transparency breeds conformity (on this argument, see Thomas Docherty's contribution to this volume). While such reductionisms betray an obsession with univocal, stable, and unmovable identities of beings, an investigation into the historical aspirations associated with transparency draws attention to other, marginalized aspects.

The insistence on transparency was long premised on superpositions, encroachments and permeability. Rather than dangling the prospect of an ultimate coincidence with the things themselves, transparency amounted to accounting for dissonant, yet overlapping realities. Many artistic avant-gardes have played with transparent materials, but their emphases were still on plural intersections and dynamic interconnections. Cubist paintings by Braque, Gris or the early Picasso experiment with the principle of depicting incompossible simultaneous viewpoints on one object on one single surface. In the Soviet constructivist art of El Lissitzky or Rodchenko, lines, planes and surfaces create a virtual space of superposing and receding objects. At the Bauhaus, artists and architects play with hovering qualities of permeable materials such as glass and cellophane. Among others, the Hungarian-born artist László Moholy-Nagy implements cross-medium experiments with light, color and space, modulating translucidity in various way, combining light projectors, mobiles, photograms and three-dimensional plexiglass sculptures. The very point of transparency, as the artist explains, is not to fix the gaze, but on the contrary, to set vision in motion, as his eponymous book title expresses (Moholy-Nagy 1947). The artist eventually starts not only to superpose the semi-transparent planes, as in Soviet constructivism, but to distort the thermoplastic planes by heating them, creating complex concave and convex shapes with changing spatial relationships, because the forms partly caught the ambient light (Fig. 2).

In his book *Space, Time and Architecture*, Moholy-Nagy's close friend Siegfried Giedion famously juxtaposed the Bauhaus building at Dessau with Picasso's *Arlésienne* (Fig. 3) suggesting that the beholder was in the presence of transparency effects that simultaneously stressed see-through qualities and the role of the supporting medium (Giedion 1949: 426-427). In other words, such an analytical Cubism contests the total dissociation of medium and content, and stresses the plurality of viewpoints. In their classic analysis on "Transparency, Literal and Phenomenal," the architecture theorists Rowe and Slutzky have put into evidence how, next to the literal transparency there is a phenomenal transparency that has to do with object in enfilade, seen through one another (Rowe & Slutzky 1964). Rather than with fully lit, but self-enclosed entities, the experiments with pellucid materials, cellophane, plexiglass and color planes gesture towards more ambiguous identities characterized by interpenetration and a dialectic of oscillating foregrounds and backgrounds. György Kepes's persuasive definition from his *Language of Vision* is invoked:

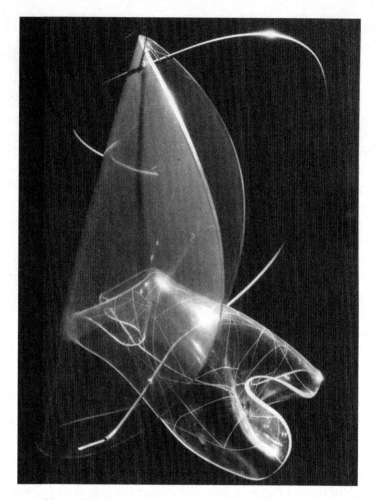

Fig. 2 László Moholy-Nagy, *Space Modulator* [*Transparency Plus!*], 1940, 33.7 × 25.4 cm. *Private Collection*. Photo: Milton Halberstadt

If one sees two or more figures overlapping one another, and each of them claims for itself the common overlapped part, then one is confronted with a contradiction of spatial dimensions. To resolve this contradiction one must assume the presence of a new optical quality. The figures are endowed with transparency; that is they are able to interpenetrate without an optical destruction of each other. Transparency however implies more than an

Fig. 3 Siegfried Giedion, *Space, Time and Architecture: The growth of the new tradition*, 2nd edition Cambridge: The Harvard University Press, 1949, pp. 426–427

optical characteristic, it implies a broader spatial order. Transparency means: a simultaneous perception of different spatial locations. Space not only recedes but fluctuates in a continuous activity. The position of the transparent figures has equivocal meaning as one sees each figure now as the closer now as the further one. (Kepes 1944: 77)

Consequently, this transparency is not so much about a unique, genuine object as about situations of partial overlapping and cross-penetration, necessitating space to be made for alternating orderings and hierarchies in space, diverse meanings and plural understandings. As Moholoy-Nagy explains in *Vision in Motion*: "Superimpositions overcome space and time fixations... They transpose insignificant singularities into meaningful complexities; banalities into vivid illumination. The transparent quality of the superimpositions often suggest transparency of content as well, revealing unnoticed structural qualities in the object" (Moholy-Nagy 1947: 210).

It would be worth recalling this other sense of transparency, as it was devised by the artistic avant-gardes in Modern Art. Rather than suggesting false unity, the superposition of different planes lets inconsistencies, partial overlaps and congruences emerge, but it also allow to jumble up and reorder what is deemd to be significant or insignificant. First and foremost, this superposition makes it possible to recapture a sense of transparency that does not preclude conflictuality. Rather than presenting transparency as a horizon where conflicts and interests would be ultimately overcome, such experiments in transparency make evident how neutrality is itself the result of a neutralization. And these experiments inspire a critical understanding of individual and social transformation, insofar as polysemy and double-entendre are not only indications of falseness and dissimulation, but indicate multiple entries as well as passageways where there seemed to be none. Accordingly, Fig. 1 might be read a new way: beyond the startling prospect of a "glassy self" in an age of surveillance, as it is often understood, Hajo Rose's self-portrait from 1930 should be considered anew in its original context, that of a photographic experimentation with multiple exposure. If the grid structure of the Dessau Bauhaus architecture built by Gropius and its characteristic radiators shine through the artist's face, it might be understood both as an act of belonging and as an act of faith in a constructivist aesthetics and its principle of diaphaneity, that is, that in every artistic appearance, the underlying construction shines through, as if to gainsay any ultimate and full transparency.

Such observations are not restricted to the field of aesthetics, far from it: they are also instructive to summon up a different sense of transparency in the context of personal and social existence. To begin with, the analysis of transparency effects in art highlights the importance of framing. Any form of phenomenal transparency requires certain framings, just as a windowpane is not unrestrictedly transparent, but only within a certain given frame. So far, the specific interventions of framing are hardly ever analyzed, when it comes to psychological, moral and social framings. Moreover, a certain given frame sets up an optic continuity between things in a row, but it also underscores, by visually superposing them, their unanticipated interconnections. The polysemy of transparency, which the history of such a "thick" concept brings to light, also points to an inherent and irreducible plurality of the phenomenon it purportedly describes. Transparency is not only about unrestricted immediacy and self-coincidence, phenomenally speaking, it stands for situations where things are seen in superposition, making evident that their borders not necessarily match. Just as our selves are entities accessible through multiple entries, social existence has to do with the overlap of domains, interests and fields, with an inner plurality of meaning which requires transactions, negotiations and revisions. Beyond the dream of total continuity and oneness on the one hand, and the dream of total segmentation and privatization of life and its domains on the other, this alternative understanding of transparency points towards the unescapable interpenetration, entanglement and overlays of our existences. Beyond the neurotic pursuit of attaining unmistakable, univocal and unshakable identities, making space for the existence of conflicting and sometimes contradictory forces is a way of making space for potential transformations too, since where there are overlays, what comes to be renegotiated are the shifting boundaries of sense.

Works Cited

Ala'i, Padideh, and Robert G. Vaughn. 2014. *Research Handbook on Transparency*. Cheltenham and Northampton: Elgar Publishing.
Alloa, Emmanuel. 2011. *Das durchscheinende Bild. Konturen einer medialen Phänomenologie*. Berlin and Zurich: diaphanes (2nd revised edition 2018).
———. 2016. What Is About to Come Will Be Dominated by Transparency. On Glass Architecture and Modernism's Ambivalent Legacy. In *TRANSPARENCIES. The ambivalence of a new visibility*, ed. Simone Neuenschwander and Thomas Thiel, 76–79. Bielefeld; Nürnberg; Berlin: Bielefelder Kunstverein; Kunstverein Nürnberg; Kulturstiftung des Bundes.
Alloa, Emmanuel, and Sara Guindani, eds. 2011. *La transparence: Esthétique et politique*, Special issue of the journal *Appareil* 7, Paris: Maison des Sciences de l'Homme Paris Nord.
Benjamin, Walter. 1929 [2005]. The Return of the Flâneur. Trans. Rodney Livingstone. In *Selected Writings, Volume 2: Part 1: 1927–1930*, ed. Michael W. Jennings, Howard Eiland, and Gary Smith, 262–267. Cambridge, MA: Belknap.

Bentham, Jeremy. 1843 [1962]. *The Works of Jeremy Bentham*. Ed. John Bowring. New York: Russell & Russell, vol. X.
———. 1995. *The Panopticon Writings*. Ed. Miran Božovič. London: Verso Press.
Birchall, Clare. 2014. Radical Transparency? *Cultural Studies ↔ Critical Methodologies* 14 (1): 77–88.
Brandeis, Louis D. 1913. What Publicity Can Do. *Harper's Weekly* 58, no. 2974.
Chambers, Simone. 2004. Behind Closed Doors: Publicity, Secrecy, and the Quality of Deliberation. *Journal of Political Philosophy* 12 (4): 389–410.
Christensen, Lars Thøger, and Joep Cornelissen. 2015. Organizational Transparency as Myth and Metaphor. *European Journal of Social Theory* 18 (2): 132–149.
Dennett, Daniel C., and Deb Roy. 2015. Our Transparent Future. *Scientific American* 312 (3): 64–69.
Fenster, Mark. 2015. Transparency in Search of a Theory. *European Journal of Social Theory* 18 (2): 150–167.
———. 2017. *The Transparency Fix. Secrets, Leaks, and Uncontrollable Government Information*. Stanford: Stanford UP.
Fox, Jonathan. 2007. The Uncertain Relationship Between Transparency and Accountability. *Development in Practice* 17 (4–5): 663–671.
Giedion, Siegfried. 1949. *Space, Time and Architecture: The Growth of the New Tradition*. 2nd ed. Cambridge: The Harvard University Press.
Götz, Norbert, and Carl Marklund, eds. 2015. *The Paradox of Openness: Transparency and Participation in Nordic Cultures of Consensus*. Leiden: Brill.
Grimmelikhuijsen, Stephan G., and Albert J. Meijer. 2014. Effects of Transparency on the Perceived Trustworthiness of a Government Organization—Evidence from an Online Experiment. *Journal of Public Administration Research and Theory* 24 (1): 137–157.
Han, Byung-Chul. 2015. *The Transparency Society*. Trans. Erik Butler. Stanford: Stanford UP.
Hansen, Hans Krause, Lars Thøger Christensen, and Mikkel Flyverbom. 2015. Introduction: Logics of Transparency in Late Modernity: Paradoxes, Mediation and Governance. *European Journal of Social Theory* 18 (2): 117–131.
Hood, Christopher. 2006. Transparency in Historical Perspective. In *Transparency: The Key to Better Governance?* ed. Christopher Hood and David Heald, 1–23. Oxford: Oxford University Press.
Hooke, Robert. 1665. *Micrographia: Or, Some Physiological Descriptions of Minute Bodies Made by Magnifying Glasses*. London: The Royal Society.
Horkheimer, Max, and Theodor W. Adorno. 1947. *Dialectic of Enlightenment. Philosophical Fragments*, trans. Edmund Jephcott. Stanford: Stanford UP.

Kepes, György. 1944. *The Language of Vision*. Chicago: Theobold.
Latour, Bruno. 1993. *We Have Never Been Modern*. Trans. Catherine Porter. Cambridge, MA: Harvard University Press.
Libaert, Thierry. 2003. *La transparence en trompe-l'oeil*. Paris: Éditions Descartes & Cie.
Luhmann, Niklas. 1995. *Social Systems*. Trans. John Bednarz with Dirk Baecker. Stanford: Stanford UP.
Lyon, David. 2009. Surveillance, Power and Everyday Life. In *The Oxford Handbook of Information and Communication Technologies*, ed. Chrisanthi Avgerou, Robin Mansell, Danny Quah, and Roger Silverstone, 449–472. Oxford: Oxford UP.
Moholy-Nagy, László. 1947. *Vision in Motion*. Chicago: P. Theobald.
Morgenstern, Oskar. 1928. *Wirtschaftsprognose. Eine Untersuchung ihrer Voraussetzungen und Möglichkeiten*. Vienna: Springer.
Newton, Isaac. 1704. *Opticks Or, A treatise of the Reflections, Refractions, Inflexions and Colours of Light. Also Two treatises of the Species and Magnitude of Curvilinear Figures*. London [New York: Dover, 1952].
Piotrowski, Suzanne J., ed. 2010. *Transparency and Secrecy. A Reader Linking Literature and Contemporary Debate*. Plymouth: Lexington Books.
Pitkin, Hannah. 1990. Slippery Bentham. Some Neglected Cracks in the Foundation of Utilitarianism. In *Jeremy Bentham. Critical Assessments*, ed. Bhiku Pareth, vol. 3: Laws and Politics, London and New York: Routledge 1993, 534–560.
Pollitt, Christopher, and Peter Hupe. 2011. Talking About Government. The Role of Magic Concepts. *Public Management Review* 13: 641–658.
Pozen, David. 2018. Transparency's Ideological Drift. Yale Law Journal 128 (forthcoming)
Rousseau, Jean-Jacques. 1995. *The Confessions and Correspondence, including the letters to Malesherbes*. Trans. Christopher Kelly, The Collected Writings of Rousseau, vol. 5, Hanover: New England.
Rowe, Colin, and Robert Slutzky. 1964. 'Transparency: Literal and Phenomenal,' *Transparency*. Ed. B. Hoesli. Basel-Boston-Berlin: Birkhäuser, 1997: 21–56.
Sartre, Jean-Paul. 1975. *Sartre at Seventy: An Interview with Michel Contat*. Trans. Paul Auster and Lydia Davis, *New York Review of Books*, August 7, 1975, 10–17.
Starobinski, Jean. 1972 [1988]. *Jean-Jacques Rousseau: Transparency and Obstruction*. Trans. Arthur Goldhammer. Chicago: University of Chicago Press.
Vasiliu, Anca. 1997. *Du diaphane*. Paris: Vrin.

Seeing It All, Doing It All, Saying It All: Transparency, Subject, and the World

Dieter Thomä

A critical reading of transparency takes issue with the dream of *seeing it all*. On the most fundamental level, it requires a discussion of the status of *seeing* in the context of a subject's activities in general, and of its access to *all* there is or, for lack of a better word, to "all-ness."

As will become clear in the first section of this paper, the reaching out to the world is by no means limited to "seeing" but takes on different forms. Three such cases will be analyzed: the attempts of doing it all, saying it all, and seeing it all. While exerting these activities, the subject takes on different forms, and so does its field of operation or the envisaged allness. The "dictatorship of transparency" (Pingeot 2016) may hate competition, but given the plurality of subjective activities directed at all-ness or the world its primacy is in question.

Whereas the first section is based on historical findings from Sophocles to Bentham, the second section will turn to today's regime of transparency, discuss its various forms, and question its appeal to an unimpeded,

---

D. Thomä (✉)
School of Humanities and Social Sciences, University of St. Gallen,
St. Gallen, Switzerland
e-mail: dieter.thomae@unisg.ch

© The Author(s) 2018
E. Alloa, D. Thomä (eds.), *Transparency, Society and Subjectivity*,
https://doi.org/10.1007/978-3-319-77161-8_4

unmediated access to the objective sphere. It will be shown that transparency is based on a distorted model of the subject and of all-ness.

Much Ado About Everything

Doing It All: From Sophocles to Shelley

Well-behaved, good-natured people do what they are supposed to do. They learn what is right, abide by the law, and do not go off limits. Their choices stay within the canon of admissible, recommendable, laudable deeds. Their perceptions stick to the ordinary; everything else is not of this world. Their ontology—if they have any—can be condensed to the assertion "that which *must* not, *can* not be [*dass nicht sein* kann, *was nicht sein* darf]." (A less poetical, but probably more comprehensible translation of this line coined by the humorous poet Christian Morgenstern reads: "that those things which are not supposed to be here, cannot exist"; Morgenstern 1933: 34–35.)

Against the backdrop of this concededly blunt picture, those who do not care much about this customary framework can be depicted in two different ways. As they infringe rules, they can be called bad or evil. As their horizon is not constricted to preconceived precepts, they can be regarded as people entitled to consider and do everything. The first variant stands for normative judgment, the second emphasizes agency.

This scrupulous, as of yet concededly enigmatic distinction serves the purpose of doing justice to a fascinating word in ancient Greek and, specifically, to its use in Sophocles' *Antigone*. Literally speaking, this word—*panourgia*—just means the ability to do everything. Its roots are *pan* (all, everything) and *ergon* (work, deed, action). This literal meaning recedes in the everyday use of *panourgia* when it is meant to designate the activity of a wily villain or knave.[1] In this word, the focus on an agent or subject

---

[1] Inevitably, this semantic setting brings to mind another, equally prominent example from Greek literature. Homer, in the very first line of his *Odyssey*, calls Odysseus *polutropos* and introduces him as a master of schemes, a versatile hero turning many ways: "Polytropy is synonymous with [...] 'cunning,' 'shrewdness'" (Pucci 1987: 16). Compared to *polutropos*, the meaning of *panourgos* is decidedly more negative though. Here the idea that "everything" can be done is paired with the

and the reference to normative criteria are intertwined in a strange manner.

Panourgia comes up in a decisive scene at the beginning of Sophocles' tragedy. The conflict unfolds as Antigone decides to bury her beloved brother Polyneices in Thebes. This is an outright breach of the law enforced by King Creon who regards him as an enemy not deserving a grave on city grounds. Antigone does not side with her sister Ismene who—following the authoritative translation of Sophocles' play by Hugh Lloyd-Jones—"obey[s] those in authority; for there is no sense in actions that exceed our powers." Antigone replies: "It is honourable for me to do this." She is willing to die after having buried her brother and "having committed a crime that is holy [*hosia panourgésas*]" (Sophocles 1994: 11). Just to state the fact: Antigone's provocation consists in the fact that she combines *panourgia* with holiness. When translated as "committing a crime,"[2] *pan* or "everything" becomes unrecognizable, but the colloquial meaning of *panourgia* is rendered properly. This translation also helps set the stage for the tragic confrontation triggered by the ambivalence of the deed in question: "Antigone's act is the holiest to which woman can accede. It is also [...] a crime" (Steiner 1984: 34; see Honig 2013: 158–160). Both the emphasis on agency and the pejorative meaning of *panourgia* also come to the fore in a distinction drawn by Aristotle in the *Nicomachean Ethics*: "There is a faculty which is called cleverness [*deinótês*]; and this is such as to be able to do the things that tend towards the mark we have set before ourselves, and to hit it. Now if the mark be noble, the cleverness is laudable, but if the mark be bad, the cleverness is mere smartness [*panourgía*]" (Aristotle 1954: 1144a 26–27).

It is commendable to pay attention to the semantic range of *panourgia*. The two layers of literal meaning and everyday use—doing everything and committing a crime—are incisive for understanding Antigone's

---

suspicion that such delimitation leads to crime and mischief. This negative image is not carved in stone though: The most prominent example for a far more generous account of *panourgia* is the intriguing figure of Panurge making its appearance in Rabelais's novel *Gargantua et Pantagruel*.

[2] Many widely used translations come up with versions similar to the one by Lloyd-Jones: Antigone is presented as "dar[ing] the crime of piety," "committing a holy crime," or acting as a "sinless sinner" (Sophocles 2013: 24, 2003: 56, 1952: 321). The exception that proves the rule is an online translation by William Tyrrell which reads: "I have done anything and everything holy." (Sophocles 2002)

action. Friedrich Hölderlin is the most prominent spokesman for preferring the literal over the colloquial meaning. According to his translation, Antigone has fully accomplished a holy deed by burying her brother ("Wenn Heiligs ich vollbracht [...]"—Hölderlin 1992: 321). The negative connotation is gone, and *pan* is aptly mirrored in the German "voll." (It could be said that "vollbracht" is the active counterpart to "fulfilled."[3]) To be sure: Hölderlin is well aware of the moral conflict waging between Antigone and Creon. But by insisting on not labeling her deed as a crime he creates some leeway for taking a step back and not being entangled in moral considerations on whether her deed is a misdeed at the outset.

This is the decisive point: Hölderlin's translation reveals the polemical nature of *panourgia*. The deed which exceeds the realm of morally admissible actions may well turn out to be wrong or evil, but whether this is the case or not remains to be seen. Before reaching the point of moral judgment, we first have to unleash agency and create a situation in which everything becomes possible, thinkable, doable: a situation "without any foothold" (*ohne allen Halt*; 1992: 375). It does not come with the claim for having access to a totality of objects, but consists in the gesture empowering an agent or subject to break out of a predefined, preordained world. It could be said that this distinction draws on Anaximander's opposition between a well-ordered *kosmos* on the one hand, an infinite, boundless, unseizable *apeiron* on the other hand (Buchheim 1994: 58).

Hölderlin's radical translation turns Antigone into a role-model for modern-day heroes. When Ismene comments on her sister's "rebellion" (*Aufstand*), she "points not only to the mystery of 'pious rebellion' but initiates what Hölderlin takes to be the theme of political revolution along republican lines" (Steiner 1984: 88). It could be said that the ideas of political emancipation and resurrection in the eighteenth and nineteenth century go back to *panourgia* and bring both meanings of this term back in play: empowerment on the one hand, moral evaluation on the other hand. The emphasis on agency (from Jean-Jacques Rousseau to Henry David Thoreau) takes sides with empowerment, the protracted

---

[3] Another poet remains in Hölderlin's footsteps. Bertolt Brecht's adaptation of Sophocles' play is largely based on his translation and reads: "Hinter mich hab ich/Heilig's gebracht" (Brecht and Neher 1949: 116).

debate on revolution's redemptive or satanic powers (from William Blake to Charles Baudelaire) focuses on morality.

Some advocates of modern-day emancipation seek to equip humankind with God-like omnipotence. This means that they turn away from the polemical gesture of *panourgia* and allude to a different notion of all-ness linked to total comprehension and perfect organization (discussed with reference to the panopticon below). A case in point in this respect is the new world order imagined by Robert Owen (not by coincidence an avid reader of Bentham's). Yet most of the scenarios for emancipation and empowerment stay away from omnipotence and remain faithful to "doing it all" in the polemical sense of *panourgia*. This comes to the fore, for example, in the modern reinterpretations of an ancient figure exemplifying empowerment: Prometheus. Even though he has divine powers, his agenda when taking sides with the humans retains a polemical function. Prometheus's most fervent followers in modern times, Johann Wolfgang von Goethe and Percy Shelley, see him fighting against "omnipotence" and "ill tyranny" (Shelley 1994: 159, 162)—and do not want him to become an overpowering figure himself. This is from Goethe's poem "Prometheus," 1774:

> You still must leave me/ My round earth standing,/ And my hut which you did not build [...]/ Here I sit, making men/ In my own image,/ A race that shall be like me,/ A race that shall suffer and weep/ And know joy and delight too,/ And heed you no more/ Than I do! (2005: 11–13)

And this is from Shelley's lyrical drama "Prometheus Unbound," 1820:

> The man remains— / Sceptreless, free, uncircumscribed, but man / Equal, unclassed, tribeless, and nationless, / Exempt from awe, worship, degree, the king / Over himself; just, gentle, wise: but man [...]. / To defy Power, which seems omnipotent; / [...] Neither to change, nor falter, nor repent; / This, like thy glory, Titan! Is to be / Good, great and joyous, beautiful and free; / This is alone Life, Joy, Empire, and Victory! (1994: 195, 205)

These two poets settle for self-containedness (Goethe) or anarchic harmony (Shelley). Implicitly, their calls for emancipation appeal to the tradition of Antigone's *panourgia*. They also stand in stark contrast to omnipotent "seeing it all" and to transparency.

Saying It All: From Euripides to Diderot

The faculty of "saying it all" has received much more attention in antiquity than Antigone's *panourgia*. It is discussed under the name of *parrhesia*, a compound of *pan* and *rhêsis* ("speech"). If Sophocles is the crown witness for *panourgia*, the main ancient source for *parrhesia* is Euripides (Foucault 2001: 25–74, 2012: 33–56). One of the many scenes where it comes up in his plays features Polyneices, Antigone's brother, who, while still struggling with his status of being an outlaw, complains: "The worst is this: right of free speech does not exist [*oùk échei parrhêsían*]" (Foucault 2001: 29). Beside Euripides, authors like Plato, Isocrates, or Plutarch have contributed to the debate on *parrhesia*. One of its high points is the answer given by the Cynic Diogenes of Sinope when "being asked what was the most beautiful thing in the world:" "Freedom of speech [*parrhesia*]" (Diogenes Laertius 1925: 71). This section will not further investigate these ancient sources, however, but limit itself to a few systematic observations and remarks on the early modern revival of *parrhesia*. Like *panourgia*, *parrhesia* can be conceived as a subjective stance toward allness serving as a counter-model to "seeing it all" and to transparency.

The *parrhesiast* is a courageous person who speaks up and speaks her mind. Her "saying it all" does not serve the purpose of gathering all the world's knowledge in an encyclopedic manner. Like in *panourgia*, the allness contained in *parrhesia* does not allude to the objective world but to a subject's unrestrained, unfettered practice. *Parrhesia* is polemical in nature, it stands for an intervention in the social or political realm challenging common sense and common knowledge. This polemical relation between free speech and customary language does not necessarily lead to blunt confrontation. A community may defend its customs, but it may also be willing to admit free speech under certain limiting conditions.

A first limitation concerns the group of people entitled to *parrhesia*. The license to say it "all" is not necessarily granted to "all" persons, but to a select group only. (In ancient Greece, *parrhesia* was a privilege of male citizens.) A second limitation does not consider the speaker but the social impact of speech-acts. When free speech takes on an impertinent form its permissibility is questioned. (This is why there is a juxtaposition of a suspiciously anarchic, less well regarded *parrhesia* and a supposedly more civilized, legally recognized form of free speech named *isegoria*; Foucault 2001: 72.) A third limitation does not account for the social compatibility of speech acts but for their epistemological value. It suggests that unsubstantiated assertions should be banned. (It could be said that the juridical system in the U.S. remains more faithful to ancient *parrhesia* and endorses a "game of ideas," whereas most European systems find restrictions based on an apparent lack of "cognitive" value more admissible; Belavusau 2013: 89–91.) It goes without saying that all those limitations are highly controversial.

Generally speaking, *parrhesia* is regarded as an ambivalent phenomenon in ancient Greece (Foucault 2012: 9–11). It is frequently used in a positive manner and attributed to speakers taking a stance, assuming responsibility, and exposing themselves in the public sphere. Their seriousness is approved as they are willing to face criticisms and even contempt. They deserve respect for cutting through the thicket of pretentious speech and questioning conventional wisdom. Yet *parrhesia* is also used in a negative sense and linked to impudence, willfulness, and chatter. The "endless babbler, who cannot keep quiet, and is prone to say whatever comes to mind" (Foucault 2001: 63) may not have much on his "mind" after all. In such a pejorative sense, *parrhesia* appears in Plato's *Symposium* (222c) as the frankness of a drunkard (Hülsewiesche 2002: 111).

What happens to *parrhesia* in "the modern epoch"? Foucault responds: "I don't really know" (2012: 29). It is safe to say that the above-mentioned ambivalence plays out in its early modern uses as well. In 1514, Erasmus of Rotterdam, following the footsteps of Plutarch, highlights the *positive* effects of *parrhesia*: "Adulation poisons friendship instantly, and that what neutralizes that poison is the habit of speaking one's mind, which Greek calls *parrhesia*, outspokenness" (Erasmus 1514: 134; Colclough 1999: 193). In 1609, Francis Bacon stresses the *negative* effects of *parrhesia* in the first chapter of his *Wisdom of the Ancients*, titled in Latin "Cassandra, sive Parrhesia." He admonishes against the "unreasonable and unprofitable liberty in giving advice and admonition" and asks "to observe [...] times when to speak and when to be silent" (Bacon 1858: 629, 701; Colclough 1999: 211). As if he were intervening in the current debate on fake news, Bacon states in his essay "Of Seditions and Troubles": "Libels and licentious discourses against the state, [...] false news often running up and down to the disadvantage of the state [...] are amongst the signs of trouble" (Bacon 1858: 407; Hülsewiesche 2002: 121). It should not go unnoticed that Bacon makes use of the standard Latin translation of *parrhesia*, namely *licentia*. This word makes it easy for Bacon to caution against free speech, as a license or permit is generally granted under certain provisos only. Along these lines, the generous invitation to speak one's mind can be restricted or even revoked.

The controversy on the ambivalence of *parrhesia* maintains its momentum in the seventeenth and eighteenth century. The reservations against *parrhesia* are brought into canonical form by John Locke. In his *Essay Concerning Human Understanding*, he states: "Boldness is the Power to speak or do what we intend, before others, without fear or disorder; and the *Greeks* call the confidence of speaking by a peculiar name *parrhesia*" (1690a: 293 [book II, chapter 22, § 10]). In his *Two Treatises of Government*, Locke refers to *parrhesia* under the label of "licence" and introduces a distinction between civic "liberty" and "licence" or "uncontroleable liberty" (1690b: 270 [II.6]). Locke's caveat is clear: Freedom of speech is to be used responsibly. The boundlessness of *parrhesia* is regarded as dangerous.

Those who come to the defense of *parrhesia* or *licentia* question the idea that a clear-cut distinction can be drawn between good and bad liberty. They resent the idea that free speech should be conditional, and seek to loosen the grip of institutions holding speakers accountable. This liberalization or liberation does not mean that the *parrhesiasts* get out of control altogether. Their ethos still requires them to speak their mind, so they stay away from faking or flattering, that is, from internal or external insincerity. This defense of the *parrhesiastic* ethos moves into difficult territory: It needs to consider the person behind the speaker and contend that there is a match between existence and speech. But how do we get hold of this person or existence? The modern defenders of *parrhesia* know of two different ways for accounting for this person. Denis Diderot describes them in a particularly succinct manner.

The first strategy is exemplified by the ancient Cynics. Diderot says: "The audacity [...] of their discourses [...] mainly consisted in the fact that they transferred the morals of the natural state into the midst of the society." Among "corrupted and delicate people," their manners of acting and speaking represented the "innocence of earlier epochs" and "churlishness" (1876: 253). Accordingly, *parrhesiastic* interventions express the simple truths of undistorted humanity in opposition to artificial conventions and social roles.

The second strategy also takes offense at conformity, yet it does not exploit the distinction between artificial conventions and robust nature, but between customary habits and spontaneous interventions. The paramount example for this mode of *parrhesia* (or *franc parler*, in French) is the eponymous hero of Diderot's novel *Rameau's Nephew*. Michel Foucault mentions this nephew in passing as a successor to the ancient Cynics and also as a representative of timeless, "trans-historical Cynicism" (2012: 189–192, 174; for another reading of Diderot's figure, see Foucault 1961: 199–201). But this line of succession obscures the difference between the ancient *parrhesiast* and Diderot's hero. The nephew says: "I'll be damned if I know what I am, deep down. [...] I say whatever comes into my head: if there's any sense in it, so much the better; if it's absurd, nobody takes any notice. I take every opportunity to speak my mind. [*J'use en plein de mon franc-parler.*] Never in my life have I reflected, before, during or after speaking" (Diderot 2014: 48; Shea 2010: 59; Thomä 2018). The nephew says what he thinks, but he does so on the spur of the moment. His modes of existing and speaking lack consistency. He does not care about being called irresponsible when practicing unharnessed experimentation. His speech stands for the liberation of expressive faculties and the exploration of worldviews.

Hegel's distinction between different character types can be adopted for clarifying the distinction between the two figures presented by Diderot. *Either* the *parrhesiast* appears as "a subject entire in itself" (1835: I, 237; see I, 244; II, 1129). Such subjects "act out of this character of theirs [...], because this character [...] is precisely what they are," or out of their "already established nature" (1835: II, 1214, 1226). *Or* the *parrhesiast* enjoys "adventurous independence" and shows signs of "vagueness" and "immaturity" (1835: I, 196; II, 1228).

It is conceivable that these notions of the subject give rise to a quandary about identity. Like the venture of doing it all, the venture of saying it all points back to the question of how to conceive the self or agent being the source of such activities. The modern portraits of *parrhesiasts* give different answers to this question. They are called upon (by Locke) to act responsibly, to justify assertions and to join the conversation of mankind. They are welcomed (by Diderot) as undeformed misfits acting out of their nature or whim. Either way, their positions as subjects depend on their ability of taking a stance in the public sphere, be it in its center or at its margins.

How do these self-conceptions relate to the paradigm of transparency? This paradigm is based on a method warranting access to everything and on a subject capable of total overview. It is safe to say that the claim for all-ness implied in *parrhesiastic* activity does not comply with these demands. Whether this refusal is to be regarded as a weakness or strength remains to be seen. In any case, the *parrhesiasts* do not seek access to an objective sphere in its completeness. Their claim for all-ness appears as an unfinished or unfinishable business. They contribute to enhancing or upsetting our understanding of the state of affairs. Moreover, they do not feel entitled to assume a position which grants them total overview.

Those who seek to solve the quandary about identity by establishing a subject equipped with self-certainty and having access to the objective world in its entirety heavily rely on the idea of transparency.

Seeing It All: From Descartes to Bentham

The shift from *parrhesia* to transparency can be explained by going back to Foucault one more time. His definition of *parrhesia* runs as follows:

> The one who uses *parrhesia*, the *parrhesiastes*, is someone who says everything he has in mind: he does not hide anything, but opens his heart and mind completely to other people through his discourse. In *parrhesia*, the speaker is supposed to give a complete and exact account of what he has in mind so that the audience is able to comprehend exactly what the speaker thinks. The word *parrhesia*, then, refers to a type of relationship between

the speaker and what he says. For in *parrhesia*, the speaker makes it manifestly clear and obvious that what he says is his *own* opinion. (Foucault 2001: 12)

There is something odd about this definition. That *parrhesia* should be based on a "complete and exact account" of a speaker's mindset strangely alludes to Descartes's ideal of exactitude, which is a world apart from many ancient sources and also from important claims made by Foucault himself. He rightly contends that the truth and truthfulness ascribed to *parrhesia* are at odds with Cartesian "evidence" and that modern epistemology has marginalized *parrhesia* (Foucault 2001: 14–15). But it is confusing that he talks about completeness and exactness himself. These qualifications do not play any role whatsoever in the ancient sources nor in his own interpretation of them. They inadvertently shift the focus from *parrhesia* to transparency.

The *parrhesiasts* claim that what they say is what they think. Their genuineness (to avoid the term "authenticity") gets approved based on their willingness to put themselves on the line and "expose" themselves to risks (Foucault 2001: 15). But what about Foucault's talk about giving a "complete and exact account of what he has in mind"? This sounds as if there were some unfinished business left which required self-inspection. Yet this is not the *parrhesiast*'s but Descartes's agenda: "I do not yet have a sufficient understanding of what this 'I' is."—"What am I to say about this mind, or about myself?" (Descartes 1641: 17, 22)

Descartes's answer to this question leads away from the polemical conception of all-ness known from *panourgia* and *parrhesia*. It does not envisage a self meddling with the world, disrupting common sense, or breaking new ground. The Cartesian subject is not in the midst of things but retreats from the world altogether. It could be said that this move serves the purpose of securing subjective transparency. During its first steps on the way to itself, the "I" does not care about all-ness, only about the one-ness of the subject taking everything in view: "When the mind understands, it in some way turns towards itself and inspects one of the ideas which are within it" (1641: 51).

Much has been said about Descartes's *ego* and its status between thinking and existing. It is neither possible nor necessary to summarize the different interpretations of *cogito ergo sum* as an inference, a mode of introspection, or a performative act ensuring "self-verifiability" (Hintikka 1962: 17). (For a discussion of these readings, see Williams 1978: 57–114.[4]) Suffice it to say that Descartes does not care about a life in full but about an *ego* without qualities—except for the one quality of thinking: "Thus, simply by knowing that I exist and seeing at the same time that absolutely nothing else belongs to my nature or essence except that I am a thinking thing, I can infer correctly that my essence consists solely in the fact that I am a thinking thing."—"Thought; this alone is inseparable from me" (1641: 54, 18). The immediacy or unmediatedness of Cartesian self-apprehension is based on the fact that the thinking *ego* has to do with nothing but itself.

This notion of the *ego* has been subject to criticisms. Maurice Merleau-Ponty takes issue with "an eternal subject perceiving itself in absolute transparency, for any such subject would be utterly incapable of making its descent into time, and would, therefore have nothing in common with our experience" (1945: 493). Accordingly, it could be said that the Cartesian *ego*, whether it exists or not, does not really matter and remains alien to human life. It should not go unnoticed that Merleau-Ponty speaks of—and turns against—the "absolute transparency" of the *ego*. This choice of words is debatable. It could be argued that it is based on a category mistake as the phrase *cogito ergo sum* aims at the self-confirmation of a thinking thing and stays away from the logic of visibility which is the true homestead of transparency. But even if one dismisses the introspective, that is, vision-oriented reading of Descartes's *ego*, it makes sense to follow Merleau-Ponty in this point. It is safe to say that Descartes does not settle for an unmediated act of "self-positing" (in the sense of Fichte) but envisages a self-apprehension of the *ego* very much resembling the

---

[4] It should be mentioned that Stanley Cavell takes side with the performative reading of Descartes in order to draw him back into the *parrhesiastic* camp (without labeling it in this manner). Cavell links subjective self-assertion to the courage to take a stance and speak up. His reading is based on a reference to Descartes in Emerson's essay "Self-Reliance:" "At the center of the essay is a paragraph that begins: 'Man is timid and apologetic; he is no longer upright; he dares not say "I think," "I am," but quotes some saint or sage.' [...] Now I think one can describe Emerson's progress as his having posed Descartes's question for himself and provided a fresh line of answer, one you might call a grammatical answer: I am a being who to exist must say it exist, or must acknowledge my existence—claim it, stake it, enact it" (1988: 106, 109).

situation of a person seeing herself in a mirror. The *ego*'s access to itself could be aptly characterized by the word used by a real estate agent praising the view from a villa overlooking the ocean: it is unobstructable.

Descartes's language is soaked with visual vocabulary. Next to the most conspicuous examples—"clear" and "evident"—he also uses the term *perspicuus* which has been rightly translated into English as "transparent." (Strictly speaking, the latter term indicates the property of a see-through material, while the former stands for the ability of a person to see right through it.) Merleau-Ponty's talk about Cartesian transparency is anteceded by Descartes's use of *perspicuus* which features in his description of self-apprehension. It turns out to be no purely intellectual procedure after all: "The one thing that I set myself to prove," he says, is that the objects of "knowledge for the human intellect" which are "the most certain and evident" or the most "solid" and "transparent [*perspicuas*]" are "our own minds" (1641: 11). The transparency of the *cogito* is then extended to the transparency of the world: "Everything which I clearly and distinctly perceive is of necessity true. [...] I now know that I am incapable of error in those cases where my understanding is transparently clear [*quae perspicue intelligo*]" (1641: 48).

Descartes who has been called the founding father of the ideal of transparency (Schneider 2013: 61) takes two steps. First, he establishes a subject which retreats from the world and finds itself in a situation unaffected by any distractions or delusions. Secondly, the subject does not stay in isolation but uses its newly gained stance as an "unshakeable" vantage point for perceiving the external world and gaining knowledge as "clear and distinct" as self-knowledge (Descartes 1641: 16, 42). Descartes's "disengaged reason" is capable of "hegemony" (Taylor 1989: 149).

When this conception is transferred from the epistemological to the social realm, it finds its fitting complement in the model of the panopticon. The focus now shifts from the person doing everything (*panourgos*) or saying everything (*parrhêsiastês*) to the person seeing everything (*panoptês*). The subject in the center of Bentham's panopticon very much resembles the Cartesian *ego*. By varying the phrase from the *Meditations* quoted above, it could be said that the essence of the observer or inspector consists solely in the fact that he is a seeing thing. His other occupations besides watching the underlings are negligible and impalpable.

Moreover, the observer emulates the *ego*'s remoteness. He is detached from the objects in view and enjoys "concealment," he exerts the "unbounded faculty of seeing without being seen" (Bentham 1995: 80, 101). "The Panopticon is a machine for dissociating the see/being seen dyad" (Foucault 1975: 201–202). In "the all-transparent, light-flooded universe of the panopticon" (Božovič 1995: 18), the objects are exposed to a gaze without even knowing whether the "inspector's lodge" in the center is occupied or empty, whether there is somebody watching or not (Bentham 1995: 35, 43).

The panoptical regime differs from the ideas of doing or saying it all in important respects. It goes beyond the notion of all-ness attributed to a subject and turns to the objective sphere accessible to an observer. All-ness is regarded as something given. Primarily, the goal of total transparency is linked to a strangely limited notion of all-ness: the small world of the panoptical building. Even if this logic were extended to the world outside its walls, it would be bound to the single perspective of one observer. Moreover, the panoptical regime eliminates the actual interaction between the persons concerned. The wardens are not forced "to come [...] in contact with each inhabitant" and to conduct "minute and troublesome investigation[s]." They are thus saved from a "great load of trouble and disgust" (Bentham 1995: 46). Interaction is replaced by supervision on the one side, submission on the other: "Visibility is a trap" (Foucault 1975: 200).

The persons living in a panopticon are reduced to physical objects or, in Descartes's language, to *res extensae*. This reduction is particularly fitting when these persons are not just held in custody—like in the "penitentiary-house"—but assembled in a "work-house" (Bentham 1995: 76–77). The production process in such a "work-house" depends on the mechanical precision of movements taking place quasi-automatically. As the laborers are reduced to bodily functions, their only concern is bodily survival:

> The part taken by each workman is reduced to some one single operation of such perfect simplicity, that one might defy the awkwardest and most helpless idler that ever existed to avoid succeeding in it. Among the eighteen or twenty operations into which the process of pin-making has been

divided, I question whether there is any one that is not reduced to such a state. [...] What hold can any other manufacturer have upon his workmen, equal to what my manufacturer would have upon his? What other master is there that can reduce his workmen, if idle, to a situation next to starving, without suffering them to go elsewhere? (Bentham 1995: 71)

The panopticon exemplifies a major shift in the relation to everything or all-ness. The practices of *panourgia* and *parrhesia* refer to such all-ness in a polemical mode. They do not entail omnipotence or omniscience. Their claim for all-ness is linked to the transgression of a given condition and to the appeal to a boundless, indeterminate whole (*apeiron*; see above). It comes down to the pretension that "there are more things in heaven and earth, [...] / Than are dreamt of in your philosophy" (Shakespeare 1998: 301 [*Hamlet* I.5]). This improvisational stance is countered by the panoptical scheme which serves the purpose of suppressing transgression. It stands for a turn-around in which all-ness is not linked to a polemical gesture but to unlimited power. The centralized vantage point grants total overview and total control:

Your prisoner will make experiments [...]. He will hazard a venial transgression at a venture: that unnoticed, he will go on to more material ones. Will he? I will soon put an end to his experiments: or rather, to be beforehand with him, I will take care he shall not think of making any. [...] In this house transgression never can be safe. (Bentham 1995: 105)

As an admirer of Helvétius, Bentham is fond of the idea of perfecting the human machine. But reducing the inmates of a panopticon to mere physical objects is not his last word. He is aware of the fact that the inhabitants of a panopticon are not just objects, but thinking or seeing things as well, if only to a minor extent. Bentham even takes this as an opportunity to make his model more effective and resilient—and the job of the inspector a lot easier.

It is clear what the inmates in the panopticon have on their mind: the fact that they are under surveillance. In order to evade punishment, they prefer to live by the rules and anticipate institutional expectations and demands. This means that they internalize the *ego* installed in the center.

Prevention and deterrence work smoothly (Bentham 1995: 105). To a certain extent, this internalization can be understood by means of Freudian theory: the *ego* of the observer becomes the *superego* of the people observed. Yet the social and political bearings of the panoptical setting go way beyond the practice of internalizing rules. It enforces the preponderance of observable behavior. The inmates appropriate the very attitude exerted by the inspector: the attitude of looking at them. Their self-relation emulates the transparency reigning between the inspector and themselves. They become self-observers. Generally speaking, the panoptical setting anticipates a world in which both self-relation and social relations surrender to the regime of visibility, observation, and transparency.

Transparency and All-ness

It could be said that the panopticon's rise to fame in cultural theory is largely undeserved: Bentham's outlandish thought experiment was no success story in the real world. Only a few prisons were built based on his proposal. Its simplicity is as compelling as it is deceptive and unsatisfactory (Lyon 2006). Yet the model of the panopticon retains a diagnostic value. First, the very simplicity of this model is of methodological value, as it serves as a basic structure which can be amended and complicated in order to create a more comprehensive model of strategies of surveillance, exposure, and behavioral control. Secondly, the fact that the panopticon is embedded in a framework shaped by Cartesian epistemology provides a good reason for going beyond the political issues normally raised in the discourse on transparency and turning to the bigger picture of social theory and the theory of the subject. Thirdly, the peculiar notion of all-ness employed in the *panopsia* of the panopticon can be confronted with its much-neglected contenders: the accounts of all-ness implied in *panourgia* and *parrhesia*.

This section is dedicated to the task of complicating and extending the panoptical regime of total visibility in order to push the limits of current transparency studies. Transparency appears in various contexts deploying different social actors and accommodating a wide range of social relations. Four such contexts will be analyzed. They are marked by more or less incisive alterations of the old panoptical model. The titles for these different regimes of transparency are *Preserving Surveillance, Inverting Surveillance, Hybridization,* and *Internalization*.

Preserving Surveillance

The first regime of transparency stays close to the original panoptical model. Two central features remain intact: (1) Transparency is bound to the relation between an invisible observer and plainly visible objects or actors; (2) it serves the purpose of somehow steering and manipulating the actors' behavior.

With the wealth of data collected via web browsers, tracking technologies, intelligent things, social media platforms, surveillance cameras in the public, commercial and private sphere, and so on, the lives of observed objects become what, in another epoch, would have been called an "open book." In this panopticon 2.0, the data are not made accessible to a single, invisible observer anymore but gathered and computed by reclusive institutions. They fall in two different classes: Governments target the population, private institutions deal with employees, customers, and consumers. An early commentary on the first variant is George Orwell's portrait of an elusive, overpowering state in his novel *1984*. An early commentary on the second variant is Charlie Chaplin's movie *Modern Times*, where even the employee's visit to the restroom is minutely monitored.

Government institutions collect data in the name of national interest. Intelligence Agencies, Homeland Security, and so on, see transparency as a key requisite for securing security and tracking down suspects, criminals, or dissenters. The scope of government activities is about to be extended to various kinds of behavioral irregularities, including health issues and the like.

Private companies compute data for commercial purposes. They take stock of the performance of employees, keep track of the activities of consumers and web users, try to nudge their behavior, and so forth. A new variant of such private strategies falls back on the political field: Interest groups, campaign managers, and lobbyists use data for influencing elections or other forms of decision-making. (The services of Cambridge Analytica for Trump's presidential campaign are a case in point here.)

Formally speaking, all these institutions follow the same pattern: Transparency is regarded as a means to gain access to information, but their own activities and procedures (algorithms, etc.) remain largely secret. This setting resembles an observation desk equipped with a one-way mirror. The observers can see everything and remain invisible. It is important to note that this setting is not just reminiscent of Bentham's panopticon, but also of the Cartesian model featuring a detached *ego* getting hold of the world. In his—controversial—reading of Descartes, Martin Heidegger illustrates this point by drawing a line from the detached, "non-indigen[t]" *ego* (1985: 172, see 1927: 92, 254) to the subject aiming at "a mastery of beings that are everywhere surveyable" (1961: Vol. III, 230–231): "Descartes, with his principle of the *cogito sum*, forced open the gates" leading to "the institution of absolute dominion over the earth" (1961: Vol. IV, 117). Heidegger's focus is on technology and mechanization, but he builds on the panoptical image of a "surveyable" world in "The Age of the World Picture": "The fundamental event of modernity is the conquest of the world as picture" (1950: 71).

Today's strategies of preserving the panoptical setting aim at curtailing *panourgia* and abusing *parrhesia*. Agency is disempowered and transformed to observable and manipulable behavior. Deregulated speech is regarded as a stream of information monitored and exploited for administrative or commercial purposes.

Inverting Surveillance

The most popular response to state surveillance, the screening of customers and related phenomena is based on the idea of turning the tables. Those who are subjected to institutional control and manipulation use transparency as a battle cry for uncovering such operations. A wide range of initiatives from Transparency International to WikiLeaks targets government institutions. Consumer organizations, anti-Google groups, and so on, launch similar initiatives in the commercial sphere. Generally speaking, such bottom-up campaigns seek to demystify the inner workings of powerful institutions and hold them accountable. Two main problems occur when transparency is inverted in this manner.

First, the newly established subject acting as the observer's observer deserves scrutiny. In what could be called the early golden age of transparency, this subject's fight against powerful institutions exemplified active citizenship. The view from above was countered by vigilance from below. This reading of emancipatory transparency is not a thing of the past altogether, but the pure intentions of the subjects collecting and leaking information today cannot be taken for granted any longer. They may have a hidden agenda themselves. This leads to the problem of framing effects. We have learnt everything about, for example, the content of Hillary Clinton's e-mails, but the transparency produced in such a case concerns particular, often carefully selected targets only. The enlightening effects of a revelation is devaluated when it serves obscure interests or belongs to a diversionary tactic. After the recent scandals mainly concerning the role of Russia in certain data leaks, the legitimacy of inverted transparency is largely in shambles. Translated into the framework used in this paper, this means that the observing subject's attempt to borrow its impeccable epistemological reputation from the Cartesian *cogito* fails blatantly.

Secondly, and more importantly, even a good-natured campaign for making institutions transparent falls short of serving emancipation. The seemingly powerful idea of revealing dirty little secrets and casting light in every dark corner conceals an embarrassing weakness. If, for instance, citizens want their government to be transparent, they can test for its compliance only when adhering to the role of observers or onlookers (Rosanvallon 2006: 258). Their agenda is limited to seeing, watching, and monitoring. Empowerment in the sense of *panourgia* is not considered. Reclaiming political agency needs to take a step beyond transparency.

Hybridization

Formally speaking, the settings discussed so far stay within the realm defined by the panoptical model. In one way or another, they still work with the distinction between institutions and individuals. The social setting created by social media breaks with this premise. According to the most generous readings, social media overcome the distance or disconnect between observers and their objects. Social media are even entrusted with the task to get rid of the observational model altogether and replace it by a communicative, cooperative realm. Mark Zuckerberg sees Facebook as a "social infrastructure for community—for supporting us, for keeping us safe, for informing us, for civic engagement, and for inclusion" (Zuckerberg 2017). This claim conceals the fact that social media still heavily rely on the paradigm of visibility, observability, and transparency. This paradigm is revised but by no means disempowered. As the users of social media act as observers and are being observed at once, they become hybrid figures or observed observers. The panopticon is transformed into a polyopticon.

Social media create a multiplication or diffusion of the observers. The single "inspector" or compact institution is replaced by a multitude of onlookers. On Facebook, YouNow, Periscope, and other platforms for user-generated content, live streaming, and so on, the behavior of a person exposing herself is gauged based on popularity. This popularity serves as an indistinct surrogate for the old-fashioned *superego*. An example illustrating this legacy and still adhering to the moral behaviorism of the original panopticon is given in Dave Eggers's novel *The Circle*, where the main character, Mae Holland, goes transparent (as she puts it) and makes her daily life visible to millions of viewers. Her subsequent change of behavior is summed up as follows:

> She'd given up soda, energy drinks, processed foods. At Circle social events, she nursed one drink only, and tried each time to leave it unfinished. Anything immoderate would provoke a flurry of zings of concern, so she stayed within the bounds of moderation. And she found it freeing. She was liberated from bad behavior. She was liberated from doing things she didn't want to be doing, eating and drinking things that did her no good. Since she'd gone transparent, she'd become more noble. (2013: 329)

Approval does not necessarily depend on "noble" behavior. As long as the audience is regarded as the ultimate source for recognition, people will be prone to do whatever is deemed attractive. In principle, such approval could be based on positions taken by the person on view, by her loving a certain film or endorsing a political decision, for example. But given the prevalence of visibility, the performance of the objects is frequently measured based on their willingness to expose themselves as completely as possible. The whole setting remains limited to observable behavior and abides by the regime of visibility. The agency of the people exposing themselves is limited to their willingness to become transparent. Their capital is their outside appearance, their looks, and what could be called the trophies of everyday life. There is a strong discrepancy between the millions of dinner plates and sunsets posted on Facebook and the fact that one does not learn a whole lot about how people are doing. This means that the transition from the panopticon to the polyopticon still comes with a bias against *panourgia*. The obsession with looks runs against agency. Moreover, cooperation among the observer and the observed remains largely indirect.

A frequent, typical setting on YouNow, for instance, consists of a female self-presenter or actor and mostly anonymous male viewers. An example documented by a journalist features a certain "Jasmina" sitting on her bed and a viewer asking "Show me your legs" (Haupt 2015). A widespread attitude among onlookers is what could be labeled as judgmental consumerism. It is symbolized by "Thumbs up," "Thumbs down," and other gestures and comments. The behavior of the onlookers can be described as a revised version of the panoptical observer. They maintain the privilege of invisibility or anonymity, but the pretended purity attributed to the Cartesian ego and, to a lesser extent, to the Benthamite "inspector" collapses and is replaced by voyeuristic interests.

The passage from Dave Eggers's novel quoted above already hints at the fact that the person going transparent does not just submit to the judgment of the audience but initiates a power shift in her favor. Eggers's heroine Mae Holland becomes a role model exerting considerable influence on her audience. Both the panoptical power game between the inspector and the multitude of inmates and the polyoptical power game between the multitude of viewers and an actor desperately seeking recognition are turned upside down when a singular person has millions of followers (!) and assumes a powerful position herself.

A case in point are so-called digital influencers. Their success depends on a condition aptly illustrating the working of transparency and its discontents. These influencers have to conceal the fact that they, in fact, act as representatives for certain brands or products. As opposed to, for example, an actor praising a product in a TV commercial, they seem to genuinely enjoy, say, the use of a shampoo or the visit to a hotel. Their contractual duties to sponsors stay off the record, that is, remain intransparent. What they do in plain view, then, is presenting themselves as leading a life which becomes ever more exciting thanks to the terrific products they use or the locations they visit. As seemingly independent individuals, digital influencers do not stay in the position of being passively exposed to observers. They have their own agenda—and they eagerly keep track of their success by monitoring their followers or observing their observers.

The concealment of economic constraints is complemented by the fact that digital influencers volunteer to reveal their supposedly unambiguous, whole-hearted, transparent preferences. Digital influencers hasten to affirm that they show themselves as they are. A digital influencer with more than 2.5 million followers on YouTube claims that, when promoting a wide range of products, "I am always myself" (Reinbold 2015). Another digital influencer with more than one million followers on Instagram says: "I do what I personally like. This is how I decide on content." It is telling how she further explains this relation between herself and the commercial content: In a somewhat awkward formulation, she concedes that "the content is my personality as formed by my environment and my profession" (Lang 2017). This means that the seemingly transparent personality actually coincides with commercial role play. The digital influencer has an appearance or surface—and eventually becomes this surface, like Nietzsche's "actors" who "turn their coat with *every* wind and thus virtually [...] *become* a coat" (1882: 316). Transparency reaches its high point: Such a person does not have any depth, there is nothing behind what she is doing. Her self is on the table. The match between existence and speech is realized by way of a perversion of classical *parrhesia*: Existence ("personality") is a dependent variable of speech ("content"), with the latter being a dependent variable of contractual agreements.

The polyoptical setting with many observers and many people exposing themselves gives rise to new modes of actorship and agency in the political sphere as well. A paramount example are media outlets inviting people to contribute online comments. They facilitate yet another perversion of *parrhesia*. At first glance, such platforms seem to serve the cause of free speech. They do not limit the public sphere to officially assigned and authorized contributors but open it up to each and every one. (In the current debates on legislation against hate speech, this issue plays an important role.) Several factors demolish the image of such media outlets as promoters of an extended public sphere.

According to the policy of many platforms, those who post comments are entitled to use pseudonyms. As a consequence, many comments are particularly outspoken—to say the least. Often they are just nasty and offensive. People use the opportunity to say what they really think (about immigrants, politicians, intellectuals, sportsmen, managers, etc.). By claiming that they finally tell the "truth" about something, they pretend to increase transparency. Unfortunately, the *parrhesiastic* quality of such contributions is devaluated by the fact that those who make public statements by using pseudonyms lack the "courage" to put themselves on the line and to assume accountability.

According to recent empirical findings, people are increasingly willing to post aggressive and hurtful statements even when they cannot hide behind a pseudonym. This may have to do with another feature of this mode of self-presentation. Even though social media are praised for being bidirectional (as opposed to old-fashioned TV broadcasts), the back and forth of statements is hampered by the fact that the "web" of communication (Arendt 1958: 184) is thinned out or ripped in pieces. Direct encounters—a core element of *parrhesia*—do not happen. Those cursing at others online resemble car drivers ranting about traffic participants whom they will never see again.

The willingness of people to post extreme comments further increases when they meet a particular kind of approval deviating from classical moral appreciation and from mass popularity alike. This approval stems from like-minded people who create an echo chamber of confirmations and encouragements. The observed observers belonging to such a group talk to each other, look at each other, and nod approvingly. When fully identifying with a small world, people create their own constricted, illusionary version of all-ness. What matters takes place in their universe, the rest is conversation.

Internalization

The observed observers emerging as hybrid figures in the field of social media are complemented by individuals observing themselves. In the panoptical setting, such internalization takes place when the persons observed internalize the inspector's gaze. Strictly speaking, this introspective mode (prepared, at least to a certain extent, by Descartes) does not stand for an exploration of the "internal ocean" (Emerson 1987: 272), but for exact and distinct self-observation and self-control. As this auto-optical approach emulates the detached position of the "inspector" its scope is confined to objectively accessible, observable data. The individuals adopt a form of self-relation in which they exclusively focus on features which can be measured. Whereas the "internal ocean" remains troubling and opaque, the self-knowledge obtained via data is crystal-clear. This means that the "quantified self" is part of the legacy of the panopticon and that "the technologies of self-surveillance" (Lupton 2015: 181) can be regarded as a means for creating self-transparency:

> Nowhere is the concept of self-imposed digital veillance more apparent than in the discourses and practices of self-tracking, life logging or quantifying the self. These concepts refer to the practice of gathering data about oneself on a regular basis and then recording and analysing the data to produce statistics and other data (such as images) relating to one's bodily functions and everyday habits. (Lupton 2015: 180–181)

At first glance, these methods generate self-knowledge and pave the way to self-enhancement or "self-improvement" (Lupton 2015: 180). These claims are in line with empowerment, agency, and *panourgia*. But this alignment is deceptive as the concept of the quantified self is limited to aspects which can be reduced to bodily movements and observable behavior. Agency is excluded from this picture at the outset.

* * *

To sum up: The many variants of the current use of transparency come with the promise of providing unlimited access to information. The subjects entitled to benefit from such information vary: They can be government institutions, companies, political activists, consumer groups, social media users, or self-enhancers. In any of these applications, transparency creates blind spots itself. These blind spots cannot be removed by making transparency ever more comprehensive. They come into being for the very reason that self-conceptions and social relations embrace the paradigm of transparency. What is left out in this paradigm are free speech and free agency, and their respective claims for all-ness enshrined in *parrhesia* and *panourgia*.

Works Cited

Arendt, Hannah. 1958. *The Human Condition*. Chicago: University of Chicago Press.
Aristotle. 1954. *The Works, Vol. 9: Ethica Nicomachea—Magna Moralia—Ethica Eudemia*. Ed. W.D. Ross. London: Oxford University Press.
Bacon, Francis. 1858. *The Works, Vol. 6*. Ed. James Spedding, Robert Leslie Ellis, and Douglas Denon Heath. London: Longman and Co.
Belavusau, Uladzislau. 2013. *Freedom of Speech: Importing European and US Constitutional Models in Transitional Democracies*. London and New York: Routledge.
Bentham, Jeremy. 1995. *The Panopticon Writings*. Ed. Miran Božovič. London and New York: Verso.
Božovič, Miran. 1995. Introduction. In *The Panopticon Writings*, ed. Miran Božovič and Jeremy Bentham, 1–27. London and New York: Verso.
Brecht, Bertolt, and Caspar Neher. 1949. *Antigonemodell 1948*. Berlin: Weiss.
Buchheim, Thomas. 1994. *Die Vorsokratiker: Ein philosophisches Porträt*. Munich: Beck.
Cavell, Stanley. 1988. *In Quest of the Ordinary: Lines of Skepticism and Romanticism*. Chicago and London: University of Chicago Press.
Colclough, David. 1999. Parrhesia: The Rhetoric of Free Speech in Early Modern England. *Rhetoric* 17 (2): 177–212.
Descartes, René. 1641 [1996]. *Meditations on First Philosophy*. Trans. and Ed. John Cottingham. Cambridge: Cambridge University Press.
Diderot, Denis. 1876. *Œuvres complètes, Vol. 14: Encyclopédie, C-E*. Ed. Jules Assézat. Paris: Garnier Frères.

———. 2014. *Rameau's Nephew: A Multi-Media Edition*. Ed. Marian Hobson, Trans. Kate E. Tunstall and Caroline Warman. Cambridge: Open Book Publishers.
Diogenes, Laertius. 1925. *Lives of Eminent Philosophers, Vol. II*. Trans. R.D. Hicks. London and New York: Heinemann/Putnam.
Eggers, Dave. 2013. *The Circle: A Novel*. New York: Knopf.
Emerson, Ralph Wald. 1987. *Essays & Lectures*. Ed. Joel Porte. New York: Library of America.
Erasmus. 1514. *Parallels. Parabolae sive similia*. Trans. R.A.B. Mynors, in Erasmus, *Collected Works, Vol. 23*, ed. Craig R. Thompson, Toronto: University of Toronto Press, 1978: 122–277.
Foucault, Michel. 1961 [1988]. *Madness and Civilization: A History of Insanity in the Age of Reason*. Trans. Richard Howard. New York: Random House.
———. 1975 [1977]. *Discipline and Punish: The Birth of the Prison*. Trans. Alan Sheridan. New York: Random House.
———. 2001. *Fearless Speech*. Ed. Joseph Pearson. Los Angeles: Semiotext(e).
———. 2012. *The Courage of Truth (The Government of Self and Others II): Lectures at the Collège de France 1983–1984*. Trans. Graham Burchell. New York: Palgrave Macmillan.
von Goethe, Johann Wolfgang. 2005. *Selected Poetry*. Trans. David Luke. London: Penguin.
Haupt, Friederike. 2015. *Videporal "You Now:" Zeig doch mal deine Beine*. http://www.faz.net/aktuell/feuilleton/familie/was-eine-14-jaehrige-auf-dem-videoportal-younow-macht-13441879.html. Accessed 15 Mar 2017.
Hegel, Georg Wilhelm Friedrich. 1835 [1975]. *Aesthetics: Lectures on Fine Art, Vol. I/II*. Trans. T.M. Knox. Oxford: Clarendon Press.
Heidegger, Martin. 1927 [1962]. *Being and Time*. Trans. John Macquarrie and Edward Robinson. Oxford: Blackwell.
———. 1950 [2002]. *Off the Beaten Track*. Ed. and Trans. Julian Young and Kenneth Haynes. Cambridge: Cambridge University Press.
———. 1961 [1991]. *Nietzsche, Vol. III/IV: The Will to Power as Knowledge and as Metaphysiks—Nihilism*. Ed. David Farrell Krell. New York: Harper.
———. 1985. *The History of the Concept of Time: Prolegomena*. Trans. Theodore Kisiel. Bloomington: Indiana University Press.
Hintikka, Jaakko. 1962. Cogito, Ergo Sum: Inference or Performance? *Philosophical Review* 71 (1): 3–32.
Hölderlin, Friedrich. 1992. *Sämtliche Werke und Briefe, Vol. II*. Ed. Michael Knaupp. Munich and Vienna: Hanser.

Honig, Bonnie. 2013. *Antigone, Interrupted*. Cambridge: Cambridge University Press.
Hülsewiesche, Reinhold. 2002. Redefreiheit. *Archiv für Begriffsgeschichte* 44: 103–143.
Lang, Bianca. 2017. Instagram-Star Caro Daur: Die Daur-Werbesendung. http://www.spiegel.de/wirtschaft/instagram-star-caro-daur-die-daur-werbesendung-a-1155916.html. Accessed 10 Jul 2017.
Locke, John. 1690a [1975]. *An Essay Concerning Human Understanding*. Ed. Peter H. Nidditch. Oxford: Oxford University Press.
———. 1690b [1988]. *Two Treatises on Government*. Ed. Peter Laslett. Cambridge: Cambridge University Press.
Lupton, Deborah. 2015. *Digital Sociology*. London and New York: Routledge.
Lyon, David, ed. 2006. *Theorizing Surveillance: The Panopticon and Beyond*. Cullompton: Willan.
Merleau-Ponty, Maurice. 1945 [2005]. *Phenomenology of Perception*. Trans. Colin Smith. London and New York: Routledge.
Morgenstern, Christian. 1933 [1963]. *The Gallow Songs: A Selection*. Trans. Max Knight. Berkeley and Los Angeles and London: University of California Press.
Nietzsche, Friedrich. 1882 [1974]. *The Gay Science*. Trans. Walter Kaufmann. New York: Vintage.
Pingeot, Mazarine. 2016. *La dictature de la transparence*. Paris: Laffont.
Pucci, Pietro. 1987. *Odysseus Polutropos: Intertextual Readings in the* Odyssey *and the* Iliad. Ithaca and London: Cornell University Press.
Reinbold, Fabian. 2015. YouTube-Star Bibi: "Daran ist doch nichts verwerflich". http://www.spiegel.de/netzwelt/web/youtube-star-bibi-ueber-duschschaum-bibiphone-produktplatzierungen-a-1067059.html. Accessed 15 Mar 2017.
Rosanvallon, Pierre. 2006. *La contre-démocratie: La politique à l'âge de la défiance*. Paris: Seuil.
Schneider, Manfred. 2013. *Transparenztraum: Literatur, Politik, Medien und das Unmögliche*. Berlin: Matthes & Seitz.
Shakespeare, William. 1998. *Complete Works*. Ed. Richard Proudfoot, Ann Thompson, and David Scott Kastan. Walton-on-Thames: Nelson.
Shea, Louisa. 2010. *The Cynic Enlightenment: Diogenes in the Salon*. Baltimore: Johns Hopkins University Press.
Shelley, Percy Bysshe. 1994. *The Works*. Ware: Wordsworth.
Sophocles. 1952. *Oedipus the King. Oedipus at Colonus. Antigone*. Trans. F. Storr. London and New York: Heinemann and Harvard University Press (Loeb Classical Library, 1st ed. 1912).

———. 1994. *Antigone. Women of Trachis. Philoctetes. Oedipus at Colonus.* Trans. Hugh Lloyd-Jones. Cambridge: Loeb Classical Library.

———. 2002. *Antigone.* Trans. William Blake Tyrrell. https://msu.edu/~tyrrell/antigone.pdf. Accessed 15 Mar 2017.

———. 2003. *Antigone.* Trans. Reginald Gibbons and Charles Segal. Oxford and New York: Oxford University Press.

———. 2013. *Antigone. Oedipus the King. Oedipus at Colonus.* Trans. Elizabeth Wyckoff, David Grene, and Robert Fitzgerald. Chicago: University of Chicago Press.

Steiner, George. 1984 [1996]. *Antigones: How the Antigone Legend Has Endured in Western Literature, Art, and Thought.* New Haven and London: Yale University Press.

Taylor, Charles. 1989. *Sources of the Self: The Making of the Modern Identity.* Cambridge: Cambridge University Press.

Thomä, Dieter. 2018. *The Troublemakers: A Philosophy of "puer robustus".* London: Polity.

Williams, Bernard. 1978 [2005]. *Descartes: The Project of Pure Enquiry.* London and New York: Routledge.

Zuckerberg, Mark. 2017. *Building Global Community.* https://www.facebook.com/notes/mark-zuckerberg/building-global-community/10154544292806634. Accessed 15 Mar 2017.

The Dream of Transparency: Aquinas, Rousseau, Sartre

Manfred Schneider

I

In his 1897 novel *The Year 3000: A Dream*, the Italian physician and author Paolo Mantegazza sketches a future society with its political institutions, energy plants, laboratories and technical inventions. At the end of his novel, the reader attends the annual Meeting of the Academy of Science at Andropolis. The Academy awards him the cosmic prize for a brand-new invention, a "psychoscope," which is an optical device providing precise insights in man's brain so that everybody's thoughts become readable. The Academy's president praises this invention, that it achieves this "sogno di tutti i secoli," namely that moral progress should parallel intellectual progress:

Quando noi tutti sapremo, che chiunque può leggere nel nostro cervello, faremo sì che pensieri e opere non si contraddicono, e noi saremo buoni nel

---

M. Schneider (✉)
Ruhr-Universität Bochum Germansitisches Institut, Bochum, Germany

© The Author(s) 2018
E. Alloa, D. Thomä (eds.), *Transparency, Society and Subjectivity*,
https://doi.org/10.1007/978-3-319-77161-8_5

pensiero, come cerchiamo di esserlo nelle opere. È a sperare che col' psichoscopio la menzogna sarà bandita del mondo [...]. (Mantegazza 1897: 321)[1]

The psychoscope indeed is a fantastic implementation of what I call the *Dream of Transparency* (Schneider 2013). This dream is a fundamental component of the Western political, philosophical and moral imagination. The earliest ironic allusions to this dream can be found in Greek and Latin literature. In Hesiod's *Theogony* (c. 700 BC) Momos is one of the many sons of νύξ, of the night, like death, dream, and sleep.[2] He is the god of blame and harsh criticism (*Theogony*, v. 214). The Greek collector of fables Babrios (c. second century) shares the tale of how Momos has to judge the competition of inventions between three gods. Zeus constructed a man, Poseidon a bull and Athena a house. However, Momos condemns all three inventions, most especially the man. His main complaint of the man is that he had no window (θυρωτά) in his chest allowing others to read his thoughts and evil intentions (Babrius and Phaedrus 1990: 74ff.). Momos's criticism recurs in various twentieth-century reincarnations of this story of the dream of transparency.

The name of Momos still stands for a desire for complete justice and truth that insistently hounds intellectuals, poets, and politicians. Momos has remained a central allusion through the centuries: in 1605, the English statesman and theorist Francis Bacon published his epochal work *Of the Advancement and Proficience of Learning*, in which he lays out the principles of a new science founded on empiricism and experimentation.

Citing Momos, Bacon reminds the reader that according to the biblical apocalypse, the eye of God sees the world as crystal clear. This, he says, creates a special obligation when it comes to research on man and all matter of things: the eye of man should become like the eye of God, for

---

[1] "When we all know that anyone can read into our brain, we will have to overcome contradictions between our thoughts and our actions; we will be as good in our thoughts as we will try to be in our actions. It is to be hoped that with the psychoscope lying will be banished from the world [...]" (trans. David Jacobson; Mantegazza 2010: 190).

[2] "Nyx bore hateful Moros and black Ker and / Thanatos, she bore Hypnos and the tribe of Oneiroi. / Next Momos and painful Oizys were born to / the dark goddess Nyx, though she lay with no one, / and the Hesperides [...]" (trans. A.S. Caldwell; Hesiod 2015: 40).

it is the perfect law of inquiry of truth, that nothing be in the globe of matter, which should not be likewise in the globe of crystal or form; that is, that there be not anything in being and action which should not be drawn and collected into contemplation and doctrine. (Bacon 1986: 188)

Moreover, in the following paragraph Bacon continues:

[...] therefore, the precept which I conceive to be most summary towards the prevailing in fortune, is to obtain that window which Momus did require; who seeing in the frame of man's heart such angles and recesses, found fault, there was not a window to look into them; that is, to procure good information of particulars touching persons, their natures, their desires and ends, their customs and fashions, their helps and advantages, and whereby they chiefly stand, so again their weaknesses and disadvantages, and where they lie most open and obnoxious, their friends, factions, dependences; and again their opposites, enviers, competitors, their moods and times [...]. (Bacon 1986: 189)

II

I want to outline three chapters in the philosophical novel of the dream of transparency; these chapters will be anchored by Saint Thomas Aquinas, Rousseau and Sartre, who represent the elaboration of these ideas in the middle ages, in the Enlightenment and in the twentieth century. In a rather provisional attempt to systemize my quotes and remarks, I will differentiate the linguistic, political and interpersonal aspects of the dream.

Bacon's reference to biblical authority in 1605 shows that antiquity's story of Momos had by that time merged with a theological concept of the transparent; indeed, the word "transparent" can be traced to the Latin of the waning Middle Ages. The expression is not found in classical Latin. Shortly before the first millennium AD, the Roman architecture theorist Vitruvius harked back to Socrates with the word *translucidus* to illustrate the Momos idea of a window in the chest (Vitruvius 1807: 67f.).[3] Twelve

---

[3] "Is autem [i.e. Socrates] memoratur prudenter doctissimeque dixisse, oportuisse hominum pectora fenestra et aperta esse, uti non occultos haberent sensus sed patentes ad considerandum. [...]

hundred years later, the word *transparens* comes up in the flourishing comments on the Aristotelian definition of the soul. One of the first philosophers to coin the new term was the philosopher Burgundius of Pisa in his translation of the Greek treaty *De natura hominis* (1165) by Nemesios of Emesa.[4] Burgundius put *transparens* for the Greek word διαφανής which designs the properties of light and materials like air, water or glass, thereby making *transparens* the quality of a medium that cannot be seen, but has the ability to make light visible. However, it was already Aristotle who claimed in his extremely influential Treatise *De Anima* (Περὶ ψυχῆς) that beyond these materials also the celestial bodies (ἐν τῷ ἀϊδίῳ τῷ ἄνω σώματι) had the quality of being transparent (διαφανής). This idea aroused the interest of a large number of scholastic philosophers and theologians who commented on *De anima* and sought to bring the Aristotelian concept of ψυχή or *anima* in line with the Christian doctrine of the soul.

Anca Vasiliu has delineated the linguistic emergence of the word *transparent* in the scholastic discourse (Vasiliu 1991, 1994, 1997, 1999). Since this word was unknown in classical Latin, it is instructive to examine how this new term became so prominent in the scholastic discourse. The most important philosophical and theological mastermind of the thirteenth century, Thomas Aquinas, provides a preliminary answer in his Commentary on *De Anima* by Aristotle, which draws upon several translations and commentaries that had already discussed the Aristotelian treatise extensively.

However, it is not a natural scientist's interest in the physical nature of light that encourages these meditations of the nature of the transparent, but rather the urgent theological interest in the nature of the illuminated blessed *animae*, that is, the quality of the glorious souls in the paradise. They are transparent and they are light giving. The question is therefore: what is their very nature? Initially, in his *Commentary on* Aristotle's *De anima*, Aquinas states that "diaphanum autem est idem quod transparens" (the diaphane is the same as the transparent); following, he writes:

Ergo, uti Socrati placuit, si ita sensus et sententiae scientaeque disciplinis auctae perspicuae et translucidae fuissent [...]."

[4] Nemesius de Emesa, *De Natura Hominis. Traduction de Burgundio de Pise*, ed. G. Verbeke u. J. A. Moncho, Leiden 1975. Cf. Vasiliu 1997: 90. With thanks to Emmanuel Alloa. Cf. Alloa 2011.

Manifestatum est enim, quod neque aer, neque aqua, neque aliquid huiusmodi est actu transparens, nisi fuerit illuminatum. Ipsum autem diaphanum secundum se est in potentia respectu luminis et respectu tenebrae, quae est privatio luminis, sicut materia prima est ut potentia respectu formae et privationis. Lumen autem comparatur ad diaphanum, sicut color ad corpus terminatum; quia utrumque est actus et forma sui susceptivi. Et propter hoc dicit, quod lumen est quasi quidam color diaphani, secundum quod diaphanum est actu factum diaphanum ab aliquo corpore lucente, sive illud sit ignis, aut aliquid aliud huiusmodi, sive aliquod corpus caeleste. Esse enim lucens actu et illuminativum, commune est igni et corpori caelesti, sicut esse diaphanum est commune aeri et aquae, et corpori caelesti. (Aquinas 1948: 104, book II, lectio XIV)[5]

In the last sentence, Thomas touches upon the very interest of this commentary. He has to answer the question: what are the celestial bodies made of, what is their physical nature? In the Supplements to his huge *Summa Theologica* Aquinas discusses this problem. He asks to what extent the transparent souls of the redeemed can be seen with the eyes of the unredeemed: "Utrum claritas claritas corporis gloriosi possit videri ab non glorioso oculo" (Aquinas 2000, *Suppl. tertiae partis* qu. LXXXV, art. I). Thomas clarifies that the souls of the blessed can in fact be seen with the eyes of the unredeemed. They are as transparent as glass, and the soul rests within this glass-like medium as though it were made of gold. In this answer Thomas refers to the Father of the Church Gregor the Great: "Gregorius comparat corpora gloriosa auro et vitro; auro propter claritatem & vitro propter hoc quod translucebunt" (Aquinas 2000: *Suppl. tertiae partis*, art. I, ad sec.).

Thomas does not quote verbatim, since he replaces the word "transparere" used by Gregorius in his commentary on Job by the word "translucere". This erroneous quotation demonstrates why the scholars needed

---

[5] "For it is evident that neither air nor water nor anything of that sort is actually transparent unless it is luminous. Of itself the transparent is in potency to both light and darkness (the latter being a privation of light) as primary matter is in potency both to form and the privation of form. Now light is to the transparent as colour is to a body of definite dimensions: each is the act and form of that which receives it. And on this account he says that light is the colour, as it were, of the transparent, in virtue of which the transparent is made actually so by some light-giving body, such as fire, or anything else of that kind, or by a celestial body. For to be full of light and to communicate it is common to fire and to celestial bodies, just as to be diaphanous is common to air and water and the celestial bodies." (trans. K. Foster, O.P. and S. Humphries, O.P.; Aquinas 1951: 130).

this neologism. The word "translucens" does not denote the quality of something that is transparent. Light does *translucere*, it goes through something like glass. However, the glass being traversed by light is not "translucens".

So, the word *transparens* served scholasticism as a means of explaining the physical state that the blessed will assume after redemption. There is, first and foremost, the metaphysical promise: all that is *transparent* comes from the sphere of the Divine; both light and the souls that reflect it participate in its heavenly origin. This means: the historical trajectory of the concept of transparency and its utopian promise—the dream—presupposes the formidable theological work of scholasticism, which made it possible to imagine the state of the blessed or the unredeemed in the hereafter.

But the outlandish idea that a visitor to the afterlife might admire the transparent blessedness of the redeemed with his own eyes is presented in a passage in Dante's epic *Divina Commedia*. This great verse from the late Middle Ages is, as we know, a report describing a journey through the Inferno, Purgatory, and finally Paradiso. In Purgatory and in Paradise, the narrator is accompanied by Dante's deceased lover Beatrice, who introduces him to all the theological, historical, and political secrets there. In the third canto of *Paradiso*, the afterlife-wanderer encounters those blessed people whose physical condition so preoccupied scholastic thinkers.

The narrator's encounter with the first immortal souls gives an exhilarating idea of what theologians at that time presumed in terms of the lightness and transparency of souls. The wanderer does not understand what he is seeing at first. He sees the souls, but believes them to be mirror images.

However, the wanderer Dante seems not to be prepared for the perception of the transparent souls. When the first soul crosses his way, he believes to see the mirror picture of a saint, and he turns back to see the original of the mirrored person, but he is perceiving the very transparent body of the saint Piccarda Donati herself:

"Quali per vetri trasparenti e tersi,
O ver per acque nitide e tranquille,
Non sì profonde che i fondi sien persi,

Tornan d'i nostri visi le postille
Debili sì, che perla in bianca fronte
Non vien men forte a le nostre pupille;

Tali vid'io più facce a parlar pronte;
Per ch'io dentro a l'error contrario corsi
A quel ch'accese amor tra l'uomo e'l fonte.

Sùbito sì com'io di lor m'accorsi,
Quelle stimando specchiati sembianti,
Per veder di cui fosser, li occhi torsi;

E nulla vidi, e ritorsili avanti
Dritti nel lume de la dolce guida,
Che, sorridendo, ardea ne li occhi santi". (Dante Alighieri 1988: III, 30–31)[6]

The wanderer believes that he is seeing reflected pictures in a transparent medium, but it is actually a transparent and clear figure. Beatrice is smiling because of Dante's error, though the poet Dante has been an eager reader of the works of Aquinas. The moon is the first celestial sphere and any wanderer had to be introduced into the theological materiality of the glorious bodies.

This gives us a brief impression of the scholastic efforts to complete their dictionary and to prepare by a new notion a new idea of the possibility of interpersonal communication. It is the beginning of a new history of what the little god Momos claimed: the dream of unrestricted communication. For it is this very transparent world, this linguistically prepared hereafter of clarity and transparency, that will be prevalent in the dream of transparency in the ages to come.

---

[6] "Such as through polished and transparent glass, / Or waters crystalline and undisturbed, / But not so deep as that their bed be lost, / Come back again the outlines of our faces / So feeble, that a pearl on forehead white / Comes no less speedily unto our eyes; / Such saw I many faces prompt to speak, / So that I ran in error opposite / To that which kindled love 'twixt man and fountain. / As soon as I became aware of them, / Esteeming them as mirrored semblances, / To see of whom they were, my eyes I turned, / And nothing saw, and once more turned them forward / Direct into the light of my sweet Guide, / Who smiling kindled in her holy eyes" (trans. Henry Wadsworth Longfellow; Dante 1867/2017: 554 sequ.).

Nevertheless, a question remains: What exactly does *transparency* mean? Is it a metaphor or is it a notion linked to something substantial? Thomas suggests that transparency is not a quality but something comparable to "primary matter." Transparency is in potency to light, since it needs light to be actually transparent. And "primary matter" is in potency, because it needs a form in order to be something. This discussion reminds of the famous medieval dispute on universals, on whether notions are names or have their own reality. We will return to this question in discussing Rousseau's discourse of transparency.

III

My contribution to Rousseau consists only in some footnotes to the admirable book *La transparence et l'obstacle* (Starobinski 1971). Starobinski showed how the notion, the idea, the dream of transparency is crucial to Rousseau. In his political writings as well as in his autobiographical confessions Rousseau wants to submit the modern society to the law of transparency and sincerity. I will outline the three aspects of Rousseau's dream of transparency.

The first aspect is political. In his famous *Lettre à d'Alembert sur le théâtre* in 1758, a major success with the public, Rousseau translates the dream of transparency to the political domain. The main arguments Rousseau puts forward against d'Alembert's proposal to establish a theater in the republic of Geneva are well known. D'Alembert considers the theater to be the suitable forum for the self-representation of free citizens. Rousseau, however, argues that the stage will create a delusive world and lead the spectators astray. The practice of visiting a theater might turn all citizens into actors and truth as well as sincerity will vanish behind social masquerading. However, at the end of his letter Rousseau asks if the republic should be without any shared experience of the citizens: "Quoi ! ne faut-il donc aucun spectacle dans une république?" And he answers himself: "Au contraire, il en faut beaucoup." In fact, there will be many spectacles in the Republic, since they have their natural and cultural origins there, but they will make the people represent himself. "C'est dans les républiques qu'ils sont nés, c'est dans leur sein qu'on les voit briller avec un véritable air de fête." In this way Rousseau develops the idea of a theater of non-representation, for that will be a theater without deceit. Therefore, Rousseau raises the question:

> Mais quels seront enfin les objets de ces spectacles ? Qu'y montrera-t-on ? Rien, si l'on veut. Avec la liberté, partout où règne l'affluence, le bien-être y règne aussi. Plantez au milieu d'une place un piquet couronné de fleurs, rassemblez-y le peuple, et vous aurez une fête. Faites mieux encore: donnez les spectateurs en spectacle ; rendez-les acteurs eux-mêmes; faites que chacun se voie et s'aime dans les autres, afin que tous en soient mieux unis. (Rousseau 1959–1988: V, 114–115)[7]

The festival functions as a *tabula rasa*. The citizens celebrate the release from the theatre of society and the end of all representation. The true republic, based on the *volonté générale*, makes all theater and theatric communication disappear. Spectators turn into actors, and the difference between representatives and represented citizens fades. At the same time, they are actors in politics and observe of their own actions. Nonetheless their observation is not from outside, since everyone is reading in the transparent heart of the other. Rousseau again:

> Il est vif, gai, caressant; son cœur est alors dans ses yeux, comme il est toujours sur ses lèvres. Il cherche à communiquer sa joie et ses plaisirs; il invite, il presse, il force, il se dispute les survenants: Toutes les sociétés n'en font qu'une; tout devient commun à tous; [...] mais cette profusion même est alors bien placée, et l'aspect de l'abondance rend plus touchant celui de la liberté qui la produit. (Rousseau 1959–1988: V, 116)[8]

---

[7] "But what then will be the object of these spectacles? What will be shown in them? Nothing, if you please. With liberty, wherever abundance reigns, well-being also reigns. Plant a stake crowned with flowers in the middle of a square; gather the people together there, and you will have a festival. Do better, yet; let the spectators become the spectacle to themselves; make them actors themselves; do it so that each sees and loves himself in the others so that all will be better united" (Modified translation by A. Bloom; Rousseau 1968, 126).

[8] "The people are lively, gay, and tender; their hearts are in their eyes as they are always on their lips; they seek to communicate their joy and their pleasures. They invite, importune and coerce the new arrivals and dispute over them. All the societies constitute but one, all become common to all." (trans. A. Bloom; Rousseau 1968: 127)

During the festival, all citizens change completely and carry themselves to an excess of transparency. Between heart and eye, between heart and tongue there is no medium left. The wordless communication is the condition of their becoming transparent. This is understandable only against the background of Rousseau's skeptical theory of language. In his *Essai sur l'origine des langues* he claims that the emergence of language was the terrible consequence of a cosmological intrigue. "Celui qui voulut que l'homme fut sociable toucha du doigt l'axe du globe et l'inclina sur l'axe de l'univers" (Rousseau 1959–1988: V, 401).[9] The shift of the axis generated earthquakes, floods and forced men to come together. It was the beginning of societies, nations and cities. Language is the terrible result of society. In his 1754 *Discours sur l'origine et les fondements de l'inégalité parmi les hommes*, Rousseau states:

> [...] errant sans parole, sans domicile, sans guerre, et sans liaisons, sans nul besoin de ses semblables, comme sans nul désir de leur nuire, peut-être même sans jamais en reconnaître aucun individuellement, l'homme Sauvage sujet à peu de passions, et se suffisant à lui-même, n'avait que les sentiments et les lumières propres à cet état, qu'il ne sentait que des vrais besoins [...]. (Rousseau 1959–1988: III, 159–160)[10]

Therefore, the origin of language is the origin of the theatre of society and the end of natural transparency. In former times, men and women came together just when they wanted to meet, and whatever they had to communicate worked without language:

> Les mâles, et les femelles s'unissaient fortuitement, selon la rencontre, l'occasion et le désir, sans que la parole fût un interprète fort nécessaire des

---

[9] "He who willed man to be social, by a touch of a finger shifted the globe's axis into line with the axis of the universe" (trans. J.H. Moran, A. Gode; Rousseau 1966: 39).

[10] "[...] that man in a state of nature, wandering up and down the forests, without industry, without speech, and without home, an equal stranger to war and to all ties, neither standing in need of his fellow-creatures nor having any desire to hurt them, and perhaps even not distinguishing them one from another; let us conclude that, being self-sufficient and subject to so few passions, he could have no feelings or knowledge but such as befitted his situation; that he felt only his actual necessities [...]" (trans. G.D.H. Cole; Rousseau 2005: 57).

choses qu'ils avaient à se dire. Ils se quittaient avec la même facilité. (Rousseau 1959–1988: III, 147)[11]

In society, in love, and in politics, language as medium puts an end to transparency. Every child has to go through this experience of becoming a lying being, and so they all are thrown out of that paradise of transparency that the church fathers had shifted to the hereafter. Communicating without words becomes one of the main concerns in Rousseau's idea of society. Like in the case of the loving couples or the people participating in the spectacles in Geneva, happy speechlessness seems to be the only guarantee for successful communication. This makes Rousseau's fundamental idea of the destructive power of language plausible. In order to sketch the linguistic aspect of Rousseau's dream of transparency I want to look at how language is taught in the didactic novel *Emile*.

What deserves the special attention of the nurse teaching a child words and language?

The nurse needs to consider that the child only hears words and sounds connected to real existing items. At the beginning, he should only pronounce words as names; he should use them only as transparent phonetic symbols of concrete objects. Any word coming to the child's ears must be the name of something shown to his eyes: "This is a stone; this is a dog; that is a hammer."

If he does not observe this rule then trouble is in sight: bewildered with a multitude of words which he does not understand, the child's imagination begins to work on its own. It is the reverse process: passions create signs, gestures, and words. The first words of mankind's language have been natural cries of passion in case of danger or in case of suffering; words without meaning, without reference in the real world, create passions in the soul of a child, for example the passion of tyranny. A tyrant is waiting even in babies and small children. Therefore, parents have to discriminate between desires rooted in nature and desires which spring from perverse passions. If they cannot relieve the child's pain they must not caress him, because "if he finds out how to gain your attention at will,

---

[11] "[...] the sexes united without design, as accident, opportunity or inclination brought them together, nor had they any great need of words to communicate their designs to each other; and they parted with the same indifference [...]" (trans. G.D.H. Cole ; Rousseau 2005: 41).

he is your master." So, the master and tyrant may come from non-transparent words. Therefore, Rousseau in his *Emile* strongly advises parents and teachers:

> Je voudrais que les premières articulations qu'on lui fait entendre fussent rares, faciles, distinctes, souvent répétées et que les mots qu'elles expriment ne se rapportassent qu'à des objets sensibles qu'on put d'abord montrer à l'enfant. La malheureuse facilité que nous avons à nous payer de mots que nous n'entendons point commence plus tôt qu'on ne pense. [...]
> Resserrez donc le plus qu'il est possible le vocabulaire de l'enfant. C'est un très-grand inconvénient qu'il ait plus de mots que d'idées, qu'il sache dire plus de choses qu'il n'en peut penser. Je crois qu'une des raisons pourquoi les paysans ont généralement l'esprit plus juste que les gens de la ville est que leur dictionnaire est moins étendu. Ils ont peu d'idées, mais ils les comparent très-bien. (Rousseau 1959–1988: IV, 293, 298)[12]

By virtue of these guidelines, the only words that ought to be heard by the child's ears would be those whose sound bring forth the sight of the named object. Rousseau would have us understand that all abundance of words not denoting elements of the real world will create evil. Who carries his heart, Rousseau says, in the eyes or on the tongue does not need any word. All participants of the republican festival only represent the needlessness of representation.

The interpersonal aspect of Rousseau's dream of transparency is outlined in a paragraph from his *Lettre à d'Alembert*. Here the author stresses the fallacies of speech in the communication of a loving man:

> De la manière que je conçois cette passion terrible, son trouble, ses égarements, ses palpitations, ses transports, ses brûlantes expressions, son silence plus énergique, ses inexprimables regards, que leur timidité rend téméraires, et qui montrent les désirs par la crainte; il me semble qu'après un

---

[12] "I would have the first words he hears few in number, distinctly and often repeated, while the words themselves should be related to things which can first be shown to the child. That fatal facility in the use of words we do not understand begins earlier than we think. [...] Let the child's vocabulary, therefore, be limited; it is very undesirable that he should have more words than ideas, that he should be able to say more than he thinks. One of the reasons why peasants are generally shrewder than townsfolk is, I think, that their vocabulary is smaller. They have few ideas, but those few are thoroughly grasped" (trans. Barbara Foxley; Rousseau 2009: 80, 88).

langage aussi véhément, si l'amant venoit à dire une seule fois, *Je vous aime*, l'amante indignée lui diroit, *vous ne m'aimez plus*, et ne le reverroit de sa vie. (Rousseau 1959–1988: V, 95–96)[13]

Speechless communication presents the heart of the lover for the beloved to read, as Rousseau puts it; his body is strewn with signs that enable her to understand his passion.

IV

A quotation from Sartre elaborates on the same topic. From the very beginning of Sartre's writing, especially from *L'Être et le Néant* (*Being and Nothingness*), the notion of transparency is crucial in his philosophy. All aspects of his thoughts, philosophy, political theory, literature, society are in their set of problems and in their utopian dimension in touch with this idea of transparency. Sartre gave an interview in 1975, on the occasion of his seventieth birthday—he was almost blind—to his friend Michel Contat, and expressed his expectation that one day objective and subjective life might be completely transparent, when no one might keep any more secrets from anyone:

> Je pense que la transparence doit se substituer en tout temps au secret, et j'imagine assez bien le jour où deux hommes n'auront plus de secrets l'un pour l'autre. (Sartre 1976: 141)[14]

And, asked about what he thinks to be the chief obstacle to such transparency he answers:

---

[13] "In the way that I conceive of this terrible passion, its perplexity, its frenzies, its palpitations, its transports, its burning expressions, its even more energetic silence, its inexpressible looks which their timidity renders reckless and which give evidence of desires through fear, it seems to me that, after a language so vehement, if the lover only once brought himself to say, 'I love you,' the beloved, outraged, would say to him, 'you do not love me anymore,' and would never see him again in her live" (trans. Allan Bloom; Rousseau 1968: 104).

[14] "I think transparency should always be substituted for what is secret, and I can quite well imagine the day when two men will no longer have secrets from each other, because no one will have any more secrets from anyone [...]" (trans. Paul Auster and Lydia Davis; Sartre 1975: 12).

C'est d'abord le Mal. [...] Ce mal rend difficile la communication de toutes les pensées, parce que je ne sais pas dans quelle mesure l'autre part de mêmes principes que moi pour former les siennes. [...] Il faut qu'un homme existe tout entier pour son voisin, qui doit également exister tout entier pour lui, pour que s'établisse une véritable concorde sociale. Ce n'est pas réalisable aujourd'hui, mais je pense que ce le sera lorsque le changement des rapports économiques, culturels, affectifs entre les hommes aura été accompli, d'abord par la suppression de la rareté matérielle, qui es selon moi, comme je l'ai montré dans la *Critique de la raison dialectique*, le fondement de tous les antagonismes passés et actuels entre les hommes. (Sartre 1976: 142–143)[15]

This vision of a future society wherein evil in terms of scarcity and acting will have disappeared and people will communicate transparently seems to be inspired by Rousseau. Sartre is definitely a Rousseauian thinker and a Thomistic thinker, too. Not only does Sartre call to mind Thomas Aquinas's communication of the blessed within his dreams of a transparent relationship between all men; even in his autobiographical narrative *Les Mots* Sartre alludes to the scholastic conception of the soul and its glassy shape:

Dans mon joli bocal, dans mon âme, mes pensées tournaient, chacun pouvait suivre son manège: pas un coin d'ombre. Pourtant, sans mots, sans forme ni consistance, diluée dans cette innocente transparence, une transparente certitude gâchait tout: j'étais un imposteur. (Sartre 1964a: 66–67)[16]

Becoming an impostor, even a transparent impostor, is the beginning of evil. There is a religious undertone in Sartre's declaration, and

---

[15] "First of all, Evil. [...] This Evil makes communicating all thoughts difficult, because I do not know to what extent the principles which the other uses to form his thoughts are the same as mine. [...] A man's existence must be entirely visible to his neighbour, whose own existence must in turn be entirely visible to him, in order for true social harmony to be established. This cannot be realized today, but I think that it will be once there has been a change in the economic, cultural, and affective relations among men, beginning with the eradication of material scarcity, which, as I showed in *Critique de la raison dialectique*, is for me the root of the antagonisms among men, past and present" (trans. Paul Auster and Lydia Davis; Sartre 1975: 13).

[16] "My thoughts swam around in my pretty glass globe, in my soul. Everyone could follow their play. Not a shadowy corner. Yet, without words, without shape and or consistency, diluted in that innocent transparency, a transparent certainty spoiled everything: I was an impostor." (trans. Bernard Frechtman; Sartre 1964c: 83)

in his autobiography, he confesses to having believed in martyrdom, salvation and immortality. Unfortunately, his life consisted in one fundamental error, as Sartre puts it, "je confondis les choses avec leurs noms: c'est croire" (Sartre 1964a: 209).[17] Of course, it was the faith of others, but Sartre retained his faith, that there is a basic evil in society. In his three monographs on Baudelaire, Genet and Flaubert, Sartre constructs these biographies around one evil moment that turned the child (and prospective poet) into a betrayer. Moreover, that fundamental change in their being is the first step on their path to becoming poets. To be a poet means to believe in words. I will touch on this point later on; first, I want to give one example of Sartre's analysis of this change in his famous book on Genet: *Saint Genet. Comédien et martyr* (1952). The abandoned child Genet, who public welfare placed with a farming family, was happy:

> Éparpillé dans la nature, il vit 'dans une douce confusion avec le monde'. Il se caresse à l'herbe, à l'eau, il joue ; au travers de sa déserte transparence passe toute la campagne. Il se caresse à l'herbe, à l'eau, il joue; au travers de sa déserte transparence passe toute la campagne. Bref il est innocent. (Sartre 1952: 13)[18]

Unfortunately, the twelve-year-old Genet was caught stealing, and called a thief. This event, in Sartre's analysis, marked the child's banishment from paradise and subsequent metamorphosis. Being named a thief, the child acquires the being of a thief. What, up until this moment, the child thought to be his transparent nature seems now to be deceitful. Genet's conversion, a religious change, consists in his affirmation of evil. Just this desire to be evil will prevent him—in Sartre's analysis—from attaining authenticity. Genet is alienated from nature, from himself and—above all—from language. Evil, theft, deceit, and loss of reality are, in Sartre's view, synonyms of poetry:

---

[17] "I confused things with their names: that amounts to believing" (trans. Bernard Frechtman; Sartre 1964c: 251).
[18] "Adrift in nature, he lives 'in sweet confusion with the world'. He fondles himself in the grass, in the water; he plays; the whole countryside passes through his vacant transparency. In short, he is innocent" (trans. Bernard Frechtman; Sartre 1964b: 5).

Il crie 'Je suis un voleur.' Il *écoute* sa voix et, du coup, le rapport au langage s'invertit: le mot cesse d'être un indicateur, il devient un *être*. [...] De moyen le verbe passe au rang de réalité suprême; le silence, au contraire, n'est plus qu'un moyen de désigner le langage. Le tour est joué: de l'enfant truqué nous avons fait un poète. (Sartre 1952: 45f.)[19]

Being a poet means being obsessed by words, which have lost their relationship to things. They lose their transparency or they let the universe go up in smoke:

[...] exilé de l'Univers, vous n'êtes attentif qu'au corps verbal, seule réalité que vous pouvez posséder et tenir entre votre langue et vos lèvres, alors c'est la chose signifiée qui disparaît et la signification devient un évanouissement d'être, une brume qui, au-delà du mot, est en voie de se dissiper. Genet fait exprès de n'avoir d'yeux pour le mot: capté et coulé dans la phrase l'univers s'évanouirait en fumée. (Sartre 1952: 346)[20]

Fumée (smoke) is a frequently used metaphor in Sartre's *Saint Genet* for things, words, goods, universes becoming opaque by poetry or theft. As Christina Howells argues, "Sartre concentrates on Genet's creation of false communication, of false prose, of his destruction of normal language usage, in a form of revenge on the bourgeois who originally 'stole' his thought from him and excluded him from their language" (Howells 1979: 199).

So, it is evident that Sartre's political dream of transparency is, of course, the dream of re-establishing a complete transparent language. In the first collection of critical essays, *Situations I* (1947), Sartre

---

[19] "'I am a thief' he cries. He listens to his voice; whereupon the relationship to language is inverted: the word ceases to be an indicator, it becomes a being. [...] The word which was a means, rises to the rank of supreme reality. Silence on the other hand, is now only a means of designating language. The trick is done: We have made a poet of the doctored child" (trans. Bernard Frechtman; Sartre 1964b: 42).

[20] "If however, you are exiled from the universe and are attentive only to the verbal body, which is the only reality you can possess and hold between your tongue and lips, then it is the thing signified which disappears and the signification becomes a vanishing of being, a mist which, beyond the word, is in the process of being dissipated. Genet makes it his business to have eyes only for the word; the universe, captured and inserted into the statement, goes up in smoke" (trans. Bernard Frechtman; Sartre 1964b: 309).

explains these linguistic ideas. He discusses the book *Recherches sur la nature et la fonction du langage* (1942) by Brice Parain. Sartre had been friend with Parain since 1934. First, Sartre sketches in a clearly Rousseauian perspective Parain's biography. Parain was, like many of his fellow students, the son of a farmer and he came to the university as a brilliant but silent student: "un de ces fils de paysans que leur intelligence exceptionnelle avait arrachés à la terre" (Sartre 1947: 181). In secondary school, the taciturn Parain turned into an eloquent speaker who could talk and communicate about everything. Later, as theoretician of language, Sartre states, Parain became alienated from language, as had Genet and many other poets. However, this is the result of Parain's experience in society and politic. As a speaking man, it is possible to be expelled from the state of nature of words. What is the linguistic state of nature? It is the state of transparent words. Sartre claims that only as a part in a chain of expressions words are transparent and keep unheard and unseen. This unnoticed language carries in itself what Sartre calls the infra-silence:

> Ainsi Parain, pour avoir abandonné à la recherche de ce que j'appellerai l'infra-silence, ce silence qui coïnciderait avec je ne sais quel 'état de nature' et qui serait *avant* le langage, n'a pas pour autant renoncé au projet de se taire. Le silence auquel il atteint à présent s'étend sur tout le domaine du langage, il s'identifie au langage même, il est bruissant de murmures, d'ordres, d'appels. Il s'obtient, cette fois, non par la destruction impossible des mots, mais par leur dévalorisation radicale. (Sartre 1947: 192–193)[21]

Language, for Sartre, has these two sides: on the one hand, communication, transparency and reference to reality; and on the other, the (poetic, material) language turning words into things, objects, sounds. This idea of language is just the contrary of those traditional ideas of poetry like Vico's or Hölderlin's who claimed poetry to be the original language, the transparent language of the paradise. For Sartre, poetic

---

[21] "So Parain, though having given up his search for what I will call l'infra-silence, a silence that coincides with I don't know which 'state of nature' and that would have existed *before* language, did not abandon the project to remain silent. The silence he reaches right now extends to the whole field of language. It is language itself, noise of murmurs, commands, calls. This time, it does not come from an impossible destruction of the words, but from their radical depreciation" (my trans.).

language belongs to the non-transparent world, to what he calls in *L'Être et le Néant* "la part du diable," the devil's part, that is "une multiplicité de significations qui se hiérarchisent ou s'opposent pour une même phrase" (Sartre 1943: 600).[22] The devil's part is, so to say, the dark side of language, or, coming back to our topic, the opaque and non-transparent mode of communication.

I come to an end with a very short remark, since I believe that it has become evident that the scholastic idea of an absolutely transparent and wordless communication between the blessed can be observed in Rousseau und in Sartre as well. I am committed to think that in the current belief in *transparency* as a promise of perfect government, management and of communication without deceit, Momos's claim and especially the religious and utopian qualities of διαφαίνω in the wordless paradise, remains a constant presence.

Works Cited

Alloa, Emmanuel. 2011. *Das durchscheinende Bild: Konturen einer medialen Phänomenologie*. Zurich: diaphanes.
Aquinas, Thomas. 1948. *Sancti Thomae Aquinatis (...) In Aristotelis librum de anima commentarium*. Ed. P.F. Angeli and M. Pirotta. Torino: Marietti.
———. 1951. *Commentary on Aristotle's De anima*. Trans. Kenelm Foster and Sylvester Humphries. New Haven: Yale University Press.
———. 2000. *Corpus Thomisticum. S. Thomae de Aquino Opera Omnia*. Ed. Enrique Alarcón. Pamplona. www.corpusthomisticum.org.
Babrius and Phaedrus. 1990. *Fables*. Trans. Ben Edwin Perry. Cambridge: Harvard University Press.
Bacon, Francis. 1986. *The Advancement of Learning*. Ed. G.W. Kitchin. London: Everyman's Library.
Dante, Alighieri. 1867/2017. *The Divine Comedy*. Trans. Henry Wadsworth Longfellow. Mineola NY: Dover Publications. (Reprint of the first edition 1867; London: Routledge).
———. 1988. *Divina Commedia. Die Göttliche Komödie*, Italian and German, trans. Hermann Gmelin, München: dtv.

---

[22] "A diversity of meaning that rank and contrast for just one sentence" (my trans.).

Hesiod. 2015. *Hesiod's Theogony*. Trans. Richard S. Caldwell. Indianapolis: Hackett Publishing.
Howells, Christina. 1979. *Sartre's Theory of Literature*. London: Modern Humanities Research Association.
Mantegazza, Paolo. 1897. *L'anno 3000: Sogno di P.M.* Milano: Fratelli Treves.
———— 2010. *The Year 3000: A Dream*. Trans. David Jacobson. Nebraska: University of Nebraska Press.
Pollio, Vitruvius, Marcus Cetius Faventinus, and Valentin Rose. 1807. *Marci Vitruvii Pollionis De architectura libri decem*. Vol. 1. Leipzig: Göschen.
Rousseau, Jean-Jacques. 1959–1988. *Œuvres complètes I-V*. Ed. Bernard Gagnebin and Marcel Raymond. Paris : Bibliothèque de la Pléiade.
————. 1966. On the Origin of Language. *Jean-Jacques Rousseau 'Essay on the Origin of Languages'—Johann Gottfried Herder 'Essay on the Origin of Language'*. Trans. J.H. Moran and A. Gode. Chicago: Chicago University Press.
————. 1968. *Politics and the Arts: Letter to M. d'Alembert on the Theatre*. trans. Allan Bloom. Ithaca, NY: Cornell.
————. 2005. *On the Origin of Inequality*. Trans. G.D.H. Cole. New York: Cosimo Classics.
————. 2009. *Emile, or Education*. Trans. Barbara Foxley. e-book: The Floating Press (Reprint of the Edition in 1921; New York: Dutton).
Sartre, Jean-Paul. 1943. *L'Être et le Néant: Essai d'ontologie phénoménologique*. Paris: Gallimard.
————. 1947. Aller et retour. In *Situations I: Essais critiques*, 175–225. Paris: Gallimard.
————. 1952. Saint Genet. Comédien et martyr. In *Œuvres complètes de Jean Genet*. Paris: Gallimard.
————. 1964a. *Les Mots*. Paris: Gallimard.
————. 1964b. *Saint Genet, Actor and Martyr*. Trans. Bernard Frechtman. New York: Mentor Books.
————. 1964c. *The Words: An Autobiography*. Trans. Bernard Frechtman. New York: George Braziller.
————. 1975. Sartre at Seventy: An Interview with Michel Contat. Trans. Paul Auster and Lydia Davis, *New York Review of Books*, August 7, 10–17. nybooks.com.
————. 1976. *Situations X: Politique et Autobiographie*. Paris: Gallimard.
Schneider, Manfred. 2013. *Transparenztraum: Literatur, Politik, Medien und das Unmögliche*. Berlin: Matthes & Seitz.

Vasiliu, Anca. 1991. La parole du 'diaphane' chez Dante (*Convivio* II et III). *Archives d'histoire doctrinale et littéraire du Moyen Age*, Paris: 189–212.

———. 1994. Le mot et le verre. Une définition médiévale du 'diaphane'. *Journal des Savants*: 135–162.

———. 1997. *Du diaphane. Image, milieu, lumière dans la pensée antique et médiévale*. Paris: Vrin.

———. 1999. Le transparent, le diaphane et l'image. *Transparences*, Paris: Éditions de la Passion: 15–29.

The Unbounded Confession

Noreen Khawaja

So soon as man declares himself to be free he at once feels bound by circumstances. If he dares to declare himself bound, he feels himself free.
(Goethe [1809] 1999: 151)

When Heinrich Voss brought a copy of Luther's *Table Talk* to the home of his friend, Johann Wolfgang von Goethe, in February 1805, Goethe spent an hour poring irritably over the dicta of the man who had succeeded in "populating the entire visible world with the devil." What followed was a broad, extemporaneous discourse on the failings of Protestantism. "I completely agreed with him," Voss reports, "when Goethe accused the Protestant religion of having given the single individual too much to bear [...] 'Auricular confession ought never to have been taken from human beings'" (Voss 1895: 72). Voss was enthusiastic about this interpretation, but also seemed worried about having spoiled

N. Khawaja (✉)
Yale University, New Haven, CT, USA
e-mail: noreen.khawaja@yale.edu

© The Author(s) 2018
E. Alloa, D. Thomä (eds.), *Transparency, Society and Subjectivity*,
https://doi.org/10.1007/978-3-319-77161-8_6

his friend's otherwise peaceful afternoon by having encouraged him to reflect on such gloomy Teutonic moralism. Voss also comes to realize, in relaying the events of the day, that there is something of a "father confessor" to Goethe himself, noting that their conversations have often brought him to "pour out his entire heart," permitting him to "return to himself strengthened in his solitude," and even in some cases to have allowed him to feel forgiveness for certain sins. "If such confessors were more numerous in this world," Voss continues, "there would be fewer heartsick souls" (Voss 1895: 72–73). It is with a discernible air of relief that he adds, in his final observation of the day, that "Goethe is now reading the novellas of Cervantes, which bring him joy" (Voss 1895: 73).

Goethe would find other occasions to mourn the weakening of sacramental traditions in Protestant lands and to reflect on the connection between religious reform and broader cultural shifts in the practice of confession.[1] But he would come to be known less for the critique of Protestantism such statements demonstrate than for having seen, within the cultural crisis, an opportunity to develop the spiritual potential of secular literature in a more coherent way than had previously been imagined. In his late autobiographical work, *Dichtung und Wahrheit*, Goethe compared his first novel *The Sorrows of Young Werther* to a sort of literary *Confiteor*. Finishing the work left him feeling "glad and free again as after a general confession," his spirit flowing with that ultimate affect of Lutheran devotion: "entitled to a new life" (Goethe [1811–1833] 1994: 432). A bit earlier in *Poetry and Truth*, Goethe had relied on this notion of literary confession in offering what would become one of the most famous lines about his overall artistic production: "Therefore all my published works are but fragments of one great confession, which this little book is a bold attempt to complete" (Goethe [1811–1833] 1994: 214). The lifelong work is his confession; the autobiography is the confession of his confession, which renders that confession complete.

---

[1] "It will be found that Protestants have too few sacraments, and indeed only one in which they actively participate, the Lord's Supper, for they see only baptism performed on others and are not personally benefited by it. The sacraments are the most sublime part of religion, the physical symbol of extraordinary divine grace and favor…[The Christian] must be accustomed to view the inner religion of the heart as completely one with that of the visible church, as the great universal sacrament, which is divided again into a multitude of others, but communicates to each of these parts its holiness, indestructibility, and eternity" (Goethe [1811–1833] 1994: 218–219).

Alongside Rousseau, Goethe is often credited with having developed a typically modern style of writing, in which the lyric "I" and the autobiographical "I" become increasingly difficult to distinguish (Perloff 1970). Following the literal sense of Goethe's disclosure (or, in this case, his metadisclosure), such a mingling of lyric and autobiographical voices has frequently been described—and just as frequently lamented—as a turn toward the "confessional" and autobiographical within modern fiction writing (Perloff 1970: 265–267). And yet as with any putative historical shift there is nothing to prevent us from viewing things in a quite different way—rather than a turn of the lyric *toward* the confessional and autobiographical, that is, we may be looking at a lyrical or poetic inflection of the confessional voice. "If *Dichtung und Wahrheit* teaches anything," Peter Gay once noted, "it is that explicitness is not the only qualified, and often not the best, escort to the interior" (Gay 1996: 118). With Goethe, as with Rousseau, the more contact we have with that sanguine, jaunty "I," the first-person voice whose raison d'être is to serve as our guide to the truth, the more decidedly our suspicion begins to form, and the more difficult it becomes to navigate the distinction between fact and representation.

Aristotle famously held that when we say, "something changes," what we mean is that a movement or change occurs in the *subject*, but not in the quality or relation that renders such change intelligible. He used physical examples to establish this principle but it was meant to apply widely: whitening is always a change in the thing that becomes white, not in the whiteness it becomes (Aristotle 1999: [5.1.224b], 118–120). Modern historical existence, however, involves a double interpretive condition that confounds this sort of physic. As literature becomes "more" confessional, the nature of confession itself submits to change. And as confessional practice shifts from the sacramental to the secular scene, it is not only confession that changes but the character of the distinction between the sacred and the secular, as well. Oswald Spengler would spin Goethe's literary metaconfession into a template for interpreting Western history as a broad dramatic narrative.[2] His *leitwort* would come from the

---

[2] The title of the present essay derives from Spengler's discussion of Pythagoras, Mohammad, and Cromwell: "And as the need of the soul to be relieved of its past and to be redirected remained

final verse of *Faust*, "All that passes is but symbol" [*Alles Vergängliche ist nur ein Gleichnis*], but it was Goethe's principle of "artistic confession," as Spengler termed it, that unlocked the vast symbolic trove of European history and revealed its inner sense:

> A tomb by one of those great Netherlanders who worked on the Royal graves of St. Denis from 1260, a portrait by Holbein or Titian or Rembrandt or Goya, is a *biography*, and a self-portrait is a historical *confession*. To make one's confession is not to avow an act but to lay before the Judge the inner history of that act...When the Protestant or the Freethinker opposes auricular confession, it never occurs to him that he is rejecting merely the outward form of the idea and not the idea itself. He declines to confess to the priest, but he confesses to himself, to a friend, or to all and sundry...What Raphael and Calderon and Haydn told to the priests, [Rembrandt and Beethoven] put into the language of their works...Western man lives in the *consciousness* of his becoming and his eyes are constantly upon past and future. (Spengler [1918–1923] 1947: 1, 264)

Spengler adored Goethe, and Goethe's name appears littered throughout the two volumes of Spengler's dark historical rhapsody, *The Decline of the West*. One might say that the work mirrors what Voss observed about Goethe's talents as a confessor, but extends the scene of acts and intentions confessed from the personal to the civilizational scale. For Spengler, Goethe's "artistic confession" is not just a good theory of or response to the secular culture that emerged in post-Reformation Germany. Goethe's great confession is what makes him *our* great confessor. His art liberates the latent truth of European history, accomplishing the paradoxical revelation at the heart of Protestant piety—that it is not a form of religion, after all, but a form of historical consciousness.

As these passages may suggest, the double interpretive condition I alluded to above—the inseparability of deciding about what has changed, and about how that change changes the criteria according to which we measure change—becomes relevant in a particularly striking way in the case of Protestant modernity. To put the matter succinctly: it is here that

---

urgent as ever, all the higher forms of communication were transmuted, and in Protestant countries music and painting, letter-writing and memoirs, from being modes of description became modes of self-denunciation, penance, and unbounded confession" (Spengler [1918–1923] 1947: 2, 295).

the project of political ecclesiastical reform is tied up with a long and complex commitment to invisibility as a site of spiritual value. The extent to which invisibility plays into the modern history of confession will become clearer over the course of this essay. But we may begin with a glimmer of the end—the end of this essay, in one sense, but also of the end of a certain arc of Protestant thinking that grapples with the tension between a confessional, missionary, and expressive faith, and a hidden God, who came to earth in the form of an unremarkable man (what Kierkegaard called the divine "incognito"). The following passage comes from Kierkegaard's *Fear and Trembling*. In the lucid swirl of awe that opens the work, Kierkegaard's pseudonym, Johannes de Silentio, imagines that he has at last found that "knight of faith," the improbable man whose way of being can unite the sublime with the pedestrian, the great "leap of life" with the ordinary afternoon stroll. "Here he is. Acquaintance made, I am introduced to him," Johannes imagines, and yet,

> the moment I set eyes on him I instantly push him from me, I myself leap backwards, I clasp my hands and say half aloud, 'Good Lord, is this the man? Is it really he? Why, he looks like a tax-collector!' […] I draw closer to him, watching his least movements to see whether there might not be visible a little heterogeneous fractional telegraphic message from the infinite, a glance, a look, a gesture, a note of sadness, a smile, which betrayed the infinite in its heterogeneity with the finite. No! I examine his figure from tip to toe to see if there might not be a cranny through which the infinite was peeping. No! […] No heavenly glance or any other token of the incommensurable betrays him; if one did not know him, it would be impossible to distinguish him from the rest. (Kierkegaard [1843] 1983: 81–82)

Let us nonetheless give it a try.

Reforming Confession

What exactly is a confession? And what does confession entail in the context of the Reformation? At the beginning, at least, we find a picture with relatively tidy outlines. The rite of confession was at the center of lively debate among reformers, and like many other Christian rites, individual confession of sins was stripped of its sacramental status by both Lutheran and Reformed traditions, and lost its clear place within Christian liturgy. The practice of auricular confession to an authorized priest was widely criticized among reformers both for being too lax and for being too rigid—for treating absolution in a formulaic way, that is, and for subjecting the penitent to harsh, in some cases even abusive examinations of conscience. Zwingli would deny categorically the ability of any human being (including priests) to offer the remission of sins; Calvin would propose a variety of positions over the course of his life, all relatively close to Zwingli's; Luther, as was typical of him in such contexts, would appeal to the virtual dimension, instructing the penitent to treat the priest's word of absolution "as though" it were a voice from heaven, offered directly from God to the penitent herself (Lea 1896: 516).[3]

While the reformers were busy dismantling the sacrament of confession, making it less and less central to the operation of the liturgy, Roman Catholic churches were moving in something like the opposite direction, securing the sacramental function of confession by installing the first iterations of that now emblematic ecclesial structure, the confessional booth. To look at such a structure from within the open space of a church may give one an impression of privacy and enclosure. It has three or four walls, separated from the rest of the church by a curtain or even a door. But in fact, as church historians remind us, this impression is misleading: the confessional was developed during the Borromean Counterreformation as an elaborate moral technology designed to keep the act of penance as *public* as possible while at the same time avoiding unnecessary contact between confessor and penitent (who was, with increasing frequency, female) (De Boer 2001: 85). Such reforms have their background in the Council of Trent, which implemented a new, juridical interpretation of the rite of confession, and cast the confessor in a jurisdictional role, assessing the sinner's particular deeds and proposing an appropriate form of penance. The confessional is not simply a closed or private space, but a conspicuous anchor of invisibility, a technology of physical control

---

[3] Lea is here citing from the Lutheran *Sächsische Kirchenordnung* of 1539. See also his discussion of other reformers' critiques of the rite of confession (Lea 1896: 517ff.). Thomas Tentler's account of these debates offers helpful basic orientation (Tentler 1977).

leveraging secrecy for the sake of surveillance.[4] Thus while reformers in Protestant contexts were demanding the liturgical marginalization of confession, which was transformed from an official sacrament to a contested and amorphous practice, we find in the Roman church a pronounced affirmation of confession's liturgical role, defined and protected by increasingly elaborate juridical, ecclesial, and architectural structures (Myers 2006: 245–246).

It is at this point that the outlines of our story begin to blur. Does the formal, sacramental defense of confession tell us that confession in the Catholic Church has a more public and collective dimension than in its Protestant counterparts? Or are the Borromean reforms a response to the tendency, already on the rise across European Christendom, to view the rite of confession in individual, psychological terms (Bossy 1975: 27–30)? While one familiar view has it that the treatment of confession in Protestant contexts diminished the "social vitality" (Bossy 1975: 27) of this ritual, what does that really mean? It is tempting to insert a familiar narrative form at this point—salvation restricted by such reforms to the scene of a private, individual conscience in Protestant Christianity—a narrative that will lead us, if we are inclined to follow, right to the door of twentieth-century liberal individualism. And yet confession did not disappear in Protestant contexts. In fact, it was sidelined within church liturgy to the precise extent that—or at least, on the precise grounds that—it might become ubiquitous. Luther explicitly imagined that a sort of everyday public and communal discourse might take the place of the liturgical confession, in which neighbors would be expected to mutually confess their guilt as well as their desire for forgiveness (Luther [1529] 2000: 477 para. 10). The privatization narrative, in other words, will not bring us closer to understanding what confession meant in Reformation contexts.[5]

We may come to see around this point by considering how the new attitudes toward confession proposed by reformers such as Luther and

---

[4] John Bossy offers a crisp study of the spread of the Borromean technology across other Catholic lands in the ensuing years, and particularly on the relation of this new technology to conditions of privacy (Bossy 1975).

[5] For an important set of tools to rethink the distinction between public and private at the heart of this narrative, see Michael Warner's *Publics and Counterpublics* (Warner 2002).

Calvin were formulated not as criticisms of confession itself, but of the pastoral power central to its operation in the Roman church. To propose a limit to this power, as Luther put it in his brief treatise on confession first appended to the 1529 edition of the catechism, is to propose a corresponding increase in the freedom of the penitent sinner: "Concerning confession, we have always taught that it should be voluntary and purged of the pope's tyranny" (Luther [1529] 2000: 476 para. 1). In the broadest sense, what Luther is suggesting here is that the church should no longer be in the business of monitoring its monitoring. Instead of stipulating that the penitent should go to confession once a week or once a month, instead of stipulating the precise circumstances in which a confession ought to take place, "My advice would be to ignore all 'circumstances' whatsoever. With Christians there is only one circumstance—that a fellow Christian has sinned…the observance of places, times, days, persons, and all other rank superstition only magnifies the things that are nothing, to the injury of the things which are everything" (Luther [1520] 2016: 92). Having the doubled vision proper to a media age, we may not find it terribly difficult to see in such overt gestures at emancipation the outlines of a now-familiar ambivalence: the monitoring of monitoring stops when we are considered able to monitor ourselves. We have a conscience, Luther tells us—that is, a personal spiritual faculty designed to know when, how, and to what extent penitence should take place. The conscience "frees" us from the obligation to confess to a priest, on this or that given occasion, because it calls us to recognize that "confession should and must take place continuously as long as we live" (Luther [1529] 2000: 477 para. 9). The connection between these two aspects of Protestant reform—freedom from conspicuous constraint and freedom for inconspicuous obligation—reflects a historical trope familiar to the study of modern ideology: the suppressed norm that does not stand outside but comes to mediate, color, define the whole. This is the trope that dominates Spengler's *Decline*, the great symbolic poem of Western history, as Northrop Frye would describe it (Frye [1965] 2010: 260). In what follows, I would like to highlight two somewhat less familiar aspects of Protestant reforms of the practice of confession that will help us to understand what is at stake in this history for us today, in the context of a critical rethinking of the ideal of transparency.

The first element is an interpretive shift on the part of Reformers from treating confession as an enumeration and avowal of specific acts and thoughts considered to be sins, to viewing confession as a recognition or avowal of *oneself* as a sinner. "Up to now, as we all know from experience," Luther wrote, citing the most widely criticized aspect of Roman confessional practice, "there has been no law quite so oppressive as that which…so greatly burdened and tortured consciences with the enumeration of all kinds of sin that no one was able to confess purely enough" (Luther [1529] 2000: 476 paras. 1–2). But Luther's aim in such criticism was not only to minimize the penitent's torment. The rite of confession should be reformatted, he thought, because its current form constitutes a misunderstanding of the true nature and power of confession. Confession is nothing short of "the essence of a genuinely Christian life," namely, "to recognize ourselves as sinners and to pray for grace" (Luther [1529] 2000: 477 para. 9). One perhaps unexpected implication of this proposal to view repentance as the recognition of the sinning self (rather than of the sin one has committed) is that it strengthens the connection between postures of confession and profession. To own up to my past is also to profess what I am: "When I exhort you to go to confession, I am doing nothing but exhorting you *to be a Christian*" (Luther [1529] 2000: 479 para. 32; my emphasis). As a speech act, profession does not normally appear suited to the penitential attitude. To make a statement about who one is and what one stands for seems more likely born of pride or confidence than of contrition. What distinguishes the professing confession from a prideful act, theologically at least, is what the repentant sinner affirms: not her individual, historical self, but the faithful corporate into which contrition inscribes her. For the "papists," Luther writes in the Smalcald Articles, confession produced "torments, rascality, and idolatry," in that, "there was neither faith nor Christ, and the power of the absolution was not explained to [the penitent]. Rather, their comfort was based on the enumeration of sins and humiliation" (Luther [1537] 2000: [3.3 para. 20] 315). For Luther, it is the Roman Christians who are left to themselves. The Protestants keep their sights on "the glory of Christian fellowship." Christ, faith, and the community inscribed by those powers—these are the eminent things of "the things which are everything" (Luther [1520] 2016: 92). Through faith, the confessing sinner is able to occupy a professional posture—partly affirmative, partly polemical.

The "confessional age" [*konfessionelles Zeitalter*], as historians have come to describe the era between the Peace of Augsburg (1555) and Peace of Westphalia (1648), was a period characterized by intense ideological and political competition among the rapidly multiplying movements of reform across both Protestant and Catholic zones. In such circumstances, all manner of religious discourse came to bear a polemical sense. To indicate or affirm right thinking or conduct was also to take up a position in the competition between distinct communities—or as they then began to be called, "confessions" [*Konfessionen, Bekenntnisse*]—of faith.[6] By appreciating how profession or avowal comes to shape the definition of confession in Lutheran contexts, we come up against the second aspect of Protestant treatments of confession that I'd like to focus on here. Through the deeply personal acts of surveying the contents of one's conscience, of experiencing contrition, and of expressing it, the sinner also determines a particular sort of a relation to her community:

> In short, we want nothing to do with compulsion. However, if anyone does not hear and heed our preaching and warning, we shall have nothing to do with such a person who ought not have any part of the gospel. If you are a Christian, you should be glad to run more than a hundred miles for confession, not under compulsion but rather coming and compelling us to offer it. For here the compulsion must be reversed; we are the ones who must come under the command and you must come in freedom. We compel no one, but allow ourselves to be compelled, just as we are compelled to preach and administer the sacrament.... (Luther [1529] 2000: 479 paras. 30–31)

Here Luther imagines Christianity as a community without constraint, a community of free desire (that is, insofar as desire can be free). You do not take part in this community because you are a human being, nor because you are God's creation. You are a member of this community insofar as you *recognize* yourself, your own proper and free desire, in what

---

[6] Klueting offers helpful, synthetic overview of how a "confessionalizing process [*Prozeß der Konfessionalisierung*]" defined this period (Klueting 1989: esp. ch. 1).

is nonetheless an obligation. Auricular confession is to be performed in one's neighborhood, not in one's church. But what makes the neighbor a neighbor is not geographical proximity ("more than a hundred miles") but rather the intimate, affective proximity of desire and satisfaction. In this way the practice of confession helps define a dispersed and as yet largely imaginary community, in part by distinguishing it from others ("If anyone does not hear and heed our preaching and warning, we shall have nothing to do with such a person."). Confession of sins is tied with the recognition of oneself as sinner and the profession of oneself as a Christian (which means, especially in this period, as a certain sort of Christian, connected with some, disconnected from others).

To call the long century following the conclusion of the German Peasants' War an age of "confessionalization" is not only to point to the high degree of ideological competition in the period. It also marks, in response to these competitive conditions, the emergence of confession as a new discursive form. As doctrinal debates proliferated over the course of the Reformation, the most important ideas and problems were formulated through the work of various theological councils. The catechisms or systems of instruction produced by such meetings began to be known by the title, "confessions of faith" [*Glaubensbekenntnisse*] (principal examples being the Helvetic Confessions, the Augsburg Confession or the *Confessio Augustana*, the Westminster Confession). These confessional or creedal statements then come to serve as the basis, over the ensuing centuries, for the formation of distinct Christian communities—denominations, as we tend to describe them now, but known in Protestant societies as distinct "confessions" ("the Lutheran confession," "the Reformed confession," "the Roman Catholic confession," and, formerly more common, "the Jewish confession"). The speech act indexed by this use of the term "confession" is not an accounting of past wrongs or an expression of contrition. This confession is a positive movement, an affirmation of the truth to which one holds oneself in standing before the eyes of the world. To ask what confession meant to Protestant reformers is thus also to ask about the way in which confession becomes the site of a wide range of discursive possibilities. German theologians will later try to demarcate some of these possibilities from one another by using distinct terms (*Beichte* for the confession of sins, *Konfession* for the confessional community, *Bekenntnis* for the confession of faith). But it is never quite so tidy. For *Bekenntnis* can also refer to the confession of sins, as to the confessional community itself. And *confessio/confession* remains the official Latin/French term for all three senses throughout the period (as in the English and French editions that would soon appear).[7]

To appreciate what it means to view the rise of confession as a polemical discourse, let us consider one rather influential text edited by the Swiss reformer Guillaume Farel. His 1536 *La Confession de foi* served as a handy, didactic distillation of Calvin's *Institutes*, and was distributed widely around Geneva, particularly in preparation for Calvin's visit to Geneva in the following year. Farel's *Confession* presents the principal tenets of Christian faith through a limited array of first-person plural verbs: *nous confessons, nous protestons, nous reconnaissons* [we confess, we protest, we recognize…] (Farel [1536] 1986). The document's primary aim is to communicate the most important elements of the Christian faith. But in doing so, the text also constitutes "confession" as the form through which these essential doctrines and practices may be defined, adopted, and affirmed. Even the two rites that retain their sacramental status in Calvin's vision of the church—baptism and the holy feast—are inscribed neatly within the overall confessional frame of the text (Farel [1536] 1986: 49–50). The sacraments are now confession's discursive content—*what* the faithful Christian confesses as having sacramental value—while confession is now a way of *conferring* that value (or of denying it). To put it most boldly: this sort of confession is less a discrete speech-act than a discourse, a medium or frame of reference through which religious self-consciousness articulates itself in a plural world. "As there is no greater division than that of faith," reads a memorandum from the Swiss reformers to the Small Council in 1537, "we ask that you arrange for all inhabitants of your city to make confession and to give reasons for their faith." Farel's *Confession* was not only distributed throughout Genevan society but was treated as inviting an obligatory

---

[7] Brooke Conti has made a compelling argument for the connection between the self-revealing discourse of confession tied to autobiography and repentance with the social and polemical confessionalizing discourse in early modern England, noting in her introduction that these senses have often been seen as distinct or even incompatible. She focuses on the polyvalence and instability of the autobiographical genre to make this case (Conti 2014).

response. Only by visiting houses one by one, as nineteenth-century historian Albert Rilliet once put it, asking each resident not only to pronounce but to explain their beliefs, would it be possible to know "what a person's doctrine actually is, which is at any rate the correct beginning of a church" (cited in Backus and Chimelli 1986: 41).

In such cases confession names the discursive form through which a Christian community addresses itself to the wider world. This sense of the term would remain central over the course of the ensuing "confessional" era, and would continue to resurface in contexts of intense ideological conflict or competition. It became particularly important to the dialectical theologians of the early twentieth century, who were dealing with the challenges of modernization, secularization, and the uncertain role of the church within the rising tide of political nationalism. Speaking to the pastoral meeting of the Reformed Churches in St. Gallen in 1935, Karl Barth delivered a lecture entitled "The Confession of the Reformation and our Confession," aimed at mobilizing his fellow pastors against National Socialism. His argument was a religious one: "Confession, in the sense that concerns us here, is the action of a *church*. A church exists where people have listened together to Jesus Christ in such a way that they belong to him and in this way that they are all responsible for their knowledge. Only a church can confess" (Barth 1935: 5). On this view, confession is defined as a corporate and public speech act. It is, as he observes, intrinsically polemical: "Whether explicit or implicit, confession always contains a *polemic*, a negation, a *damnamus*" (Barth 1935: 9). And yet the penitential dimension of confession remains central to this view, for when the church confesses, "it confesses as a church of sinners" (Barth 1935: 10). Barth's theological aim here is to argue for the interdependence of church and confession: "As for a church that does not confess, insofar as such a thing exists, one should describe it not as a lack or deficit, but rather as a form of inactivity...A truly and literally confessionless church...would be—if there were such a thing—*ipso facto* a dead church" (Barth 1935: 7). With this syllogism Barth intensifies the view of confession as discursive form which we saw in Farel's *Confession de foi*. What scholars have described as the historical process of confessionalization, Barth here turns into a theological principle, an absolute criterion of religious legitimacy (Barth 1935: 29).

Developing a similar view in a lecture delivered a few months earlier, entitled "Confession and Living Community," Eduard Thurneysen, a friend and close collaborator of Barth's, would ground the principle of communal confession in a communal characterization of faith, itself: "Faith concerns the community. Faith cannot remain solitary. Nor can it remain with a few people. It must communicate itself, just as an infection communicates itself. It lays hold of one person here and another there, and it drives him to break free from the world and to take others with him, those who share his faith...Faith is no private matter" (Thurneysen 1935: 9–10). One may not be surprised to find an Evangelical pastor and theologian defending the view that faith must and ought to propagate. Things become more curious when we try to square this notion of faith as a contagious, communal profession, with the polyvalent notion of confession we began examining in relation to Protestant reform. In the works of early reformers such as Luther and Farel we considered the way in which de-sacramentalization went along with an interlacing of the penitential and polemical senses of confession. For Luther, recall, the confession of sin and the profession of faith were linked because the confessing-recognition of oneself as a sinner came to take the place of the confessing-enumeration of one's sinful deeds, and because auricular confession had been rerouted along more horizontal circuits of fellow, brother, neighbor, community. If a Christian does not come, "compelling us to offer [confession]," then he is not in fact a Christian, for Luther. Rather, he is something with whom Christians "have nothing to do." Thus we may wonder, in the twentieth-century situation of Barth and Thurneysen, whether we have not simply moved on here to a theology in which these two senses of confession have split off more fully from one another? What do their accounts of *Bekenntnis* as the public action of a church vis-à-vis the world have to do with penitence or the conscience-clearing confession of sin? The remark from *Elective Affinities* which opens this essay may help us begin to reflect on this question. Confession can be liberating, on the view Goethe expresses, on the condition that one declares oneself to be bound. To declare oneself free has the opposite effect. And yet this is less an asymmetry than a kind of circle. The bind *from* which penitential confession frees a Christian is reproduced by the professional confession, which thrusts her into the polemical fellowship of worldly life.

Authenticating Confession

Thurneysen will address the point about penitence explicitly, stating that "confession is always first of all the confession of sins" (Thurneysen 1935: 7). How he understands this connection may become clearer when we recall an example from the start of his lecture: "There he is," Thurneysen exclaims, before introducing the well-known story of Zwingli, the Protestant theologian who was killed in the Battle of Kappel, where he had been fighting to defend a newly reformed Zurich. "Zwingli lies on the battlefield at Kappel, late in the evening of October 10, 1531. Marauding enemies found him, not far from the abbey, among the bodies of his comrades. There he was—still alive, hands folded, lips moving silently. The enemies asked him if they should fetch a priest, so that he might confess. He remained silent, his gaze fixed on the heavens. This infuriated the bystanders, and a captain from Unterwalden dealt him the final blow. This final silence of Zwingli—that was confession!" (Thurneysen 1935: 4).[8] With this example Thurneysen shows that the doubled meaning of confession—the repentance-confession of sin and the profession-confession of faith—persists even under the most polemical circumstances (an actual *polemos*). A confession of sin should aim at sincerity; a confession of faith should aim at persuasion (enabling the "contagion" of faith to spread). To take Zwingli's conduct as a model of true confession is to locate the conjunction between penitence and persuasion in a discourse that is evident (it takes place before their eyes) but imperceptible (it excludes them). The example of Zwingli thus modifies the bombastic missionary image we might have from Thurneysen's discussion of faith as contagion. On the primitive secular stage of the battlefield, Zwingli's confession of faith is constituted by his silence. Zwingli

---

[8] Barth likely has Thurneysen's speech in mind when he notes that the requirement that confession be polemical need not mean it be voiced. "Confession may also be a being-silent," he specifies, before citing Zwingli's final hour as an eminent example (Barth 1935: 8).

(or at least the version of him taken up in Thurneysen's parable) not only refuses the comfort of auricular confession to a priest, he refuses even to engage with the men offering him this potential comfort. And for Thurneysen, we might say, while the first refusal is an action Zwingli takes with regard to his own conscience, the second refusal is a performance, addressing an audience of those who are not his neighbors, communicating the sincerity of the first performance by rejecting the opportunity to persuade.

The problem of authenticity had been a central part of the history of confession long before the Reformation: how to be sure that the sinner who confesses does not merely say the words, but actually repents? One of the thorniest aspects of this problem—which worried Catholic and Protestant theologians alike—was the fact that it could cause significant trouble for the penitent sinner herself. I go to confession. I examine my conscience and account for the sinful deeds and thoughts that appear to this examining gaze. But how can I be sure that I have confessed *all* my sins? What if I have forgotten something, and it comes back to me later? What if I have forgotten something, and it never comes back? Where exactly does it go? Somewhere in "me"? Somewhere that "I" am still responsible for? Providing an initial framework to legislate such tangles was one of the principal achievements of the discussion of confession at the Council of Trent. On the Protestant side, the practical difficulty in assessing the fullness and validity of a confession, coupled with a resistance to formulating stable juridical and punitive norms that might apply to ambiguous situations, became a salient feature in the efforts to remove from confession its sacramental status. Calvin would hold, for example, that the Roman church was unable to maintain a meaningful distinction between "compunction of heart" and "confession of mouth" (Calvin [1559] 2006: [3.4.2] 625). What the Zwingli example demonstrates is how the Reformers, so far from eliminating the problem, have given it an upgrade. While the challenges of transparency and completeness in confession are arguably made less acute by Protestants' focus on confessing one's own being-a-sinner, rather than on enumerating the sins one has committed, this model also invites the norm of profession, of a declaration or affirmation of one's nature and communal identity, into the discursive practice of penitence. Insofar as confession marks not only the repentant sinner from her former, unrepentant self, but also the free church from the unfree community, the anxiety of authenticity is reflected through the tension of a confession that must also serve *polemical* purposes. To confess the truth for which one lives (and dies) is not only to communicate and hold to what one believes but to do so under a social gaze that will (by definition) not see you as you are, to an audience that will not hear what you are really saying.

The resonance between Thurneysen's tribute to Zwingli and the passage from Kierkegaard about the invisibility of the knight of faith, quoted at the start of this essay, is hardly coincidental. Barth and Thurneysen were profoundly influenced by Kierkegaard, and particularly by his presentation of the incommensurability of faith with worldly virtue. That Thurneysen renders Kierkegaard's characterization so literally—the "knight of faith" as an actual *knight…of faith*—is perhaps the subject for an essay on secular religion and the hyperreal. Most important in both cases is the connection between the devotional and worldly attitudes: confession involves the laying bare of one's heart directly to God, but it also involves the public profession of one's faith, an act with intrinsically polemical significance. The proof of sincerity in the first case is opacity in the second. Thurneysen honors Zwingli, not for the martyrdom of having died for his faith, but for the martyrdom of living misunderstood.

Fictionalizing Confession

In the art of literary confession whose development Goethe saw as the consequence of Protestant reform, Zwingli's eloquent silence is thrust to the heart of the literary subject itself. The tension between confession and profession, disavowal and self-avowal, the indistinguishability even in analytic terms between repentance and affirmation—it is precisely this set of issues that will come to define the work of Goethe's most celebrated partner in the passage from sacramental to secular confession, Jean-Jacques Rousseau. Twentieth-century readers have generally considered modern modes of autobiographical writing as fundamentally shaped by the model of Rousseau's *Confessions*. Generations of scholars have looked to Rousseau to understand something about the paradoxes and ironies of the attempt to establish a *literature* of intimacy. Rousseau represents the central paradox of modern literature, for someone like Lionel Trilling, insofar as the quality of literariness, of writing that asks to be interpreted in aesthetic terms, is dependent on a certain disavowal of intimacy within the text, on our inability to reduce the words in front of us to a straightforward address between author and reader, a conversation between me and you (Trilling 1972: 7–8).[9] Readers have also looked to Rousseau's writing as a context in which the nature of the self and its relation to language and to writing has been defined in formative ways for European modernity. From Starobinski to Derrida and de Man, Trilling to Coetzee, Rousseau's writing is both the temple and the archive. It is the story defined by inhibition, fact, and control, from which emerge our most persistent myths about truth, self, and representation, and it is the unwieldy and uncontrollable register of the writer's shame and desire, a register which can be deployed at any time, by Rousseau as by any of his readers, to profane his story and the myths it generates. What most interests these twentieth-century readers is the problem of where and how Rousseau's confession comes undone—where the moral demand for transparency that animates the whole discourse founders, and what that foundering shows us (about Rousseau, about language, about truth). In semiotic terms, Rousseau's confession functions in these readings as a broken icon. Here, instead of disappearing before the greater reality behind it (the "truth" of Rousseau's self), the sign itself appears and remains conspicuous, calling attention to its symbolic work.

Among all the famous anecdotes of the *Confessions* none has received more attention in this regard than the story of the stolen ribbon. This passage, along with the few other instances of petty theft in Rousseau's story, has often drawn comparison to similar passages in Augustine's *Confessions*.[10] When Augustine tells the story of the pears he stole as a

---

[9] Dorothea E. von Mücke offers a compelling new version of the Rousseau-Goethe genealogy, pointing to the two figures not as the origin of a certain style of literature but of a certain style of publicity: "Together with the birth of the celebrity author such as Rousseau or Goethe, the eighteenth century witnessed the emergence of the concept of an active, critical public" (von Mücke 2015: xiii).

[10] Derrida uses the stolen fruit parallel in particular to illustrate what he calls the "délicat et abyssal problème d'archivation—consciente ou inconsciente," which emphasizes how a text, autobiographical or not, always exceeds its author. Far from an intentional pact between author and reader

youth, he confesses his sin and his crime, he explains his former attitude in stern and distant tones, and expresses remorse. Above all he introduces and excludes any potential mitigating factors that might qualify or be seen to excuse his act (hunger, poverty, even simple desire to enjoy the fruit). By constructing such an unforgiving perspective on his past deed, we perceive a sharp and stable perspectival difference—between the sinning self being confessed and the repentant self that does the confessing:

> Theft receives punishment by your law, Lord, and by the law written in the hearts of men…I wanted to carry out an act of theft and did so, driven by no kind of need other than my inner lack of any sense of, or feeling for, justice. Wickedness filled me. I stole something which I had in plenty and of much better quality. My desire was to enjoy not what I sought by stealing but merely the excitement of thieving and the doing of what was wrong. There was a pear tree near our vineyard laden with fruit, though attractive in neither colour nor taste. To shake the fruit off the tree and carry off the pears, I and a gang of naughty adolescents set off late at night after (in our usual pestilential way) we continued our game in the streets. We carried off a huge load of pears. But they were not for our feasts but merely to throw to the pigs. Even if we ate a few, nevertheless our pleasure lay in doing what was not allowed.
> Such was my heart, O God, such was my heart, which You had pity on it when it was at the bottom of the abyss. Now let my heart tell you what it was seeking there that I became evil for no reason. I had no motive for my wickedness except wickedness itself. It was foul, and I loved it. I loved the self-destruction, I loved my fall, not the object for which I had fallen but my fall itself. (Augustine 2008: 28–29)

When Rousseau confesses his theft, however, the perspective of his narration is far more difficult to fix. As he tells us: At sixteen years old, working as a valet in the house of Madame de Vercellis, he covets a ribbon and steals it. Having chosen not to hide the evidence, he is quickly found out by his employers, and asked to come clean. Instead of admitting his crime, however, he commits a much greater one, accusing Marion, the

---

(as Philippe Lejeune would read Rousseau's *Confessions* around the same time), what the *Confessions* demonstrate is how the referential arena of a text multiplies without clear boundaries (Derrida 2001: 48ff). See also Derrida [1967] 1976.

innocent kitchen maid, of the theft, thereby compounding his childish sin of covetousness with a lucid and sadistic crime. His lie is believed, he tells us, and Marion is dismissed from the household service. It is at this point in Rousseau's narrative that the difference from Augustine becomes most apparent. Rousseau begins to imagine, with palpable relish, the sordid ends to which poor Marion must surely have been driven after her dismissal. The more detail he offers about his theft and its possible effects on her, and the more transparently he appears to relay his own present state of mind, the less certain we become of what he is really doing: is this confession a sinner's act of penitence or a writer's self-characterization? Is he expressing contrition for his sin, or pride in the power of his conscience? With Rousseau's pen, in other words, the tension between the professional and penitential economies of Protestant confession is pushed to its hermeneutic breaking point: How can a profession ever achieve penitence, we wonder? Or conversely, if there is concrete spiritual value in the act of declaring oneself a sinner, how bad can sin really be? "In the economy of confession," as J.M. Coetzee puts it, in describing the fundamental tension of Rousseau's *Confessions*, "a shameful desire is a valuable desire. Conversely, for a desire to have a value it must have a secret, shameful component. Confession consists of a double movement of offering to spend 'inconsistencies' and holding back enough to maintain the 'freedom' that comes from having capital" (Coetzee 1985: 212–213).

The tension between (or the superimposition of) the professional and confessional economies in Rousseau's writing is also what pushes Paul de Man to the claim that Rousseau's confessions are not really confessions at all, but rather exhibitionist "excuses," an essentially fictive discourse in which sin is not the referent of the confession but something "produced" by the confession, an outcome of one's attempt to alleviate the weight of a moral imbalance (de Man 1979).[11] For de Man, the normative instability of Rousseau's discourse distinguishes it from a "true" confession. Confession, for him, is always referential, in that it expresses contrition and can draw on reasons. Opposed to this referential discourse is

---

[11] In this remark we can hear the closing bell of a particular history of intentionality, one which comes to grief, as Sartre theorized some decades before de Man, in the recognition of finitude as the ultimate inability to distinguish between a reason and a pretext.

"confession" à la Rousseau—a form of fiction which cannot draw on reasons but whose failure nonetheless bears the potential for a different kind of truth, as the problem-text becomes a privileged site where language reveals its deepest nature, not as a system of meaning, reference, expression, but of rupture, difference, irony. But to insist that confession is referential discourse, as de Man does, is to allow the phenomenon of confession to be defined by the confession of sins. But in Protestant contexts, as we have seen, this penitential form of confession came to coexist with a confessional discourse that had strongly professional tendencies: you confess what you have done in order to square your account, not only to square the debt of the deed, but to square the debt of the deed with the debt of who you are—despite the sin, given the sin, even because of the sin.[12] Rousseau tells us this on the very first page. What the *Confessions* concerns—what the work of confession in the *Confessions* concerns—is the onto-genealogy of himself, "un homme d'après nature."

Jean Starobinski was perhaps the first to consider the *Confessions* in light of the drive toward exhibitionism and, unlike de Man, he did not tend to see a tension between this drive and the task of confession itself. Examining Rousseau as an originator of rather than as an aspirant to the genre of confessional writing, Starobinski emphasized the way in which confessional writing seems inherently to straddle the divide between two discursive ideals—the ideal of the true, where confession is referential, and the ideal of the authentic, where language must generate its "own" sort of truth. Rousseau would regularly affirm the clarity of his mind and feelings by describing the transparency of his heart—"transparent as crystal," as Starobinski locates Rousseau's favored simile (Starobinski [1957] 1971: 301ff.). But Rousseau was no mystic. Transparency was never satisfying as a mere state of being. It had to be recognized, to propagate itself, to catch on—or else it was not transparency at all. "It is not enough to live in the gracious condition of transparency," as Starobinski put it,

---

[12] Coetzee makes a related point about de Man: "Though de Man errs in asserting that the truth one confesses must in principle be verifiable (one can confess impure thoughts, for example), his distinction between confession proper and excuse does allow one to see why confessions of the kind we encounter in Rousseau raise problems of certainty not raised by confessions of fact" (Coetzee 1985: 207).

"one must also relate one's own transparency, convince others of it" (Starobinski [1957] 1971: 219).

The problem went even deeper than this, however. For to desire transparency and to desire to be seen—even to be seen *correctly*—are at some level opposing drives. If others see me other than as I am, then they do not see me, then "I am invisible to them, and they impose on me an opacity which is foreign" (Starobinski [1957] 1971: 302). For Starobinski this is one of the core libidinal tensions (transparency vs visibility) that organizes Rousseau's literary confession. The desire for transparency is connected to the question that sets up Rousseau's confessional project: "Why does this inner feeling, immediately evident, not find its echo in an immediately accorded recognition? Why is it so difficult to make agree what one is for oneself and what one is for others?" (Starobinski [1957] 1971: 218–219). But Rousseau's attempt to fulfill this desire, Starobinski maintains, is much less about those others than it might seem. He does not take up writing in order to show *them* or convince *them*, that is, to finally become as transparent to others as he feels to himself. Rousseau's goal is in fact to transform *himself* into a pure mode of vision, seeing all things, and yet itself opaque—to "become a gaze which knows no interdiction; it is truly 'to become a living eye'" (Starobinski [1957] 1971: 302). This is why Rousseau, in writing his confessions, must also invent a new form of writing, "must mark his difference from others by means of *a different language*, which he would be the first and the only to use" (Starobinski [1957] 1971: 229).[13] Rousseau's writing, for this reason, should be strictly differentiated from classical rhetorical discourse. Here, speech is not deployed to *reveal* Rousseau's character in a compelling way, but to *realize* it, as the site of his own becoming. Language *is* the locus of Rousseau's "authentic self," as Starobinski would have it, but for one who aspires to establish one's home in the force of absolute difference, language is a bad

---

[13] Starobinski cites a passage from the *Annales* at this point: "Il faudrait pour ce que j'ai à dire inventer un langage aussi nouveau que mon projet: car quel ton, quel style prendre pour débrouiller ce chaos immense de sentiments si divers, si contradictoires, souvent si vils et quelquefois si sublimes dont je fus sans cesse agité?" (Starobinski [1957] 1971: 229). We see the idea here that will appear throughout Romantic preoccupations with authenticity and expressive singularity, culminating in Schlegel's infamous apology for the style of the *Athenæum*, which declares an isomorphism between truth and incomprehensibility (Schlegel [1800] 1971).

place to build. For language is also what is bound to reveal, for any subject, again and again, that "authenticity is still lacking, that plenitude is still to be conquered, that nothing is assured if the witness refuses to consent" (Starobinski [1957] 1971: 239).

Here we see a shift, not only in the content of the confession (from deeds to doer, or actions to identity), but also in how the confession relates to its intended audience. Going back to the passage from Augustine, we can note that the addressee of his confession is God. We are as if not there—we overhear his confession. Rousseau, however, addresses us directly:

> Let the trumpet of judgment sound when it will, I will present myself with this book in my hand before the Supreme Judge. I will say boldly: "Here is what I have done, what I have thought, what I was. I have told the good and the bad with equal frankness. I concealed nothing that was ill, added nothing that was good...I have showed myself as I was, contemptible and vile when that is how I was, good, generous, sublime, when that is how I was; I have disclosed my innermost self as you alone know it to be. Assemble about me, Eternal Being, the numberless host of my fellow-men; let them hear my confessions, let them groan at my unworthiness, let them blush at my wretchedness. Let each of them, here on the steps of your throne, in turn reveal his heart with the same sincerity; and then let one of them say to you, if he dares: *I was better than that man.* (Rousseau [1782–1789] 2000: 5)

God sees, but is not addressed. We are addressed, but we do not see, or do not see Rousseau as he *really* is. We might think, here, of Mill's famous distinction between eloquence and poetry: eloquent speech is to be heard, poetry is *over*heard; eloquence reaches out to other minds, poetry is a feeling that *confesses itself* (Mill 1860: 95). Yet as we saw with Thurneysen's parable about Zwingli, the poetic or overheard confession may also be the most eloquent or rhetorical—it is through silence that Zwingli offered his most authentic and most compelling confession of faith. Viewing Rousseau's work as a "secular" confession may tempt us to consider that *we*—the public, the human audience, the reader—have replaced God. But this is not quite right. For a confessant who addresses God, God already knows what the confessant is struggling to articulate. The confessing subject is always catching up to the perfect transparency of a divine perspective. This is what all the techniques and strategies, the lists and times and dates are meant to indicate, that we do not see ourselves as we are seen by God. In the passage from Rousseau above, God's knowledge is an embellishment. It is Rousseau who *knows* himself in the exemplary way—"No one in the world knows me, but I myself" (cited in Starobinski [1957] 1971: 218)[14]—and it is the reader who must catch up to the author's self-knowledge. The public does replace God, in Rousseau's rendering; we have become the sinning subject, himself.

Observing this curious triangle may also help us explain the hall of mirrors into which Rousseau's criticism matriculated in the second half of the twentieth century. When Coetzee notes certain patterns in what postmodern readers have made of Rousseau, he suggests that "the only kind of reader who can judge between truth and falsity in Rousseau while accepting—even if only provisionally—the premises of his confessional project, must be one like de Man, who tries to detect inauthentic moments in Rousseau via inauthentic moments in his language. De Man's analysis of the ribbon episode depends on the premise that confession betrays inauthenticity when the confessant lapses into the language of the Other" (Coetzee 1985: 209). By "language of the Other" Coetzee and de Man are referring to public language—accessible to anyone, able to be criticized by anyone. This is the language of eloquence and rhetoric, not the language of the heart in its immediate transparency to God. These critics follow the traces left by a will to persuade so as to uncover the differential conditions of Rousseau's (and, by extension, anyone's) attempt at self-revelation. But the element they identify as at odds with genuinely confessional speech is an element that has been central to the history of confession since the Reformation. To understand the deep ironies of confessional culture, of the will to render oneself transparent to others, we should begin by refusing to suppose that confession has a simple ur-norm which an all-too-human genius such as Rousseau or Kierkegaard betrays. We should consider that the problems and paradoxa of transparency have a history tied to the ironies of our ongoing confessional age (religious

---

[14] Starobinski is here quoting from Rousseau's "First Letter to Malesherbes."

modernity, polemical fellowship, and its discontents). Here the question cannot take its cue from a tidy analytical opposition between public discourses and private truths. The question is about the forms of publicity a private truth entails.

Works Cited

Aristotle. 1999. *Physics*. Trans. Robin Waterfield. Oxford: Oxford University Press.
Augustine. 2008. *Confessions*. Trans. Henry Chadwick. Oxford: Oxford University Press.
Backus, Irene, and Claire Chimelli, eds. 1986. *La Vraie piété*. Geneva: Labor et Fides.
Barth, Karl. 1935. Das Bekenntnis der Reformation und unser Bekennen. *Theologische Existenz Heute*, vol. 29. Munich, Kaiser.
Bossy, John. 1975. The Social History of Confession in the Age of the Reformation. *Transactions of the Royal Historical Society* 25: 21–38.
Calvin, Jean. 1559 [2006]. *Institutes of the Christian Religion*, vol. 1, ed. John T. McNeill, trans. Ford Lewis Battles. Louisville: Westminster John Knox Press.
Coetzee, J.M. 1985. Confession and Double Thoughts: Tolstoy, Rousseau, and Dostoevsky. *Comparative Literature* 37 (3): 193–232.
Conti, Brooke. 2014. *Confessions of Faith in Early Modern England*. Philadelphia: University of Pennsylvania Press.
De Boer, Wietse. 2001. *The Conquest of the Soul: Confession, Discipline, and Public Order in Counter-Reformation Milan*. Leiden: Brill.
Derrida, Jacques. 1967 [1976]. ...That Dangerous Supplement... In *Of Grammatology*, trans. Gayarti Chakravorty Spivak, 141–164. Baltimore: The Johns Hopkins University Press.
——— (2001) 'Le ruban de machine à écrire,' in *Papier Machine*, Paris: Galilée.
Farel, Guillaume. 1536 [1986]. Confession de la Foi, laquelle tous bourgeois et habitants de Genève et sujets du pays doivent jurer de farder et tenir, extradite de l'Instruction dont on use l'Eglise de la dite ville. In *La Vraie piété*, ed. Irene Backus and Claire Chimelli, 45–53. Geneva: Labor et Fides.
Frye, Northrop. 1965 [2010]. The Rising of the Moon: A Study of Vision. In *Northrop Frye on Twentieth-Century Literature*, ed. Glen Robert Gill. Toronto: University of Toronto Press.

Gay, Peter. 1996. *The Naked Heart: The Bourgeois Experience, Victoria to Freud*. New York: Norton.
von Goethe, Johann Wolfgang. 1809 [1999]. *Elective Affinities*. Trans. David Constantine. Oxford: Oxford University Press.
———. 1811–1833. From My Life: Poetry and Truth (Parts One to Three). In *Goethe: The Collected Works*, vol. 3, ed. Thomas P. Saine and Jeffrey L. Sammons. Princeton: Princeton University Press, 1994.
Kierkegaard, Søren. 1843 [1983]. *Fear and Trembling and Repetition*, Trans. Walter Lowrie. Princeton: Princeton University Press.
Klueting, Harm. 1989. *Das Konfessionelle Zeitalter 1625–1648*. Stuttgart: Eugen Ulmer.
Lea, Henry Charles. 1896. *A History of Auricular Confession and Indulgences in the Latin Church*. Vol. 1. Philadelphia: Lea Brothers.
Luther, Martin. 1520 [2016]. *The Babylonian Captivity of the Church*. In *The Annotated Luther*, ed. Paul W. Robinson, vol. 3. Minneapolis: Augsburg Fortress Press.
———. 1529 [2000]. A Brief Exhortation to Confession. In *The Book of Concord*, ed. Robert Kolb and Timothy J. Wengert, 476–480. Minneapolis: Fortress Press.
———. 1537 [2000]. Smalcald Articles. In *The Book of Concord*, ed. Robert Kolb and Timothy J. Wengert, 297–328. Minneapolis: Fortress Press.
de Man, Paul. 1979. Excuses (*Confessions*). In *Allegories of Reading: Figural Language in Rousseau, Nietzsche, Rilke, and Proust*, 278–301. New Haven: Yale University Press.
Mill, John Stuart. 1860. Thoughts on Poetry and its Varieties. *The Crayon* 7 (4): 93–97.
von Mücke, Dorothea E. 2015. *The Practices of the Enlightenment: Aesthetics, Authorship, and the Public*. Columbia: Columbia University Press.
Myers, W. David. 2006. From Confession to Reconciliation and Back: Sacramental Penance. In *From Trent to Vatican II: Historical and Theological Investigations*, ed. Raymond F. Bulman and Frederick J. Parrella, 241–266. Oxford: Oxford University Press.
Perloff, Marjorie G. 1970. The Autobiographical Mode of Goethe: *Dichtung und Wahrheit* and the Lyric Poems. *Comparative Literature Studies* 7 (3): 265–296.
Rousseau, Jean-Jacques. 1782–1789. *Confessions*. Trans. Angela Scholar. Oxford: Oxford University Press.

Schlegel, Friedrich 1800 [1971]. On Incomprehensibility. In *Friedrich Schlegel's Lucinde and the Fragments*, trans. Peter Firchow, 259–271. Minneapolis: University of Minnesota Press.

Spengler, Oswald. 1918–1923. *The Decline of the West*, 2 vols., trans. Charles Francis Atkinson. New York: Knopf, 1947.

Starobinski, Jean. 1957 [1971]. *Jean-Jacques Rousseau: La transparence et l'obstacle*. Paris: Gallimard.

Tentler, Thomas N. 1977. *Sin and Confession on the Eve of the Reformation*. Princeton: Princeton University Press.

Thurneysen, Eduard. 1935. Lebendige Gemeinde und Bekenntnis. *Theologische Existenz Heute*, vol. 21. Munich: Kaiser.

Trilling, Lionel. 1972. *Sincerity and Authenticity*. Cambridge: Harvard University Press.

Voss, Heinrich. 1895. *Goethe und Schiller in Briefen*. Ed. Hans Gerhard Gräf. Leipzig: Philipp Reclam.

Warner, Michael. 2002. *Publics and Counterpublics*. Brooklyn: Zone Books.

Seeing It All: Bentham's Panopticon and the Dark Spots of Enlightenment

Miran Božovič

> ... *but even transparency is of no avail without eyes to look at it.*
> Jeremy Bentham, Panopticon; Postscript, Part II

In this paper, I compare Jeremy Bentham's panopticon writings with Denis Diderot's early novel *Les Bijoux indiscrets* (1748) and his later work *Le Rêve de d'Alembert* (written in 1769 and published in 1830). Although a comparison of works so radically different in all respects and written by authors as unalike as Bentham and Diderot may seem absurd, there are nevertheless more parallels between the works—as well as between their authors—than generally might be expected. In *Les Bijoux indiscrets,* Diderot depicts an exotic African empire that could be considered an epitome of a transparent society and an unpar-

M. Božovič (✉)
Department of Philosophy, Faculty of Arts, University of Lkubljana, Ljubljana, Slovenia
e-mail: miran.bozovic@guest.arnes.si

alleled embodiment of constant surveillance. In the female population of the empire, the organs of speech have been duplicated; that is, the power of speech has been granted to their sex organs. Each one of these unseen voices of the new speech organs is aware of every sexual transgression and impure thought of its bearer. Unlike the seen voice issuing from the mouth, which can lie, hide the truth or confabulate, the unseen voice of the sex organ speaks only the truth, even against the will of its bearer. Thus, chastity and the purity of morals in the empire are established and maintained by the possibility that the unseen voice of any woman may intervene at any time and publicly reveal her immoral sexual behavior and lustful thoughts. Roughly four decades later, Diderot's fantasy of a transparent empire governed by a ruler who enjoys privileged access to the hidden sexual activities and the most intimate thoughts of his (female) subjects was realized by Bentham in his plans for the panopticon prison, whose smooth running is ensured by a voice that seems to be as all-knowing with regard to the entire panopticon as each of the voices of the female sex organs is all-knowing with regard to the body from which it stems. The subjects of Diderot's transparent empire recognize God at work in the all-knowing voice of the female sex organs. Similarly, in Bentham's panopticon, it is the all-knowing voice that elevates the invisible inspector, in the eyes of prisoners, to the status of a deity. Bentham's panopticon writings portray the process of production or construction of God, which is what this work has in common with Diderot's *Le Rêve de d'Alembert*, where the same process seems to be taking place. In both instances, God is an incidental result, a by-product of the architectonics of the universe itself. Both works could be said to make God and his workings more manifest than any other work, even religious and theological. In the course of both these works, readers witness nothing less than the process of God's coming into existence, but with a notable difference: once God has materialized himself in Diderot's universe, there would be nobody left to behold the theophany; if, on the other hand, God materialized in the universe of Bentham's panopticon, it is God himself that would cease to exist.

Transparent Bodies

Not only did Diderot write in his *Pensées sur l'interprétation de la nature*: "l'Utile circonscrit tout" (Diderot 1994–1997: 1, 563), that is, utility circumscribes (marks off, characterizes, defines) everything, and thereby coined what might have easily been adopted as an emblematic motto by the later Utilitarians; not only was he himself a votary *avant la lettre* of what became the Benthamite greatest happiness principle,[1] but there are numerous other similarities and parallels between the materialist thinker and the utilitarian sage, at least with regard to the internal logic of their ideas. Far from being widely accepted, some of the ideas they shared were dismissed by their contemporaries as downright unorthodox. It could even be said that in developing some of these ideas, they complement each other in a very special way, each carrying the other's ideas to their logical conclusion. That is, it seems as if the ideas of the one were only followed through to the end by the other.

One of the more unorthodox ideas they shared was a belief in the frequent dissection of dead human bodies as a means of acquiring anatomical knowledge and achieving medical progress. The materialist thinker and the utilitarian sage both believed that the dissection and study of the dead would spare the living numerous severe pains. This idea is advocated by Diderot in his articles on "Anatomie" and "Cadavre" in the *Encyclopédie* and by Bentham in the last and possibly the most undeservedly neglected of his works, that is, *Auto-Icon; or, Farther Uses of the Dead to the Living* of 1832. Although it might seem unnecessary for Diderot and Bentham to have to persuade anyone about the utility of the dead in teaching anatomy, neither in the France of Diderot's time nor in the Great Britain of Bentham's time was this idea widely shared. What they had in common was not only their boundless enthusiasm for dissection; moreover,

---

[1] See, for example, *Histoire des deux Indes*: "Chaque enfant qui naît dans l'État, chaque nouveau citoyen qui vient respirer l'air de la patrie qu'il s'est faite, ou que lui a donné la nature, a droit au plus grand bonheur dont il puisse jouir" (Diderot 1994–1997: 3, 717). In several other respects, their views widely differed, of course—for example, in their attitudes to public opinion: while Bentham thought highly of the "Public-opinion Tribunal" (see Bentham 1838–1843: 9, 41), such a "tribunal" was dismissed outright by Diderot in 'Madame de la Carlière' as "le sot public," the stupid public (see Diderot 1994–1997: 2, 522).

in their keen desire to further anatomical knowledge, they both set a personal example for that which Bentham, in his *Auto-Icon*, termed the "anatomical, or dissectional" (Bentham n.d.: 2) purpose of dead bodies. It is well known that in his will, Bentham left his own body to an anatomist, who was to dissect it and use it

> as the means of illustrating a series of lectures to which scientific & literary men are to be invited.... These lectures are to expound the situation structure & functions of the different organs.... The object of these lectures being two fold first to communicate curious interesting & highly important knowledge & secondly to show that the primitive horror at dissection originates in ignorance... (Bentham MSS Box 155, UC Library; quoted in Marmoy 1958: 80)

Diderot, as is perhaps less known, had done the same almost half a century before Bentham: it was his wish too that, after his death, his own body be dissected and studied by anatomists to the benefit of the living. Before quoting from Diderot's autopsy report, his daughter Angélique writes in her *Mémoires*: "My father believed that it was wise to open up the bodies of the dead. He believed that this procedure was of use to the living. More than once he urged me to have him opened up after death; so he was indeed opened up" (Vandeul 1875: lviii).

Interestingly enough, in the article titled "Anatomie," Diderot toys with the daring idea that anatomists should be allowed to dissect not only the bodies of the insensible dead, but also those of the susceptible living, that is, the bodies of live convicts condemned to death (Diderot and d'Alembert 1751–1772: 1, 409–410).[2] Instead of executing the convicts, their bodies could be put to an alternative use: they could serve for practicing surgical procedures and thereby spare humanity numerous severe pains in the future. The deterrence of the innocent from committing

---

[2] In the mid-eighteenth century, this idea was not as uncommon as it might seem. The use of live criminals for practicing surgical procedures was also recommended by Pierre-Louis Moreau de Maupertuis in his *Lettre sur le progrès des sciences* (see Maupertuis 1752: 375–381). Dissection of live malefactors was apparently a well-recognized punishment in the African empire of the Congo, as depicted in Diderot's *Les Bijoux indiscrets*: in the novel, one of the former emperors is said to have had "his surgeon and his chief physician dissected alive" for having prescribed him a purgative at the wrong moment (see Diderot 1748: 46).

crimes achieved through the exemplary punishment of the convicted criminals is thus clearly not the only good that can be extracted from their bodies—anatomical knowledge, gained by what Diderot calls "la dissection d'un méchant," the dissection of a malefactor, constitutes a good of no lesser magnitude. In the unlikely event of the convict dying during the surgical procedure being tested on him, his death in the dissecting theater would be as useful to society as his death on the scaffold, says Diderot.

In one of his dialogues, *De tranquillitate animi*, Seneca recounts a brilliant anecdote about a Stoic philosopher named Julius Canus. To summarize very briefly, having been condemned to death by the emperor Caligula, the said philosopher had to wait ten days for execution. He is said to have spent the entire time without the slightest anxiety, playing checkers, completely unperturbed by his imminent death and openly mocking it. He tried to console his friends, who were understandably sorrowful at the prospect of losing him, by saying: "Why are you sad? You are wondering whether souls are immortal: I shall soon know" (Seneca 1997: 53). Canus's positive, heroic attitude in facing death is not due to a comforting belief in the immortality of the soul formed beforehand; he does not know yet whether the soul is immortal, but looks forward to finding out the truth. He eagerly awaits death, even though it may still transpire that the soul perishes with the body. On the way to the execution ground, his teacher asks about his state of mind, to which Canus calmly replies that he is preparing to observe the sensations in his soul at the fleeting moment of its presumed separation from the body. At the same time, he promises his friends that, if the soul survives the death of its body, he (or, rather, his soul) will return from the other world and bring them news he knows they are longing to hear, the news of the immortality of the soul. By enthusiastically anticipating the knowledge he will acquire at the death of his body, even though it may mean the utter end of him as well; by persisting in his search for truth to the very last, by striving to learn something not only up to the time of death, but from the very death itself, that is, by making his own death a learning experience, a subject of inquiry, he earns Seneca's deep respect and admiration. As Seneca admiringly declares: "No one ever pursued philosophy longer" (Seneca 1997: 53).

No one except, one might add from a later perspective, Bentham himself. Bentham can perhaps be said to have pursued philosophy even longer than Canus. Not only did Bentham make his own death a subject for examination—thus, Bentham says of his own death, and of the fate of his body after death, that "for many a year the subject has been a favourite one at my table" (Bentham n.d.: 2)—but moreover, he pursued philosophy, as it were, beyond death and well into the after-life. Canus, who had promised his friends to return from the other world and bring them news of life after death, has never been heard from again—it is either that, for one reason or another, he failed to keep his word, or that the soul is not really immortal and there is no life after death. Bentham, on the other hand, has been resurrected through the process of "auto-iconization," and may still be seen today enjoying precisely the sort of post-mortem fate he anticipated in *Auto-Icon*: he sits in a glass and mahogany case in a corridor of University College London, still "presid[ing] bodily" (Bentham n.d.: 5), as he had foreseen, over the sect of his followers more than 180 years after his death. Bentham even toyed with the idea of actively taking part in philosophical dialogues after death; in these dialogues, his auto-iconized body, "animated" by means of strings and wires operated by technicians under the stage, would perform as himself, while the voice would be lent by an actor reciting the lines scripted for him in advance by Bentham (see Bentham n.d.: 12–14).[3] In *Auto-Icon*, he even coined a new term for the description of one's own death and the subsequent fate of the body, that is, *auto-thanatography* as a natural sequel to one's autobiography (see Bentham n.d.: 2).

While it is true that it was only his body that rose from the dead, as it were, and that the immortality he attained was therefore merely a corporeal one, it is no less true that it was a person's dissected and preserved—that is, "auto-iconized"—dead body that, in Bentham's eyes, constituted the person's self after death. As he succinctly puts it, "A man's Auto-Icon

---

[3] An important and, as it were, vital enrichment of Bentham's already busy afterlife is provided by an online camera placed in March 2015 on top of the case containing his auto-icon, as a part of an interdisciplinary research project being conducted at University College London. The camera, most happily termed by the research team "PanoptiCam," streams live images of visitors observing the auto-icon. Since the observers are themselves being observed from the point of view of Bentham's auto-icon, the "PanoptiCam" project could, perhaps, alternatively be called "On the Observing of the Observer of the Observers," to borrow the subtitle of Friedrich Dürrenmatt's 1986 novel *Der Auftrag*. (Dürrenmatt 1986 [2008])

is his own self" (Bentham n.d.: 10). For Bentham, one's "auto-iconized" dead body is so much one's self that people while still alive will take into account the judgement they will receive after death in the eyes of their fellow human beings when deciding upon any course of action: "What will be said of my Auto-Icon hereafter?" (Bentham n.d.: 7) is the question that people will typically ask themselves. That is, even though the utilitarian eschatology cannot threaten with pain or entice with pleasure after death—auto-icons are merely "senseless" carcasses—it can, nevertheless, by exposing the auto-icons to the public eye, introduce "into the field of thought and action ... motives both moral and political" (Bentham n.d.: 7), Bentham believed.

Thus, on the one hand, the materialist thinker's attitude to living bodies turns out to be more utilitarian than Bentham's own, for, unlike Bentham, Diderot believed that anatomists should be allowed to dissect not only the bodies of the dead but also those of the living. The utilitarian sage's attitude to dead bodies, on the other hand, turns out to be more materialist than Diderot's, since Bentham believed that it is the dissected and preserved dead body, the "auto-icon," that constitutes one's self after death, whereas for Diderot one's "self" passes away together with one's body, and the "self" of each of the molecules into which the body has split itself takes over.

The Transparent Empire

For Bentham, as is well known, the main objective of the panopticon as a penal institution was to deter the innocent on the outside from offending, rather than the processing of prisoners within.[4] And for the

---

[4] Incidentally, the firm belief that a criminal, strictly speaking, does not deserve punishment, and that the punishment is less intended for the criminal being punished than it is for everyone else, that is, the innocent, or in other words, that the setting of an example by far outweighs reformation, is another idea Diderot and Bentham shared, although each of them embraced it for different reasons. For Bentham, reformation is useless because it is aimed at a comparatively small number of individuals, that is, at those who have already offended, whereas setting an example is aimed at all those exposed to the temptation of offending, that is, "all mankind" (Bentham 1838–1843: 4: 174n). For Diderot, on the other hand, reformation is quite impossible: "Can one cease to be wicked at will?" asks Diderot in his letter to Landois of 29 June 1956, and goes on to answer: "Once the crease is taken, the fabric will keep it forever." And later on in the same letter, he adds that it is for the "beneficial effects of example" that the malefactor must be "destroyed in a public place" (Diderot 1994–1997: 5, 56).

panopticon to achieve its external objective, which is to effectively deter the innocent from offending, it must, obviously, first achieve its internal objective, which is to deter the prisoners themselves from transgressing. Bentham achieves the internal objective of his prison by creating, within the universe of the panopticon, the fiction—or, as Jacques-Alain Miller has put it, "a semblance" (Miller 1975: 5)—of God with all his attributes. By amplifying and inflating the inspector's finite attributes, Bentham elevates him in the eyes of the prisoners to an apparently all-seeing, all-knowing, and omnipresent being. Bentham creates the idea of God in the panopticon through a gaze and a voice that are desubjectivized and detached from their bearer, that is, through gaze and voice as objects.[5] In the panopticon, gaze and voice are produced by means of two devices that are as brilliant as they are simple: by the "inspection-lantern,"[6] or, more precisely, by the dark spot therein that returns the prisoners' gaze, and by the so-called "conversation-tubes" (Bentham 1838–1843: 4, 84) leading from the central inspection-tower into each individual cell. These two devices are of such stunning simplicity that the God produced by them could perhaps be said to be nothing more than an inevitable by-product of putting this "simple idea in Architecture" (Bentham 1838–1843: 4, 39 and 66) into effect. In short, upon completion, the panopticon is already inhabited by God. By means of these two devices, the prisoners are seen without seeing the one who sees them, and they hear a voice without seeing the one who speaks.

Let us take a brief look at the "conversation-tubes," a contraption whose idea, as Janet Semple observes (Semple 1993: 304), Bentham probably owes to Francis Bacon, who in his *New Atlantis* mentions in passing the "tubes and pipes" by means of which the inhabitants of Bensalem are able to convey sounds "in irregular lines and distances"

---

[5] For a more extensive treatment of the role of gaze and voice in creating the fiction of God in the panopticon, see Bozovic 1995: 11–18.

[6] The "inspection-lantern," a device introduced in *Postscript* I, has the shape of "two short-necked funnels joined together at their necks"; it is pierced in certain places , and pieces of colored or smoked glass, through which the inspector looks, are inserted into the holes. The lantern is just big enough for the inspector to see everything around him without having to move—a turn of the head or body is sufficient. Although the lantern is translucent and the inspector's body within it is to a certain degree discernible, this does not allow the prisoner to determine whether the eye of the inspector is at that moment directed towards him any more than he can if the inspector is invisible. All that the prisoner can see inside the lantern is a dark spot that is always gazing back at him. And this dark spot that returns the prisoners' gaze can, in Bentham's words, be constituted by "any opaque object" placed in the translucent lantern (see Bentham, 1838–1843: 4, 82).

(Bacon 1627: 266). By means of "conversation-tubes" the inspector is able to communicate with the prisoners in their cells without having to expose himself to their view. The prisoners can hear him, but cannot see him. He is able to communicate with each of the prisoners individually without the others knowing. Since no one except for the prisoner being addressed can know whom the inspector is addressing at any given moment, no one can know for sure that he himself is not at that time under surveillance. Although all the inspector's attention may be focused on the one prisoner to whom he is talking, none of the others can be certain that the inspector's eyes are not at that moment directed toward them.

Thus, by preserving the inspector's apparent omnipresence intact—in the panopticon, the inspector is apparently omnipresent precisely insofar as he is not really present: the moment the inspector materializes anywhere in the panopticon, he loses his omnipresence in the eyes of those who see him[7]—the "conversation-tubes," obviously, help sustain the illusion of constant surveillance. What is more, the "conversation-tubes" not only sustain the illusion of constant surveillance, but in their turn they also contribute in an important way to its creation in the prisoners' minds. That is, it is largely to the voice coming through the "conversation-tubes" that the inspector owes his divine attributes in the eyes of those who hear it.

The voice coming through the "conversation-tubes" is a good example of what Michel Chion called "the acousmatic voice" (Chion 1982: 23–28). In the mind of someone who hears it, a voice whose source of production is invisible is automatically assigned exceptional powers. Such a voice seems to have "the ability to be everywhere, to see all, to know all, and to have complete power" (Chion 1982: 24). In short, this is a voice possessed of divine attributes. And this voice is possessed of divine attributes as long as it remains unseen; the moment the source of its production is seen, the voice loses these attributes.

Diderot apparently well understood at least the concept of the acousmatic voice and its exceptional powers as a way of producing the idea of

---

[7] Although Bentham saw one of the "fundamental advantages" of the panopticon in that it combines "the *apparent omnipresence* of the inspector" with "the extreme facility of his *real presence*" (Bentham, 1838–1843: 4, 45; Bentham's emphases), he was, it goes without saying, well aware that by showing himself at any particular spot in the panopticon, the inspector "los[es] thereby his omnipresence for the time" (Bentham, 1838–1843: 4, 83).

God in the mind by means of endowing a finite and powerless creature with divine attributes. This is evident from two of his *Encyclopédie* articles, "Pythagorisme" and "Acousmatiques," where he deals with the way Pythagoras's visibility affected the weight and persuasiveness of his words in the eyes of his disciples. The upshot of the two articles is that, as long as the disciples only heard Pythagoras speak from behind the curtain, he had the aura of an all-knowing sage. It was as though every word heard from behind the curtain was a word coming directly from God, which to them had the status of divine revelation. A sufficient guarantee of the truth of his cryptic words was provided by the mere fact that "Pythagoras has said so." But when his disciples also saw him speak, they were no longer willing to believe him and he had to clarify things he talked about and give reasons for them. Also, from that moment on, appealing to the all-knowing voice—that is, claiming that "Pythagoras has said so"—was no longer sufficient, as Pythagoras was now forced to answer the objections of his disciples that he had arrogantly disregarded before (Diderot and d'Alembert 1751–1772: 13: 615b and 1: 111a). In short, having become visible, Pythagoras's voice lost its magical power and he himself lost the divine attributes that he had when he spoke from behind the curtain.

The concept of the acousmatic voice and its "magical powers" can be found at work in Diderot's *Les Bijoux indiscrets*, which might alternately be titled *On the Divine Attributes of the Unseen Voice*. As already noted above, in the African empire of the Congo, women's speech organs have been duplicated, that is, the power of speech has been conferred on their sex organs or "jewels," as they are euphemistically called in the novel. The explanation for this bizarre phenomenon is simple: the sultan, pondering the question of feminine fidelity, has come into possession of a magic ring by means of which he is able to make the women's genitals speak, that is, to render their jewels "indiscreet." In order to find out whether the virtue of the women of his empire is only an illusion, he conducts a series of "interviews" in which every woman asserts fidelity to her partner. However, on the basis of the testimony obtained during "cross-examination"—that is to say, by alternately questioning the women's jewels by means of the magic ring—it turns out that none has been speaking the truth; they all prove to be sexually promiscuous. The virtue of the women of the Congo, in short, is only an illusion. And this is more or less the entire story.

Unlike the voice from the mouth, the jewels' voices remain unseen throughout the novel: in the novel, we never see the jewels speak, we only hear them. And, as might be expected, the unseen voices of the jewels are viewed by the people of Congo in precisely the same way as Pythagoras's voice was viewed by "the acousmatics," that is, by those of his disciples who had not yet seen Pythagoras speak, but only heard him. For the people of Congo, the words uttered by the unseen voices of the jewels have a special weight that words uttered by the seen voice of the mouth do not have. For example, if the testimony of the mouth and that of the jewel are contrary to each other, for the people of Congo the truth is always unreservedly on the side of the unseen voice of the jewel. The unseen voice of the jewel has a "power" that the seen voice of the mouth does not have, even when it speaks about precisely the same things as the unseen voice. Furthermore, they believe the unseen voice not only when its testimony contradicts the testimony of the seen voice of the same person, but also when its testimony is contrary to the testimony of the seen voice of another individual. In short, the jewels always have the last word.

If the people of Congo listen to every word of the unseen voice of the jewels as if it were a divine revelation, it is because this voice does, in fact, appear to have the complete power and ability to be everywhere, to see and know all. First, this voice is more powerful than the woman whose jewel has come to speak; although the voice speaks through a part of her own body, she has no power over it, and cannot silence it—it speaks independently of, and even against, her will (see Diderot 1748: 32). In short, once her jewel has spoken, the woman can only listen helplessly as it exposes her misdeeds. Secondly, this voice is indeed ubiquitous—it is impossible to escape or hide from it: the voice will find the women wherever they may go, since they literally carry the source of its production within themselves. Thirdly, this voice's knowledge seems to far surpass the woman's own: this voice seems to be aware also of her body's encounters with bodies of the opposite sex that she herself has already forgotten (see Diderot 1748: 36)—thus, when the invisible voice reminds her of these encounters, she can only realize with horror that this voice knows more about her than she knows about herself. And, finally, not only is this voice more powerful than she is and follows her wherever she may go and knows things about her that she herself does not know, it has the uncanny ability to read her thoughts: it is obviously aware of her innermost secret thoughts, thoughts that she firmly believes no one but she is aware of. And the explanation—provided by the jewel itself—as to precisely how the body "reads" the mind of the woman it embodies, that is, the explanation as to how, for example, the jewel "knows" that the woman is thinking impure thoughts, is a masterstroke of materialist philosophy: "her little finger told me so" (Diderot 1748: 27).

It is on the basis of their own affections that the jewels know everything they know. As a rule, their "indiscretion" is limited to the interpretation of their own affections. The jewels speak as the mouth would speak if it were to describe only its own affections, such as the sensations accompanying the intake of food or drink. If the jewels merely verbalize their own first-hand, empirical "knowledge" and never digress from the subject, it is because "they lack ideas or terms" (Diderot 1748: 32), as an anatomist in the novel succinctly explains the apparently puzzling fact that the jewels blindly keep to a single topic and tend to repeat themselves. Unable to invent or express anything that they have not experienced themselves, the jewels can speak only the truth.

It is no surprise, then, that the people of Congo come to regard the words of the unseen voice of the jewels as divine revelation and the jewels themselves as "altars" (Diderot 1748: 23) and "oracles" (Diderot 1748: 24); it is no surprise that they come to believe that it is none other than God Brahma himself who speaks through women's bodies, and to interpret the acousmatic voice of the jewels as the "latest proof" (Diderot 1748: 49) of God's existence. With regard to the body from which it stems and its affections, this voice is as all-seeing, all-knowing and omnipotent as the voice of Bentham's inspector—conveyed from the central lantern by means of the "conversation-tubes" into each individual cell—is all-seeing, all-knowing and omnipotent with regard to the universe of the panopticon.

Just as the people of Congo recognize God Brahma at work in a voice which is more powerful than they are, from which they cannot escape or hide, but which finds them wherever they go, and which knows more about them than they do about themselves and also seems to be able to read their thoughts, so too would the prisoners in

Bentham's panopticon recognize God in the inspector's acousmatic voice which, heard through the "conversation-tubes," seems to be endowed with analogous attributes.

Upon hearing the unseen voice spitefully enumerate, in front of everyone present, all their sins and infidelities, the women in Diderot's novel—who themselves claim to have been either virtuous or faithful to their partners—are made to mend their ways immediately and become chaste. Once the unseen voice of the jewels has spoken, nothing in the empire of the Congo is as it had been: the days of debauchery, infidelity, and adultery are irrevocably over, and virtue, chastity and devotion begin to reign in their place. Indeed, as the sultan aptly observes, "society can only benefit tremendously from this duplication of faculties" (Diderot 1748: 24), that is, from the duplication of the speech organs in women. In much the same way, and by the same means, Bentham suppresses violations of discipline and restores order in the panopticon in a single, clever move: assuming the role of the inspector, in the famous thought experiment in *Postscript* I, Bentham fixes his gaze on one of the prisoners who is trying to determine whether the inspector's hidden, invisible eye is in fact always directed at him, whether the inspector is really all-seeing, by first hazarding, entirely at random, a less serious transgression, and if this transgression goes unnoticed, he then commits another, this time more serious transgression. Bentham writes:

> I will single out one of the most untoward of the prisoners. I will keep an unintermitted watch upon him. I will watch until I observe a transgression. I will minute it down. I will wait for another: I will note that down too. I will lie by for a whole day: he shall do as he pleases that day, so long as he does not venture at something too serious to be endured. The next day I produce the list to him. (Bentham 1838–1843: 4, 81–82n)

Whereupon, in the prison cells, a voice coming out of the "conversation-tubes" can be heard to say:

> —*You thought yourself undiscovered: you abused my indulgence: see how you were mistaken. Another time, you may have rope for two days, ten days: the longer it is, the heavier it will fall upon you. Learn from this, all of you, that in*

this house transgression never can be safe. (Bentham 1838–1843: 4, 81–82n: Bentham's emphasis)

Once the unseen voice of either the jewels or of Bentham's inspector has spoken, it is never safe to transgress in either the empire of the Congo or in the panopticon. Only one such intervention of the unseen voice is needed for its bearer to appear all-seeing, all-knowing or, in a word, god-like in the eyes of the women of Congo or in the eyes of the prisoners; only one such intervention of the unseen voice is needed for the prisoners to fully internalize discipline and for the women to internalize chastity, that is, "to make them," as Bentham put it, "not only *suspect*, but be *assured*, that whatever they do is known, even though that should not be the case" (Bentham 1838–1843: 4, 66; Bentham's emphases). In both instances, an unseen voice comes to speak and enumerates the transgressions which the perpetrator—an unfaithful woman or an "untoward" prisoner—believes to have passed unnoticed. Nevertheless, in establishing and maintaining discipline through the unseen voice, Bentham's panopticon prison does seem to be a marked, purely utilitarian improvement on Diderot's empire of the Congo: in Bentham, Diderot's multitude of unseen voices, each of whose knowledge is limited to the sinful actions and thoughts of its bearer, is replaced by a single never-seen voice, which, of itself, seems to know everything about everyone in the universe of the panopticon. Even if the inspector or the jewels never again intervene, the prisoners' discipline and the women's chastity are now guaranteed. Although the unseen voice falls silent at this moment, its impact will not cease for that reason to be felt in the minds of the prisoners or the subjects of the empire of the Congo, but rather the contrary: the longer the unseen voice keeps silent, the more it resonates within the panopticon and throughout the empire. Rather than disappearing, it only grows more ominous and threatening with each passing moment of silence. From this moment on, in the eyes of a woman or a prisoner who has committed a transgression and has not been immediately chastised for it by the unseen voice, the jewel's or the inspector's silence—which may now well be a result of the jewel's or the inspector's inattention—will be interpreted as a deferral of the inevitable chastisement. And the chastisement will be all the more severe the longer it is deferred. From this moment on, no one needs to watch over them and surveillance may safely be ended—in an act of what may perhaps best be termed "autoveillance," each woman in the empire watches over herself and each prisoner in the panopticon preys upon himself, all the while keeping in mind a list of their own transgressions and anticipating the chastisement that will sooner or later befall them, knowing that the longer it is postponed, the more severe it will eventually be.

The Transparent Universe

In Bentham's vision, the panopticon, governed by the semblance of God produced through the all-seeing gaze of the dark spot in the lantern and the unseen voice transmitted into each individual cell by means of the "conversation-tubes," would run with "clock-work regularity," displaying "certainty, promptitude, and uniformity … in the extreme" (Bentham 1838–1843: 4, 85), that is, so flawlessly that Bentham even calls it an "artificial body" (Bentham 1838–1843: 4, 84), adding that "action scarcely follows thought, quicker than execution might here be made to follow upon command" (Bentham 1838–1843: 4, 85).

At the sight of the "compact … microcosm" (Bentham 1838–1843: 4, 85) of the panopticon, which is so functionally integrated as to appear as a single living entity, a unified superorganism, Diderot would probably be reminded of what he himself called "le tout" (Diderot 1994–1997: 1, 631), the whole, that is, the whole of nature or material universe as a single great individual, while the inspector himself, as the central consciousness of the universe of the panopticon, would most likely remind him of his own material God, that is, the paradoxical deity, briefly discussed in *Le Rêve de d'Alembert*, as the subject of what he termed "la conscience du *tout*" (Diderot 1994–1997: 1, 589; Diderot's emphasis), the consciousness of the *whole*.

According to Diderot, matter—that is, the only existing substance in the universe—produces life and develops sensibility by itself. The transition from inert matter to sentient being and from a sentient being to a thinking being occurs solely by means of "material agents" and through "purely mechanical operations" (Diderot 1830: 53). In *Observations sur*

Hemsterhuis, Diderot writes: "I have never seen sensibility, soul, thought, and reasoning produce matter. But I have seen a hundred times, a thousand times, inert matter transform itself into active sensibility, into soul, into thought, and into reasoning solely by means of material agents or intermediaries" (Diderot 1994–1997: 1, 706–707). Similarly, in *Entretien d'un philosophe avec Madame la Maréchale de ****, Diderot counters the Maréchale's claim that God made the world, or, in other words, that a spirit made matter by observing: "If a spirit can make matter, why could not matter make a spirit?" (Diderot 1777: 228). And he corroborates his materialist position simply by saying that he sees matter "do it every day" (Diderot 1777: 228). That is, while no one has yet seen a spirit produce matter, or God create the material world, we can, by contrast, see matter produce a spirit every day with our own eyes; that is, we can see bodies develop their own soul—and perhaps at some point in the future we might even be able to see the material world produce God before our own eyes.

The "mind" produced by matter, or the "soul" produced by the body, is not an entity distinct from the body, but identical with the body or its organization, and therefore material. Unlike the spiritual soul, the material soul cannot exist without the body, since it is itself nothing other than "l'organisation et la vie" (Diderot 1994–1997: 1, 1316), the organization and life of the body. By associating the "soul" with bodily organization, the materialist means to say that what produces thought is not matter in and of itself, but rather certain material entities endowed with a specific physical structure, first and foremost the brain. It is in the "meninges" of the brain that Diderot places memory, and therefore the being's consciousness of itself through time, that is, its "self" (see Diderot 1830: 90–91 and 105–106).

Just as the internally diversified and complex matter that makes up the human body develops its own "mind," so too the matter that makes up the universe as a whole, if properly organized, could at some point develop *its* own "mind," that is, its "meninges" or center of consciousness of the whole of nature. It seems that in Diderot's "immense ocean of matter" there is at work a tendency towards the self-organization of matter at ever higher levels, in increasingly higher and more complex organisms, even in yet entirely unknown and hitherto unseen super-organisms. That is, living entities combine into unities, which in turn combine into higher unities, and so on. Unified into a new whole, each part loses its former self. At each level, the resulting whole can develop awareness of itself as a unity. If this were to happen on a cosmic scale, that is, if all entities comprising the universe were to amalgamate to form a continuous whole, a single entity, a single great individual, which would develop its "mind" and become conscious of itself as a unity, such a "world-soul" would, in Diderot's view, be God.

This sort of "material" God that results from the self-organization of living matter at the level of the universe would be to the universe what the "meninges" of the brain are to the human body (Diderot 1830: 82). The "meninges" of the universe would indeed make for a paradoxical deity: as a portion of the universe, the material God would be "subject to vicissitudes" and would "grow old and die" (Diderot 1830: 82), and so on. Nevertheless, in the eyes of the materialist sage, this is "the only sort [of God] that is conceivable" (Diderot 1830: 82). In an important aspect, Diderot's material God would fall short of the God of traditional theism. Admittedly, through his "identity with all things in nature" the material God would be aware of "all that happens" in the universe. Furthermore, through his memory, the material God would know "all that has happened" in the past. About the future, however, he would be able to form only "conjectures that were likely but liable to error" (Diderot 1830: 82); in his knowledge of the future, then, he would resemble us, ordinary mortals who are trying to guess what is going to happen inside ourselves, for example, at the tip of our foot or our hand.

For Diderot, it is quite possible that there was in the past, or there will be in the future, such a God. Nevertheless such a God's imminent manifestation is not very likely. In a universe in which "everything is in perpetual flux" (Diderot 1830: 79), including perhaps the laws governing the flux, the tendency towards the self-organization of living matter into ever higher organisms, which seems to be at work at present, is unlikely to last long enough for the entities that make up the universe to amalgamate into a single entity that would then become aware of itself as a unity. While matter transforming itself into a soul at the level of the human body is a common and widely observed phenomenon, the material universe transforming itself into God is certainly not something one sees "every day."

Although in Diderot's universe the process of the self-organization of matter at the level of the universe, that is, at a level where it could lead to the materialization of God, is unlikely to begin any time soon, nevertheless that is precisely what d'Alembert sees in his eponymous dream. Judging by his words, uttered in feverish sleep, the process of the universal self-organization of living matter appears to be well underway; moreover, it appears to have reached a point at which it could lead to the universe's acquiring self-consciousness or to the materialization of God. In the sleeping d'Alembert's eyes, everything in nature is linked to such an extent that the whole of nature is a single individual. Particular beings by themselves are not true individuals, but rather "parts" of a much wider "whole," of nature or the material universe as the "great individual" (Diderot 1830: 79). In d'Alembert's exalted vision, entities, including himself, have clearly lost much of their individuality; desubstantialized and desubjectified, they are gradually becoming one with nature or the material universe. That is, entities making up the great whole are gradually losing their former selves and the emerging self of the whole, that is, the material God, increasingly takes over.

But if the process of self-organization of living matter ultimately did lead to the universe becoming self-conscious, or to the materialization of God—that is, even if we were to see the world and ourselves actually constitute God—we most probably would not be aware of it. According to Diderot, upon every formation of the consciousness of the whole, every single one of the parts that make up the whole loses its former self. Thus, it may well be that in the future, d'Alembert—along with all other beings in the universe—will form "a whole" or compose "un être commun" (Diderot 1994–1997: 5: 172), a common being, that is, a single unique being that will develop its own "meninges" and its own "self," but he will not know it, since with the advent of the fully-formed "consciousness of the whole" the consciousnesses of its "parts" will be extinguished.

If the God of the panopticon were to reveal himself at any particular spot, that is, if his "apparent omnipresence" were replaced by the "real presence," in the eyes of the prisoners who saw him, he would cease to exist as God. Owing his divine attributes to his invisibility, the inspector exists as God only insofar as he is not "really present." On the other hand, once God materialized himself in Diderot's universe, there would be no one left to witness the theophany. Admittedly, in Diderot's universe, we are still there, constituting God with our bodies, which have amalgamated into the great whole, the universe as a single unified entity, while our former selves have dissolved into the consciousness of the newly formed whole. In short, we have actually become one with God—but we do not know it, since we no longer exist as individual consciousnesses.

For Diderot, God is the ideal end result of the process of complete integration, the total coalescence of all beings in the universe into a single living entity, a unified whole. It is only when the whole universe becomes what Diderot called "un être un" (Diderot 1994–1997: 1: 624), a being that has unity, a single living being—when the link between the bodies making up the material universe is one of continuity and not merely contiguity (see Diderot 1830: 82)—that God emerges. For Bentham, it is rather the reverse: it is the emergence of God, that is, the inspector's momentary exposure to the eyes of the prisoners that potentially triggers the disintegration of the universe of the panopticon. This is because the inspector can sustain the smooth running of the "compact … microcosm" of the panopticon only insofar as, in the eyes of the prisoners, he is endowed with divine attributes, and he owes the latter, first and foremost, to his invisibility.

Furthermore, there is usually no contact between the inmates in Bentham's panopticon; there is no "horizontal" communication between the prisoners themselves, but only "vertical" communication between the inspector and the prisoners in their cells. The prisoners are separated from one another by walls, but exposed—all alike—to the view of the inspector. Or, in Diderot's terms, the link between the entities making up the "compact…microcosm" of the panopticon is one of mere contiguity, not one of continuity. Yet it is precisely contiguity that seems to be a necessary prerequisite for the universe of the panopticon to persist in existence and run smoothly; paradoxically, it is continuity that would bring about its disintegration. That is, it is to its parts being merely contiguous, not continuous, that the "microcosm" of the panopticon owes its "compactness." If the contiguous condition the prisoners are in changed so that they become continuous, that is, if the horizontal contact between prisoners occurred, the universe of the panopticon would probably collapse. Angela Carter's novel *Nights at the Circus* (1984), for example, illustrates this point most vividly. This beautifully written and complex novel contains a chapter describing in detail the inner workings of the panopticon prison; it is an all-female prison somewhere in Siberia run by a female inspector (Carter 1984: 210–218). The inspector, herself a murderess, stretches the principle of utility even further than Bentham, by having the convicts build the panopticon prison for themselves. The breakdown of an otherwise perfectly functioning universe of the panopticon, and the downfall of the inspector herself, is initiated by a simple touch of hands—and a mute exchange of glances—between a prisoner and a guard delivering meals to cells, followed by further contacts between the inmates themselves carried out surreptitiously by means of illicit notes and drawings executed in blood or excrement on rags of clothing. This is an ironic reversal of the act of creation as depicted by Michelangelo in his fresco in the Sistine Chapel of the creation of Adam, in which God gives life to the first man by stretching out his hand and (almost) touching Adam's finger. In Michelangelo's painting, the touch of hands between God and the first man is an allegory of creation, whereas in Carter's novel, the slight, fleeting touch of hands between the subjects of the universe of the panopticon triggers the destruction of the universe and the demise of God in it. Ultimately, in one sublime moment the prisoners bring the universe of the panopticon to a complete and final halt by jointly turning towards the inspector in the inspection-tower "in one great, united look of accusation" (Carter 1984: 218), that is, by returning the gaze of the dark spot at the center of the transparent universe. One can only regret that—even though God appears to be present in both Diderot's universe and in the universe of Bentham's panopticon to an unparalleled degree—the face-to-face encounter between God and human individuals, subjects of the universe is, inevitably, a failed one.

* * *

Having applied "the Panopticon principle" to the manufactories, madhouses, hospitals, and so on, it was only a matter of time before Bentham would apply it to a seraglio, which is perhaps one of the most obvious uses to which it could be put. And he does in fact do so, at the end of the last of the panopticon letters, where he says that a "bare hint of such an establishment [i.e., a panoptically arranged seraglio] in any of the Constantinople papers" would cause the price of eunuchs in Turkey to fall "at least ten per cent.," since "one trusty one [i.e., eunuch] in the inspection-lodge would be as good as half a hundred" (Bentham 1838–1843: 4: 65). Bentham's seraglio is, of course, still an enclosure, with strictly limited access to the women within, where surveillance is carried out from the central inspection-tower by a single guard. Diderot's seraglio, on the other hand, is open and freely accessible to all. Apparently having no fear for the chastity of his women, the sultan of the empire of the Congo "broke down the gates" of his seraglio and "banished" its guards; one entered the sultan's seraglio "as freely as one might any convent of Flemish canonesses" (Diderot 1748: 8–9). Being able at any time to make the women's sex organs talk and publicly reveal their disorderly conduct and impure thoughts, the sultan could certainly entrust each of the women—not only in his seraglio, but throughout the empire—"with her own fidelity" (Diderot 1748: 9). If ever there was an apt embodiment of "autoveillance" at work, this was it. Not only would Diderot's talking jewels make even Bentham's single eunuch in seraglio redundant—they would also make the seraglio itself redundant, since the whole empire had been transformed into one giant seraglio guarded by their unseen voice.

Works Cited

Bacon, Francis. 1627 [1999]. New Atlantis. In *Selected Philosophical Works*, ed. Rose-Mary Sargent, 21–268. Indianapolis: Hackett.
Bentham, Jeremy. 1838–1843. *The Works of Jeremy Bentham*, 11 vols., ed. John Bowring Edinburgh: William Tait.
———. n.d. *Auto-Icon; or Farther Uses of the Dead to the Living. A Fragment. From the MSS of Jeremy Bentham*, privately printed.
Bozovic, Miran. 1995. An Utterly Dark Spot. In *The Panopticon Writings*, ed. Miran Bozovic and Jeremy Bentham, 1–27. London: Verso.
Carter, Angela. 1984 [1994]. *Nights at the Circus*. London: Vintage.
Chion, Michel. 1982 [1999]. *The Voice in Cinema*. Trans. Claudia Gorbman. New York: Columbia University Press.

Diderot, Denis. 1748 [1993]. *The Indiscreet Jewels.* Trans. Sophie Hawkes. New York: Marsilio.

———. 1777 [1979]. Conversation of a Philosopher with The Marechale de X. In *Diderot: Interpreter of Nature; Selected Writings*, trans. Jean Stewart and Jonathan Kemp, 218–234. Westport, CT: Hyperion Press.

———. 1830 [1979]. D'Alembert's Dream. In *Diderot: Interpreter of Nature; Selected Writings*, trans. Jean Stewart and Jonathan Kemp, 49–126. Westport, CT: Hyperion Press.

———. 1994–1997. *Œuvres*, 5 vols., ed. Laurent Versini. Paris: Robert Laffont.

Diderot, Denis, and Jean Le Rond d'Alembert, eds. 1751–1772. *Encyclopédie, ou Dictionnaire raisonné des sciences, des arts et des métiers, par une société des gens de lettres*, 17 vols. text and 11 vols. plates. Paris: Briasson/David/Le Breton/Durand.

Dürrenmatt, Friedrich. 1986 [2008]. *The Assignment or, On the Observing of the Observer of the Observers.* Trans. Joel Agee. Chicago: The University of Chicago Press.

Marmoy, C.F.A. 1958. The "Auto-Icon" of Jeremy Bentham at University College, London. *Medical History* 2: 77–86.

de Maupertuis, Pierre-Louis Moreau. 1752 [1756]. Lettre sur le progrès des sciences. In *Œuvres de Mr. de Maupertuis*, vol. II, 343–399. Lyon: Jean-Marie Bruyset.

Miller, Jacques-Alain. 1975. Jeremy Bentham's Panoptic Device. Trans. Richard Miller, *October* 41, Summer 1987: 3–29.

Semple, Janet. 1993. *Bentham's Prison: A Study of the Panopticon Penitentiary.* Oxford: Clarendon Press.

Seneca. 1997. On Tranquillity of Mind. In *Dialogues and Letters*, trans. C.D.N. Costa, 29–58. Harmondsworth: Penguin.

de Vandeul, Mme. 1875. Mémoires pour servir à l'histoire de la vie et des ouvrages de Diderot. In *Œuvres complètes de Diderot*, ed. Jules Assézat, vol. I, xxix–lxviii. Paris: Garnier frères.

Transparency, Humanism, and the Politics of the Future Before and After May '68

Stefanos Geroulanos

In his 1975 *Discipline and Punish*, Michel Foucault famously presented Jeremy Bentham's Panopticon, the "celebrated, transparent, circular cage, with its high tower, powerful and knowing" (Foucault 1975: 208) as a microcosm of modern power—something that began as a heterotopia and became a naturalized model. Already in a 1973 discussion of that prison in his Collège de France lectures, he had described the Panopticon in terms of "transparency" and "permanent visibility" (Foucault 2008: 77). Now, he gave it the famous genealogy that framed the Enlightenment more broadly as his target, as the birth of both the promise and illusion of modernity as transparency.

> Bentham is the complement to Rousseau. [Rousseau too had] the dream of a transparent society, visible and legible in each of its parts, the dream of

---

This essay pursues further problems developed in my *Transparency in Postwar France: A Critical History of the Present* (Palo Alto, CA: Stanford University Press, 2017); some discussion here reworks (considerably) passages from that book.

S. Geroulanos (✉)
New York University, New York, NY, USA
e-mail: sg127@nyu.edu

there no longer existing any zones of darkness, zones established by the privileges of royal power or the prerogatives of some corporation, zones of disorder. It was the dream that each individual be able to see the whole of society from whatever position he occupied, that men's hearts communicate each with the other, that gazes not encounter obstacles, and that opinion of all reign over each. Starobinski has written some most interesting pages about this. (Foucault 1981: 152, translation modified)

Bentham/Rousseau: Foucault saw the duet's ostensible dream of a transparent society that would eliminate superstition, social hierarchy, masking, sovereign and unjustified power as a historical turning point for the invention of a power dynamic that would not rest until all sense of individuality and space had been regulated, with all disorder or heterogeneity subsumed under the dynamic itself.

A second, more contemporary and similarly French genealogy also emerges in this claim, and the reference to Jean Starobinski is far from incidental: his *Jean-Jacques Rousseau: Transparency and Obstruction* had presented Rousseau's pursuit of a crystalline heart and social transparency as the effective cause of his later paranoia. The single-minded commitment to purity had led Rousseau to the projection of all action and all guilt onto others: he could maintain transparency in his self-affection only by treating it as contaminated by worldly action among those others who imprisoned him in an "impregnable asylum" of solitude and dispossession (Starobinski 1957: 240). And Starobinski was far from alone in offering a bleak diagnosis for transparency—indeed the postwar French use of the term "transparency," and related concepts and figures was astonishingly different from the long Christian and Enlightenment traditions that had advocated a transparent life and a transparent society, and it was also quite different as well from our contemporary use of the term. We speak of transparency as a matter of ethical, democratic governance, and as an issue of freedom of information: Barack Obama, in his inaugural memorandum as president, declared that "My Administration is committed to creating an unprecedented level of openness in Government. We will work together to ensure the public trust and establish a system of transparency, public participation, and collaboration. [...] Government should be transparent. Transparency promotes accountability and provides information for citizens about what their Government is doing"

(Obama 2009). Similarly we find it hard to believe that Donald Trump cannot recognize the expectation that he releases tax returns or the authoritarianism ostensibly inherent in a government that refuses to make its acts, deliberations, and finances public. When he brazenly unloads a convulsive stream of consciousness on Twitter, he too celebrates a vision of personal transparency coded in terms of exposure, which dovetails and is in many ways entirely concomitant with the one he disavows, all the while claiming unmediated appeal and retaining for himself a measure of control over the systems for divulging information.

By comparison to the current celebration of transparency, the postwar French use of the term spiraled around the deep suspicion that transparency was philosophically violent and distortive, politically perilous, ethically misguided. Jean-Paul Sartre and Maurice Merleau-Ponty had begun their magnum opuses of the mid-1940s by establishing the opacity of the world to consciousness—*this* was the necessary premise of phenomenological ontology.[1] Michel Leiris, Claude Lévi-Strauss, and Georges Bataille in different ways identified Western thought with an imposed, colonizing, distortive transparency that forced a reductive social homogeneity. Lévi-Strauss found transparency only in communicating—as a displaced anthropologist, forced into loneliness, distorted in his relations with others, out of sync with his world—with "the feeblest and humblest of others" (Lévi-Strauss 1963: 39). Louis Althusser identified transparency with ideology: "But what, concretely, is this uncriticized ideology if not simply the 'familiar,' 'well known,' transparent myths in which a society or an age can recognize itself (but not know itself), the mirror it looks into for self-recognition, precisely the mirror it must break if it is to know itself" (Althusser 1990: 144)? Jacques Derrida in turn accused Lévi-Strauss of concocting a language of transparent communion with his subjects in the Nambikwara tribe in the Amazon and of treating them as living in a "crystalline community" (Derrida 1967: 119 et al). Jean-François Lyotard identified transparency with neoliberal economic and epistemic systems, warning that

---

[1] My reading of Sartre's treatment of transparency differs considerably from Manfred Schneider's, which he pursues further in his contribution to this volume. I do not have the space to establish these differences or the reading itself in all its necessary complexity here, and ask the reader to please consult Geroulanos 2017: 48–63.

[...] the ideology of communicational "transparency," which goes hand in hand with the commercialization of knowledge, will begin to perceive the State as a factor of opacity and "noise." It is from this point of view that the problem of the relationship between economic and State powers threatens to arise with a new urgency. (Lyotard 1979: 6)

Claude Lefort pronounced "the myth of the self-transparency of society" to be a key element of totalitarianism, and his associates from Pierre Rosanvallon to François Furet used this as a key heuristic argument—in Furet's case for rethinking the Terror of 1793–94 as an attempt by Robespierre to enforce a transparent post-revolutionary society.[2] By the later 1980s, Edouard Glissant wrote of a "right to opacity" (Glissant 2006: 189–192), Gilles Deleuze and Jacques Derrida declared themselves in favor of a certain personal "secrecy" (Deleuze 1995: 11; Derrida and Ferraris 2001: 59) and Derrida also complained that the new "master discourses" of European integration

> impose the homogeneity of a medium, of discursive norms and models [...]. Under the pretext of pleading for transparency (along with 'consensus,' 'transparency' is one of the master words of the 'cultural' discourse I just mentioned), for the univocity of democratic discussion, for communication in public space, for 'communicative action,' such a discourse tends to impose a model of language that is supposedly favorable to this communication [...]. Claiming to speak in the name of intelligibility, good sense, common sense, or the democratic ethic, this discourse tends, by means of these very things, and as if naturally, to discredit anything that complicates this model [...] to suspect or repress anything that bends, overdetermines, or even questions, in theory or in practice, this idea of language. (Derrida 1992: 54–55)

To put it more curtly, French thinkers were consistently hostile to transparency—they used the term in a systematically pejorative sense. From Marxists to "post-structuralists" to the democrats of the 1970s, postwar French thinkers bared their talons whenever even a specter of transparency arose. First, they regarded "transparency" as a false ideal in ethics. In

---

[2] Rosanvallon 1979. Note that the second edition, published in 1999, removes the entire critique of transparency in the preface of the original edition. François Furet 1981: 16, 19, 50, 60.

ethics, they scoffed at the romantic fantasy of a "heart-to-heart" and pushed instead for a heightened attention to "the other," whether a phenomenological, psychoanalytic, or colonized other: this other was unattainable, unreachable, and the pretense that it could be simply embraced or fully understood posed profound ethical challenges. By extension, they increasingly argued that the self too was fundamentally opaque to itself: it could not simply know itself without erasing the unconscious or society (or both). Second, they routinely used the term "transparency" as a characteristic of positivist science and idealist philosophy, which a new generation of epistemologists and existentialists charged with reducing the world to the mind. This, they argued, removed the essential distortion that shakes and structures the relationship of the subject to the world. New philosophies from existentialism and the "new" epistemology through structuralism and democratic thought in the 1970s were profoundly committed to rethinking knowledge and society by taking this distortion into account as a given that rendered transparent representation and knowledge impossible. And third, even before Lefort disparaged it as a totalitarian sociopolitical ideal and Foucault identified it with the Panopticon, political thinkers from Merleau-Ponty and Lévi-Strauss presented transparency as de-differentiation, as a homogenizing reduction of individuality and difference that aimed to eradicate any privacy or distance from the community.

In my book *Transparency in Postwar France: A Critical History of the Present* (2017), I trace the history of this suspicion in the works of philosophers, literary authors, political thinkers, anthropologists, filmmakers, criminologists, and psychiatrists. I argue that only in the mid-1980s did transparency enter the French intellectual sphere with a positive hue, and this largely because it became a useful substitute for the post-1983 socialist government's modernization project and the entry into the information age. Here I want to press two specific points: first, how this critique, which before was a largely epistemological and ethical critique, became for philosophers after 1968 a distinctly political resistance to the demands of the day. (This happened at a time when elsewhere in Europe transparency had achieved a largely "positive" status.) Second, how the pre-68 moment—on which I will focus for much of the paper—offers tools for thinking past humanist commitments that returned with the post-68 moment and that eventually allowed the acceptance of "transparent government" dicta in France as well.

After the War Was Over

Critiques of transparency published in France before 1968 were first and foremost epistemological and ethical—one often grounding the other—and their political claws grasped generally at what have been called side-effects of postwar modernity, namely homogenization and normalization. The philosophical generation that had come of age in the 1930s and early 1940s—including Jean-Paul Sartre, Georges Bataille, Georges Canguilhem, Claude Lévi-Strauss, Maurice Merleau-Ponty, Emmanuel Levinas, André Leroi-Gourhan, Jacques Lacan, and others—famously refused the idealism of their "mandarin" predecessors. Particularly in their crosshairs were the progressivist formulations of Léon Brunschvicg, who had promised transparency in a mathematical and philosophically idealist perfection of thought, but also of Alain with his pacifism. Speaking in very broad terms, the antifoundationalism and skepticism expressed toward these earlier positions mobilized both a Bachelardian concern with the "obstacle" (which doubled as a concern with the limits of the cogito) and a secondary concern with the capacity of consciousness and norms to adequately represent the complexity of the world experienced and conceived by that consciousness.

As was the case with most other postwar democracies and people's republics in Europe, France dealt with governmental and social transparency in the postwar consensus and settlement. The Fourth Republic's constitution of October 27, 1946 declared in Article 2 as a "principle" (principe) of the Republic the *gouvernement du peuple, par le peuple et pour le peuple*. Enshrining this fragment of Lincoln's Gettysburg Address in the constitution gave a semblance of coextensiveness between government and governed, although today it strikes us as an attempted formalization of the contrast with Vichy, a recognition of French reliance on American support for liberation, and a convenient expression of republican rhetoric. To protest the inapplicability or vagueness of the principle misses the point—namely, the republican attempt to draw legitimacy on the basis of this mirroring effect and to designate alternative systems, including communism, Vichy, and the Third Republic, as compelled to make such government "perish from the Earth." This article was reiterated in the Fifth Republic's constitution of October 4, 1958, which also proposed in Article 3 (an article that was savagely mocked for its pretense of the legitimacy of de Gaulle's presidency): "National sovereignty belongs to the people which exercises it through its representatives and by way of a referendum. No part of the people and no individual can appropriate its exercise." The distance of this basic constitutional consensus from the postwar everyday experience of government was easy to accentuate as was made evident by the continuation of rationing until 1948, the fragmentation of political opinion, the division of Gaullists from communists, the seemingly slow reversal of the industrial collapse, the policy for rural populations, the reliance on the United States and the Marshall Plan, which also seemed to threaten domestic discord and war with the USSR, and the Purge (whose political meaning as purification is clearer in the original French term *épuration*). One way to understand the negative valences of "transparency" in the early postwar period was precisely that it was socially and politically promised, in different ways, by every claimant to political and theo-anthropological power. Indeed, the ideological re-coalescence that occurred in both Marxist and Catholic thought posed similar problems of immanent belief. The explicit claim of communist regimes to be *perfectly* expressing the proletariat, realizing Marx's and Lenin's thought and to have instituted a transparent society demanded far too much of an intellectual milieu or field comprising competitive intellectuals that were both taken with phenomenology and existentialism and that identified either as victims of Nazi and Vichy rule or with the résistance to it (the "Republic of Silence" or "Republic of the Night" as Sartre put it). Meanwhile Catholic Neo-Thomism, with its theory of community and a metahistory that saw decline having begun with the Renaissance, seemed dated and limited.

Compare to these positions the skepticism proposed by existentialism and carried over, partly thanks to *Les temps modernes*, into non-orthodox Marxism. Sartre's refusal (akin to Bachelard, Canguilhem, Koyré, Merleau-Ponty, and others) that the world and objects in it are delivered over to consciousness without mediation or obstacles doubled onto a vision of personal responsibility and agency. "How you cling to your purity, young man! ...Well, I have dirty hands. Right up to the elbows. I've plunged them in filth and blood... Do you think you can govern innocently?" declared his character Hoederer in *Les mains sales* (Sartre 1989: 218). Merleau-Ponty decried transparent society as a society of statues; "arraying the world before us in perfect transparency," entailed "destroying the world's 'worldliness.'" In *Le Très-Haut* (*The Most High*), Maurice Blanchot described a society and a subjectivity so profoundly permeated by the state that only an epidemic like that described by Albert Camus in *The Plague* could disrupt their union (Blanchot 1948).

Such positions present with some clarity the overall situation of the concept shortly after the *libération*, and into the early 1950s, when anticolonial thinkers like Frantz Fanon and anthropologists like Lévi-Strauss struggled against a homogenizing and normalizing quality of discourses of unveiling and unmasking, equality, modernization and progress. These positions remained first and foremost ethical and epistemological as differentiation—the production of stark oppositions—became the order of the day. Even political claims relied in great part on these distinctions. And with the rise of structuralism in the mid-1950s, this skepticism became formalized.

Transparency and Futurity in the Mid-1960s

Rather than examine this point further, or consider the appeal of poujadisme, anti-colonial thought, and unorthodox Marxism, I would like to move at this point to the mid-1960s and look quickly at certain publications preceding May 1968. Three classic works published in 1965–67 offer a quite clear sense of the problem with transparency as perceived at the time: Foucault's *The Order of Things*, Jacques Derrida's *Of Grammatology*, and André Leroi-Gourhan's *Gesture and Speech*. All three texts took for granted that no mind/world transparency was available to the human subject, and that certain kinds of dynamically emergent structures undergird that relation, and indeed make its reframing, and with it the reframing of all knowledge, possible. All three works, however, signaled that a certain transparency *might* be possible—even imminent—in the near future, provided humanism was jettisoned, and with it the expectation that this transparency would be achievable by human beings themselves.

Thus Michel Foucault handled the term "transparency" with remarkable rigor, deploying it as a key to the conceptual and epistemological rupture of modernity with a pre-1800 Classical Age as well as for the consequences of that rupture in his day. Transparency, he argued, had been unavailable, even pointless, in the Renaissance, where knowledge operated on principles of similitude: the lack of transparency in the book of the world was explained through an appeal to Babel. Language, having lost its original transparency at Babel, was merely an object *within* discourse, not one premised on, or exhausted by, its representative value (Foucault 1966: 35–36). In the Classical Age, language "has withdrawn from the midst of beings themselves and has entered a period of transparency and neutrality" to the point that it "does not exist [but] it functions" (Foucault 1966: 56, 79). Representations generated by systems of signs are now premised on an essential transparency between them and nature, a transparency whose reign must now itself be made transparent.

> In its perfect state, the system of signs is that simple, absolutely transparent language which is capable of naming what is elementary; it is also that complex of operations which defines all possible conjunctions. (Foucault 1966: 62; also 64–66, 208)

This change, Foucault insisted, is not limited to an abstract understanding of representation; it is the foundation of language. Now, "language is deployed within representation" (Foucault 1966: 79); its transparency is essential in that language resides *with* what it expresses *in* the movement of expression, and does not form a double, a crust of thought as before. With the invention of human finitude and historicity in the early nineteenth century—that is, with the "anthropologization of knowledge" that marked the beginning and dominance of the human sciences—that transparency in representation disappeared. This was either because it descended into paroxysm, as demonstrated by Sade, who captured "the fresh violence of desire in the deployment of a representation that is transparent and without flaw" (Foucault 1966: 242),[3] or because new

---

[3] See also Foucault 1966: 210, where Foucault interprets the understanding of desire and the "table of representation" again by way of transparency.

comparative, historical, humanist elements undermined it. For example, in linguistics after Franz Bopp, "grammatical composition has regularities which are not transparent to the signification of the discourse" (Foucault 1966: 283; also 293, 299). The same was the case in other modes of elucidation, such that the Classical Age "collapsed," and knowledge lost its definitive attributes:

> At the time of Descartes or Leibniz, the reciprocal transparency of knowledge and philosophy was total, to the point that the universalization of knowledge in a philosophical system of thought did not require a specific mode of reflection. From Kant onward, the problem is quite different; knowledge can no longer be deployed against the background of a unified and unifying *mathesis*. (Foucault 1966: 247)

Remaining as rigorous as before, Foucault's use of "transparency" and related terms and metaphors shifted at this point, proposing that the order of language has "has lost its transparency" and that

> the order of Classical thought can now be eclipsed [...] it enters a region of shade. Even so, we should speak not of darkness but of a somewhat blurred light, deceptive in its apparent clarity, and hiding more than it reveals. (Foucault 1966: 295, 303)

The structural shift in knowledge and representation generated the new matrix of labor, life, and language, out of which developed the human sciences. With their emergence, and thanks to finitude and historicity, transparency became inoperative. The introduction of Man into the structural foundations of knowledge generates a new order that has a distinct use for transparency. Insofar as it is now structurally displaced, insofar as its transparency now becomes a device for pretending that the erstwhile continuity between speaker, language, representation, and world continues undistorted. This is why, "deceptive in its apparent clarity," the blurred light no longer offers access but infuses knowledge with Man and history.

This entire schema regarding transparency reaches its extremely ambiguous apex in the concluding pages of *The Order of Things* where it becomes key to the future of the human. Foucault famously asserted in his last two chapters that the anthropomorphization of thought was essentially over, that the human sciences had gone over to the other side and that linguistics, psychoanalysis, and ethnology were doing away with the anthropoid hybrid that had dominated representation and interpretation. Coextensively, yet also contrastively, he described language and representation in terms of a newly arising transparency—this was precisely what could be expected in the future, yet this transparency would not be captured by man, by the subject, by the contemporary culture that sought it: it was unthinkable, perilous, self-contained and detached, truly other. It reached its crescendo in two poles of "our culture:" literature à la Antonin Artaud and Raymond Roussel, which is "language stripped naked," and formal languages, notably mathematics and logic (Foucault 1966: 383). The latter, newly evolved out of structuralism, "open up the possibility, and the task, of purifying the old empirical reason by constituting formal languages." It is this purity, this form (which was not, he insisted, a formalism) that, being so different from the modern episteme, guaranteed what Foucault imagined as a truly new order of knowledge. Purity guaranteed this new order by arising out of the current order of knowledge which "still serves as the positive ground of our knowledge" (Foucault 1966: 385) and by showing "our" inability to think outside of the modern episteme: "we" remained to wallow within the space of the Last Man, while this new order developed as a very nearly absolute other. Knowledge could thus acquire a new purity, spared of Man; yet we *only* "think in that area" (Foucault 1966: 384), and could not imagine an outside or a beyond; "our reflection" remains within the distortive immanence of the human sciences. From this perspective, we might sample the concluding questions of Foucault's argument less as announcements of the dispersion of the human (which is the evident stylistic drive of the famous concluding passage about man being "erased like a face drawn in sand at the edge of the sea") than as ambiguities imposed by the new "unity" of language—a language that, except in its utter unavailability to "us," mirrors that of Classical transparent representation:

> If *this same language is now emerging with greater and greater insistence in a unity that we ought to think but cannot as yet do so*, is this not the sign that

the whole of this configuration is now about to topple, and that man is in the process of perishing *as the being of language continues to shine ever brighter upon our horizon?* Since man was constituted at a time when language was doomed to dispersion, will he not be dispersed when language regains its unity? And if that were true, *would it not be an error—a profound error, since it could hide from us what should now be thought—to interpret our actual experience as an application of the forms of language to the human order?* (Foucault 1966: 386, emphasis mine)

The final question here marks the absolute disconnect: the death of Man is no longer an overcoming of the human but a decisive loss of the human—and of "us" within that lost human—in a bifurcated present that stares in fear at the near-future that remains absolutely apart from us.

Like *The Order of Things*, Jacques Derrida's *Of Grammatology* and André Leroi-Gourhan's *Gesture and Speech* made political and metapolitical claims on the present and coming future, all the while relying on epistemological forms of the transparency problem to structure these claims.

Leroi-Gourhan's *Gesture and Speech* remains the least-known of the three works. Nor is it, with minor exceptions, explicit on matters of transparency.[4] What it did do, however, is produce a theory of the advent of the human across of the emergence of the species called *Homo sapiens* that traced to the present and near future a major shift, at once epistemological and ontological. Taken cumulatively, the human would either have to fold upon itself or to transform in a manner that would make it seem largely incomprehensible.

This shift may be traced in part to three developments. First, the advent of cybernetic thought, which allowed Leroi-Gourhan to move away from the Durkheimian organicism characteristic of his *Milieu et techniques* (1943) and to outdo Marcel Mauss's concept of "techniques of the body" by discussing the different forms of individual and social memory that underpin the establishment of society in terms such as "human operational behavior," "operational memory," "human technical behavior", and "the mechanical operational sequences" that "form

---

[4] See Leroi-Gourhan's sense that material and social evidence should be understood in terms of complementarity rather than transparency or co-dependence (Leroi-Gourhan 1964–1965: 147).

the basis of individual behavior" (Leroi-Gourhan 1964–1965: 225, 227, 230, 231). Second was the rise and decline of early transhumanist thought, such as that of Julian Huxley, J.B.S. Haldane, J.D. Bernal, or especially Pierre Teilhard de Chardin (Leroi-Gourhan 1964–1965: 407). Their anticipation of a post-human future largely incomprehensible to "us" was largely in keeping with biological, and paleoanthropological imaginations of a technologized future; the popular versions in Stanley Kubrick's *2001: A Space Odyssey* (1968) and Chris Marker's *La Jetée* (1961) retained some of the concerns that Leroi-Gourhan also exhibited. For him, this vision of radical overcoming of present humanity was based on paleontological and ethnological prehistory, and it hoped for very little. Unlike the transhumanists and their popularizers, Leroi-Gourhan expressed profound doubts about the capacity of human beings to manage their environment and offered a stark—starker than either Foucault or Derrida—antihumanist vision of the near future. He had argued as much already in 1962, declaring that an ethnographic approach to prehistory offered a thorough historical and ethnological interpretation of human activity on the entire planet. The only major transformation since the birth of *Homo sapiens* concerned the experience of distance, the practice of techniques, and the use of the human body; and it had occurred in the past century. The present was characterized by an exteriorization of the nervous system (in modern technology), an elimination of distances, and an ever-complicating entanglement of individuals within societies, with a resulting homogenization, a loss of "ethnic values." Now the threat transformed into the destruction of the natural world and the capacity for individuation. Leroi-Gourhan veered between two alternatives. First,

> human society became the chief consumer of humans, through violence or through work, with the result that the human has gradually gained complete possession of the natural world. If we project the technical and economic terms of today into the future, we see the process ending in total victory, with the last small oil deposit being emptied for the purpose of cooking the last handful of grass to accompany the last rat. The prospect is not so much a utopia as the acknowledgment of the singular properties of the human economy. (Leroi-Gourhan 1964–1965: 184–185)

Second:

> We must expect a completely transposed *Homo sapiens* to come into existence, and what we are witnessing today may well be the last free interchanges between humans and the natural world. Freed from tools, gestures, muscles, from programming actions, from memory, freed from imagination by the perfection of the broadcasting media, freed from the animal world, the plant world, from cold, from microbes, from the unknown world of mountains and seas, zoological *Homo sapiens* is probably nearing the end of his career. (Leroi-Gourhan 1964–1965: 407)

While this overcoming was possible—if one assumed that "the individual is infinitely socializable and that an artificial world functioning toward the well-being of all its cells is more desirable for the individual than the world of the cave dweller"—it was by no means guaranteed. Instead, "We can imagine the human of the near future as being determined by a new awareness and the will to remain *sapiens*" (Leroi-Gourhan 1964–1965: 407–408). Foucault did not play on the term *homo sapiens* but surely the analogy between his options and Leroi-Gourhan's amused him. Leroi-Gourhan suggested that humans were more likely to recoil from the consequences and pick the last of these solutions even if this meant that an altogether new management of human relations with life and nature were necessary and just as unlikely to be pursued. The world would remain somewhere between the deeply troubled solution of self-overcoming, and the worse alternative of remaining on the same shore and trying out a limited management of earth and life.

Jacques Derrida, for his part, peppered *Of Grammatology* with discussions of transparency: on Leibniz and the early modern Cartesian dream of a universal language, on Rousseau and linguistic transparency, and especially on Lévi-Strauss's attempt to overcome Western reduction of "the other" through the near-mystical Rousseauistic attachment to the "crystalline community" of the Nambikwara—the people who ostensibly do not write.

> Self-presence, transparent proximity in the face-to-face of countenances and the immediate range of the voice, this determination of social authenticity is therefore classical: Rousseauistic but already the inheritor of

Platonism, it relates, we recall, to the anarchistic and libertarian protestations against Law, the Powers, and the State in general, and also with the dream of the nineteenth-century utopian socialisms, most specifically with the dream of Fourierism. In his laboratory, or rather in his studio, the anthropologist too uses this dream, as one weapon or instrument among others. (Derrida 1967: 138)

Lévi-Strauss's construct of a "crystalline structure" and "complete self-presence" excised the basic forms of mediation and violence that characterize all societies. Across numerous examples, transparency turned out to be a carrier of the illusion that a community could survive without violence. In Lévi-Strauss's Rousseau-influenced reading, he charged, the Nambikwara lacked writing, hence they lived in a particular kind of authenticity and purity; violence within that society was supposedly incidental, and in essence it came from without (Derrida 1967: 112). Against Lévi-Strauss's solution, Derrida championed Leroi-Gourhan, who had pronounced that the structural transformation of the hands from instruments of movement into instruments for the use of tools (and eventually writing) were "liberations." Well aware of the importance that "liberation" had for Leroi-Gourhan in the context of the emergence of writing—he also credited Leroi-Gourhan with a theory of the "liberation" or exteriorization of memory—he clearly contrasted it to Lévi-Strauss's view that the invention of writing was a form of enslavement: "What is going to be called enslavement [by Lévi-Strauss] can equally legitimately be called liberation" (Derrida 1967: 131). If the speech-writing duet was thought of in terms of transparency, it ended up right back at the hands of a humanism that failed to think society, violence, transformation, power, possibility in noise. If, instead, it was thought of in terms of a cybernetically inspired program, it moved toward complexity, and this complexity reached beyond "man." Once again, the human proved inadequate to grasp the future that was just out of its reach, as Derrida emphasized in his "exergue":

it is a peculiarity of our epoch that, at the moment when the phoneticization of writing—the historical origin and structural possibility of philosophy as of science, the condition of the epistémè—begins to lay hold on world culture, science in its advancements can no longer be satisfied with it. This inadequation had always already begun to make its presence felt. But today something lets it appear as such, allows it a kind of takeover, without our being able to translate this novelty into clear cut notions of mutation, explicitation, accumulation, revolution, or tradition. These values belong no doubt to the system whose dislocation is today presented as such, they describe the styles of an historical movement which was meaningful—like the concept of history itself—only within a logocentric epoch… For that future world and for that within it which will have put into question the values of sign, word, and writing, for that which guides our future anterior, there is as yet no exergue. (Derrida 1967: 5)

The present time indicated an opening out of the heavy burden of modernity: difference was inscribed within it, and a future based on it was at least imaginable—even if no preface for it existed "as yet."

1968: The Breakup of the Future

I have been tracking the emergence of this entire arrangement or rationality by which, thanks to the failure and outdatedness of transparency, the future became unavailable and opaque to the human, yet which promised to yield a novel complexity. This arrangement evaporated around May '68. By that May—speaking in New York—Jacques Derrida already doubted the capacity for real change in this direction: criticizing the hope Foucault had put in the beach and the waves, he wrote in *The Ends of Man* that "we are still on the same shore" (Derrida 1972: 119). What is "the economy of the eve," he asked—the eve in which "we are" (Derrida 1972: 136). Indeed May 1968 and its aftermath transformed this sense of the future quite radically, suggesting it to be at most the misguided hope of a few intellectuals cloistered from the world and the impending and imminent revolution. Writing four years later, Gilles Deleuze asked "How do we Recognize Structuralism?" and began answering his own question with "This is 1967" (Deleuze 1972: 170). He wasn't altogether facetious to consign these questions to the pre-68 era: so much had changed.

This is not because May reintroduced transparency into politics. On the contrary: its mistrust did not cease, instead the state became the explicit target. The promise and eventhood of revolution required and enabled the revival of a unitary agent of history, now explicitly aimed against a homogenizing and too-powerful state. This "agent" was a conglomerate of student and proletarian movements, which, defined above all in its opposition to the state, became a decisive force in political opposition: the whole philosophical tine of the critique of transparency was sidelined as an abstract matter of discourse and epistemology. The student–worker movement was the first and most general incarnation of this agent; in the radical 1969–1973 period, it swelled and was supplanted by other figures, perhaps most famously by the Chinese proletariat, which Maoists treated as the clearest expression of a new, revolutionary and universal general will, capable of changing the structure of Western society.

As a "live" demonstration of the logic of revolution and of the Marxist approach to history, "May '68," as a confrontation, turned the public's rapt attention to a much more immediate politics of the Left, which prioritized very different lineages, images, and tropes. The state-society conflict, rather than complementing the promises of philosophy, largely sidelined the non-humanist future as vague. Thus some authors, notably the situationists around Guy Debord, retroactively identified May with the Paris Commune and treated it as a Rousseauian "festival" in which the distortion of representation, knowledge, and humanity that occurred with the capitalist relations peculiar to the age of the "spectacle." But as Debord too argued, a true festival could not last. Althusser and his disciples had decried transparency as a goal of utopian and non-scientific pre-1850 Marxism, yet they identified in the Chinese proletariat a new agent.[5] Self-management (*autogestion*) in factories, rejection of governmental repression, and an aspiration to new norms inherent in society characterized this antistatist tendency. As significantly, Claude Lefort, Merleau-Ponty's former student, who would spearhead a movement of

---

[5] See the fourth point of the founding declaration of the *Union des Jeunesses communistes Marxistes-Léninistes* which proposed to form revolutionary intellectuals linked to "the workers and the working people" and to institute "new forms of organization" that would realize this "task." In Résolution (1967).

democratic thought in the 1970s that involved in different ways Pierre Clastres, Marcel Gauchet, Pierre Rosanvallon, François Furet, and others, began speaking regularly and (after 1968) very disparagingly of the "self-transparency of society" (Geroulanos 2017: ch. 21). It served, he thought, as a founding myth of totalitarian states that pretended to rule in continuity with their populations, to mirror them perfectly, when as a matter of fact they enforced this impossible transparency through (physically and symbolically) violent means. Clastres gave the post-68 moment a forceful name: *Society against the State* (Clastres 1974). Foucault turned to power, and the surveillant imposition of social transparency as a mechanism in human production and control.

Conclusion: Transparency and the 1968 Bifurcation

A lot could be said to complicate the distinction I have offered in the critique of transparency, between the antihumanist direction given it in the mid-1960s and the revolutionary, anti-statist alternative pursued after 1968. I have also insisted here that the two should be seen less as stark opposites—even if the thinkers to be grouped on each side tended to disparage those on the other—than as oscillations in the same impulse, each with different targets and hopes, one complementing the other. Each unfolded differently, and the fundamental characteristic of the post-1968 approach was the commitment to the reality, urgency, and transformability of the present and the near future through new forms of political and sociopolitical action.

This turn of events nevertheless left the questions raised by Foucault, Leroi-Gourhan, and Derrida somewhat behind and somewhat in place. In this last section, I want to ask about that direction, which seemed to confront man with complexity and a realm of representation beyond "his" reach: how are we supposed to understand the moment, or trajectory, that proposed that an epistemological transparency in the same move might be recovered but refused it to the subject, and left behind the hopelessly confused, opaque, anthropomorphic system of knowledge in which humans were entangled? Was it the construction of a system that had abandoned any hopes of political action, or that arrogated, with debonair insouciance, history and systemic movement for structuralist historicism, denying it to humans and humanism—as it was soon thereafter accused of doing? Was it a misguided reconstruction of a "historical stages" approach, which, unable to see the current stage continuing, anxiously jumped over into a post-bureaucratic, post-cybernetic complexity as though the transcendental movement to a new stage? Was it, as Jean-François Lyotard later hinted, perhaps fulfilled in the adoption of neoliberal policies and knowledge? (Lyotard 1979: 5–6, also 82; Lyotard 1986: 24–25).[6]

Whatever the merits of such answers, they leave much aside, and they largely follow the direction of May. (The advent of "theory" in the 1970s and 1980s also nurtured the political affiliation with the moment of May as essential to its own credentials.) To briefly rest in the 1967 moment is to derive from its epistemological claim consequences that were deeply political. In the 1940s, the key quality of the critique of transparency had been skepticism—doubt at the way the world presents itself, the way the subject perceives it, the strength of obstacles to interpreting or experiencing this world directly. The intensifying critique of norms in the 1950s— as non-transparent, man-made, and authoritarian—and the conceptual wrangling of the symbolic as unavailable to the subject in Lévi-Strauss's and Lacan's structuralism resolved that problem by strengthening and rendering positive the assemblage of the subject's limitations. By the development of the positions of Foucault, Derrida, and Leroi-Gourhan, the epistemological and ethical critique had acquired a distinct futural quality which delegitimized humanism not on behalf of some "truer" humanism or political program, as had been the case thus far, but specifically on the principle that knowledge (and politics) had to pivot to these systems as though it were directly—historically, anthropologically—to overcome the human and humanist limit. If systems of (now non-human) cognition were to rule the day after tomorrow—if they were to bring forth an alternative form of representation and life that would be spared

---

[6] See also Lyotard's treatment of social transparency in *Economie libidinale* of Marx's theorization of "the mystery of labor" and its "erasure" in *Capital* (Lyotard 1974: 134).

the anthropocentric and anthropomorphic transformation of language and representation, this needed to be seen as a world historical event that would drive human history without deriving from it.

One consequence was the promise of a future that would be better able to remedy the scars of the century and to conceptualize the information, language, and computing innovations that were rapidly changing the present. Foucault, Derrida, and Leroi-Gourhan always accentuating the danger ("peril") of this exciting possibility, wrote as if they were beginning a new Enlightenment, jumping ahead to look back at the present through a new lens, which could pull thought out of the homogenizing, destructive, shortsighted humanism of past centuries. But this gesture was also the opposite of a regulative ideal, and the implication is compelling: the 1967 moment asked whether systems (bureaucratic, administrative, computing, governmental, abstract conceptual) were to be judged against a level of non-human complexity. In a recalibration of the "Who comes after the subject?" question and its consequences, it asked precisely on what basis would such systems be judged. (One might object that the question of judgment is too classical; yet it was certainly implicit and present in the three arguments discussed here.) If transparency were altogether impossible for an agent or for consciousness, the philosophical and structuralist critique of transparency was now wording new sciences of language, society, and representation and turning them into the tools for something new, dynamic, more hybrid—something as yet unclear, except in its inhuman sovereignty, its pursuit of new castles, codes and grids that are vital to the deployment of knowledge.

Without forgetting the limitations of this approach, we can acknowledge that its vision of complexity cuts harshly across the problem presented today by the political force of the Trump administration and by the new media that transform citizenship. Now that the liberal dream of transparency has been inverted into a technologically dominated and financially promoted imaginary of self-exposure (whether by Trump or social networking), it seems that 1967 has once more much to teach of the necessary direction of critique against the simplification of political alternatives, the reliance on outdated political hermeneutics and the transformation of the human. The proliferation of systems, the rapid expansion of computing power, and the sheer opacity of a future that now seems dominated by evermore elusive forms of complexity have ceased to be a distant, nontransparent future, and become motors dragging away a present that—to us—becomes more opaque by the day.

Works Cited

Althusser, Louis. 1990. *For Marx*. London: Verso.
Blanchot, Maurice. 1948 [1996]. *The Most High*. Trans. Allan Stoekl. Lincoln, NE: University of Nebraska Press.
Clastres, Pierre. 1974 [1987]. *Society against the State: Essays in Political Anthropology*. New York: Zone Books.
Deleuze, Gilles. 1972 [2004]. How Do We Recognize Structuralism? In *Desert Islands and Other Texts*, 170–192. New York: Semiotext(e).
———. 1995. Letter to a Harsh Critic. In *Negotiations*, 3–12. New York: Columbia University Press.
Derrida, Jacques. 1967 [1997]. *Of Grammatology*. Baltimore: Johns Hopkins University Press.
———. 1972 [1980]. *Margins of Philosophy*. Trans. Alan Bass. Chicago: University of Chicago Press.
———. 1992. *The Other Heading: Reflections on Today's Europe*. Trans. Pascale-Anne Brault and Michael B. Naas. Bloomington: Indiana University Press.
Derrida, Jacques, and Maurizio Ferraris. 2001. *A Taste for the Secret*. Malden, MA: Polity Press.
Foucault, Michel. 1966 [1994]. *The Order of Things*. New York: Vintage.
——— 1975 [1995]. *Discipline and Punish: The Birth of the Prison*. Trans. Alan Sheridan. New York: Vintage.
———. 1981. The Eye of Power. In *Power/Knowledge*, 146–165. New York: Pantheon.
———. 2008. *Psychiatric Power*. Trans. Graham Burchell. New York: Picador.
Furet, François. 1978 [1981]. *Interpreting the French Revolution*. Cambridge: Cambridge University Press.
Geroulanos, Stefanos. 2017. *Transparency in Postwar France: A Critical History of the Present*. Stanford: Stanford University Press.
Glissant, Édouard. 2006. *Poetics of Relation*. Ann Arbor: University of Michigan Press.
Leroi-Gourhan, André. 1964–1965 [1993]. *Gesture and Speech*. Trans. Anna Bostock Berger. Cambridge, MA: MIT Press.

Lévi-Strauss, Claude. 1963 [1983]. Jean-Jacques Rousseau, Founder of the Sciences of Man. In *Structural Anthropology*, vol. 2, trans. Monique Layton, 33–43. Chicago: University of Chicago Press.

Lyotard, Jean-François. 1974 [1993]. *Libidinal Economy*. Bloomington: Indiana University Press.

———. 1979 [1984]. *The Postmodern Condition: A Report on Knowledge*. Minneapolis: University of Minnesota Press.

———. 1986 [1992]. *The Postmodern Explained to Children*. London: Turnaround.

Obama, Barack. 2009. Transparency and Open Government: Memorandum for the Heads of Executive Departments and Agencies. January 21. www.whitehouse.gov/the_press_office/TransparencyandOpenGovernment. Last accessed 10 Jan 2017.

Résolution politique de la première session du premier Congrès de l'UJC (ml). 1967. In *Les Cahiers marxistes-léninistes* 15 (1967).

Rosanvallon, Pierre. 1979. *Le Capitalisme utopique*. Paris: Seuil.

Sartre, Jean-Paul. 1989. *Dirty Hands*. In *No Exit and Three Other Plays*. New York: Vintage Books.

Starobinski, Jean. 1957 [1988]. *Jean-Jacques Rousseau: Transparency and Obstruction*. Trans. Arthur Goldhammer. Chicago: University of Chicago Press.

Part II

Under the Crystal Dome

The Limits of Transparency

Amitai Etzioni

This chapter takes as its starting point the very widely held conception that transparency is a major good. Moreover, it observes that leading scholars and policymakers hold that it could replace major parts—if not all forms—of government regulation. Regulation is widely criticized as being coercive while transparency is said to achieve behavioral and social change by sharing information but leaving the choices and actions that follow to the individual (i.e. is much more compatible with liberty than regulation). The chapter challenges this core assumption on several grounds ranging from prudential issues to matters of political theory.

I am indebted to Rory Donnelly for research assistance and to Erin Syring for comments on a previous draft. An earlier version has been published in the *Public Administration Review* (Volume 74, Issue 6 November/December 2014, 687–688).

A. Etzioni (✉)
The George Washington University, Washington, DC, USA
e-mail: etzioni@gwu.edu

Transparency as a Major Good

Transparency Defined

Transparency is generally defined by political scientists as the principle of enabling the public to gain information about the operations and structures of a given entity (Heald 2006; Finel and Lord 1999). It has also been defined as "a lack of secrecy and an openness to public scrutiny" (Dawes 2010). Other definitions refer to "lifting the veil of secrecy," "the ability to look clearly through the windows of an institution," or "the conduct of public affairs in the open or otherwise subject to public scrutiny" (Meijer 2009: 258). Governmental transparency has been associated with "the degree to which access to government information is available" (Piotrowski and Borry 2010: 138 and 140). In the campaign finance context, the terms "transparency" and "disclosure" (of political spending) are often used interchangeably (e.g. 'Campaign Finance and Disclosure," *Sunlight Foundation,* 2015).

Transparency Has Long Been Recognized as a Major Good

Transparency has long been considered an unmitigated, incontestable "good" by public intellectuals and scholars in liberal democratic societies. James Madison wrote in 1822 that any "popular Government, without popular information, or the means of acquiring it is but a Prologue to a Farce or a Tragedy; or, perhaps both." In this same vein, he held that "people who mean to be their own Governors, must arm themselves with the power which knowledge gives" (Madison 1822). Similar ideas are found in the works of Locke, Mill, Rousseau, Bentham, and Kant (Fenster 2005: 895–896). Supreme Court Justice Louis Brandeis famously declared that "Publicity is justly commended as a remedy for social and industrial diseases. Sunlight is said to be the best of disinfectants" (Brandeis 1913; see also Hood 2006: 9; Fenster 2005).

Much of transparency's appeal comes from its association with effective democratic government (Brito and Perrault 2009: 2; Piotrowski and

Van Ryzin 2007; Rosendorff 2004; Hale 2008). According to John C. Bertot, Paul T. Jaeger, and Justin M. Grimes, over the course of the twentieth century, transparency has become "internationally regarded as essential to democratic participation, trust in government, prevention of corruption, informed decision-making, accuracy of government information, and provision of information to the public, companies, and journalists" (Bertot et al. 2010). Sharon S. Dawes adds that in recent years, the "idea that democratic governments should be open, accessible, and transparent to the governed is receiving renewed emphasis through the combination of government reform efforts and the emergence of advanced technology tools for information access" (Dawes 2010: 377).

Transparency in the Public Mind

Transparency is held in high regard by large segments of the American public. In a 2012 poll, 76 percent of Americans supported mandatory disclosure requirements for corporate political spending.[1] In an earlier poll, between 60 and 75 percent of Americans supported the mandatory disclosure of the names of lobbyists who raised money for candidates for public office, as well as mandatory disclosure by members of Congress of all communications with regulatory agencies related to policy changes that might benefit their campaign contributors (The Sunlight Foundation 2006). In 2013, a poll found that mandatory disclosure of easy-to-understand summaries of health care plans was the most popular feature of the Affordable Care Act (Kaiser Family Foundation 2013).

The rise in the support for libertarian and laissez-faire conservative positions has undermined support for government regulation. Regulation may be defined simply as "an official rule or law that says how something should be done," a definition that does not include indirect efforts to control behavior (such as tax breaks), or the voluntary adoption of high standards, "self-regulation" (Merriam-Webster 2015). For instance, a 2013 poll showed that a majority of Americans (53 percent) presently

---

[1] Corporate Reform Coalition. 'Support for Reform of Corporate Political Spending Practices,' Bannon Communications Research, October 18, 2012. Accessed at http://www.citizen.org/documents/bannon-communications-research-executive-summary.pdf.

"favor less government involvement in addressing the nation's problems in order to reduce taxes, while 13% favor more government involvement to address the nation's problems."[2] While libertarians strongly oppose government regulation, they have no principled objections to transparency. The Cato Institute, for example, a think tank closely associated with libertarian thought, has repeatedly called for a more transparent government (e.g. Harper 2013).

At the same time, transparency is also popular among civil libertarians and left-liberal reform groups. These groups promoted the Sunshine Laws in the 1970s, which required that government meetings be open to the public and the press.[3] Following the Snowden leaks in 2013, they rallied to demand greater transparency of the activities of the NSA, calling for companies to be allowed to disclose when they turn over customer information to the government, and for the government to engage in more comprehensive reporting of its surveillance activities.[4] Transparency fits into their political philosophy because it is grounded in the sort of democratic populism whereby the people are empowered to rule themselves and to prevent private power and special interests from corrupting or dominating the state.[5]

In his first election campaign, President Barack Obama promised "to run the most transparent White House in history" (Beam 2008; Cillizza 2013). In a memo for department heads shortly after taking office in 2009, Obama stated, "My Administration is committed to creating an unprecedented level of openness in Government. We will work together

---

[2] Jeffrey M. Jones, 'Americans Remain Divided on Role They Want Gov't to Play,' *Gallup*, September 19, 2013 http://www.gallup.com/poll/164444/americans-remain-divided-role-gov-play.aspx.

[3] Fleming, Joseph Z. and Joes I. Leon. 2008. 'The Federal Government in the Sunshine Act: A Federal Mandate for Open Meetings,' The Florida Bar, August. http://www.floridabar.org/DIVCOM/PI/RHandbook01.nsf/1119bd38ae090a748525676f0053b606/33db31567bc6b028852569cb004c8736!OpenDocument.

[4] Mike Mansick. 'Large Coalition of Tech Companies and Advocacy Groups Demand Greater Transparency About NSA Surveillance,' *TechDirt*, September 30, 2013. http://www.techdirt.com/articles/20130930/12195224700/large-coalition-tech-companies-advocacy-groups-demand-greater-transparency-about-nsa-surveillance.shtml; Center for Democracy and Technology. 2013. 'Coalition of Major Internet Companies and Advocates Rallies Around Surveillance Transparency Legislation,' September 30. https://cdt.org/press/coalition-of-major-internet-companies-and-advocates-rallies-around-surveillance-transparency-legislation/.

[5] For further evidence of this claim, see Democratic National Committee, "Open Government," http://www.democrats.org/issues/open_government Accessed March 5, 2014.

to ensure the public trust and establish a system of transparency, public participation, and collaboration."[6] He followed up with several measures to enhance transparency (Ginsberg 2011; Obama 2009a; Obama 2009b) although his administration was criticized for not being transparent enough.[7]

Transparency as an Alternative to Regulation

The Changing Mix

The increasing popularity of transparency coincided with a broader movement in favor of deregulation. The Kennedy, Johnson, and Nixon administrations greatly expanded regulation, including in matters as different as affirmative action and environmental protection. The Carter administration, however, revealed some signs of a counter-movement, with Alfred Kahn championing, and Carter signing the 1978 Airline Deregulation Act. Deregulation increased greatly during the following administrations, particularly in the financial sector. With the support of Federal Reserve Chairman Alan Greenspan, large banks pushed through extensive deregulation of their sector, culminating in the repeal of the Glass-Steagall Act in 1999. These deregulations are held to be a major cause of the 2007–2008 Great Recession.[8] As deregulation expanded, transparency was increasingly promoted as an *alternative* to regulation.

---

[6] 'Memorandum for the Heads of Executive Departments and Agencies,' White House, Office of the Press Secretary, March 9, 2009.

[7] Jordy Yaeger (2011) 'Watchdogs say Obama has not done enough on government transparency,' *The Hill*, December 25, 2011. Accessed at http://thehill.com/homenews/administration/201295-watchdogs-say-obama-has-not-done-enough-on-transparency; John Dickerson, 'Obama's New Toy,' *Slate*, November 14. 2008, accessed at http://www.slate.com/articles/news_and_politics/politics/2008/11/obamas_new_toy.html; David Sobel (2009) 'Obama's Transparency Promise: We're Still Waiting,' Electronic Frontier Foundation, April 19; Eric Lithbau (2010) 'Report Faults U.S.'s Efforts at Transparency,' *The New York Times*, March 14, 2010; Sharon Theimer (2010) 'Obama's Broken Promise: Federal Agencies Not More Transparent Under Obama Administration,' *The Huffington Post*, March 17.

[8] 'The Financial Crisis Inquiry Report,' Financial Crisis Inquiry Commission, January 2011, accessed at http://www.gpo.gov/fdsys/pkg/GPO-FCIC/pdf/GPO-FCIC.pdf.

In Campaign Finance

Along these lines, some scholars have called for completely replacing caps on political spending with disclosure requirements. Thus, Matthew Melone held that "disclosure rules, consistently upheld by the [Supreme] Court, should be adequate to assure that corporations cannot avoid the constraints imposed upon open advocacy," with the solution for abuses being to "strengthen the disclosure rules, not ban the speech" (Melone 2010: 96). Cecil C. Kuhne proposed deregulating campaign finance spending, while strengthening transparency: "Complete disclosure of contributions and political activity allows the electorate to be informed of any attempts at political maneuvering, with any quid pro quo corruption by politicians to be prosecuted to the fullest extent of the law," while the "quantity and substance of campaign speech ought to be determined by private choices" (Kuhne 2004: 647).[9]

According to the Congressional Research Service, using disclosure to reduce conflicts of interest and corruption has been among "the least controversial aspects" in an "otherwise often-contentious debate" on campaign finance policy, with a bipartisan "pro-disclosure consensus" in Congress between 1971 and 2002 managing to quickly close loopholes in disclosure legislation as they emerged (Garrett 2014). Herbert Alexander and Brian Haggerty called disclosure an "essential cornerstone" of campaign finance reform and "an automatic regulator, inducing self-discipline among political contenders and arming the electorate with important information" (Alexander and Haggerty 1981: 37).

In 2010, the Supreme Court greatly further curtailed restrictions on campaign spending in *Citizens United v. FEC*, stating that disclosure was sufficient for preventing corruption, as "[w]ith the advent of the Internet, prompt disclosure of expenditures can provide shareholders and citizens with the information needed to hold corporations and elected officials accountable for their positions and supporters. Shareholders can

---

[9] See also Carson Griffis (2011) 'Ending a Peculiar Evil: The Constitution, Campaign Finance Reform, and the Need for Change in Focus after Citizens United v. FEC,' *John Marshall Law Review* 773: 773 ("disclosure requirements are a more agreeable and workable method of reform" than spending caps, as they "help combat the negative effects that reformers believe money has on campaigns by allowing voters to keep candidates and contributors in check" and better informing voters about "the ideology and policy of candidates").

determine whether their corporation's political speech advances the corporation's interest in making profits, and citizens can see whether elected officials are 'in the pocket' of so-called moneyed interests."[10] *Citizens United* and a subsequent ruling, *McCutcheon v. FEC* (2014) overturned limits on political spending, affirming, respectively, that "disclosure is a less restrictive alternative to more comprehensive regulations," the "transparency" of which "enables the electorate to make informed decisions," and that "disclosure of contributions minimizes the potential for abuse of the campaign finance system" and "offers much more robust protections against corruption" thanks to "modern technology."[11] As a result, note that Michael Gilbert and Lili Levy, campaign finance reformers in both politics and academia, have "shifted their focus" (Levy 2012: 100) and "rested their hopes on disclosure" (Gilbert 2012: 1847).[12]

More Generally

Support for transparency as an alternative to regulation is by no means limited to campaign finance. Scholars, policymakers, and activists have called for greater transparency within government agencies in general—either completely or partially replacing regulation. In 2013, a presidential task force called for "information about surveillance programs to be made available to the Congress and to the American people to the greatest extent possible (subject only to the need to protect classified information)" (Cillizza 2013). Others have called for greater transparency from the IRS in response to accusations that it unfairly targeted conservative groups. (Korte 2013). There has been considerable support for calls on the White House to be more transparent about the legal basis, implementation, and results of U.S. drone strikes in the Middle East and North

---

[10] *Citizens United v. Federal Election Commission*, 558 U.S. 310 (2010).
[11] *McCutcheon v. Federal Election Commission*, 572 U.S. (2014).
[12] See also Torres-Spelliscy (2011): abstract: "in order for voters to make informed choices at the ballot box, they must know who is paying for each side of a political fight. Campaign finance disclosure and disclaimer laws should be adopted at the federal level to achieve this end". Hasen 2014: 14: "a 'strong disclosure regime, which deters corruption and provides valuable information to voters,' is a vital aspect of campaign finance reform".

Africa.[13] More broadly, according to a study published in 2013 "government transparency has been on the rise over the last two decades" as a result of new freedom of information legislation and "various transparency initiatives" such as *Data.gov* (Meijer 2009). Cass Sunstein observed that "mandatory disclosure is an increasingly pervasive and important regulatory tool" and that "regulation through disclosure" has become "one of the most striking developments in the last generation of American law" (Sunstein 1999: 613 and 625). And Elizabeth Gilbert noted that disclosure not only leads corruption to "wither in the light of day," but also "is an effective solution if the existence of institutional corruption is not clear cut" (Gilbert 2001: 665).

Better than Regulation

We saw that both scholars and the Court held that transparency can replace regulation or at least serve an alternative means for accomplishing much of what regulation is supposed to achieve. Some scholars have explicitly spelled out the substitution thesis. The most prominent advocate of this approach is Cass Sunstein, who served both as an academic and as the head of the Obama administration's White House Office of Information and Regulatory Affairs from 2009 to 2012. Given the high regard in which he is held among scholars, and the pivotal role he served in the White House, he is next quoted at some length. Sunstein stated:

> It is increasingly recognized that information is often a far less expensive and more efficient strategy than command-and-control, which consists of rigid mandates about regulatory ends (a certain percentage reduction in sulfur dioxide, for example), regulatory means (a technological mandate for cars, for example), or both. A chief advantage of informational regulation is its comparative flexibility. If consumers are informed of the salt or sugar content of foods, they can proceed as they wish, trading off various product characteristics however they see fit. If workers are given information about the risks posed by their workplace, then they can trade safety against

---

[13] 'UN rights experts call for transparency in the use of armed drones, citing risks of illegal use,' United Nations News Centre, October 25, 2013, accessed at http://www.un.org/apps/news/story.asp?NewsID=46338&Cr=terror&Cr1=drone#.Usw_o9KIxJk.

other possible variables (such as salary, investments for children or retirement, and leisure). From the standpoint of efficiency, information remedies can be better than either command-and-control regulation or reliance on unregulated markets alone. From the democratic point of view, informational regulation also has substantial advantages. (Sunstein 1999: 32)[14]

Sunstein considers it a point of pride that the government *avoided* regulation, noting that Obama issued fewer regulations than did any of his four predecessors—a downsizing of government that Sunstein lauds as saving money. In a column for the *Wall Street Journal*, Sunstein decried the "red tape" that characterizes regulation and which, according to him, risks "compromising economic growth and job creation" (Sunstein 2012).

In addition to promoting transparency as an alternative to regulation, Sunstein has also advocated for a more transparent government, arguing that it ensures government accountability:

> Each new step is a small mark toward making the government more accountable to the public. Each new set of information making public in easy to read formats, and each removal of arcane barriers to participation helps to restore the confidence of the American people and their government and also to improve its management and operation. (Sunstein 2010)

He recognized, though, that in some contexts transparency is "inferior to command and-control regulation" or "reliance on markets unaccompanied by disclosure requirements," either because it is too expensive, or because it is "ineffectual, or even counterproductive" (Sunstein 1999: 613, 626).

Transparency vs. Competing Goods

Political scientists have long recognized that transparency—as "good" as it may be—can clash with other public goods or individual rights. This is true both for transparency in the public sector, as with open government

---

[14] See also Sunstein 2010: "Each new step is a small mark toward making the government more accountable to the public. Each new set of information making public in easy to read formats, and each removal of arcane barriers to participation helps to restore the confidence of the American people and their government and also to improve its management and operation".

initiatives, and in the private sector, for instance when corporations are expected to disclose that their databases have been hacked. That is not to suggest that transparency does not play a central role in liberal democratic governments, but rather that, like all other goods and rights, transparency must be squared with other normative concerns. Key examples follow. Because they are familiar, they are only briefly discussed.

Transparency can clash with privacy: In order to perform the functions of a modern state, governments collect great amounts of personal information about their citizens. For example, Medicare requires each medication taken, procedure carried out, and treatment rendered to be reported in order for the institution or the person to be reimbursed. Similarly, in support of taxation, governments collect a great amount of data about individuals' financial status. In both realms, the privacy of what is considered "sensitive" information is prioritized over transparency (Coglianese et al. 2008). This principle is recognized in the exception to the Freedom of Information Act for "disclosure [that] would constitute a clearly unwarranted invasion of personal privacy."[15]

Transparency can clash with national security: While there is very widespread agreement that some matters should not be disclosed (e.g. names of CIA agents in the field) and that others should not have been kept secret (e.g. legal briefs that justify the use of drones), there is an intense debate among scholars and policymakers on where lies the proper balance between national security and transparency.

Transparency can encumber internal deliberations: The White House long held that internal deliberations and memos should be kept confidential in order to ensure that the president, the president's staff, and their advisors could explore a variety of options and candidly discuss those options' merits and demerits without fearing disclosures to the public.[16] At the same time critics held that such claims are used to prevent the media from reporting, and the public from finding out, about poor deliberations and improper influences.

---

[15] "Freedom of Information Act Exemptions," United States Department of Justice, Accessed April 8, 2015 at http://www.justice.gov/

[16] 'Press Briefing by Press Secretary Jay Carney," White House Office of the Press Secretary, May 10, 2013.

All these and other such observations serve as recognition that the weight accorded to transparency as a core value must be assessed against the weight given to other core values. However, these observations alone do not disprove assertions that transparency is essentially a common good, or that it can replace some of regulation. The chapter next turns to showing that, for several reasons, transparency cannot carry much of the load regulations were supposed to carry. Transparency can make some such contributions, but they are much more limited than often suggested. Often regulation is required.

Transparency Is Itself a Form of Regulation

We have seen that transparency is strongly favored as an alternative to regulation because transparency is held to leave the choices and actions that follow to the individual, following the sharing of information, whereas regulation relies on coercion. (It is sometimes referred to as part of the 'command and control system,' a term used to describe the Soviet centralized, tyrannical, hugely inefficient form of government.)

However, this argument does not take into account that transparency *itself* is a form of regulation. Unless the government requires it, and ensures that this requirement is observed by employing the same coercive means that other forms of regulations draw upon, and sees to it that transparency is properly implemented—there will be precious little transparency.

Businesses tend not issue audits or disclose how often their employees suffered work accidents, if their databases were invaded, or their products caused harm—unless regulations so require. And government agencies are not prone to allow the public to learn about their failures, cost overruns, and illegal actions unless such disclosure is required. Moreover, it is not enough for Congress, state legislatures, or regulatory agencies to mandate disclosure; there must also be penalties for non-compliance just as there are for disregarding other regulations. Last but not least, disclosure regulations must ensure that the information released is (1) accessible, (2) communicative, and (3) reliable (Brito and Perrault 2009: 2).

Lacking proper penalties, the government is often slow to respond to Freedom of Information Act requests, with many responses left outstanding for years (Wald 2012). In other cases, information is disclosed but deliberately in ways that make access difficult. Thus, the Bureau of Alcohol, Tobacco, Firearms, and Explosives (ATF) maintains information about gun purchases, but is prohibited from keeping them in paper format rather than in a searchable computer database (Horwitz and Grimaldi 2010). Often transparency measures provide users with the illusion of disclosure while actually serving to obfuscate (Fung et al. 2007: 174). Mortgage statements that are 47 pages long lead people to believe that such details mean that they have been fully informed, while actually the information is overwhelming, hard to digest, and contains negative information hidden in late paragraphs and obscure text. Many privacy policies—crafted by lawyers—are very difficult to understand and are so lengthy that it would take the typical person roughly *250 hours* to read all the policies they encounter each year (Mansick 2003, 2012). Hence, advocates of disclosure hold that such forms must be standardized and use terms consumers and citizens are able to understand (Zweig 2009).

Evidence supports the rather obvious observation that uncommunicative transparency initiatives are ineffective. For example, "a major problem of workplace hazards disclosure is that information is provided to workers in a highly technical format and after they have already made employment decisions," and as a result does not "become embedded in most [worker]'s decisions" (Weil et al. 2006: 155 and 164). The same is true of toxic pollution, as there is no established *simple* metric that adequately conveys the interaction of the multiple factors that contribute to the pollution's danger (Fung et al. 2007: 174).

Finally, the reliability of the information released in the name of transparency cannot be taken for granted and must be mandated (Harper 2011; see also Fung et al. 2007: 174, noting the lack of consensus on which metrics should be used to evaluate public schools; Prat 2005). For example, campaign finance disclosure through the Federal Election Commission (FEC) was found to lack reliability both because "contributor compliance with providing required information—such as address and occupation—is often both inconsistent and partial" and because there is "insufficient accuracy and completeness for social scientists, engaged citizens, or informational intermediaries to confidently infer broader patterns of political influence" (Heerwig and Shaw 2014: 1443). Just as firms with poor reputations often change their names rather than their practices (McDevitt 2011), transparency in campaign finance is hindered when political action committees and other advocacy groups use generic-sounding names that conceal their ideological or partisan affiliation, such as "Democracy Alliance," "Americans for Prosperity," or "Committee on Political Education."[17]

In short, in order for this information to be available and useable, a measure of regulation (i.e. coercion) is needed. Transparency may well be significantly less coercive than other kinds of regulation, but it is a difference of degree rather than in kind.

People's Cognitive Capabilities Are Limited

A much more serious challenge faced by the thesis that transparency can replace much if not all of regulation than it itself is a form of regulation—is that the thesis assumes that people are rational actors. That is, that they are able to absorb complex information, and draw logical conclusions from it.

There is no need to rehash here the long and profound debate in social science about the differing definitions of rationality—some assume a much higher ability to collect, absorb, and process information than others—and about the extent to which people draw proper conclusions from the information they command (Evans 2004). Suffice it to note that the field of behavioral economics has assembled a robust body of data on this issue, much of it based on experiments, indicating that people are *hardwired* in such a way that they are *unable* to make rational decisions—however one dilutes the definition of rationality. People are found to regularly and systematically misread information and draw unwarranted conclusions from it. (The findings of behavioral economics have been

---

[17] "COPE," United Federation of Teachers, 2015, http://www.uft.org/political-action/cope; "Americans For Prosperity," 2015, http://americansforprosperity.org/; "Democracy Alliance," http://www.democracyalliance.org/.

reviewed in a popular book by Nobel laureate Daniel Kahneman [Kahneman 2011: 59–60 and 103]. See also Simon 1955; Kahneman et al. 1982. For a discussion of the relevance of rationality to transparency, see Fung et al. 2007.) If this is the case, then both individuals and society would benefit from addressing particularly harmful market failures or forms of misconduct by public officials through outright regulation rather than increased transparency.

For example, with respect to Cass Sunstein's point that "If consumers are informed of the salt or sugar content of foods, they can proceed as they wish" (Sunstein 1999: 613), Michael Moss has amassed a great deal of evidence that show that the American food industry, which spends billions on advertising, appeals to consumers' urges, below the radar screen of their rational deliberations, to buy foods that are unhealthy but profitable. Sugar, salt, and fats are laced into products in order to make them more addictive, labels on products are misleading, boxes are given bright colors because studies associate these colors with impulse buying, and so on (Moss 2013). Such techniques have proven effective regardless of federal requirements that food be labeled to disclose its nutritional value—in other words, despite transparency.

Intermediaries Can Alleviate but Not Eliminate the Cognitive Limitations

In response to the evidence about people's hardwired cognitive limitations, champions of transparency argue that even if the information disclosed is not comprehensible to or actionable by the general public, it can be analyzed and explained by third parties, allowing the public to make informed decisions. For example, the Sunlight Foundation's Alexander Furnas writes:

> In contrast to the average citizen, the media and existing interest groups—be they public-interest advocates, labor unions, or trade associations—can pay attention and evaluate complex policy issues, which they are able to observe because of the existence of relatively robust transparency regimes.... By presenting targeted and timely information to their constituents,

interest groups can help concerned but time-crunched citizens act according to their beliefs without all of the overhead of being a full-time politico. (Furnas 2014)[18]

However, the question arises if people can judge the veracity of these intermediaries and trust them. The often-cited question "who will guard the guardians?" applies here. The issue at hand is illustrated by those investors and regulators who relied on the "Big Three" credit ratings agencies, Standard & Poor's, Moody's, and Fitch Group in the years leading up to the 2007–2008 financial crisis. They were found to suffer from "flawed computer models, the pressure from financial firms that paid for the ratings, the relentless drive for market share, the lack of resources to do the job despite record profits, and the absence of meaningful public oversight," even as investors "relied on them, often blindly" and in some cases "were obligated to use them."[19]

Similarly, consumer reports have been found to suffer from built-in biases. For example, Nicholas A. Bowman and Michael N. Bastedo point out that the *U.S. News* rankings of colleges seem to be misleading, with the rated institutions seeking to "to manipulate the data," rankings and institutional reputations having a circular dynamic, and "marginal differences in performance" leading to "large differences in reputation and resources" (Bastedo and Bowman 2010).

A study of four ratings lists of U.S. hospitals found little consistency, as "each system uses its own rating methods, has a different focus to its ratings, and stresses different measures of performance," threatening to

---

[18] See also David G. Robinson et al. (2009: 160) who argue that the government should "understand providing reusable data, rather than providing websites" to be "the core" of its "online publishing responsibility," as "Private actors, either nonprofit or commercial, are better suited to deliver government information to citizens and can constantly create and reshape the tools individuals use to find and leverage public data" [...] "As long as there is vigorous competition between third party sites [...] we expect most citizens will be able to find a site provider they trust"). See also Adam Liptak, "A Blockbuster Case Yields an Unexpected Result," *New York Times*, September 19 2011 (Richard Hasen argues that "If all I tell you about a candidate is that he is backed by the N.R.A. or Planned Parenthood, that is all many voters need to know... The disclosure serves a shortcut function").
[19] 'Conclusions of The Financial Crisis Inquiry Commission,' Stanford University's Rock Center for Corporate Governance, 2011, accessed at http://fcic.law.stanford.edu/report/conclusions. See also Hau et al. (2013).

"confuse patients, providers, and purchasers" (Austin et al. 2015). Angie's List, a website for reviewing local businesses, is reported to place those businesses that pay to advertise higher in its search results (Consumer Reports 2013; see also Szper 2013). According to Jennifer Heerwig and Katherine Shaw, "systemic flaws" in the FEC's collection of campaign finance data, "pose a serious obstacle to the ability of both voters and intermediaries to translate potentially valuable campaign finance disclosure information into credible signals, or shortcuts, to guide voter choice" (Heerwig and Shaw 2014: 1488; see also May 2002).

All this does not suggest that all or even most intermediaries are unreliable. Many seem to provide trustworthy rankings and evaluations. However, the evidence suggests that information about their veracity is subject to many of the same challenges faced by information about specific policies. Hence it is difficult for the public to determine which intermediary to rely upon.

Transparency Assumes Direct Democracy

We have seen that transparency may well fall short of being able to serve in the ways its advocates assume for a number of practical reasons—disclosed information may be inaccessible or difficult to process, and intermediaries may not be reliable. In addition, transparency is limited by built-in assumptions about the political process that are usually overlooked. These assumptions are next explored.

Transparency can achieve desired outcomes in two ways. First, transparency can inform individuals' choices, leading them to freely adopt healthier lifestyles or prefer more socially responsible businesses, for example, rather than coercing them to do so. Second, transparency can inform political action, leading voters to support or reject particular policies ranging from Affirmative Action to waterboarding, from foreign aid to allowing same-sex marriages. This second understanding of transparency in effect assumes a measure of direct democracy, in which the government is guided directly by the people rather than through elected representatives (O'Neill 2009: 170 and Islam 2006). Thus Joseph Stiglitz holds that "If data suggest that unemployment is soaring, they [the people] will be concerned that the government is mismanaging macroeconomic policy. If data suggest that inequality is increasing, then their concerns about distribution policies and whether the government is doing enough to help the poor will be heightened" (Stiglitz 2002: 29; Sen 1987; Vishwanath and Kaufmann 2001; O'Neill 2009: 170; Islam 2006: 123–127).

Yet political scientists and others have long recognized that direct democracy of this kind is not practical for societies of even relatively low size and complexity, let alone nation states (Madison 1787; Buchanan and Tullock 1962; Clarke and Linzey 1996: 226–230). This is not to dismiss direct democracy entirely (Barber 1984). Some elements of direct democracy exist in the Swiss government and in the United States at the state and local level, such as propositions and referendums on school bonds or same-sex marriage. However these are exceptions that help remind of the rule. No modern state is governed wholly, or even mainly, through direct democracy. For the most part, on all levels of government, but especially on the national one, people can vote only for or against a particular representative or political party, but not for or against any particular policy.

Hence, most times that transparency reveals the defects of a given policy, such information cannot be converted into action that affects that policy. Given that people have one vote, they cannot vote for Affirmative Action but against the invasion of Iraq, and for increased foreign aid but against the use of drones, and on and on—as Stiglitz implies. Hence, additional information about these and other such policies, even if valid and properly understood, cannot lead directly to remedial consequence, to realigning these policies with the preferences of the people. This point has been well captured by Bernard Manin, Adam Prszeworski, and Susan C. Stokes, who observed that "Governments make thousands of decisions that affect individual welfare; citizens have only one instrument to control these decisions: the vote. One cannot control a thousand targets with one instrument" (Manin et al. 1999: 50. See also Maravall 1999: 161 and Besley and Coate 2000).

One may argue instead that transparency facilitates democracy in a two-step process: first, voters use transparency to better evaluate various policies their representatives support; then, come elections, people combine the scores they grant to various policies in a sort of an index that reveals which party or candidates scores better, and they vote for that representative. Hence, the more the public knows about the various policies, the more the public will direct their representatives to heed their preferences. However, this assumption ignores that (1) most people vote most times for the same party they voted for previously, without building such indexes; (2) that their choices are affected by beliefs and peer pressure and not just information; and (3) that those voters that are affected by specific policies seem to take into account a very small number, and ignore the information about most others (sometimes referred to as lexicographic choices; Colman 2008).

In other words, issues raised about direct democracy in societies of greater size and complexity than small local communities (Madison 1787: 78; Buchanan and Tullock 1962: 213; Clarke and Linzey 1996: 226–230), apply to the thesis that transparency can replace much, if not all, of regulation. People, most times, can choose only among elected officials and political parties, not policies. They can hence judge, in general, if their representatives favor too much regulation or not enough, but not more. Hence, increased transparency about most policies has little direct effect and serves mainly as one source of information and judgment about the overall reputation of the representative in question. That means when a particular condition has serious harmful effects, or a policy is needed to ensure major benefits, these choices under most circumstances have to be delegated and therefore regulated rather than subject to informed individual choices by the citizens.

Work Cited

Alexander, Herbert, and Brian Haggerty. 1981. *The Federal Election Campaign Act: After a Decade of Political Reform*. Washington, DC: Citizens' Research Foundation.

Austin, J. Matthew, et al. 2015. National Hospital Ratings Systems Share Few Common Scores and May Generate Confusion Instead of Clarity. *Health Affairs* 34 (3): 423–430.

Barber, Benjamin R. 1984. *Strong Democracy: Participatory Politics for a New Age*. Oakland: University of California Press.

Bastedo, Michael N., and Nicholas A. Bowman. 2010. U.S. News & World Report College Rankings: Modeling Institutional Effects on Organizational Reputation. *American Journal of Education* 116 (2): 163–183.

Beam, Christopher. 2008. The TMI Presidency. *Slate*, November 12. http://www.slate.com/articles/news_and_politics/politics/2008/11/the_tmi_presidency.html.

Bertot, John C., et al. 2010. Using ICTs to Create a Culture of Transparency: E-government and Social Media as Openness and Anti-corruption Tools for Societies. *Government Information Quarterly* 27: 264–271.

Besley, Timothy, and Stephen Coate. 2000. Issue Unbundling via Citizens' Initiatives. *National Bureau of Economic Research Working Paper Series*, Working Paper no. 8036, December. http://www.international.ucla.edu/cms/files/besley_coate.pdf.

Brito, Jerry, and Drew Perrault. 2009. Transparency and Performance in Government. Working paper no. 09-38, Mercatus Center.

Buchanan, James M., and Gordon Tullock. 1962. *The Calculus of Consent: Logical Foundations of Constitutional Democracy.* Ann Arbor: University of Michigan Press.

Cillizza, Chris. 2013. The Least Productive Congress Ever. *The Washington Post*, July 17. http://www.washingtonpost.com/blogs/the-fix/wp/2013/07/17/the-least-productive-congress-ever/.

Clarke, Paul A.B., and Andrew Linzey. 1996. *Dictionary of Ethics, Theology and Society*. London: Routledge.

Coglianese, Cary et al. 2008. Transparency and Public Participation in the Rulemaking Process: A Nonpartisan Presidential Transition Task Force Report. University of Pennsylvania Law School, July.

Colman, Andrew M. 2008. Lexicographic Choice. In *A Dictionary of Psychology*, 3rd ed., 420. Oxford: Oxford University Press.

Consumer Reports. 2013. The Truth About Angie's List, Yelp, and more. September. http://www.consumerreports.org.

Dawes, Sharon S. 2010. Stewardship and Usefulness: Policy Principles for Information-Based Transparency. *Government Information Quarterly* 27 (4): 377–383.

Evans, Jocelyn A.J. 2004. *Voters & Voting: An Introduction*. London: Sage Publications.

Fenster, Mark. 2005. The Opacity of Transparency. *Iowa Law Review* 91: 885–949.

Finel, Bernard I., and Kristin M. Lord. 1999. The Surprising Logic of Transparency. *International Studies Quarterly* 43: 315–339.

Fung, Archon, Mary Graham, and David Weil. 2007. *Full Disclosure: The Perils and Promise of Transparency*. New York: Cambridge University Press.

Furnas, Alexander. 2014. Why Representative Democracies Can't Write Off Transparency. *The Atlantic*, January 16. http://www.theatlantic.com/politics/archive/2014/01/why-representative-democracies-cant-write-off-transparency/283143/.

Garrett, R. Sam. 2014. The State of Campaign Finance Policy: Recent Developments and Issues for Congress. *Congressional Research Service*, June 23.

Gilbert, Elizabeth. 2001. *The William J. Brennan Lecture in Constitutional Law: The Future of Campaign Finance Laws in the Courts and in Congress*. Working Paper No. 19 in the Chicago Public Law Working Paper Series, Oklahoma City University Law School.

Gilbert, Michael D. 2012. Campaign Finance Disclosure and the Information Tradeoff. *Iowa Law Review* 98: 1847–1894.

Ginsberg, Wendy R. 2011 The Obama Administration's Open Government Initiative: Issues for Congress. *Congressional Research Service*, January 28; ii, 14; http://www.fas.org/sgp/crs/secrecy/R41361.pdf.

Hale, Thomas N. 2008. Transparency, Accountability, and Global Governance. *Global Governance* 14: 73–94.

Harper, Jim. 2011. Publication Practices for Transparent Government. CATO Institute Briefing Paper no. 121, September 23. http://object.cato.org/sites/cato.org/files/pubs/pdf/bp121.pdf.

———. 2013. Addressing Transparency in the Federal Bureaucracy: Moving Toward a More Open Government. Cato Institute, March 13.

Hasen, Richard L. 2014. Three Wrong Progressive Approaches (and One Right One) to Campaign Finance Reform. *Harvard Law & Policy Review* 21: 21–37.

Hau, Harald, Sam Langfield, and David Marques-Ibanez. 2013. Bank Ratings: What Determines Their Quality? *Economic Policy* (April): 289–333.

Heald, David. 2006. Varieties of Transparency. In *Transparency: The Key to Better Governance?* ed. Christopher Hood and David Heald, 23–45. Oxford: Oxford University Press.

Heerwig, Jennifer, and Katherine Shaw. 2014. Through a Glass, Darkly: The Rhetoric and Reality of Campaign Finance Disclosure. *Georgetown Law Journal* 102: 1443–1500.

Hood, Christopher. 2006. Transparency in Historical Perspective. In *Transparency: The Key to Better Governance?* 3–23. Oxford: Oxford University Press.

Horwitz, Sari, and James V. Grimaldi. 2010. ATF's Oversight Limited in Face of Gun Lobby. *The Washington Post*, October 26. http://www.washingtonpost.com/wp-dyn/content/article/2010/10/25/AR2010102505823.html; http://www.techdirt.com/articles/20030625/0158245.shtml.

Islam, Roumeen. 2006. Does More Transparency Go Along with Better Governance? *Economics & Politics* 18 (2): 121–167.

Kahneman, Daniel, Paul Slovic, and Amos Tversky. 1982. *Judgement Under Uncertainty: Heuristics and Biases*. Cambridge: Cambridge University Press.

Kahneman, Daniel. 2011. *Thinking, Fast and Slow*. New York, NY: Farrar, Straus, and Giroux.

Korte, Gregory. 2013. IRS Assailed from All Sides for Lack of Transparency. *USA Today*, August 19. http://www.usatoday.com/story/news/politics/2013/08/18/irs-transparency-tea-party/2668193/.

Kuhne, Cecil C. 2004. Rethinking Campaign-Finance Reform: The Pressing Need for Deregulation and Disclosure. *John Marshall Law Review*, 633–647.

Levy, Lili. 2012. Plan B for Campaign Finance Reform: Can the FCC Help Save American Politics After Citizens United? *Catholic University Law Review* 61 (1): 97–173.

Madison, James. 1787. The Federalist no. 10. *The Federalist Papers* 78.

———. 1822. Letter to W.T. Barry, August 4 1822. In *The Complete Madison: His Basic Writings*, ed. Saul K. Padover, 1953. New York: Harper.

Manin, Bernard, Adam Prszeworski, and Susan C. Stokes. 1999. Elections and Representation. In *Democracy Accountability, and Representation*, ed. Adam Prszeworski, Susan C. Stokes, and Bernard Manin, 29–54. Cambridge: Cambridge University Press.

Mansick, Mike. 2003. Web Privacy Policies Confuse Net Surfers. *TechDirt*, June 25.

———. 2012. To Read All of the Privacy Policies You Encounter, You'd Need to Take a Month Off from Work Each Year. *TechDirt*, April 23. http://www.techdirt.com/articles/20120420/10560418585/to-read-all-privacy-policies-you-encounter-youd-need-to-take-month-off-work-each-year.shtml.

Maravall, Jose Maria. 1999. Accountability and Manipulation. In *Democracy Accountability, and Representation*, ed. Adam Prszeworski, Susan C. Stokes, and Bernard Manin, 154–196. Cambridge: Cambridge University Press.

May, Albert L. 2002. The Virtual Trail: Political Journalism on the Internet. Institute for Politics, Democracy and the Internet. http://www.pewtrusts.org/uploadedFiles/wwwpewtrustsorg/Reports/The-practice of-journalism/pp-online-journalist.pdf.

McDevitt, Ryan C. 2011. Names and Reputations: An Empirical Analysis. *American Economic Journal: Microeconomics* 3 (3): 193–209.

Meijer, Albert. 2009. Understanding Modern Transparency. *International Review of Administrative Sciences* 75 (2): 255–269.

Melone, Matthew A. 2010. Citizens United and Corporate Political Speech: Did the Supreme Court Enhance Political Discourse or Invite Corruption? *DePaul Law Review* 60: 29–97.

Moss, Michael. 2013. *Salt Sugar Fat: How the Food Giants Hooked Us*. New York: Random House.

O'Neill, Onora. 2009. Ethics for Communication? *European Journal of Philosophy* 17 (2): 167–180.

Obama, Barack. 2009a. Executive Order 13489—Presidential Records. January 21. http://www.whitehouse.gov/the_press_office/ExecutiveOrderPresidentialRecords/.

———. 2009b. Executive Order 13562—Classified National Security Information. December 29. http://www.whitehouse.gov/the-press-office/executive-order-classified-national-security-information.

Piotrowski, Suzanne J., and Erin Borry. 2010. An Analytic Framework for Open Meetings and Transparency. *Public Administration and Management* 15 (1): 138–176.

Piotrowski Suzanne, J., and Gregg G. Van Ryzin. 2007. Citizen Attitudes Toward Transparency in Local Government. *The American Review of Public Administration* 37 (3): 306–323.

Prat, Andrea. 2005. The Wrong Kind of Transparency. *The American Economic Review* 95 (3): 862–877.

Robinson, David G. et al. (2009: 160). Government Data and the Invisible Hand. *Yale Journal of Law & Technology* 11: 159–175.

Rosendorff, Peter B. 2004. Democracy and the Supply of Transparency. *Annual Meeting of the International Studies Association in Montreal*, Quebec, Canada. March 14. http://www.nyu.edu/gsas/dept/politics/faculty/rosendorff/Transparency.pdf.

Sen, Amartya. 1987. Food and Freedom. Sir John Crawford Memorial Lecture, Washington, DC, October 29. http://library.cgiar.org/bitstream/handle/10947/556/craw3.pdf?sequence.pdf.

Simon, Herbert A. 1955. A Behavioral Model of Rational Choice. '*Quarterly Journal of Economics* 69: 99–118.

Stiglitz, Joseph E. 2002. Transparency in Government. In *The Right to Tell: The Role of Mass Media in Economic Development*, ed. Alisa Clapp-Itnyre,

Roumeen Islam, and Caralee McLiesh, 27–44. Washington: World Bank Publications.

Sunstein, Cass. 1999. Informational Regulation and Informational Standing: Akins and Beyond. *University of Pennsylvania Law Review* 147: 613–675.

———. 2010. The Power of Open Government. Speech, *The Brookings Institution*, Washington, DC, March 10.

———. 2012. The White House vs. Red Tape. *Wall Street Journal*, April 30.

Szper, Rebecca. 2013. Playing to the Test: Organizational Responses to Third Party Ratings. *Voluntas: International Journal of Voluntary and Nonprofit Organizations* 24 (4): 935–952.

Torres-Spelliscy, Ciara. 2011. Hiding Behind the Tax Code, the Dark Election of 2010 and Why Tax-Exempt Entities Should Be Subject to Robust Federal Campaign Finance Disclosure Laws. *Nexus: Chapman's Journal of Law & Policy* 16: 59–98.

Vishwanath, Tara, and Daniel Kaufmann. 2001. Toward Transparency: New Approaches and Their Application to Financial Markets. *The World Bank Research Observer* 16: 41–57.

Wald, Matthew L. 2012. Slow Responses Cloud a Window into Washington. *The New York Times*, January 28.

Weil, David, et al. 2006. The Effectiveness of Regulatory Disclosure Policies. *Journal of Policy Analysis and Management* 25 (1): 155–181.

Zweig, Jason. 2009. About Time: Regulation Based on Human Nature. *The Wall Street Journal*, June 20.

Publicity and Transparency: The Itinerary of a Subtle Distinction

Sandrine Baume

Introduction

Transparency and publicity are generally held to be two major requirements in public affairs. The two are often mentioned in the same breath, but it would be reasonable to wonder whether they really refer to one and the same thing. In scholarly literature too, transparency and publicity are often used interchangeably, and the few attempts that have been made to distinguish the two notions have not been developed extensively. There have been repeated calls for a clear differentiation in the growing literature on transparency, and such thinkers as Elster, Erkkilä, Kelly, and Naurin have proposed their own explicit attempts at conceptual distinction. The question I will investigate here is whether there is a discontinuity of meaning between the principle of publicity, which appears in classical writings notably of Jeremy Bentham, Immanuel Kant, and Benjamin Constant, and the call for transparency emerging in parallel as

S. Baume (✉)
Centre for Public Law, University of Lausanne, Lausanne, Switzerland
e-mail: sandrine.baume@unil.ch

© The Author(s) 2018
E. Alloa, D. Thomä (eds.), *Transparency, Society and Subjectivity*,
https://doi.org/10.1007/978-3-319-77161-8_10

a metaphor in the eighteenth century. The contemporary use of the notion of transparency does display some similarity to the classical early modern concept of publicity, but the differences between the two, no matter how small or subtle, need to be elaborated. Compounding the challenge is the fact that the existing literature, even by well-established and highly esteemed authors, largely remains insensitive to such distinctions. Axel Gosseries, for example, uses both concepts interchangeably, giving the impression that the two are one and the same: "Publicity can be opposed both to privacy and to secrecy. This entry will mostly be dealing with the latter meaning. In everyday life, calls for more transparency or openness in political and economic life may seem rather uncontroversial" (Gosseries 2010).

The empirical evidence affirms that in the 1980s "publicity" started being gradually replaced by the term "transparency," which has now become significantly more present. Figure 1 (based on Google Books) shows an exponential increase of the use of "publicity" in the first part of the twentieth century, followed by a decline since the 1940s, and then by a significant increase of the use of "transparency" since the 1980s.[1]

In economics and politics, debates that used to refer to the problem of "publicity" now tend to refer to the problem of "transparency." In the 1950s and '60s, debates about the freedom of access to administrative information did not result in a demand for "transparency," but rather in requests for "publicity." For example, in 1951, Finland adopted the Publicity of Official Documents Act, whereas in the United States the Freedom of Information Act (FOIA) adopted in 1966 did not mention the words transparency or transparent. If we consider the recent Swiss law on the transparency of administrative information (2004), it is the word "transparency"[2] which is used. These instances illustrate how the term "transparency" has progressively replaced that of "publicity" in official

---

[1] I would like to thank Yannis Papadopoulos for suggesting this instrument to me in order to understand the evolution of the popularity of "transparency" and "publicity."
[2] Federal Act on Freedom of Information in the Administration (2004, Switzerland): "Art. 1 (Aim and subject matter): This Act seeks to promote transparency with regard to the mandate, organisation and activities of the Administration. To this end, it contributes to informing the public by ensuring access to official documents."

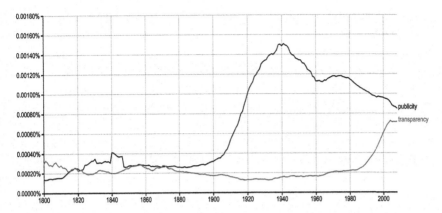

Fig. 1 Google Books Ngram Viewer, instances of publicity and transparency, 1800–2008. Source: Ngram/Sandrine Baume

documents and ultimately taken over the signification of information publicity.

While the two terms "transparency" and "publicity" often refer to similar measures regulating information and relate to the same expected outcomes, the need to keep the two distinct remains. I will start by presenting different attempts of distinguishing them by scholars, notably by Naurin, Elster, Erkkilä, and Kelly. Then I will assess such attempts with regard to their respective merits and weaknesses. And, finally, I will suggest yet a different way of distinguishing publicity from transparency, by drawing on the polyvalence in the semantics of the latter.

Theoretical Distinctions Between Transparency and Publicity

In 2006, Daniel Naurin produced an interesting attempt to define "transparency" as the availability of information, even though such access to information is not necessarily exercised (2006: 90–98). By contrast, he referred to "publicity" as a situation in which information is not only available but also received, processed and digested by the public. Transparency is thus a prerequisite *for* but not a guarantee *of* publicity, a necessary but not sufficient condition for publicity. Naurin identifies three factors accounting for possible gaps between transparency and publicity: First, the absence of intermediaries between actions and discourses of officials and the public opinion, which would enable the activities of the latter to become visible and readable (this role being traditionally devoted to media). Secondly, rational ignorance could be a factor in the discrepancy between transparency and publicity, as citizens do not invest in information-seeking if the cost of acquiring information exceeds the potential benefit that the knowledge would provide. Thirdly, citizens' cognitive limits could explain why available information is not processed. As shown by Baume and Papadopoulos (2018: 171), there is another distinction that is not mentioned by Naurin. People tend to ignore or neglect information which is non-convergent with their beliefs (Lord 2006: 12).

Does Naurin's distinction find some confirmation in the classical literature? In Jeremy Bentham's writings, elements of validation can be found in various occurrences, when he affirms, for example, that publicity requires that the public "take cognizance of the question, whatever it may be" (Bentham 1983: 35; see also Baume and Papadopoulos [2018:171]). However, in other occurrences, Bentham gives the impression that he does not have a distinction in mind between transparency and publicity and that these two notions are fairly interchangeable. Bentham does contrast transparency with "opakeness" in this quotation: "Opakeness. Want of transparency, disturbance given [to] the transparency of the whole business, hence facilities afforded throughout for the secret and successful operation of sinister interest" (Bentham 1989: 102). In another passage, he contrasts publicity with the "darkness of secrecy": "In the darkness of secrecy, sinister interest and evil in every shape, have full swing [...] Where there is no publicity there is no justice" (Bentham 1962: 493). These quotations, however, do not show a clear distinction between the two concepts: publicity and transparency seem to be equally and similarly opposed to "darkness," "secrecy," and "opakeness." It is telling to see that a negative characterization of publicity is being mobilized here, giving the impression that "publicity" reveals itself all the better when contrasted with its opposite. Bentham rarely uses the term "transparency" in its metaphorical meaning in comparison to the word "publicity." For Immanuel Kant and Benjamin

Constant—two other main thinkers on publicity—the notion of transparency is wholly absent. Kant uses the notion of *Publicität*,[3] whereas Constant speaks about *publicité*.[4] For Rousseau, the notion of publicity is, to the best of our knowledge, absent, while the concept of transparency is less frequent than generally thought. Revealingly, *Le Dictionnaire de Jean-Jacques Rousseau* (Eigeldinger and Trousson 1996) doesn't even feature an entry on "transparency." Nevertheless, in line with Foucault's (1980) and Starobinski's influential readings (1988),[5] I would propose that Rousseau occupies a significant place in the elaboration of transparency. While the classical corpus has much to say about the values and the expectations associated with the notion of publicity—and much less frequently with transparency (Baume 2011, 2013; Baume and Papadopoulos 2018)—then it must be acknowledged that it does not offer many occasions to distinguish the two concepts.

Given this background, how should one assess Naurin's distinction between transparency and publicity? It certainly does boast the advantage of being both parsimonious and analytically clear. But the main weakness of this distinction is that the literature remains largely insensitive to it, given that authors do not choose one concept or another in accordance to Naurin's differentiation (see Gosseries 2010 and Fenster 2006). Consequently, this distinction is not useful to systematizing the occurrences that have led to the emergence of "transparency" and "publicity" either in the literature or in political discourses, as is unfortunately often the case for theoretical attempts to distinguish publicity from transparency. As I will discuss later, Naurin's proposal bears some similarities with Kelly's distinction, namely that publicity is more demanding than

---

[3] "Von der Schwierigkeit der auf das Fortschreiten zum Weltbesten angelegten Maximen in Unsehung ihrer Publicität" (Kant 1992: 160).

[4] "Toutes les barrières civiles, politiques, judiciaires deviennent illusoires sans liberté de la presse. L'indépendance des tribunaux peut être violée au mépris de la constitution la mieux rédigée. Si la publicité n'est pas garantie, ce délit ne sera pas réprimé, car il restera couvert d'un voile. Les tribunaux eux-mêmes peuvent prévariquer dans leurs jugements ou bouleverser les formes. La seule sauvegarde des formes est encore la publicité. L'innocence peut être plongée dans les fers. Si la publicité n'avertit pas les citoyens du danger qui plane sur toutes les têtes, les cachots retiendront indéfiniment leurs victimes à la faveur du silence universel" (Constant 1980: 136).

[5] Regarding Starobinski's contribution, Hammann mentioned that "Starobinski a mis en lumière la permanence du rêve de transparence et l'angoisse de l'obstacle dans l'œuvre de Rousseau" (2006: 516)

transparency and that the latter could even be considered an ingredient of publicity. Publicity would be more than revealing but includes a specific and public treatment of information.

In 2012, Tero Erkkilä suggested another distinction which assumes that publicity has to be understood as a democratic concept, whereas the current widespread use of transparency would rather be linked to economics literature concerned with lowering transaction costs, improving market information and increasing efficiency (Erkkilä 2012: 5).[6] In my view, Erkkilä's distinction does not account for contemporary usage. The use of the term "publicity" was originally—and it still is—used in both economic and political fields.[7] The availability and accessibility of information is simultaneously a device for decreasing the risk of corruption and inefficiency in the economic and political fields. Consequently, it would be erroneous to consider—as Erkkilä does—publicity as primarily associated with politics. The economic angle in the classical literature has authors claiming, as William Stanley Jevons does in *The Theory of Political Economy*, that "publicity, whenever it can thus be enforced on markets by public authority, tends almost always to the advantage of everybody except perhaps a few speculators and financiers" (Jevons 1888: chap. IV).[8] For Jevons, wherever information is imperfect and secrecy reigns, prices are "unnatural ratios of exchange" (Jevons 1888: chap. IV). In a well-organized economy, publicizing market information will make conspiracies impossible. That is why Jevons supported government intervention to encourage publicizing economic information, which involved the publication of market prices, whether by supporting business newspapers or by laws requiring the maintenance and publication of company accounts. In this situation, the market price is set by an accurate reflection of the conditions of production, and publicity becomes the primary pillar of competition policy.

---

[6] "Whereas publicity has been primarily understood as a democratic concept, the notion of transparency increasingly carries economic connotations" (Erkkilä 2012: 5).
[7] Gosseries underlines today the fact the transparency is associated to both fields: "In everyday life, calls for more transparency or openness in political and economic life may seem rather uncontroversial" (2010).
[8] Regarding Jevons' contribution, I am particularly grateful to Amanar Akhabbar, with whom I elaborated a research project that partly responded to the question raised here.

Regarding the rationalities of publicity but from a political side, Bentham is probably the most explicit author at the threshold of the late eighteenth century and the early nineteenth century. In Bentham's argument, publicity is a very effective way to fight the effects of bad governance. In *Securities against Misrule and Other Constitutional Writings for Tripoli and Greece*, Bentham lists cases of bad administration or "misrule" where publicity remains the best antidote. These include cases where the victim is an individual, as in banishment, homicide, or imprisonment, and collective cases such as generalized misinformation or waste of public money. Publicity is in his opinion the only remedy for all these examples (Bentham 1990: 26). Moreover, in *Of Publicity*, Bentham lists six reasons to encourage and apply the principle of publicity in public life, most notably the ability "to constrain the members of the assembly to perform their duty" (Bentham 1999: 29).[9]

Broadly speaking, the unequal or limited distribution of information yields problems that are partly similar in governments or in markets and in public or private bureaucracies. Unequal distribution of information among economic as well as political actors distorts the incentive structure, and the interplay among particular interests then encourages opportunistic behavior that goes against collective interests. Moral hazard and adverse selection[10] introduce mechanisms of corruption into public life and undermine economic prosperity, among other things. In the scholarly literature, but also in political discourses, one of the main solutions put forward to eschew these deleterious phenomena has been to call on making information publicly available. Such call is usually expressed today in terms of transparency, as in the principle "the more information, the better." By making behavior visible, especially in social organizations,

---

[9] There are five other reasons: second, "to secure the confidence of the people and their assent to the measures of the legislature"; third, "to enable the governors to know the wishes of the governed"; fourth, "to enable the electors to act from knowledge"; fifth, "to provide the assembly with the means of profiting by the information of the public"; sixth, and probably the anecdotical reason, "the amusement with results from [the appliance of the principle of publicity]" (Bentham 1999: 30–34). For a development regarding these six reasons, see Baume and Papadopoulos (2018).

[10] "Rasmusen (1989: 133) describes these terms as follows: 'Moral hazard with hidden actions: Smith and Brown begin with symmetric information and agree to a contract, but then Smith takes an action unobserved by Brown. Adverse selection: (Smith knows things about himself that Brown does not). Smith and Brown then agree to a contract. Information is incomplete'," cited in Lupia (2003: 41).

publicity makes it possible to observe and to monitor agents. For Bentham, one of the essential functions of publicity is to protect us from wrongful behavior. In *Of Publicity*, that is an important reason why he argues in favor of this principle. Publicity forces elected officials to comply with their duties; it turns into a guarantee of integrity:

> The greater the number of temptations to which the exercise of political power is exposed, the more necessary is it to give to those who possess it, the most powerful reasons for resisting them. But there is no reason more constant and more universal than the superintendence of the public. (Bentham 1999: 29)

Specifically, transparency devices tend to govern relationships between principals and agents (i.e. relationships involving delegation by instructing parties to their instructed representatives). Such relations of delegation are common in public life, where, for example, it is expected that elected officials will act in compliance with voters' interests, as they are in the business world, where it is hoped that managers will act in the interest of shareholders. In these principal–agent relationships, uncertainty and the unequal distribution of information create an acute problem of misalignment between the interests of agents and those of principals. For example, a manager maximizes the short-term share price and drives up the volume of business, disregarding prudential considerations and a long-term perspective; a political representative betrays the voters' interests by serving those of interest groups; a corrupt official administers affairs not by the rules of law and justice but by a system of favoritism and private profits. How then to evaluate Erkkilä's distinction between publicity and transparency? It turns out that his attempt does not resist the confrontation with both classical and contemporary sources, which testify that publicity was always both used in political and economic perspectives.

In his 2013 book *Securities against Misrule*, Jon Elster also attempted to distinguish publicity and transparency, all the while confessing that it is hard to draw a clear border. Considering an administrative context, transparency could be associated to decisions, Elster says, which "are made known to the individual whom it concerns but not to anyone else"

(Elster 2013: 10–11, n. 41), whereas publicity would be here associated to decisions or documents which are diffused to the public. This last hypothesis could dovetail with Erin Kelly's distinction—which we shall delve into in a moment—when she affirms that publicity contains an element of public justification. Regarding the "judicial and legislative contexts," and according to Elster, it is even harder to make a distinction: "[I]n some cases, one can perhaps define transparency as what is *not hidden* (but may be costly to find) and publicity as what is *revealed* (with low or zero costs)" (Elster 2013: 11, n. 41). This last attempt at distinction conflicts with that made by Naurin. For the latter, publicity can be differentiated from transparency by the fact that the former is more demanding insofar as it requires a real and more costly access to information. Moreover, Elster's distinction does not seem to be related to the effective use of both terms in the literature, as is the case for Naurin and Erkkilä.

Finally, in 2013, Erin Kelly made the pitch for a promising distinction between transparency and publicity, affirming that publicity is inherently associated with political or public justification, which would not be the case for transparency. According to Kelly, public justification would contain three elements. The first is transparency, for which "the public interest should be open to public scrutiny and challenge, and the public's interest itself should be identified through measures that are open to public deliberation" (Kelly 2013: 2). As the author mentions, "these possibilities require certain institutional protections: freedom of conscience, freedom of speech and of the press, freedom of association, freedom of information, and rights to political participation" (Kelly 2013: 2). According to her, the second dimension of public justification "is dependence on common knowledge" (Kelly 2013: 3), which means that "[j]ustification is not the province of experts and specialists, but of the common judgment of political subjects" (Kelly 2013: 3). Finally, public justification supposes a third element, the requirement of "shared values." Kelly's definition has some affinities with Naurin's distinction because publicity, viewed here as a requirement of public justification, is shown as something more demanding than transparency. As a result, transparency would be a necessary although not a sufficient condition of publicity.

Is Kelly's thesis, according to which publicity can be differentiated from transparency because the former necessarily contains an element of political justification, validated by other definitions of transparency emerging in the literature? To address this question, we shall turn to Christopher Hood's definition, which is devoid of any element of political justification: "In fact, it [transparency] is commonly used to mean a number of different things, such as disclosure, policy clarity, consistency or a culture of candour" (Hood 2001: 701). Hood's characterization of transparency contains three chief elements: revelation of information, integrity, and intelligibility. There is no element of public justification. The same holds true for Anoeska Buijze's characterization of transparency, which focuses on the availability, accessibility, and comprehensibility of information[11] and does not mention any element of justification. If I consider the institutional definitions of transparency, as formulated and examined carefully by Meijer (2013: 430)[12] and represented notably by Den Boer[13] or Moser,[14] the element of justification is not present either. Finally, when transparency is perceived through the specific relationship of delegation, as is the case for Oliver or Prat, the element of justification does not appear explicitly either. However, when the idea of surveillance becomes tangible, as in the case in principal–agent relations, the idea of justification is never far behind.[15]

The doctrinal sources of Kelly's differentiation between publicity and transparency are not completely clear. In other words, on what grounds should publicity imply public justification? What are the textual sources

---

[11] "All transparency obligations seem to have a common core. They are all concerned with the availability, accessibility, and comprehensibility of information. A transparent government is one that provides people with the information they need to ascertain and understand the state of the world and to predict how their actions will affect that world, and that does not unnecessarily complicate that world" (Buijze, 2013: 4). Note that Buijze, in opposition to Naurin (2006: 91), added the element of accessibility of information to her definition of transparency.

[12] The following definitions of transparency given by Den Boer; Moser; Oliver; Prat are all quoted by Meijer (2013: 430).

[13] Transparency is "the ability to look clearly through the windows of an institution" (Den Boer 1998: 105).

[14] Moser defines being transparent as "to open up the working procedures not immediately visible to those not directly involved in order to demonstrate the good working of an institution" (2001: 3).

[15] "Oliver (2004: 2) indicates that transparency can be described as having three elements: an observer, something available to be observed, and a means or method for observation. This type of definition builds on the principal–agent theory: a principal requires information about the agent to check whether the agent adheres to the 'contract' (Prat 2006: 92)" (Meijer 2013: 430).

for such an assumption? Although he is never mentioned, Immanuel Kant is crucially inspirational. As is known, for Kant, publicity represents a criterion to evaluate whether the agent's principle is apriorically grounded in reason.[16] Publicity then rises to the level of a transcendental formula, once it comes to public law: "All actions that affect the rights of other men are wrong if their maxim is not consistent with publicity" (Kant 1983: 135). Consequently, whenever a political action or a maxim cannot be disclosed, it is because of its deleterious character:

> Every claim of right must have this capacity for publicity, and since one can easily judge whether or not it is present in a particular case, i.e., whether or not publicity is compatible with the agent's principles, it provides us with a readily applicable criterion that is found a priori in reason; for the purported claim's (*praetensio iuris*) falseness (contrariness to right) is immediately recognized by an experiment of pure reason. (Kant 1983: 135)

The pivotal role played by the concept of publicity in Kant, notably in *Perpetual Peace*, is based on the fact that publicity guarantees the convergence of politics and morality (Habermas 1991: 104). If the doctrinal roots of the intrinsic relation between publicity and political justification hark back to the Kantian corpus, this elicits another question: to what extent must political justification be related to a social need or, drawing on Reinhart Koselleck's *Begriffsgeschichte* (*Conceptual History*), to social uses and social functions of concepts? As indeed, according to Koselleck's historical semantics, concepts express social necessities or needs, while these language practices in turn significantly affect reality. In short, our reality and our experience are dependent on the meanings given to concepts.[17] As expressed by Christina Nadeau in reference to Koselleck, "society appropriates or creates the concepts that it needs in order to

---

[16] "Every claim of right must have this capacity for publicity, and since one can easily judge whether or not it is present in a particular case, i.e., whether or not publicity is compatible with the agent's principles, it provides us with a readily applicable criterion that is found a priori in reason; for the purported claim's (*praetensio iuris*) falseness (contrariness to right) is immediately recognized by an experiment of pure reason" (Kant 1983: 135).

[17] Koselleck (1988, 1972–1997, 1997).

understand itself and to 'give itself' to the understanding of others (future generations and other societies)" (Nadeau 2013: our translation).[18]

On this background, I want to put forward the hypothesis that publicity develops in regard to the social and political necessity to control public officials, to foster the accountability for policymakers and require them to justify their actions. Historically speaking, it is when representative governments begin to emerge in Europe that a full-fledged discourse articulated around the norm of publicity begins to develop. The rise of representative governments led to a growing desire among represented citizens to achieve greater visibility, demanding that their representatives' actions comply with the general interest or their electoral promises. As such, there is a strong link between the emergence of representative governments and the requirement of publicity. The necessity of publicity as an emerging value coincides with a questioning of and an objection to absolute authority, the strength of which lay in part in State secrets—the *arcana imperii*. At the time publicity established its legitimacy in Europe during the second half of the eighteenth century, an important step had been taken, one which diverged from previous theories of the State that, until then, had been bolstered by the idea of secrecy: theories that the birth of contemporary states and their development were underpinned by the practice of secrecy. For citizens of representative governments, publicity constitutes a counterpart for the decisional power that they have delegated to their "agents." In other words, in return for the mandate given to representatives, citizens keep the right of surveillance, evaluation and the right to request public justifications of public officials. The requirement of accountability contains precisely these elements, if we take Bovens' definition into account (Baume and Papadopoulos 2018). This definition sees accountability as "a relationship between an actor and a forum, in which the actor has an obligation to explain and to justify his or her conduct, the forum can pose questions and pass judgment, and the actor may face consequences" (Bovens 2007: 450).

---

[18] Original version: [Chaque] "société s'approprie ou crée les concepts dont elle a besoin afin de se comprendre elle-même et [de] 'se donner' à la compréhension des autres (des générations futures, des autres sociétés)" (Nadeau 2013: 14).

At the end of the eighteenth and beginning of the nineteenth centuries, Jeremy Bentham and Benjamin Constant explicitly addressed the issue of accountability or, to use a less contemporary terminology, the issue of responsibility. In Constant's understanding, visibility is the main lever of control public opinion can play on, and "publicity" protects against the State and its exercise of authority. The responsibility of those in power can only take effect under this condition. What is more, Constant adds that all levels of hierarchy are subject to political responsibility.[19] In *Political Principles*, he outlines what the objectives of ministerial responsibility should be: they aim to "depriv[e] guilty ministers of their power" through the nation's watchfulness, which operates through publicity and freedom of speech.[20] By virtue of the sanction it allows and the civic spirit it creates, watchfulness (conceived here as a control by the people) lies at the very heart of political life. The Benthamian understanding of publicity is very close to Constant's position, which posits that publicity requires control for opinions to develop and political responsibilities to establish themselves, especially by public opinion, which, for Constant as for Bentham, plays the role of a non-instituted, fictitious tribunal. As systematized by Cutler (1999: 328), Bentham assigns four functions to the public opinion tribunal, as described in *Constitutional Code* (Bentham 1983: 36–37): (1) "All persons have the right to seek information and evidence (the 'statistic or evidence-furnishing function')"; (2) "The tribunal renders judgments (the 'censorial function')"; (3) "It punishes and rewards the people involved by establishing their reputations (the 'executive function')"; (4) "It proposes improvements on any public matter (the 'melioration-suggestive function')." As developed by Baume and Papadopoulos (2018: 175), "the first three functions are currently considered to be the main functions of

---

[19] "It is not sufficient to have established the responsibility of ministers; this responsibility has no existence unless it begins with the immediate executor of the act which is its object. It must weigh upon all the levels of the constitutional hierarchy" (Constant 1988: 244).

[20] "It seems to me that responsibility must, above all, secure two aims: that of depriving guilty ministers of their power, and that of keeping alive in the nation—through the watchfulness of her representatives, the openness of their debates and the exercise of freedom of the press applied to the analysis of all ministerial actions—a spirit of inquiry, a habitual interest in the maintenance of the constitution of the state, a constant participation in public affairs, in a word a vivid sense of political life" (Constant 1988: 239).

accountability mechanisms: information provision, debate, and sanctioning."[21] Kelly's distinction between publicity and transparency captures an essential element regarding the definition of publicity: the component of justification, which does not really emerge in the numerous definitions of transparency. This characterization tallies with Kant's understanding of publicity, itself strongly associated with public reason, although Kelly strangely enough makes no mention it. It should be noted that in *The Structural Transformation of the Public Sphere*, Jürgen Habermas states that while the practice of secrecy serves "sovereignty based on *voluntas* [arbitrariness]," publicity aims to serve "the promotion of legislation based on *ratio* [reason]" (Habermas 1991: 53).

Transparency as a Metaphor

There is one other significant and substantial difference between transparency and publicity: transparency is an image or a metaphor, whereas publicity is not. Surprisingly, this distinction—although it appears obvious—is not deeply elaborated in the literature. Transparency is primarily a technical term in optics (a synonym of diaphanousness and an antonym of opacity), meaning the quality of something that is transparent; the terms "transparency" and "transparent" also refer to statements or intentions with meanings that are easily discoverable. Since the eighteenth century, these two terms—the noun and the adjective—have been extensively used in this metaphorical sense.[22] For example, Littré's *Dictionary* (1863–1877), in its entry "transparency," quotes Rousseau: "[T]he scorn they feign is not real, that it is only the very transparent veil covering an

---

[21] See (Bovens 2007: 463–464). As shown by (Baume and Papadopoulos 2018: 175), "the fourth function can be understood as one of the possible additional functions of such mechanisms: those having to provide account may use the feedback they receive for learning purposes."

[22] However, if the concept of transparency is clearly based on visual metaphors, the concept of publicity is also, if less obviously, associated with such metaphors. For example, for Bentham, "publicity" means "exposure—the completest exposure of the whole system of procedure—whatever is done by anybody, being done before the eyes of the universal public" (Bentham 1843: 8). For him and his contemporaries, publicity was associated with light and sight, for it illuminates and makes visible. Bentham speaks of "the light of *publicity* shining in full splendour" (Bentham 1843: 75). Thus, in its usage since the late eighteenth century, the term "publicity" is closely linked with visual metaphors: to become public is to become visible, to place oneself in the public eye.

esteem which tears them apart and a rage which they hide very badly" (Rousseau 1990: 184). And again Rousseau: "His heart, transparent as crystal, can hide nothing about what happens within it" (Rousseau 1990: 155). In this last quotation, "transparency" is conceived of as a state opposed to the hidden, the secret, the inaccessible and the impenetrable. Here, what is seen, perceived, recognized is given without any effort. This would confirm Naurin's intuition that publicity—in opposition to transparency—is accompanied by an effort, an intention, a specific will and ability to access to an information (Naurin 2006: 91).

By opposing transparency to opacity, Rousseau identifies two relational models: transparency characterizes an immediate relationship with the self or with others, by which "nothing comes between one mind and another" (Starobinski 1988: 23). Yet, relations in which personal interest interferes lose this immediate quality; they move away from transparency, which remains for Rousseau the virtue of "beautiful souls."[23] If this is valid on an individual level, it is also relevant from a collective perspective. It can, for instance, explain Rousseau's preference for small States: "Almost all small States, republics as well as monarchies, prosper simply because they are small, because all their citizens know and watch one another, because the chiefs can see for themselves the evil being done, the good they have to do; and because their orders are carried out within their sight" (Rousseau 1997: 193). Foucault very finely expressed what the "Rousseauist" dream of a transparent society consists of:

> What in fact was the Rousseauist dream that motivated many of the revolutionaries?[24] It was the dream of a transparent society, visible and legible in each of its parts, the dream of there no longer existing any zones of darkness, zones established by the privileges of royal power of the prerogatives of some corporation, zones of disorder. It was the dream that each individual, whatever position he occupied, might be able to see the whole of society, that men's hearts should communicate, their vision be

---

[23] See Starobinski (1988: 262) and Bredin (2001: 5). In the *Confessions*, Rousseau re-examines the issue of the heart's transparency (1981: 446).
[24] According to Richir, the failures of past revolutions can be assessed by their incapacity to achieve transparency: "[C]'est toute la pensée 'révolutionnaire' qui est animée de la croyance en une transparence de la société à elle-même" (Richir 1973: 10).

unobstructed by obstacles, and that opinion of all reign over each... (Foucault 1980: 152)

In *Jean-Jacques Rousseau. Transparency and Obstruction*, Jean Starobinski notes that in the course of the eighteenth century, the rejection of opacity coincides with the denunciation of appearance, lies and social masks: "In the theatre and the Church, in novels and in newspapers, sham, convention, hypocrisy, and masks were denounced in a variety of ways" (Starobinski 1988: 3). According to Sophie Wahnich, such a stigmatization of the mask, the appearance of the "costume," marks a new turn from the culture of court society, a "society of representation where everyone had to keep his place, [...] [it] was the ideal stage for this kind of role-play."[25]

The omnipotence of visibility in Rousseau's work explains the omnipresence of the eyes as organs of surveillance, public evaluation, and emulation. In *Considerations on the Government of Poland*, Rousseau indicates that civic life takes place "under the eyes" of the public (Rousseau 1997: 185) of the citizen,[26] or of the legislator.[27] For example, when Rousseau speaks about the best means to "bring patriotism to the highest pitch in every Polish heart," he indicates:

[i]t remains for me to detail here the means I believe to be the strongest, the most powerful, and even infallibly successful, if well implemented. It is to

---

[25] Our translation of: '[S]ociété de représentation où chacun devait tenir sa place, [...elle] était la scène par excellence de ce jeu de rôles' (Wahnich 1997: 32).

[26] In *Considerations on the Government of Poland*, and specifically in the chapter dedicated to "Education," Rousseau indicates that "[t]heir instruction may be domestic and individual, but their games ought always to be public and common to all; for the point here is not only to keep them busy, to give them a robust constitution, to make them agile and limber, but to accustom them from early on to rule, to equality, to fraternity, to competitions, to living under the eyes of their fellow-citizens and to seeking public approbation. To this end, the winners' prizes and rewards should be distributed not arbitrarily by the coaches or school principals, but by acclamation and the judgment of the spectators; and these judgments can be trusted always to be just especially if care is taken to make these games attractive to the public by organizing them with some pomp and so that they become a spectacle. In which case it is a fair assumption that all honest folk and good patriots will regard it a duty and a pleasure to attend them" (1997: 191).

[27] "For the administration to be strong, good and efficient in the pursuit of its aims, the entire executive power has to be in the same hands: but it is not enough that these hands change; if possible they should act only under the eyes of the Lawgiver and that it be he who guides them. This is the true secret of keeping them from usurping his authority" (Rousseau 1997: 200).

see to it that all Citizens constantly fell under the public's eyes, that no one advance or succeed save by public favor, that no position, no office be filled save by the nation's wish, and finally, that everyone, from the least nobleman, even the least peasant up to the King, if possible, be so dependent on public esteem, that no one can do anything, acquire anything, achieve anything without it. (Rousseau 1997: 238)

Significantly, Rousseau considers vigilance a natural attribute of political liberty, mobilizing, on a massive scale, the visual organ[28] more than the auditory one. Rousseau's conception of transparency contributes largely to the understanding of the contemporary predilection for the word "transparency" more than for the word "publicity." As shown by the Swiss philosopher, the lexical fields associated with transparency are broader and vaster than those associated with publicity. In the definition of transparency given by Hood, this was tangible when he affirmed that transparency has to be associated notably with "disclosure, policy clarity, consistency or a culture of candor" (Hood 2001: 701). Bredin evokes also the multifaceted aspects of transparency in saying that "transparency" is associated with "truth, clarity, lucidity, pureness even" (Bredin 2001: 5). As I surmise, part of the fascination with transparency is related to its semantic polyvalence, gathering several crucial values. This polyvalent feature is aptly captured by Foucault when he asserts that in the second part of the eighteenth century, the reign of visibility is conceived as preventing us from numerous and diverse problems, such as lies, arbitrariness, monarchical caprices, superstitions, tyranny, plots, epidemics, illusions, and ignorance.[29] As a matter of fact, such diversity of expectations, virtues and facets associated with "hypervisibility" finds a much broader echo in the notion of "transparency" than in the concept of

---

[28] "In France it is an accepted maxim of State to turn a blind eye on many things; that is what despotism always obliges one to do; but in a free Government it is a sure way to weaken the legislation and upset the constitution" (Rousseau 1997: 223).

[29] "A fear haunted the latter half of the eighteenth century: the fear of darkened spaces, of the pall of gloom which prevents the full visibility of things, men and truths. It sought to break up the patches of darkness that blocked the light, eliminate the shadowy areas of society, demolish the unlit chambers where arbitrary political acts, monarchical caprice, religious superstitions, tyrannical and priestly plots, epidemics and the illusions of ignorance were fomented" (Foucault 1980: 153).

"publicity." This may explain the overwhelming success of this metaphor, which is of course polyvalent, polymorphic, and polysemic, but above all always virtuous. Mark Fenster has insisted on the melioristic potentialities associated with the demand of transparency in public affairs when he argued that "[t]ransparency thus serves as more than a mere technical concept that provides the basis for constitutional, legislative, and regulatory rules. It also acts as a powerful metaphor that drives and shapes the desire for a more perfect democratic order" (Fenster 2006: 621).

Conclusion

In this paper, I have discussed the reasons for distinguishing between the concepts of transparency and publicity, building first on Erkkilä, Elster, Kelly, and Naurin's suggestions. As this assessment showed, Kelly's and Naurin's proposals appear to be the most promising and moreover, from a certain perspective, they seem convergent. Both Kelly and Naurin consider transparency to be part of publicity, with publicity representing a more comprehensive demanding than transparency. For Naurin, publicity demands a real access to information and not only an availability of information, which would characterize transparency. For Kelly, transparency is a necessary but not sufficient condition for public justification, which is here equated with publicity. When Naurin affirms that "publicity [...] is a causal mechanism linking transparency and accountability" (2006: 91), we can sense the idea of public justification, as it is comprised in the notion of accountability, according to Bovens' definition (2007: 450).

Erkkilä's contribution is misleading in the sense that it gives the impression that publicity is the privilege of political spheres. This is refuted by a genealogical approach which confirms that classical economics were engaged in considerations of publicity, as was seen with Jevons' work. As in the case of strictly political matters, that is, administrative actions, the discussion on economic regulations is linked, from the 1980s on, with the concept of "transparency" rather than with the notion of "publicity." Such discussion has continued from the 1980s through today, but the term "transparency" has become ubiquitous. In this contribution, I contest the idea that publicity is the exclusive domain of political actors. Finally, the value of Elster's position consists of highlighting the difficulty of distinguishing both concepts, even though he attempts at making some subtle distinctions.[30]

To conclude, I would like to raise my own contribution with respect to differentiating both notions. As I have laid out, the polyvalence of transparency, which is allowed by its metaphorical character, plays a decisive role. In my view, the "multifunctionality" of transparency constitutes an important appeal, the publicity of which is lacking. Transparency lies in the capacity to absorb numerous virtues or aspirations, such as sincerity, clarity, consistency, truthiness, pureness, and efficiency. Simultaneously, transparency should be able to protect us from diverse and multiple problems, such as ignorance, tyranny, arbitrariness, and inefficiency. It is no exaggeration to say that transparency became, in the second part of the eighteenth century, a political, legal, and moral project, and it remains so today. To achieve such a major ambition, the metaphor of transparency was better qualified than the notion of publicity. However, the outsized expectations associated with transparency may have a flip side. State activities cannot keep up with the hopes and ambitions displayed by transparency simply because "the state is too big, too remote, and too enclosed to be completely visible. The very nature of the state, in other words, creates the conditions of its obscurity" (Fenster 2006: 622–623). That is, transparency and its correlated expectations invariably give rise to disappointment, because transparency as a metaphor applies to "materials," such as institutions, organizations, persons, and behaviors, which, by definition, cannot be transparent.

Works Cited

Baume, Sandrine. 2011. La transparence dans la conduite des affaires publiques. Origines et sens d'une exigence. *Raison publique* (Dossier: transparence). http://www.raison-publique.fr/article459.html. Accessed 10 May 2017.

---

[30] "There does not seem to be a well-established distinction between publicity and transparency as features of decision-making processes" (Elster 2013: 10, n. 41).

———. 2013. Exposer les affaires publiques au regard des citoyens: les raisons justificatives du principe de transparence. In *La transparence en Suisse et dans le monde. Contributions à l'action publique*, ed. M. Pasquier, 3–18. Lausanne: PPUR.

Baume, Sandrine and Yannis Papadopoulos. 2018. Transparency: From Bentham's Inventory of Virtuous Effects to Contemporary Evidence-Based Scepticism. *Critical Review of International Social and Political Philosophy* 21 (2): 169–192.

Bentham, Jeremy. 1843. Principles of Judicial Procedure, with the Outlines of a Procedure Code. In *The Works of Jeremy Bentham*, ed. J. Bowring, vol. 2, 1838–1843. Edinburgh: William Tait.

———. 1962. Constitutional Code [1843]. In *The Works of Jeremy Bentham*, ed. J. Bowring, vol. 9. New York: Russell & Russell.

———. 1983. Constitutional Code [1843]. In *The Collected Works of Jeremy Bentham*, ed. F. Rosen and J.H. Burns, vol. 1. Oxford: Clarendon Press.

———. 1989. *First Principles Preparatory to Constitutional Code*. Ed. P. Schofield. Oxford: Clarendon Press.

———. 1990. *Securities against Misrule and other Constitutional Writings for Tripoli and Greece*. Ed. P. Schofield. Oxford: Clarendon Press.

———. 1999. Of Publicity. In *Political Tactics*, ed. J.C. Blamires, 29–44. Oxford: Clarendon Press.

Bovens, Mark. 2007. Analysing and Assessing Accountability: A Conceptual Framework. *European Law Journal* 13 (4): 447–468.

Bredin, Jean-Denis. 2001. Secret, transparence et démocratie. *Pouvoirs* 97: 5–15.

Buijze, Anoeska. 2013. The Six Faces of Transparency. *Utrecht Law Review* 9 (3): 3–25.

Constant, Benjamin. 1980. *Les principes de politique*. Ed. Etienne Hoffmann. Genève: Droz.

———. 1988. Principles of Politics Applicable to all Representative Governments. In *Political Writings*, trans. and ed. B. Fontana, 169–305. Cambridge: Cambridge University Press.

Cutler, Fred. 1999. Jeremy Bentham and the Public Opinion Tribunal. *The Public Opinion Quarterly* 63 (3): 321–346.

Den Boer, Monica. 1998. Steamy Windows: Transparency and Openness in Justice and Home Affairs. In *Openness and Transparency in the European Union*, ed. V. Deckmyn and I. Thomson, 91–105. Maastricht: European Institute of Public Administration.

Eigeldinger, Frédéric, and Raymond Trousson, eds. 1996. *Dictionnaire de Jean-Jacques Rousseau*. Paris: Honoré Champion.
Elster, Jon. 2013. *Securities Against Misrule. Juries, Assemblies, Elections*. Cambridge: Cambridge University Press.
Erkkilä, Tero. 2012. *Government Transparency. Impacts and Unintended Consequences*. New York: Palgrave Macmillan.
Federal Act on Freedom of Information in the Administration of 17 December 2004 (Status as of 19 August 2014, Swiss Confederation).
Fenster, Mark. 2006. The Opacity of Transparency. *Iowa Law Review* 91: 885–949.
Foucault, Michel. 1980. The Eye of Power. In *Power/Knowledge: Selected Interviews & Other Writings 1972–1977*, ed. C. Gordon, 146–165. New York: Pantheon Books.
Gosseries, Axel. 2010. Publicity. In *The Stanford Encyclopedia of Philosophy*, ed. E.N. Zalt. http://plato.stanford.edu/archives/fall2010/entries/publicity/. Accessed 27 Apr 2017.
Habermas, Jürgen. 1991 [1963]. *The Structural Transformation of the Public Sphere. An Inquiry into a Category of Bourgeois Society*. Cambridge, MA: MIT Press.
Hammann, Christine. 2006. Rousseau citant le Tasse, ou les séductions de l'artifice. *Dix-huitième siècle* 1 (38): 511–528.
Hood, Christopher. 2001. Transparency. In *Encyclopedia of Democratic Thought*, ed. Paul Barry Clark and Joe Foweraker, 700–704. London: Routledge.
Jevons, William Stanley. 1888 [1871]. Theory of Exchange (chap. IV). In *The Theory of Political Economy*, Library of Economics and Liberty. http://www.econlib.org/library/YPDBooks/Jevons/jvnPE4.html. Accessed 10 May 2017.
Kant, Immanuel. 1983. *Perpetual Peace and Other Essays on Politics, History, and Moral*, translated with an introduction by Ted Humphrey. Indianapolis and Cambridge: Hackett Publishing Company.
———. 1992. *Der Streit der Fakultäten/The Conflict of the Faculties*. Lincoln, NE: University of Nebraska Press.
Kelly, E.I. 2013. Publicity. *The International Encyclopedia of Ethics*, 1–8.
Koselleck, Reinhart. 1988 [1959]. *Critique and Crisis: Enlightenment and the Pathogenesis of Modern Society*. Cambridge, MA: MIT Press.
———. 1997. *L'expérience de l'histoire*. Paris: Seuil/Gallimard.
Koselleck, Reinhart, Brunner Otto, and Werner Conze, eds. 1972–1997. *Geschichtliche Grundbegriffe. Historisches Lexikon zur politisch-sozialen Sprache in Deutschland*. Stuttgart: Ernst Klett/J.G. Gotta.
Lord, Kristin M. 2006. *The Perils and Promise of Global Transparency*. New York: Suny Press.

Lupia, Arthur. 2003. Delegation and its Perils. In *Delegation and Accountability in Parliamentary Democracies*, ed. Kaare Strøm, Wolfgang C. Müller, and Torbjörn Bergen, 33–54. Oxford: Oxford University Press.

Meijer, Albert. 2013. Understanding the Complex Dynamics of Transparency. *Public Administration Review* 73 (3): 429–439.

Moser, Cornelia. 2001. *How Open Is "Open as Possible"? Three Different Approaches to Transparency and Openness in Regulating Access to EU Documents*. Political Science Series no. 80, Institute for Advanced Studies [working paper].

Nadeau, Christian. 2013. *L'histoire comme construction politique. Une lecture croisée de Reinhart Koselleck et Quentin Skinner*. http://www.creum.umontreal.ca/IMG/pdf/nadeau.pdf. Accessed 10 May 2017.

Naurin, Daniel. 2006. Transparency, Publicity, Accountability—The Missing Links. *Swiss Political Science Review* 12 (3): 90–98.

Oliver, Richard W. 2004. *What Is Transparency?* New York: McGraw-Hill.

Prat, Andrea. 2006. The More Closely We Are Watched, the Better We Behave? In *Transparency: The Key to Better Governance?* ed. C. Hood and D. Heald, 91–103. Oxford: Oxford University Press.

Rasmusen, Eric. 1989. *Games and Information: An Introduction to Game Theory*. Oxford: Blackwell.

Richir, Marc. 1973 [1793]. Révolution et transparence sociale. In *Considérations sur la Révolution française*, ed. Johann Gottlieb Fichte, 7–74. Paris: Payot.

Rousseau, Jean-Jacques. 1981 [1959]. Les Confessions. In *Œuvres complètes de Jean-Jacques Rousseau*, vol. I, 1–656. Paris: Gallimard.

———. 1990. *Rousseau. Judge of Jean-Jacques: Dialogues*. Hanover and London: University Press of New England.

———. 1997. Considerations on the Government of Poland. In *The Social Contract and other Later Political Writings*, translated and ed. Victor Gourevitch, 177–211. Cambridge: Cambridge University Press.

Starobinski, Jean. 1988. *Transparency and Obstruction*. Chicago and London: The University of Chicago Press.

Wahnich, Sophie. 1997. *L'impossible citoyen. L'étranger dans le discours de la Révolution française*. Paris: Albin Michel.

Regulation and Transparency as Rituals of Distrust: Reading Niklas Luhmann Against the Grain

Caspar Hirschi

> *In contrast to the course of ritual, which is without alternative, it is characteristic of procedures that the uncertainty over their outcome and its consequences and the openness of alternative behaviors are included...*
> Niklas Luhmann, Legitimation durch Verfahren *(1969)*

Whenever something scandalous unfolds in public life today, calls for tighter regulation and more transparency are part of the routine reaction by journalists and politicians. Both demands are coupled with the promise of more comprehensive procedures that will help to restore public trust and prevent similar scandals in the future. In this sense, regulation and transparency are advocated as different means for similar ends. This chapter shares the view of a functional equivalence between regulation and transparency. However, it argues that their functioning is to be seen

---

C. Hirschi (✉)
University of St. Gallen, St. Gallen, Switzerland
e-mail: caspar.hirschi@unisg.ch

© The Author(s) 2018
E. Alloa, D. Thomä (eds.), *Transparency, Society and Subjectivity*,
https://doi.org/10.1007/978-3-319-77161-8_11

less as a set of procedures to rebuild trustworthiness than as a set of rituals to express systemic distrust. In other words, this chapter suggests that regulation and transparency perpetuate and aggravate the problems which they are supposed to resolve.

The argument is made through a critical reading of two dated yet seminal studies published in quick succession by the German sociologist Niklas Luhmann: *Vertrauen* (1968; translated into English as *Trust and Power*) and *Legitimation durch Verfahren* (1969 [*Legitimation Through Procedure*]).

Trust in Trust

Luhmann's interest in trust was guided by the assumption that instead of losing significance over the course of modernization, trust had in fact become more significant.[1] Or as Luhmann's convoluted style put it:

> So it is not to be expected that scientific and technological development will bring events under control, substituting mastery over things for trust as a social mechanism and thus making it unnecessary. Instead, one should expect trust to be increasingly in demand as a means of enduring the complexity of the future, which technology will generate.[2]

This passage sheds preliminary light on Luhmann's approach. It describes a process that Luhmann expects, despite its being incomplete at the moment, to become more prominent in future. It also represents a theory of civilizational progress that Luhmann associates with an increase in technocratic complexity. Moreover, it rejects the technocratic expectation that modernization will, thanks to the rationality of scientific

---

[1] Some of the following reflections have appeared in my essays (Hirschi 2015, 2014a, 2014b, 2016).

[2] (Luhmann 1973b: 15–16) German original: "Demnach ist nicht zu erwarten, dass das Fortschreiten der technisch-wissenschaftlichen Zivilisation die Ereignisse unter Kontrolle bringen und Vertrauen als sozialen Mechanismus durch Sachbeherrschung ersetzen und erübrigen werde. Eher wird man damit rechnen müssen, dass Vertrauen mehr und mehr in Anspruch genommen werden muss, damit technisch erzeugte Komplexität der Zukunft ertragen werden kann" (Luhmann 1973a: 17).

methods, lead to better control of social and individual processes. "Trust," for Luhmann, describes an anti-technocratic category that is intended to highlight society's inability to cope with more complexity with the help of greater rationality.[3] To reduce complexity, and thus to remain capable of action, society must adapt archaic judgment and decision techniques to the conditions of modern life. Luhmann considers trust to be such an archaic technique. He also regards establishing trust in and through procedures as the successful adjustment of this technique to the challenges of modern complexity.

But how does trust work? Luhmann's definition at the end of his study stresses the contrast with the standards of scientific epistemology:

> Trust reduces social complexity by going beyond available information and generalizing expectations of behavior in that it replaces missing information with an internally guaranteed security. It thus remains dependent on other reduction mechanisms developed in parallel with it, for example those of law, of organization and, of course, those of language, but cannot, however, be reduced to them.[4]

As such, trust is always "beyond explanation" (*unbegründbar*) and needs to be understood as "a blending of knowledge and ignorance" (Luhmann 1973b: 26). If trust functions as the bets hedged by optimistic everyday gamblers, it makes little sense at first sight to think of it as a crucial device for orienting behavior in modern society, which is subject to unprecedented change. "Overdrawing" (*Überziehen*) existing information seems more hazardous, the more quickly information loses validity; just as "generalizing" expectations about behavior becomes more awkward, the less stable and conforming behavior is.

---

[3] Jürgen Habermas is mistaken in criticizing Luhmann's systems theory as an "advanced technocratic consciousness" while at the same time attacking his functionalist affirmation of the existing social order. The particularity of Luhmann's theory rather seems to be that it is both functionalist and anti-technocratic (Habermas 1971: 145).

[4] (Luhmann 1973b: 93) German original: "Vertrauen reduziert soziale Komplexität dadurch, daß es vorhandene Informationen überzieht und Verhaltenserwartungen generalisiert, indem es fehlende Information durch eine intern garantierte Sicherheit ersetzt. Es bleibt dabei auf andere, parallel ausgebildete Reduktionsleistungen angewiesen, zum Beispiel auf die des Rechts, der Organisation und natürlich auf die der Sprache, kann aber nicht auf sie zurückgeführt werden" (Luhmann 1973a: 105).

Luhmann's contrast between "simple" and "complex" social systems takes this into account. Under simple conditions, trust (*Vertrauen*) arises directly from familiarity (*Vertrautheit*) with the social surroundings:

> Familiarity in this sense makes it possible to entertain relatively reliable expectations and, as a consequence, to contain the remaining elements of risk as well. In itself, however, familiarity denotes neither favorable nor unfavorable expectations, but the conditions under which both are rendered possible. Familiarity is the precondition for trust as well as distrust, i.e. for every sort of commitment to a particular attitude towards the future.[5]

In more complex societies, however, the relative lack of precisely this type of familiarity demands a more abstract form of trust. Luhmann concludes:

> Yet the very complexity of the social order creates a greater need for coordination and hence a need to determine the future—i.e. a need for trust, a need which is now decreasingly met by familiarity. Under these circumstances, familiarity and trust must seek a new mutually stabilizing relationship which is no longer grounded in a world which is immediately experienced, assured by tradition, and close at hand. Assurance for such a relationship can no longer be provided by shutting strangers, enemies, and the unfamiliar outside some boundary. History then ceases to be remembrance of things experienced and is instead simply a predetermined structure which is the basis for trust in social systems.[6]

Luhmann explains the transformation of trust in terms of the standard formula of his modernization theory. If "personal trust" exists on the level

---

[5] (Luhmann 1973b: 19) German original: "Vertrautheit in diesem Sinne ermöglicht relativ sicheres Erwarten und damit auch ein Absorbieren verbleibender Risiken, ist aber selbst weder günstige noch ungünstige Erwartung, sondern Bedingung der Möglichkeit für beides. Vertrautheit ist Voraussetzung für Vertrauen wie für Mißtrauen, das heißt für jede Art des Sichengagierens in eine bestimmte Einstellung zur Zukunft" (Luhmann 1973a: 19).

[6] (Luhmann 1973b: 20) German original: "Vertrautheit und Vertrauen müssen unter diesen Umständen ein neues Verhältnis wechselseitiger Stabilisierung suchen, das nicht mehr in der unmittelbar erlebbaren, traditional bestimmten Nachwelt gründet, also nicht mehr durch eine Grenze zum Unvertrauten und daher Fremden und Feindlichen abgesichert werden kann. Geschichte kann dann nicht mehr als erinnerbare Erfahrung, sondern nur noch als schon entschiedene Struktur sozialer Systeme Vertrauensgrundlage sein" (Luhmann 1973a:. 21).

of an everyday familiarity with the world, and if social complexity increases, then this familiarity transforms into a "new kind of trust in systems." This, in turn, helps to reduce increased complexity again. Systemic trust is oriented not only toward social systems, but also toward humans as "personal systems." Thus, change concerns less the objects of trust than its foundations—there is a shift "from bases of trust which are defined in primarily emotional terms to those which are primarily presentational."[7]

What this might mean in more concrete terms can be devised in Luhmann's follow-up study *Legitimation durch Verfahren*, "Legitimation Through Procedure," where he specifies the functioning of modern trust with respect to the procedural character of decision-making processes. The book focuses on administrative procedures, first those at court, second those in politics. It almost entirely ignores scientific procedures, which is not quite unproblematic for his argumentation, as I shall show below. A further problem to be explored more closely is Luhmann's indifference towards the costs that its faith in procedure incurs for modern society. Ultimately, this raises the question as to whether, under certain conditions, procedures do not tend to increase rather than reduce complexity. Luhmann's indifference might be related to the fact that in the late 1960s these problems were still less evident than, say, since the sovereign debt crisis of 2008. In effect, however, this indifference stems from a particular feature of Luhmann's thinking, which Jürgen Habermas has aptly pointed out (Habermas 1971: 160–167): Luhmann cultivates an affirmative functionalism, in which everything in society is supposed to make social sense. Thus, he barely considers the possibility of modern "achievements" that produce chronic dysfunctions by serving particular interests while harming society as a whole.

As in his theory of trust, Luhmann grounds his concept of procedure on his hypothesis about the nature of historical development. However, he dates the crucial transition earlier—approximately at a stage when "archaic law" was replaced by "the law of early modern high culture." (As the corresponding footnote suggests, this would correspond to Greek

---

[7] (Luhmann 1973b: 22) German original: "Übergehen von primär emotionalen zu primär darstellungsgebundenen Vertrauensgrundlagen." (Luhmann 1973a: 23).

antiquity.) Luhmann associates this transition with the assertion of new decision structures: the ritual invocation of a "supernatural decision" yielded to codified procedures, which began with "open-ended possibilities" and resulted in binding decisions (Luhmann 1983: 40). Luhmann's next sentence explains on a theoretical level what this historical change means:

> In contrast to the course of ritual, which is without alternative, it is characteristic of procedures that the uncertainty over their outcome and its consequences and the openness of alternative behaviors are included and dealt with in the context of action and its motivational structures. Not the predefined concrete form, gesture, the correct word drive a procedure, but the selective decisions of those involved. These decisions eliminate alternatives, reduce complexity, absorb uncertainty, or transform the undefined complexity of all possibilities into a definable, graspable problematic. (Luhmann 1983: 40)

Thus, procedure is also reined in by systems theory. Yet how, then, is procedure related to trust in its modern form of "systemic trust"? For Luhmann, the answer—at least in 1969—is irritatingly simple: procedures themselves are social systems even if they are of limited duration. Luhmann's explanation, which somewhat contradicts his later systems theory, is that procedures represent "a complexity-reducing context of action" (Luhmann 1983: 41). In this logic, trusting procedures inevitably assume the character of systemic trust, which emerges from procedures that offer both participants and observers the opportunity to anticipate and to reconstruct decision processes.

For Luhmann, "how" decisions occur is crucial, rather than "what" they entail. Administrative procedures do not promise greater rationality in his eyes, but simply greater legitimacy of the decisions taken. It is an "illusion," he argues, to "interpret" the establishment of procedures "as a means of establishing the truth." It is also characteristic that, historically, he attributes this illusion to "the fact that the Enlightenment typically underestimated the problem of complexity" (Luhmann 1983: 26). Luhmann thus remains faithful to his anti-technocratic stance, which he had already adopted in his theory of trust.

Trust, Procedures, Legitimation

Soon after the publication of *Legitimation durch Verfahren*, Luhmann's stance faced staunch criticism, especially from lawyers and legal philosophers. This was hardly surprising given that he explained his theory of procedure in terms of court practice. In his preface to the new edition of *Legitimation durch Verfahren* (1975), Luhmann firmly rejected his critics' argument that the legitimacy of procedures could not be divorced from the epistemic quality of decisions (Luhmann 1975: 1–8). Yet no matter how expertly he defended his theory, his functionalism, which is characteristically devoid of any content, is not quite without pitfalls. It can be upheld only by the radical separation of administrative procedures from scientific ones. Thus, while the former establish legitimacy, the latter establish truth. Although this functional distinction is central to Luhmann's account, he never works it out in explicit detail. Besides, it is fairly unconvincing, from both a historical perspective and a sociological one. Court proceedings are first and foremost epistemic procedures, especially in criminal law: they establish justice by producing the greatest possible truth, and do so by deploying an evidential machinery that is constantly rearmed on epistemic grounds. Vice versa, scientific procedures also produce legitimation to an outstanding degree: they build trust by representing epistemological work as a systematic, entirely rationalized process and by glossing over any potential uncontrollability and coincidence, improvisation, and bricolage. Both historically and typologically, administrative and scientific procedures are more closely entwined than Luhmann's theory alleges.

A strong indication in this respect is that one particular feature of administrative procedures becomes difficult to explain if their epistemic function is denied. This, as the example of court evidence has suggested, is their structural instability. This results from their constant urge to change procedural processes. Ever since procedures have existed, they have been refashioned and expanded with the promise of "better" decisions. To this extent, their legitimation inevitably depends on how those directly involved, those affected, and those observing gauge the quality of decisions based on the existing procedure. Yet this does not mean, as some of Luhmann's critics believe, that decisions based on procedures are "objectively" better than others. It merely suggests that social belief in the qualitative superiority of procedures is needed for them to emerge in the first place, and for them to endure. This premise, however, foregrounds questions that are only of marginal interest to Luhmann's "complexity-reducing reductionism." Foremost among these questions is whether, from a certain vantage point, unquestioned faith in procedures re-ritualizes decision-making structures. This may happen because systems that neither need to nor are able to apply procedures simulate these to legitimate themselves or because quality issues not stemming from how procedures are organized are covered up by their reorganization. I shall return to this point after considering another illuminating aspect of Luhmann's theory of procedure.

Luhmann maintains that if trust in procedure is underpinned by the predictability of the decision process, while the content of a decision remains uncertain, then this is associated with a precise expectation about how those involved ought to behave: they occupy specific, clearly distinct roles; and although these roles are not entirely detached from the available possibilities for action beyond the procedure, they are nevertheless clearly distinct. The more important the autonomy of a procedure is, the stricter the role requirements are. Criteria such as impartiality and independence serve to minimize environmental influences on decision making. They prevent conflicts of interest among those involved, that is, the possible impairment of internal roles by external ones. At the same time, roles can restrict the possibilities for action available to their bearers beyond a procedure. For instance, it is difficult to participate in a procedural decision only to subsequently mount public opposition against it.[8]

On the subject of role consistency, Luhmann, for once, becomes quite specific. Considering the role of judges, he observes: "The representation of a procedure must rule out from the outset that the judge all of a sudden behaves like a dentist or the summoned party like a lottery-ticket seller" (Luhmann 1983: 92). The same applies to electoral processes: "In an election, a voter does not primarily behave as if he were a hairdresser, a

---

[8] Drawing on Luhmann, Barbara Stollberg-Rilinger offers a general explanation of this issue in her introduction (Stollberg-Rilinger 2010: 9–31, esp. 11).

husband, a stamp collector, or a Methodist. For instance, he cannot contribute to the election by offering to cut the candidates' hair or to pray for them, but remains bound to the role of the voter" (Luhmann 1983: 48). Although this may sound banal at first sight, the opposite is true: accepting a role not only involves (outwardly) fulfilling the associated behavioral expectations, but also (inwardly) adopting the corresponding behavioral norms. A defense lawyer who does not feel compelled to achieve the best possible verdict for his client undermines the legitimacy of court proceedings. The same is true of a university professor who selects his or her preferred candidate ahead of the actual appointment procedure. Each procedure involves a certain course of events and a certain code of conduct. It has both a collective component, which applies to all involved actors, and an individual one, which defines role-specific requirements. Common to all roles is that they require those involved to take an intrinsic interest in the matter under discussion. Equally fundamental is the attitude that a decision will be taken, but that no one knows in advance which one it will be.[9]

Knowing in advance that a decision will be taken while not knowing its content ensures that the procedure is synchronized with the decision process (Luhmann 1983: 3). Luhmann speaks of "synchronization" to highlight the fact that formal and actual decision-making need not be identical. In itself, this distinction is normative because it delimits a range of tolerance for informal action in procedures that, at least presumably, does not affect legitimating a decision. At the same time, it makes intuitive sense, since there is little to suggest that a decision process functions exactly as staged by the respective procedure. Even scientific experiments, which enjoy a particular status of accuracy due to the reproducibility requirement to which their results are subject, require the involved scientists to possess a high level of improvisational judgment—also because deciding when an experiment ends proves difficult in procedural terms.[10]

The range of tolerance between formal and informal decision-making increases the flexibility of those involved, and at best enhances procedural efficiency. Yet efficiency arguments alone do not suffice to explain this

---

[9] See also Luhmann's more specific assertions (Luhmann 1983: 51).
[10] For a classic study on late modern physics (Galison 1987).

range, or else one would need to assume that formal structures align themselves with informal processes. The legitimizing function of procedures, at which Luhmann's argumentation is actually aimed, is probably far more important. It implies that decisions are not simply produced in procedures, but are also represented therein (Stollberg-Rilinger 2010: 11). This dual function becomes even more pronounced the more procedures are conducted in public. In terms of a theory of legitimation, representation forces actors to engage in a formality of procedures that is not absolutely necessary for their establishment. Strikingly, however, Luhmann's treatment of representation separates this problem from the range of tolerance between formal and informal decision-making. In fact, he gives the latter very short shrift: the more the normative range of tolerance is exceeded, the more procedure congeals in ritual. It celebrates a decision that has been taken beyond its procedures. Luhmann cites two characteristic examples: political elections "involving a predefined single list of candidates" and "show trials" (Luhmann 1983: 51). These examples are significant because Luhmann pushes the problem of re-ritualized procedures behind the Iron Curtain instead of treating it as an integral part of his history of modernization in the Western world.

Legitimation by Procedural Rhetoric: The Case of Regulation

Luhmann's theoretical substantiation and ideological strengthening of procedural trust helps us to grasp the scale of the problems associated with the re-ritualization of procedures. Modern society involves an array of professions whose representatives live on this trust. Over the last three centuries, the demand for these professions has moved only in one direction: sharply upwards. Typologically, they can be divided into two groups. First, administrators and regulators, that is, procedural meta-practitioners, who apply their procedures to extraneous procedures so as to monitor processes, verify results, and enforce improvements. Second, public commentators, who appear in procedures as second-order actors: they react to, and act back on, procedures through the media. Both groups strive to maintain trust in procedures at a high level for various reasons. Moreover, they both contribute unintentionally to the ritualization of procedures. Considering each of these groups separately helps to understand how exactly they achieve their particular effects.

Let us begin with supervisory and administrative authorities: their professional capital stems largely from the legal sciences; wherever these authorities are active, work routines are permeated by the law. Historically, this professional group spearheaded the expansion of state power while at the same time it functioned as a job-creation cartel for the legal profession.[11] This group meanwhile feels equally comfortable in state regulatory bodies as in the "compliance" divisions of private enterprises. Its expansive force results largely from the fact that its representatives have turned a systemic contradiction into a strength: they appear as independent authorities whenever the concrete outcomes of their regulated procedures are concerned; at the same time, however, they have vested interests in the general status of procedures. Waning systemic trust in procedures clouds their professional prospects. This requires such authorities to always react to procedural problems in the same way: with new procedures. "New" as a rule means more elaborate and more intense monitoring, which keeps the self-regulated spiral of expansion turning. Here, then, complexity is increased, not reduced.

This is how this professional group contributes to the ritualization of procedures. The more complex the procedures, the greater the incentive to subvert them. Executing actors may consider it more efficient to cancel elaborate procedures through informal decision-making and to maintain the respective procedure merely as an apparent legitimation than to execute it within a normative range of tolerance. In such cases, the executors' systemic trust is too weak for these actors to feel obligated by the procedural code of conduct. At the same time, the regulators' systemic trust is too strong to abolish the dysfunctional procedure. Accordingly, ritualization involves a discrepancy in trust between regulators and executors. For the regulatory authority, a conflict exists between system needs and actor

---

[11] A current example is the SEC (U.S. Securities and Exchange Commission), which regulates US financial services providers and is run almost entirely by lawyers whereas the few economists in the authority are marginalized (Macey 2013: 270).

interests. An obvious solution presents itself to the authority: namely, to take disciplinary action by enforcing stricter regulations. The procedure must now also offset the diminished trust in its executors. It becomes a compensatory instrument, and as such further accelerates ritualization. The regulatory authorities maneuver themselves into a dilemma with no predefined way out. Their role as meta-practitioners requires regulators to assert new procedural modalities and processes while this leads to cancelling a basic condition for procedures to succeed: its executors' intrinsic motivation to fulfill the existing procedural norms.

Enforced procedures almost inevitably resemble ritual acts of compensation for systemic failure. What Luhmann projects onto Eastern bloc dictatorships is just as much to be verified in Western democracies, although in a different guise. What may seem to be a new problem in light of the regulatory frenzy that erupted after the collapse of the financial sector in 2008 has actually been a constant companion of modern government interventions based on the violation of the same, simple principle: any new procedural structure requires a corresponding procedural culture to fulfill the expectations placed on it. Yet since cultural change is less governable, and occurs more sluggishly in the wake of great pressure for reform than the implementation of structural measures, regulators and administrators soon struggle with the unintended consequences of their own attempts at reform. For as long as their own procedural trust does not suffer, it does not end.

This process, to cite a prominent example, is currently in full swing as regulators attempt to tame the international financial industry. Public confidence in regulatory authorities such as the U.S. Securities and Exchange Commission (SEC) still seems greater than in the regulated corporations. Nevertheless, a growing number of specialists monitoring developments in the financial industry are warning against the inefficiency and instability of a system whose lost reputation has been replaced with regulations. The economist Jonathan Macey, for instance, has criticized regulatory bodies for establishing a surveillance apparatus that their limited resources are unable to control and for therefore resorting to the symbolic policy of setting warning examples in court that are geared towards attracting media attention. In the meantime, says Macey, the regulated corporations have been relieved of the burden to cultivate their image and can now pawn their ruined reputations to pursue their business interests even more ruthlessly.[12]

Transparency as Media Ritual

How does this compare to the ritualization effect of the media on procedures? Although other forces, actors, and institutions are involved than in the regulatory spiral, the structural consequences of these processes are identical. Transparency and regulation both place the actors involved in a procedure under close external scrutiny. Such monitoring tries to prize open the "black box" of the respective procedure and to control the authorized decision-makers. The latter feel less observed by the other actors involved in the procedure than by external, unknown ones, whose actions are barely observable. From an internal perspective, this alienates the respective procedure, and thereby makes it more difficult for actors to detach their procedural role from their other social roles. Their scope for autonomous action within the procedure dwindles. Tim Neu has aptly described the effect of this process: "When a division of roles becomes impossible, genuine openness about decisions is perilous, which explains why decision-making is outsourced and why procedures are even less able to establish legitimation" (Neu 2014).

Turning to the media, whereas Luhmann detects a potential conflict for orderly procedure, he does not associate this with the threat of ritualization. This might be due to his concentration on court proceedings. The problems of media coverage, as highlighted in *Legitimation durch Verfahren*, are characteristic of the courts—from the flurry of camera-bulb flashes through the rush to judgment to the public criticism of verdicts (Luhmann 1983: 124–130). Luhmann tries to defuse the problems through positing normative media guidelines, thereby revealing that he does not consider such strictures to pose a systemic threat to administrative procedures. It is difficult to say whether he still held this

---

[12] See Macey's final chapter, "Regulation: The New Secular Religion." His analysis of the current state of affairs is stronger than his historical model, which rests on the past utopia of a financial market that exists beyond regulatory pressure because cultivating corporate reputation was the basis of all economic success (Macey 2013: 269–275).

view after 1969. In his late study *Die Realität der Massenmedien* (1995; translated as *The Reality of the Mass Media*, 2000), Luhmann, who despised television, issued a provocative assertion heavily doused with systems theory: the media construct their own, self-enclosed reality, through which they condition our knowledge of the world. In this respect, he seems to go to the other extreme. Its particular production of reality makes the media system appear so autonomous that it needs to establish a relationship with judicial and political reality only to a limited extent. What we find out via the media scarcely points to external realities: "If we hear that a leading politician has made a decision, we are still far from knowing who has made that decision—with the exception of Lady Thatcher, perhaps" (Luhmann 1995: 31). If reality is so pluralistic, the problem of one system disturbing another from functioning can hardly ever occur.

Luhmann's joke about Margaret Thatcher is well chosen in one respect: especially politics reveals just how the media can transform formal procedures into ritual spectacle. Flying the flag of transparency, the media have gained ever greater access to political bodies in recent decades. They have not, however, delivered on their promise to provide the wider public with better insights into political decision-making. The advent of "transparent" politics led to consultation processes being ousted from political committees. The presence of the media restricts what can be said to such an extent that the precept of political acumen demands that such processes be separated from formal procedures so as to safeguard a solid basis for decision-making.

This process no longer merely concerns the parliamentary institution, the first to transform into a deliberative body without a deliberative function. Expert committees have undergone a similar process in recent decades. Especially their deliberations and recommendations on controversial and hence media-hyped issues like gene technology, drug use, or nuclear energy seldom serve political decision-making any longer (Hirschi 2012). Instead they are used more than ever to retroactively legitimate decisions. In such cases, the function of expert committees is confined to politicians on camera being able to claim "expert-based" action for measures decided on without consulting the respective committee. Whenever such a system is well established, politicians in need of real advice must seek it through informal channels. This sets the course for old-style European cabinet politics to re-establish itself behind the curtains of a glossy political stage under constant media scrutiny.

Now, political procedures deprived of decision processes due to the media's creation of transparency might be expected to sooner or later also lose their public legitimation. Yet this hardly seems to be the case so far. How come? Presumably, this is due mostly to the functional logic of political media coverage. The historical and ideological point of reference for the media's campaign for transparency is the Enlightenment's aspiration to bring the actions of political decision-makers before the tribunal of public reason. This initiated the role of the public critic. The powerful promise of the eighteenth century was that reading newspapers and journals would enable citizens to pass qualified judgment on their government's achievements while politicians would, in turn, be encouraged to engage in politics in order to serve the citizenry. The Enlightenment promise rested on a particular ideology of progress: a public sphere constructed by critical media would bring forth greater reasonability and better decision-making abilities. What could have been better suited to bestowing credibility on this ideology than presenting public criticism as a well-ordered, rule-governed process? This purpose was achieved by hailing the public as a tribunal endowed with universal jurisdiction, where publicists would act as prosecutors or defense counsels, and the enlightened readership as the highest judicial authority. This picture gave the criticism voiced in the media the semblance of orderliness and fairness, and thus contributed largely to its political legitimation. However, the court metaphor was never particularly well suited to describing its functioning. Media assessments of political processes do not follow predefined steps, but may instead cover the entire spectrum from uncontrolled lynching through circumspect deliberation to heavily ritualized celebration. Just as little does the public possess the necessary homogeneity and sovereignty to reach conclusive verdicts in its judicial capacity. What emerges is a paradoxical constellation: although the language of judicial proceedings is applied to a sphere of action that eludes procedure-based organization, it still has a legitimizing effect. In a critical addendum to Luhmann, I therefore suggest that we speak of trust through procedural rhetoric.

This background makes it easier to understand why the media-generated ritualization of political procedures must receive equally media-generated legitimation. In Western democracies, procedural credibility is a constituent element of political reporting. Media culture functions according to a dual procedural principle, which applies both to the objects and to the subjects of reporting: politicians must take decisions based on transparent procedures while media professionals must verify these decisions based on critical procedures. Were the media to address its own ritualization effects, it would undermine its own legitimacy. Commentators on camera and editors in newsrooms—no matter how level-headed they might be in private—are therefore forced to continue staging the political theatre as if its main events take place in front of rather than behind the (media) scenes.

In light of this systemic coercion, I reach a different conclusion than Luhmann: When it comes to transparency, legitimation emerges from rituals that simulate procedures and thereby reduce complexity to the point of rejecting reality. At least the more naive souls among the media are likely to closely resemble the duped deceiver, who plays his role so well because he fails to recognize its political function.

Translated by Mark Kyburz

Works Cited

Galison, Peter. 1987. *How Experiments End*. Chicago: University of Chicago Press.

Habermas, Jürgen (1971) "Theorie der Gesellschaft oder Sozialtechnologie? Eine Auseinandersetzung mit Niklas Luhmann" in *Theorie der Gesellschaft oder Sozialtechnologie*. ed. Habermas, Jürgen. and Niklas Luhmann, Frankfurt/M.: Suhrkamp: 142–290.

Hirschi, Caspar. 2012. Moderne Eunuchen? Offizielle Experten im 18. und im 21. Jahrhundert. In *Wissen, maßgeschneidert. Die Geburt des Experten in der Vormoderne*, ed. Frank Rexroth and others, 290–328. München: Oldenbourg.

———. 2014a. Colberts Vertrauen in Verfahren. Bausteine für eine andere Modernisierungstheorie. *Aufklärung* 26: 259–289.

———. 2014b. Transparenz ist nur eine andere Form von Intransparenz. *Frankfurter Allgemeine Zeitung*, January 8, NR 6.

―――. 2015. Transparenz als Verschleierungsritual. Niklas Luhmanns Aktualität in der Finanzkrise. In *Auf die Wirklichkeit zeigen. Zum Problem der Evidenz in den Kulturwissenschaften*, ed. Helmuth Lethen and others, 394–403. Frankfurt/M.: Campus.

―――. 2016. Komplexität durch Verfahren. Niklas Luhmanns Aktualität in der Finanzkrise. http://www.theorieblog.de/index.php/2014/02/komplexitaet-durch-verfahren-niklas-luhmanns-aktualitaet-in-der-finanzkrise/. Accessed 16 Jun 2017.

Luhmann, Niklas. 1973a. *Vertrauen. Ein Mechanismus der Reduktion sozialer Komplexität*. Stuttgart: Ferdinand Enke.

―――. 1973b [1979]. *Trust and Power*. Transl. Howard Davis and others. Chichester etc.: Wiley.

―――. 1975. *Legitimation durch Verfahren*. Frankfurt/Main: Suhrkamp.

―――. 1983. *Legitimation durch Verfahren*. Frankfurt/Main: Suhrkamp.

―――. 1995 [2000]. *The Reality of the Mass Media*. Transl. Kathleen Gross. Stanford: Stanford UP.

Macey, Jonathan. 2013. *The Death of Corporate Reputation. How Integrity Has Been Destroyed on Wall Street*. Upper Saddle River, NJ: FT Press.

Neu, Tim. 2014. Verstrickt und verkoppelt—Rituelle Verfahren. https://www.theorieblog.de/index.php/2014/12/verstrickt-und-verkoppelt-rituelle-verfahren/. Accessed 16 June 2017.

Stollberg-Rilinger, Barbara. 2010. Einleitung. In *Herstellung und Darstellung von Entscheidungen. Verfahren, Verwalten und Verhandeln in der Vormoderne*, ed. Barbara Stollberg-Rilinger and André Krischer, 9–31. Berlin: Duncker & Humblot.

Not Individuals, Relations: What Transparency Is Really About. A Theory of Algorithmic Governmentality

Thomas Berns

In this paper, I first define the nature of the relationship transparency maintains to the real through which transparency governs, and then in the second section I outline its specificities in terms of the highly symptomatic example of "algorithmic governmentality" (Rouvroy and Berns 2013). On this backdrop, and with the help of Gilbert Simondon, in the third section I will draw on the work of Gilbert Simondon to argue that the new objects of transparency are relations, but only to the degree that these relations, by being objectified, become individual, mechanically repeatable statuses. In other words, Derrida's theory of performativity will help me to explain how these relations are citations without difference.

T. Berns (✉)
Free University of Brussels (ULB), Brussels, Belgium
e-mail: tberns@ulb.ac.be

© The Author(s) 2018
E. Alloa, D. Thomä (eds.), *Transparency, Society and Subjectivity*,
https://doi.org/10.1007/978-3-319-77161-8_12

Governing from the Real

I would like to start by establishing a preliminary, perhaps axiomatic series of paradigm shifts implied by the blurry idea of transparency, in contrast with the more well-defined principle of publicity:

1. Calls for transparency feed into the project of establishing a continuous visibility of the real, whereas the principle of publicity is essentially limited, applies to specific acts and always finds its counterpart in established spaces protected by privacy.
2. Transparency entails a rivalry with the legal norm, which determines what must be public and what must be protected as private.
3. Whereas publicity seeks to limit the forms of domination inherent to political space, transparency appeals directly to actors' goodwill and good sense, as is illustrated by the words of Eric Schmidt, Google's CEO, in an interview with CNBC on the subject of private data under the U.S. PATRIOT Act: "If you have something that you don't want anyone to know, maybe you shouldn't be doing it in the first place."
4. As opposed to publicity, petitions for transparency do not seek to broaden the polemical space of political decision-making, but rather to mitigate it or even to dilute the very idea of decision.
5. With transparency, government no longer seems to be about governing *the* real but governing *from* the real.

To understand this shift in terms of the particular relation a governmental practice entertains with the real, and how this relation ensures government's effectiveness, I would like to lay out three fundamental maneuvers within contemporary normative apparatuses and their adherence to the real, their desire to be expressions of the real:

Firstly, it may appear as if contemporary normative apparatuses were simply intent on naming things and could, as such, be considered technical specifications used to certify things based on their conformity to an ideal definition of an element of our reality. The ISO standard is a patent example of this dynamic, but another one can be found in attempts to standardize therapeutic practices, of which the DSM is an eloquent case. In these instances, the norm is nothing more than a "technical specification [...] the observation of which is not mandatory," but which is approved by an "institution recognized" for its "normative activity".[1] Ideally, norms should just be a matter of saying or recognizing things as they are and not as they should be, so much so that they should become devoid of any coercion.[2]

Secondly, contemporary normative apparatuses call upon their objects (individuals, companies, services, research centers, and so on) to give an account of their own activities. Normative action is most effective when carried out through this act of self-reporting.[3]

Thirdly, contemporary normative apparatuses fit into an actuarial rationality and are often fed, accompanied, justified, reinforced or shaped by statistical techniques. This is even more relevant in light of new statistical techniques resting upon practices of indiscriminate and massive data collection, which *mine* these *Big Data* in such a way the norms produced appear to be the very expressions of the reality they seek to represent. As I will show further on, these procedures seem to be freed of any reference to subjectivity.

Defining the real; inciting everyone to report on their activity; and statistically extracting norms from reality: these are the three fundamental, intertwined symptoms of new forms of normativity (evaluation, ranking, certification, classification, comparison, etc.) through which the norms produced can be conceived as immanent to the real. More broadly speaking, these gestures also give rise to a form of government that appears to be deeply affected by a kind of restraint or limited rationality.[4]

---

[1] Directive 98/34/CE of the European Parliament and Council.
[2] On this point, a comparison between legal acts of qualification and new practices of definition that seek to normalize the real needs to be urgently undertaken.
[3] It would be worth investigating the practice of reporting as underlying a variety of contemporary normative practices in light of the question of avowal or confession. I suggested such an approach in two articles written with G. Jeanmart (Jeanmart and Berns 2009, 2010).
[4] This restraint can be seen as a quest to govern without governing, an idea the origins of which I attempted to unearth in my book *Gouverner sans gouverner. Une archéologie politique de la statistique* (2009).

Paradoxically, this self-effacement somehow lends a powerful intensity and extensiveness to governmental acts in their ability to govern *evermore* and *without end*, in the double meaning of tracing the real without ever giving it a definite shape, but also of governing endlessly.

Before taking this analysis a step further by looking more closely at the third distinctive and fundamental gesture of new normativities, namely quantifying the real, I would like to point out a final, particularly paradoxical characteristic regarding calls for transparency and their difference with the principle of publicity:

6. The discretion of contemporary norms departs from the spirit of publicizing the norm. The apparent triviality of a government limited to perfectly adhering to the real by making it transparent, is accompanied by the ideal of its own invisibility: an efficient norm is one that does not even appear (and thus escapes debate). This is strikingly conveyed by European Commission texts: "The majority of goods and services around us have now been standardized, although this goes largely unnoticed in most cases. Standards are unseen forces that ensure that things work properly."[5] Normative action becomes invisible: it does not think of itself as the result of a decision, nor as the object of a conflict. Fundamentally, all that remains is its technical hold and footing on reality.

Algorithmic Governmentality

To understand this new form of normativity essentially dependent on quantifying the real, which Antoinette Rouvroy and I have called "algorithmic governmentality," its logic can helpfully be broken down into three steps. Of course, this analytical disjunction is artificial: the three phases interact and are all the more efficient precisely because they are intertwined. We will see how, notwithstanding these statistical techniques'

---

[5] Communication of the Commission to the European Council, "Integration of Environmental Aspects into European Standardisation."

extreme personalization, each of these steps seeks to avoid potential frictions with subjects or, rather, implies a rarefaction of subjectivation processes without ever turning into an exercise of violence. This avoidance of subjectivity requires only the most minimal form of reflexivity: a kind of tacit approval from subjects.

The first step revolves around "Big Data," the phenomenon of mass data collection and storage, which gives way to a kind of fragmented doubling of the real perfectly respectful of its heterogeneity. To grasp this phenomenon, I will simply suggest that the data constituting Big Data are neither "given" nor "stolen," two alternatives which presuppose the possibility of consent (in the second case by affirming that consent was disrespected or transgressed). Any reference to truly informed consent is inadequate because the use of the data or the ends that would justify its transmission are unknown, are fundamentally unavailable. Neither given, nor stolen, these data are instead abandoned or left behind. In contrast to a gift or a theft, it seems important to emphasize this idea of abandonment accompanied by an act which consists in *making unavailable* the implicit ends to anything we could call consent. To do so is not so much to bemoan the negation of consent as to reveal a form of tacit approval that appears to be neither consent nor extortion. In other words, we are not faced with the negation of any possible reflexivity, but only with its diminishment. This weakened reflexivity is driven, both in terms of its weakening *and* its residual reflexivity, by the trivial, "raw," heterogeneous character of the data left behind. However, the impossibility of actual consent pushed to the point where even its actual negation is inconceivable is, in the same breath, presented as proof of the data's apparent objectivity. The data's transmission is so involuntary, so fragmented and devoid of meaning that it cannot lie. This is why, even in this first moment of algorithmic governmentality, the possibilities of reflexivity and subjectivation are rarefied and *not* canceled, and why such rarefaction is by the same token proof of the normative process's strength and efficacy.

The second phase is the automated "mining" of these massive quantities of data. *Data mining* aims to statistically extract multiple correlations so as to establish fine-grained profiles. What is important to highlight here is the production of a certain type of knowledge seemingly composed of simple, automatically established correlations.[6] With this production of knowledge *it is as if* preliminary hypotheses were superfluous (and this appears to be even more so the case with *machine learning* practices). Again, we run up against the idea of knowledge that is objective *because* it is protected from subjective interventions (in this instance: formulating hypotheses). Norms (those correlations through which profiles are established) seem to emerge from the real itself, with the greatest *respect* for its variability.

The third moment is linked to the effects these norms have on individual or collective behaviors (insofar as they are related to profiles). I will simply underline that the normativity at stake here consists in ever so subtly acting on the *possible* behaviors of individual or collective subjects by discretely modulating their surrounding *environment*. This modulation is ever less expressed in terms of directly imposed and publicly expressed constraints (as modeled on the legal-discursive norm which intrinsically expects to be disobeyed by foreseeing a punishment).

In the second and third moments of algorithmic governmentality (and I insist once again that the three steps described are intertwined), it is in fact the minimization of any subjective experience that is played out. This minimization ensures the normative process's legitimacy and objectivity as well as its absence of violence or even constraint typical of the law. In this sense, the strength of the normative process unfolding within algorithmic governmentality relies on the presupposition that the real's heterogeneity can be immediately and objectively grasped. The diversity of specific needs can be met and respected precisely because there is a tacit approval to circumvent subjectivity. If indeed there is a personalization of the normative process, a claim to define normativity at an individual level and to make each individual the norm's object (thereby reconciling the government of large numbers with the government of individuals), then the logic of this personalization implies, above all, a gentle avoidance of

---

[6] While this is not tragic in and of itself—all beings, and not only human beings, have always benefited from the correlations that run through them—it is nonetheless important to underline how certain correlations, such as the one that links a certain rate of public debt to a decrease in growth (Reinhart and Rogoff), can be dangerous depending on the lessons that are drawn from them. In any case, and I will come back to this later, it is urgent to no longer be satisfied with this *sufficiency* of correlations.

subjectivization's frictions and resistances. It would seem as if norms, in the broad sense of the term, were able to emerge amidst the real itself, amidst the most mundane, variable and composite manifestations of the real, without requiring the prior expression of a project, a hypothesis or even of subjectivity that putatively feeds the information used to generate norms, which, in turn, discreetly govern the real by feeding back into it. This, of course is nothing but a fiction: norms do not spontaneously arise out of the real! As Alain Desrosières never tired of repeating, "data are not given" ("les données ne sont pas données"). Data have a cost, they are produced, they are conventional, there is always an upstream to their availability.[7] Moreover, they are sorted so as to fit statistical hypotheses that generate correlations. And behind these hypotheses, there are engineers, and behind them there are economic interests, power relations, styles, and so on. Yet, with its fiction of a gentle and inoffensive hold on the world, this new utopia of normative objectivity is a source of strength and legitimacy for algorithmic governmentality. As we have already shown, while on the one hand this new normativity appears to govern *from* the real rather than govern *the* real, on the other hand the intensity of government has perhaps never been so strong in that the very impediment of its exercise has been lifted.

Algorithmic governmentality draws its strength from the normative intensity of extracting correlations from everyday patterns. This is the price to pay for such a pretense of objectivity: correlations suffice (and must be sufficient) in order to govern (without impediment) from the real. This price is all the more irresistible given the correlations' seemingly painless nature. They are nothing more than connected fragments of our daily lives: resisting them would be schizophrenic.

What is important to underline then is the indifference of algorithmic governmentality towards individuals. Its interest lies only in controlling our "statistical double," that is, the automatically generated correlations fed by massive quantities of data that are collected by default. The problem with this indifference and its avoidances of the subject is not that the individual is jeopardized by being extorted, but that processes and opportunities of subjectivation, namely the difficulty to become a subject of,

---

[7] Even though these conventions are never questioned or debated.

and within, this algorithmic normativity, are rarefied. Simply put, it is not a question of being dispossessed of what we consider to be our *own*, nor is it about being coerced into relinquishing information that would violate our privacy or freedom; more fundamentally still, the problem comes from the fact that our statistical double is too detached from us, that we have no "relationship" with it, even though contemporary normative actions need nothing more than this statistical double to be efficient, and actually find in this sufficiency the full weight of their power.

Transparency Is All About Relations

The question that must now be asked is: if the individual is not the object or target of algorithmic governmentality, then what is? Or better yet: what is it that is governed when all friction with subjects is avoided and when the possibility of subjectivization is complicated?

The object—incapable of becoming a subject—of algorithmic governmentality is relations: the data transmitted are relations[8] and they remain such only so long as they avoid contact with the terms of the relations. The knowledge generated is a set of relations of relations and, as a set of correlations, it adds no consistency to these relationships. Likewise, the normative actions resulting from these relationships are actions upon relationships referred to relations of relations. Therefore, algorithmic governmentality's novelty, if it has one, is that it governs relations.

The incentive in approaching algorithmic governmentality by way of Gilbert Simondon's philosophy comes from the fact that this mode of government, as I will show, no longer seems to take hold on, or take aim at, subjects, but rather *relations* considered as prior to the terms by which they are constituted. In other words, the relationships at stake are not merely the sum of the inter-subjective interactions supposed to comprise individuals, but are more fundamentally the relations *themselves*, without

---

[8] The word "relation" is meant in the rawest and least affected sense of the term, by which data is qualified. It is used only to indicate an operation linking *a* to *b* while ignoring what lies behind the two terms. As we will show, the whole strength of algorithmic governmentality lies in its ability to "monadologize" this relation, to the point that it can no longer grasp the becoming that *is* the relation.

reference or assignation to the individuals they relate to, as a form of "relationality" subsisting above and beyond the individualities involved. In order to grasp what we are dealing with, we need to follow Simondon's lead and abandon a classical ontology or *metaphysics of substance*, centered on individuals and states (in which relations are attributed to an individual), for a *relational ontology* (in which relations have ontological precedence over the individuals they span) or better yet, an ontogenesis mindful of becoming and of understanding the very movement of individuation.

Simondon's philosophy of individuation presents itself as the most accomplished attempt to envision the relation for its own sake as freed from its Aristotelian understanding in which it was always preceded by substance and thereby reduced to its strictly logical content. By refusing the primacy of the substance, that is, by moving from a metaphysics of states towards a metaphysics of their modifications and becoming, Simondon confers ontological content to the relationship so as to account for the process of individuation itself. For Simondon, this means that the relationship always exceeds or overflows what it relates; it can never be reduced to inter-individual sociality. When thinking of relations one must take their ontological primacy as far as possible: "the relation does not spring from two already individuated terms," but it is always "the internal resonance of an individuation system" (Simondon 2005: 29, translation mine).[9]

For Simondon this also means that the "preindividual field"—in which individuation processes must always take place in order to be thought of as processes developing out of, and all the while conserving, this preindividual dimension prior to any differentiation movement—is potentially metastable: its equilibrium can be broken by even the most minimal internal modification of the system. This non-stability of the preindividual field is the inherent possibility of taking form through differentiation. As such, it is the very condition of a thinking that does not fall into the paralogism of presupposing and even individuating the principle for which it seeks the cause. In other words, if there is becoming it is only insofar as there is disparateness between orders of magnitude, between dissymmetrical realities.

---

[9] Muriel Combes, *Simondon. Individu et collectivité* (1999), was also of great help in our framing of Simondon.

Rather than the individual and its principle, Simondon enjoins us to envision the operations of individuation as from a preindividual being, which is also individuating itself, or must at least be seen through different individuation processes. From this perspective, the operations or processes emanating from individuals and milieus, from individuals associated with milieus (the individual is "the reality of a metastable relationship"), are perfectly real. The individual is real only because it is a relationship, because it is relative to a milieu. Or, put another way: what is relative is real. The relation therefore should in no way be considered from a subjectivist standpoint in which the relativity of the relationship is such that it dissolves its very reality. Rather, it is the reality of becoming. Likewise, the individual's associated milieu is anything but reducible to a form of measure, to the probability it has of appearing.[10]

Paradoxically, by probabilizing the real (thus turning all of reality into the substrate of statistical action) and by desubjectivizing this probabilistic perspective (which no longer bothers with preliminary hypotheses), in short by giving itself the means to directly govern behaviors without direct concern for individuals, algorithmic government "derealizes" the individual to the extent that it is only related to a series of measures standing in for reality without ever manifesting their subjective nature. The relationships marshaled by algorithmic government are measures which, by their very capacity to appear as non-mediated and non-subjective expressions of reality, make what comes of them all the more relative and less real. In fact, what comes of them is only relative to a series of measures standing in for reality. In other words, through their ability to appear disconnected from any subjectivity, relations and their measurements turn the real as well as the individual itself into something relative.

Yet, from the standpoint of Simondon's thinking, the above paradox is the result of an inversion. While for a metaphysics of substance it was impossible to know the individual through measures of its milieu because they were necessarily too subjective, this insufficiency (along with the ontological difference it revealed between the individual and its milieu)

---

[10] Simondon dedicates several pages to the dangers of a loss of reality implied by the subjectivist and probabilistic nature of contemporary physics.

would now be resolved by making the individual entirely relative to measures free of any subjectivity. Working one step further through this confrontation between a practice of government and Simondonian thinking, one could even say that, by concentrating on relations, this practice succeeds in "monadologizing" them, in transforming them into states, or even statuses, as if the relations were themselves individuals. In this way, they lose what Simondon's thinking brought about: the becoming of a metastable reality.

"Big Data," the *data* of which subsists only as a series of relations, actually turns relations into individuals or statuses. Both the knowledge generated from the data—consisting in relations linked together—*and* the normative actions implied in terms of governing relations—insofar as they refer to relations of relations—excludes the very possibility of a becoming within a metastable reality. Simondon enjoined us to stop thinking becoming from the position of an already given individual because, in doing so, we would overlook the very experience of individuation in its making. We could no longer afford to neglect the fact that "the possible does not already contain the actual," and that "the emergent individual differs from the possible that catalyzed its individuation" (Debaise 2004: 15–23, translation mine). In this light, it would seem that a true relation continues to be thinkable only on the basis of failure and deviation—the very existence of which is threatened by a reality augmented to the point of including even the possible. A relation involving dissymmetric and partially incompatible realities out of which new realities and meanings are eventuated would be a true relation, one that would remain unassignable to that which it relates.

Thinking the "Becoming-Status" of the Relation in Order to Escape Pure Repetition

To give an idea of what is entailed by this "becoming-status" of relations captured by algorithmic governmentality—which distances us from a relational ontology by excluding the relation's disparities and thereby foreclosing the possibility of any subjectivization process—it seems that a second detour is necessary, this time by way of the theory of performativity.

For J. L. Austin (1962), far from being evaluated simply as true or false, that is, in terms of their constative value describing the world, utterances can also be considered as "happy" or "unhappy" insofar as they do something and actively take part in the construction of the world. Analyzing utterances as "doing" something distances us from the descriptive illusion, be it when faced with a specifically performative utterance or when confronted with the performative dimension of any utterance. On this very general basis, upon which *saying* can be understood as *doing*, the question then is to determine what enforces these utterances. The point here is not to evoke all of the distinctions such a question implies—namely the vigorous debate which pitted Searle against Derrida (Derrida 1972)[11] as well as the political and juridical consequences Butler drew from it (Butler 1997)[12]—but rather to underscore that Derrida's sometimes unjust critique of Austin's theory of the performative was a denunciation of the contextual structure from which a performative utterance derived its force, as well as the intentional presence such a structure presupposes. Likewise, through her mobilization of the Derridean theory and by taking aim, rightly so, at certain legal and militant uses of the Austinian theory, Butler pointed out the dangers inherent to the perspective according to which performativity's source essentially lies in the conventional structure of the performative (limited as such to its illocutionary dimension) and through which the act is incorporated as a discourse only because certain conventions pertaining to certain contexts have been respected. Significantly, what Derrida's and Butler's critiques reveal is that the Austinian approach to the performative continued to think language in a logocentric, and thus metaphysical fashion (Derrida), by presupposing the sovereignty of an intentional subject with regards to its utterances (Derrida and Butler) and thereby authorizing a potential political sovereign hold on discourses, in which case the performative force of an

---

[11] For a nuanced commentary of the Austin/Derrida/Searle debate see R. Moati, *Derrida/Searle. Déconstruction et langage ordinaire* (2009).

[12] The reader may also refer to the consequences I draw from this debate in "Insulte et droit post-souverain" (2015: 120–125).

utterance is necessarily enforced by such sovereignty (more specifically, Butler questions *fighting words*). Derrida, followed by Butler, shows us how Austin essentially remains an idealist given his incapacity to consider a performance's failure as other than an accident (an inappropriate context or the disrespect of conventions) and not as an inherent possibility of the performative. This limitation forces Austin to re-establish a distinction between serious (typified by the law) and non-serious (theater, contrived utterances, etc.) languages. To these critiques, I would like to add that a conventionalist approach of performativity such as Austin's leads to explaining the law (legal utterances understood as the epitome of performatives) with the law (its performativity is explained by its very own conventions).

Derrida and Butler replace the contextual and/or conventional structure of the performative with a citational one: signs should be considered only by distancing them from the idea of communication. In other words, a sign must apprehend in terms of its split with any (therefore always differed) presence, in terms of its "its power to break away from its context," including any form of meaning that stands for an intention (Derrida 1972: 377, translation mine). The distancing of intentionality that denotes writing as independent of any communicational function, the absence of a speaker or an addressee, is what signifies its very constitution: its iterability.

Regardless of whether one accepts this approach of ordinary language (or even of all "experience"), it is impossible to deny that we are irremediably and tragically confronted with iterability's primacy whenever we try to think experience under the auspices of algorithmic governmentality. Any sign—any data—is first and foremost considered in terms of its severance with an intentional context, in terms of its possibility of being read independently of its "moment of production," that is "abandoned to its essential drifting." Equally though, a sign can function while being "drawn out" of "the sequence within which it fits" so as to be "transplanted into other sequences" (Derrida 1972: 377, translation mine). Yet, while it may look as if data were infinitely correlated to one another within algorithmic governmentality, these combinations leave no remainders. They are repetitions without alterations.

Indeed, for Derrida or Butler, the sign's essential drifting is not, or should not be, synonymous with the vanishing of any reference, which subsists but only as differed. One could even say that what is signified becomes an element of the text. The value of Butler's reading is, on the one hand, to show the inherent danger of accepting a proposition, or data in our case, as a purely mechanical and remainderless repetition by pointing out the conventionalist dynamic (reducing the performative to the illocutionary) underlying such an understanding.[13] On the other hand, Butler conversely emphasizes the possibilities of empowerment eventuated by the citational structure of the performative. As soon as iteration is not merely repetition (and sovereign hailing), but also difference, then novel appropriations of propositions, along with their afferent processes of subjectivation, must be taken into account.

It would seem that the mechanical repetition of data, and its equally mechanical transplantation into systems of correlations, must be seen as follows: if the relation of algorithmic governmentality's object or rather, algorithmic governmentality, has the power to reduce relations to objects, it is because relations are reduced to statuses that cannot be refuted precisely, in that there is nothing added to them (as this is how the three phases of algorithmic governmentality avoid subjectivity). Through this becoming-status of the relation and its absence of friction with a subject, a regime can be designated in which the problem is not so much the correlations it produces but rather their self-sufficiency, their remainderless repetition: nothing needs to be added to the correlation for it to govern or act. The idea that they are "nothing *but* correlations" ensures algorithmic governmentality's boundless strength.[14]

Translated from French by Tyler Reigeluth

---

[13] This conventionalization of the performative—which completely incorporates the saying (illocutionary) into the doing instead of seeing the action as unfolding the saying with the perlocutionary latitude it allows—is certainly a specific theoretical understanding of the performative, but it is also the encounter of several sovereign dynamics: the hailing of the subject, of the subject subjected to the hailing (and whose sovereignty is denied), the State which controls language and confirms the hailing by giving in to the fear of the unknown future of words. It is nothing else than a certain face of the law, thought in terms of sovereignty, that is defined in this manner.

[14] There is nothing tragic about this realization. It intends rather to open up new potentialities for becoming a subject within algorithmic governmentality, potentialities which necessarily rely on the ability to alter the repetitions that ensure government's performativity.

Works Cited

Austin, John L. 1962. *How to Do Things with Words*. Oxford: Ed. Urmson.
Berns, Thomas. 2009. *Gouverner sans gouverner. Une archéologie politique de la statistique*. Paris: Presses Universitaires de France.
———. 2015. Insulte et droit post-souverain. *Multitudes* 59.
Berns, Thomas, and Antoinette Rouvroy. 2013. «Gouvernementalité algorithmique et perspectives d'émancipation. Le disparate comme condition d'émancipation par la relation?», dans Réseaux, 2013/1, n° 177, éd. La Découverte, pp. 63–196 (English translation: http://www.cairn-int.info/article-E_RES_177_0163DOUBLEHYPHENalgorithmic-governmentality-and-prospect.htm).
Butler, Judith. 1997. *Excitable Speech. A Politics of the Performative*. New York: Routledge.
Combes, Muriel. 1999. *Simondon. Individu et collectivité*. Paris: Presses Universitaires de France.
Debaise, Didier. 2004. Qu'est-ce qu'une pensée relationnelle. *Multitudes* 18.
Derrida, Jacques. 1972. Signature événement contexte. In *Marges de la philosophie*. Paris: Edition Minuit (trans. 'Signature Event Context,' *Margins of Philosophy*, Chicago, Chicago UP, 1982, 307–330).
Jeanmart, Gaëlle, and Thomas Berns. 2009. *Reporting*/Confession. *Multitudes* 36.
———. 2010. Le rapport comme réponse de l'entreprise responsable : promesse ou aveu (à partir d'Austin et Foucault). *Dissensus* 3: 117–137. http://popups.ulg.ac.be/dissensus/document.php?id=701.
Moati, R. 2009. *Derrida/Searle. Déconstruction et langage ordinaire*. Paris: Presses Universitaires de France.
Simondon, Gilbert. 2005. *L'individuation à la lumière des notions de forme et d'information*. Paris: Millon.

Obfuscated Transparency

Dieter Mersch

The Ambiguity of the Concept

The necessity of transparency is one of the key philosophical, political, and ethical principles of the Enlightenment. Transparency is essential in a world that strives for complete clarity and openness and views with suspicion any attempt to distort, obscure, or relativize this principle. René Descartes stated that the language of reason had to be *clare et distincte*, a demand that was later transferred from the sciences and their discursive order to the domain of ethics and politics, opening the way for the demand that their principles too be deduced *more geometrico*. Thus, it became a mission of the Enlightenment to ground the knowledge, practices, decisions, maxims, and principles of both science and politics in nothing other than the medium of reason. This gave rationality an exceptional status among the media: it was equated with godliness and conceived of as a "medium without means," a form of pure neutrality

D. Mersch (✉)
Zürcher Hochschule der Künste, Zürich, Switzerland
e-mail: dieter.mersch@zhdk.ch

© The Author(s) 2018
E. Alloa, D. Thomä (eds.), *Transparency, Society and Subjectivity*,
https://doi.org/10.1007/978-3-319-77161-8_13

untainted by finitude and the limits imposed by death. Whether in the domain of the practical or of the theoretical, the will to transparency, the desire to be transparent came to be seen as absolute; it was linked to a historical process that seemed to stand beyond all criticism, a process associated with the image of an all-encompassing light that stood for itself and was supposed to chase away the shadows of irrationality once and for all.

Accordingly, the Enlightenment's project of making things transparent pursued two goals. First, it sought to free people from obscurantism and the resentments it gave rise to, among them the errors of mysticism and the blind acceptance of theological dogmas (and first and foremost those of the Abrahamic religions). Second, it sought to overcome tyranny and domination by freeing people from violence, oppression, and arbitrary rule. Transparency implied a double ideal and a double freedom: an epistemological freedom that refused to accept anything not sufficiently reasoned or proven, and a practical or moral freedom that revolved around a politics of unlimited discussion and participation and a social ideal of equality and justice that found its highest expression in the idea of universal human rights. Immanuel Kant connected both sides in his short essay "What is Enlightenment?" (Kant 1784a). Under the pretense of criticizing the dogmatism of the priesthood and its strategies of religious stupefaction, Kant ultimately ended up grappling with both "the prince" and his power, claiming that it was insufficient for him to merely allow for an ideal "freedom of thought," and that, in the interest of the maturity of the individual, he ought to allow freedom of speech in the public sphere. Thus, Kant was interested in protecting truth from censorship and disciplinary measures and allowing it to break through the compulsions of intrigue and manipulation. In this sense, enlightenment had political consequences. With the medium of rationality as its preferred tool, it would help emancipate the "subjects" and enable them to think for themselves, which would, according to Kant, in the end be useful for governance. Decisive is the fact that Kant did not plea for unqualified tolerance, because he did not believe that everything could be thought, claimed, said, and done—if that were the case, he would have contradicted himself by having to let esotericism and religion in again through the back door. Instead, he believed that only those judgments should be communicated that had passed the test of reason.

Dialectic of Enlightenment

Although the notion of "transparency" is often treated as though it were itself clear and unobscured, it is wrapped up in a dialectic that escapes its own grasp. Seemingly a positive project without limits, its actualization is in fact always relative, which opens a critical perspective on the rarely questioned naïve use of the concept. The key metaphor "light," and specifically the "light of reason," reveals a remainder of Platonism and Christian theology, both of which associate darkness with the diabolical (in the sense of dia-bolon, that which is in the way). But while this rhetoric of light speaks of divine qualities like innocence and purity, it takes on a cold, unrelenting shape in the context of rationalism. Its lack of mercy seems to shine into the darkest corners, uncovering and unmasking them. This too clouds its supposed positivity. Light everywhere above everything produces its own opposition, which confronts the pathos of enlightenment with its own ambiguities. Light not only "shines" and "makes visible," it also exposes and uncovers, bringing even those things into the open that might have been held back for good reason. It is this divulgement par excellence, this revelation "at any price" that shows the well-protected secrets of man to be plain old things, presenting them in their unworthy banality.

Thus, "transparency" can in no way be treated as a self-explanatory concept whose form represents its apparent content. Its Janus-faced nature might be most apparent in the consequences that this humanist ideal has for human affairs themselves, "where almost everything is considered paradoxical," as Kant wrote in his "Enlightenment" essay (Kant 1784a: 22). This is so because, as Kant later wrote in near resignation in the sixth proposition of his "Idea for a Universal History with a Cosmopolitan Aim," "out of such crooked wood as the human being is made, nothing entirely straight can be fabricated" (Kant 1784b: 113). The attempt to geometricize man with the straitjacket of reason is thus the most oxymoronic venture ever undertaken in the name of emancipation. It reveals itself as a contradiction and form of repression insofar as it tends to violate man's dignity and right to intimacy and privacy. In the end, the credo of enlightenment contains much that is inhumane and even antihuman, which has distorted its call for transparency and its emancipatory project since its very beginnings.

The same can be said of the fundamentals of modern science, whose analytic penetration is motivated by a "will to know" inseparably bound to its own immanent destructivity: what can be known of nature must first be cut open, purified, "mortified" before it can be broken down into parts and analyzed. The microscopic details of the organism first become visible after it is dyed and prepared; but these procedures leave behind nothing more than a structure, a carcass that at best only represents the appearance of life. Friedrich Nietzsche was probably the first to identify the inescapable dialectic inherent in the fact that the light that illuminates also blinds the eye that sees, showing that the unconditional nature of the will to know has an inherently nihilistic dimension (Nietzsche 1988: vol. 13, 189). Skepticism, the productive force of enlightenment, also haunts it in a very literal way, and in a certain sense, it even haunts the entire history of Western science like a doppelgänger. Nietzsche characterized nihilism as the "uncanniest of all guests" (Nietzsche 1988: vol. 12, 125). As a guest, it has been invited in, but while its host remains aloof, it transforms the most familiar and domestic into something unfamiliar and "uncanny." Others like Martin Heidegger and Theodor W. Adorno followed Nietzsche in his diagnosis of enlightenment in order to try and save the singular, the unnamable, the event and the "other of reason" from its all-consuming light. As the famous introductory passage to the Dialectic of Enlightenment reads, "the wholly enlightened earth is radiant with triumphant calamity" (Horkheimer and Adorno 1947: 1).

Responsible Transparency and the Criteria of Science

The concept of transparency therefore turns out to be in many ways opaque—to paraphrase Heidegger, it shrouds itself in a fog. Nevertheless, its key feature is its claim to resist the seductions of illusion and obscurity: enlightenment is always associated with the positive demand of making public that which is spoken and taking responsibility for it in the sense of a "capacity to respond" (Waldenfels 2007). The publicness and openness of transparency are related. Accordingly, Kant greeted the Age of Enlightenment by famously defining it as "the human being's emergence from his self-incurred minority" (Kant 1784a: 17). He sought to overcome what contemporaries criticized as the "dark middle ages," an epoch of childish irrationality and alienation that did not hesitate to use obfuscation, persecution, and inquisition to keep a grip on power and torture to force out the truth in the name of God. In doing so, it ultimately banished the transcendence that it itself claimed to represent. Of course, this image of the middle ages is grossly distorted.[1] In truth, it is the propaganda of rationalization itself, which invented its own opponents in order to be rid of their specters by using nothing more than scientific methods.

In turn, this public dimension of reason meant that science was to be made into a general means of communication, thus giving it the distinction of being a genuine instrument of transparency. The privileging of science was motivated by a politics of theory: thinkers of the Enlightenment like Kant only viewed those claims as valid that could stand the "test" of reason and its rigorous criteria (see Schnädelbach 2005: 21ff.). One might call the primacy placed on the public disputation of epistemic debates before an ideal community "responsible transparency." On the one hand, the practice of responsible transparency involves staying true to the principles of reason, while on the other, it requires "publication," an issue Kant also treated in his essay on Enlightenment:

> I reply: The public use of one's reason must always be free, and it alone can bring about enlightenment among human beings; the private use of one's reason may, however, often be very narrowly restricted without this particularly hindering the progress of enlightenment. But by the public use of one's own reason I understand that use which someone makes of it as a scholar before the entire public of the world of readers. What I call the private use of reason is that which one may make of it in a certain civil post or office with which he is entrusted. (Kant 1784a: 18)

---

[1] A corrective of the traded image of the middle ages can be found in Eco (1987) and Tuchman (1978).

Thus, the Enlightenment and the demand of transparency rest on the division between public and private, a division that finds its paradigm in the ideals of scientific community. Kant reins in the ambiguities of transparency with the principle of plausibility, which he in turn roots in the notion of participation, particularly in the realm of practical reason. Both shared by the members of a rational community and dependent upon them as individuals, participation obligates speakers to take responsibility for what they say; in the end, however, Kant does not give an account of what for him constitutes this community and the participation that seems to be so essential to it. This gap was filled in during the linguistic turn, which identified communication as the medium of publicness and the central mechanism of the social and demonstrated that language and understanding follow rules that always shape the way claims are expressed (Habermas 1978, 1979, 1981). Thinkers of the linguistic turn viewed community as a function of speech, thus supplanting scientific publication as the general form of a collective's identity with "consensus" reached through discussion. Consensus is a new principle of truth that substitutes the correspondence of subject and object with a desire to come to a general agreement. In this sense, transparency can only exist in contexts of such participation, which are in turn founded on trust and cooperation.

What is significant here is that the principle of "responsible transparency," as developed by Kant, creates its own scientific style that holds for the entire process of enlightenment all the way up through the theories of communicative consensus. Transparency follows from knowledge, knowledge follows from discursivity and proof; this notion even holds for the total accessibility of information in the digital age, which basically sets forth the same tendency. Thus, the model of participating in public discourse by scientists engaged in the passionate search for truth remains also true for new publics on the Internet, a fact exemplified by the original *Advanced Research Projects Agency Network* (Arpanet), conceived of as a network of experts. Enlightenment is governed by a prejudice for science. At the same time, the norms of science have been taken to be equally applicable to the resolution of political conflicts and the discussion of social inequalities and moral dilemmas. In other words, epistemic principles are being applied to practical problems, which is not something that should be taken for granted, because it forces to treat the dissent with the same degree of critical rigor as we do those of discursive claims. Kant was not the only one to subordinate the practical to the theoretical in this fashion, turning discursive rationality into something like a projector machine, which, for all that, nevertheless remains illegitimate, as the very premises of the projection are left unexplained. If geared towards nothing other than furthering a process of collective rationalization guided by expert participation, transparency tends to be applied to things beyond its proper domain, making politics into the task of science.

Transparency and Medialization

Thus, when reason is made identical with transparency and the claims of theoretical enlightenment are hypostasized into universalizable processes that fail to heed the specificity and limits of their applicability, they turn against themselves and bring forth the same monstrosities that they had once warded off. This is the inner dialectic of "responsible transparency." Not only are there good reasons to doubt the effectiveness of the idea of transparency in politics and in inter-human relationships, the idea of transparency also reveals its contradictory nature when it—a notion based in the world of reasons—usurps the social itself and forces upon it the same compulsion to publication as it does upon the findings of science. Kant's imperative to publish was limited to the rational accessibility of ideas. As a social or moral prescription, however, transparency tends to violate human integrity and sociality. Even more consequential may be the way in which Kant and the theorists of enlightenment believed that reason is in itself clear and transparent and thus does not need a medium, just as they thought that transparency is clear and distinct in and of itself and thus need not be obscured by a medium. This gives rise to a further dialectic, because transparency is necessarily bound up with the medial, which obscures it once more. In contrast to the supposedly immaterial illuminations of the light of reason, this dialectic inscribes a resistance into the process of enlightenment that shows it to be fractured from the start. The concept of the medium should not be understood in a superficial manner here, whether it be as means or "middle" or as tool or instrumentum; rather, the medial only reveals itself through the practical, through which it realizes its function. It is not neutral; rather, it impacts the processes and procedures that it conditions, just like an apparatus, which at once makes action possible and hinders it. With an emphasis on the "through," going through a medium means effectuating an effect in the mode of performativity. It follows that performativity constitutes the condition that both makes things public and precedes and determines rationality. In the end, transparency exists only within economies of making transparent, working through or "through composing," which implies that transparency is neither a state of being nor an attribute, but at best a medially produced operation that is bound up with its own kind of opacity.

In other words, beyond the dialectic and relativization of enlightenment and transparency, we can see that there is a necessary dependency between transparency and opacity that is indicative of the "a priori" incompleteness of both terms. The aesthetic philosophies of the early nineteenth century touched on this when they gave materiality a special status by claiming that things could only reveal themselves as things through it (see Hegel 1842). Like enlightenment and transparency, which share a visual metaphor, pure light without the resistance of material or atmosphere is an illusion that has just as little consistency as the ether or aura, neither of which can be captured by thought or the senses—only that which has a body can, like Aristotle's diaphane, be perceived and understood. Indeed, the "dia-phane" through which the light penetrates and makes "clear" structures the perceived object, allowing it to show itself in its particular appearance (Alloa 2011).

Up to this point we have uncovered three points that relativize the seemingly self-explanatory concept of transparency: transparency is limited by the public use of reason, which, however, runs the risk of being hypostasized as an absolute; transparency is determined by a preconceived conception of reason, which produces its own problems and obscurities when applied to the sphere of social practices; and transparency is bound to a universal rationality that fosters the illusion of being without media while simultaneously needing media, thus depending on the devices of a principle of a different kind. While the absolutely transparent seems to lack all resistance, it fails to recognize its necessary materiality and is thus ultimately opaque to itself. As an instrument of enlightenment, reason and its guise of immateriality is literally "not of this world," which is to say that it is "in-finitized" and without any gravity. The truth is that the medium separates itself from itself in the moment of mediating and shows itself as irresolvable difference, splitting the mediated and making itself opaque. Every mediation modifies, influences and transforms the mediated, because it "mediates" the mediated through itself, thus making its mark on it. The mediated has its own form of otherness. This is why something remains as a residue on the represented in the process of representation; for instance, the modalities of the visual leave their trace on the depicted object, and the "form" and rules of language leave their trace on concepts and the things grasped through them, without itself being able to be represented and understood through these things (Mersch 2008, 2016a). Thus, although the medium is necessary for making things appear, it itself is not an appearance; rather, it only sticks out as a trace in places where it falters or is exposed.[2] As a form of negativity, the medial does not escape its own obscuration. Thus, even in its "responsible" guise, transparency is not only a relative concept that can never be wholly realized, but also something that is constituted and thus always accompanied by obscuration or opacity.[3]

In the end, the conditions of a philosophy and politics of transparency are trickier and more complex than one might think at first. Bogged down by the contradictory, illusory burden of having to be a "medium without means," it is no surprise that the ideal of transparency (like the Enlightenment's dream of reason without a medium) has always been associated with notions like purity, freedom and truth. What is more innocent than total and complete openness that shows itself without holding anything back? All metaphysical categories—the true no less than the good, the beautiful, justice, freedom, autonomy, and self-determination—seem to be gathered together in the concept of transparency, giving power to its indestructible mythology. And yet, at

---

[2] A similar argument can be found in Heidegger's analysis of useful things. See also Rautzenberg and Wolfsteiner (2010).

[3] "Our writing tools are also working on our thoughts." Quoted in Kittler (1986: 200). See Friedrich Nietzsche, Letter to Peter Gast (Heinrich Köselitz), Feb. 1882, in Nietzsche (1988: vol. 3.1, 172).

the same time, they conspire against it, reveal its inherent paradoxes, and contaminate it.

Technological Transparency as Opacity

All this seems to give transparency a mystical dimension that it still has today and that is the cause of its failures. It began dominating emancipatory criticism and ideas of democratic openness in 1800 at the latest, and was a key element in utopias of media revolutions, from early systems of telecommunications up to contemporary digital networks. The latter above all rests on the double vision of non-hierarchical and egalitarian participation alongside limitless access to information, thus once again transferring the ideals of enlightenment to the field of technology. Fred Turner has analyzed the affinity between the counter-culture movements of the 1970s, the birth of personal computers and the development of new online communities (Turner 2006). Technology seems to fuse the ideals of a techno-centered society with those of direct democracy, in which all have an equal right to take part in making decisions—despite the fact that access cannot be equally distributed, and despite the double-sided nature of the "vision" of making visible, which combines seemingly unlimited information with the constant threat of surveillance. Technological systems seem to effortlessly make real the promises of the long, contradictory history of modernity: the freedom of knowledge, the transparency of power, the right to unhindered communication, and the scientific—cybernetic—resolution of social conflicts. Even more, their supposed neutrality—technology does not distinguish between its users—has altered the politics of transparency itself, thus repeating once again the myths of self-transparency and "indigence," or "being without means." But what takes place under its auspices forms at best an amalgam of ideologemes that dispenses with precisely those things that the old hopes were founded in. This is because the networks are run by a mathematical logic of decision-making that promotes binarity as a principle of order to an absolute, a principle that tolerates neither indeterminacy nor undecidability nor a middle way (Mersch 2013).

Technological, which is to say formal, relations thus take the place of reason, leading to a situation in which the transparency guaranteed by technology obeys a strictly mathematical logic that comes to structure the matrix of the social. This, of course, has serious implications for communication and public life. On the one hand, these formal relations enable users to forge seemingly instant connections to all kinds of actors, groups, knowledge, commodities and objects on a global level, simply by virtue of the fact that all use the same protocols, tools and formats. On the other hand, however, they make space for ignorance, lies and "alternative facts," putting them on the same footing as true statements in an increasingly indifferent world of information. After all, the mathematical syntax doesn't care if information is true or false or if a commodity is useful or useless—in the end, the only thing that matters is that they stay in circulation. This complex makes a parody of one of the key values of the Enlightenment, letting the monsters of doxology, belief, error and intrigue out of the cage, all to the detriment of the Enlightenment values of autonomy and maturity. The public nature of the sciences and their rules of publication—indeed, the public nature of reason itself—once constituted the criteria of "responsible transparency"; however, what today passes as information and is stockpiled as data dispenses with all criteria of judgment, an effect of the fact that everything comes out of the same mathematical universe. Thus, although digital transparency may rely on an implicit critique of repressive elitism, the problem is that in rejecting every form of exclusion and inequality in favor of a structure and an algorithm, facts and their filtration through reason are also affected, because every limitation falls under the general suspicion of being a form of censorship. The Enlightenment ideal—even if it lacked an adequate concept of the social and simply relied on the form of reason as its constitutive element—was that a critical public would be responsible for drawing a line between what could be said and what couldn't; contemporary digital culture, in contrast, hollows out the capacity to differentiate and the significance of difference itself in the name of universal participation. The struggle against ignorance has now handed over its spirit to a regime of mechanical procedures, which processes and devalues data—whether it be in the form of information, half-truths, scientific findings, rumors or insults—as equally computable variables.

Transparency is touted as only following from mathematization, and in turn, mathematization appears as the only source of technological enlightenment. By excepting itself from its own highest principle, however, technological transparency produces opacity as technology's blind spot.

The Concealment of the Unconcealed and the Incomputability of the Event

Under the dominance of technology, the ideal of transparency is distorted. What is more, it becomes an illusion, a failed utopia that destroys the old hopes of the Enlightenment. To speak with Byung-Chul Han, the more technology subordinates openness and transparency to the *conditio mechanica*, the more dystopian it makes them (Han 2012). Technology's domination over transparency is fatal not because it automatizes surveillance, which then runs amok like the brooms in Goethe's "The Sorcerer's Apprentice," nor because the praxis of seeing and making visible is invested with the capacity to surveil, but because, as Han states in his book *The Transparency Society*, the exposition of facts as "naked evidence" is itself "obscene" (Han 2012: 11–30). It exhibits nothing other than the "flesh" itself. What once served enlightenment has been transformed, in the most literal sense of the word, into a "per-version." In this analysis, Han draws on an argument from Nietzsche, which was less directed at the topos of transparency, but nevertheless sought to identify the abyss lurking beneath the veneer of enlightened truths in order to enlighten enlightenment. "Perhaps truth is a woman who has grounds for not showing her grounds?" (Nietzsche 1887: 8), Nietzsche writes in the preface to the second edition of *The Gay Science*. The passage connects the supposed innocence of the truth with shame by giving it the attribute of shyness, because, as Nietzsche continues, the "will to truth," "this youthful madness in the love of truth" (Nietzsche 1887: 8), is suspicious to the core: "Today we consider it a matter of decency not to wish to see everything naked, to be present everywhere, to understand and 'know' everything" (Nietzsche

1887: 8). Han concludes that the ubiquitous visibility of the "unconcealed" is nothing more than "pornography" (Han 2012: 24). Similarly, in the fifth of the "Arrows and Epigrams" in *Twilight of the Idols*, Nietzsche writes: "For once and for all, I want not to know many things. —Wisdom sets limits on knowledge too" (Nietzsche 1889: 156).

The result is that making visibility absolute and ever-present necessarily distorts it. Transparency without its opposite means constructing a concept without its negative, thus making it impossible to define and turning it into something indistinct. It is tantamount to a figure without a ground. In Heidegger's definition of the process of truth as *alētheia* or "unconcealment," the "revealed" is always limited, caught up between unconcealment and concealment. The process of *alētheia* is itself an act of negativity, as is made clear by the fact that the privative prefix "a" indicates that non-concealment has to be chiseled out of concealment. Beyond that, unconcealment is temporally preceded by a primary concealment, and the process of "revealing" is akin to a movement of deposing or wresting away from, which, as "leap," remains concealed (Heidegger 1927: 204–220 [§44, especially b and c]; Heidegger 1949/50). Thus, the above discussed dialectics of transparency is not sufficient in and of itself. With reference to Heidegger's two-fold conception of *alētheia* (separated, of course, from his analysis of useful things, which, as he shows, is wholly incompatible with the analysis of truth), we should recognize that the process of transparency is double-sided; first, because it is dependent upon a whole slew of opaque things, and second, because its sense can only be understood within a history that is different in each particular instance. In no way is transparency "clear" in and of itself; rather, it is invested with different meanings and interpretations, thus undermining once and for all the seemingly self-explanatory complex of reason, openness, freedom and participation. Moreover, transparency has to be viewed not as an ideal, but as a form of relation that is always already immanent to the social and its modes of nearness, trust and giving. At the same time, the relation of transparency can at any time be broken, both historically and in social life, because there is no universal definition that does not itself follow the logic of "becoming" and transformation. In other words, transparency should not be conceived of as something that is simply there or as something that can be attained, nor as something that could ever be guaranteed through truth. Transparency is the constant effort of mediation that makes transparent and is preceded by the various practices that carry out this effort.

From Transparency to Self-Presentation: The Rise of the "Societies of Control"

As such, transparency must confront the constant danger of becoming meaningless and being instrumentalized. This is readily apparent under contemporary conditions of technological production: although transparency technology is now widely available to everybody, it generates the opposite effects. It seems to be an inherent element of technology and its indifference that it paves the way for the abuse of the things it makes possible. The constant availability of means of communication thus implies both their disposition over other things (domination) and their disposability, which is to say that they can always be appropriated for other means. That which is communicated fosters both connection and separation and can always fall victim to misuse, and both aspects are so intertwined that it is impossible to wrest them apart.

Thus, the blind spot of the history of enlightenment, its political ambitions, and the naïveté of technological utopias that subordinate these ambitions to mathematical laws can be found in what Heidegger conceived of as the "mystery" of the event, which is constitutive of the temporality of truth but which can neither be mastered nor controlled. Technological means and mathematical models and predictions are thus by definition incapable of grasping and making disposable the concealment of unconcealment, the event that evades all attempts to make it transparent, the event's "dés-œuvrement" (Nancy 1991), and its undecidability. Although it might seem that transparency, by its very nature of being transparent, can be computerized and freely formed without incurring any loss, "transparency" is chronically lacking in mathematically and technologically produced forms of transparency based on nothing more than syntactic operations that seek to inscribe their algorithms to the point that they can no longer be controlled by rules. This is why Han claims that pure light produces only "hypervisibility" (Han 2012: 12 and 24). However, "hypervisibility" has nothing in common with what Heidegger called the "clearing," because the "clearing" is always already limited by the "path" that leads to it, a path through which we see and which enables us to see in the first place. Rather, hypervisibility indicates a loss of vision and a loss of sight, because, like the prisoner who reaches the daylight in Plato's allegory of the cave, the light of noon outshines everything, making it impossible to see the things and their forms (eidos). It thus runs counter to the reflexive search for the sources of knowledge, because looking directly into the sun blinds the eye.

In the course of our meditations we have encountered a range of similar figures, from Nietzsche's criticism of the Enlightenment's will to truth to Heidegger's critique of the domination of metaphysics, both of which Han (admittedly in a somewhat diluted form) recapitulates in his criticism of the excesses of today's technologically produced hypervisibility. The conclusion to be drawn is that full transparency is something like a form of exhibitionism. This not only shows the nefarious dimension of the digital imperatives of equality and free access propagated by leading IT companies like Google and Facebook. It also reveals that by getting users to develop an unconditional "desire to be seen," they have made real Deleuze's prophecy of the shift from "disciplinary society" to a "society of control." At any rate, "control" might be the wrong word, since what we are seeing today is a "freely" executed self-control in which people—astonishingly—surrender themselves to the dictates of technological apparatuses, naked and without protection. This complex is nothing less than a system of "fascination" in the robust, double meaning of the word. Its proponents have long stopped pleading for a politics of transparency, and instead have made themselves servants of the proliferation and boundless reproduction of narcissistic self-presentation, of a constant "look at me" that places itself in the foreground (see Etzioni 2010). The goal is not to "share" one's own life with millions of others, as the clearly superfluous justifications claim, but to increase and capitalize on one's own sense of self-worth through the sheer quantity of "shares" and "likes." The demand for openness and transparency plays into this. The content of the mere "shares," however, is neither social nor for that matter shared. Rather, the proliferation of shares turns into a form of obtrusion and compulsion that substitutes participation with the self and its affects. All of this goes hand in hand with a progressive decay of the sense of community.

This touches on the disturbing aspects of technologically generated sociality, above all in so-called "social media," and this despite widely shared slogans like "Don't be evil" or "Making the world a better place." The digital, binary format that stands at the foundation of their programming is shot through with asociality because it only permits those modes of producing "shares" and "participation" that can be organized through the discrete forms of networks. The necessary consequence is the insistence of auto-representation and the ubiquity of self-presentation and "making oneself present" that seems to have turned social life into a stage, an endless theater. All of this should not simply be dismissed as the accident of a narcissistic, self-centered society, because in actuality it is the product of a virtual schema that generates only aggregations and "swarms" and generates social capital out of presence and making present.

This lines up with a mode of "communication" that is not founded in difference and alterity and does not foster "inter-action" in the literal sense of the word. Rather, it is a mode of communication that is based on the exchange of data and the distribution of "likes" and "dislikes." The mathematical operations are primarily geared towards making sure the networks function and optimizing and accelerating the process of exchange and circulation (Mersch 2013). The specifically technological form of transparency and openness is subordinated to this. Connections in the digital world do not take the form of two-sided communication, even if they superficially resemble it. Their praxis is not one of responding and thus not one of "response-ability," which for its part is founded in inter-human relations. Instead, digital connections take the shape of diagrams and "inter-connections" that end up in a sort of eccentric excess that consumes itself and evokes the confounding image of pipes communicating with one another. These inter-connections only make public those mediated elements which are formed by the logic of exchange, so that visibility and transparency are subordinated to the diagrammatic forms of visualization producing them. Just as digital media generate hypervisibility, digital communication generates hypertextuality or hyper-linking, which always already form what is communicated. This is another reason why the capacity to judge and social creativity are chronically lacking in the digital world. In the end, it makes the allocation of means of communication and access to infrastructure the primary issues, reducing problems of sociality and transparency to questions of hardware.

Participation, Capitalization on Affects and De-Participation

The degree to which critical discourses on the fate of "open society" almost exclusively foreground the problem of free access for all is striking, because it reduces transparency to a mere function of furthering global exchange, as if this were a sufficient guarantee of "worldliness," when in fact we are currently witnessing the exact opposite, namely the destruction of trust and the distortion of facts. We are being confronted with the normalization of a "commentariat" that covers everything with its subtexts, even when they consist of mere rumor and speculation. Digital transparency is a hyper-communicability consisting of nothing more than communication-producing machines that hollow out the infinite "conversation that we are" (Hölderlin) by supplanting it with new ways of making money and new forms of entertainment. It simply reproduces the orders of enjoyment rather than working on the construction of a *communis* that can neither be given nor taken for granted but must be brought into "becoming" through common work (see Nancy 1991).

Hyper-communicability thus contributes to the erosion and destruction of the social by formalizing it, overloading it, and accelerating it. It is a consequence of the forceful incision of digital networks into the body of communication. Although digital networks are often seen as being one of the basic conditions of sociality, their structure qua networks supplants "having a part in" social life with "taking part in" it, reducing the "part" to a mere quantity. The claim being made here is that the reality and context of hyper-communicability qua connectivity is a mere vestige of dialogue and communication. Moreover, it is constituted by the ensemble of conditions forming the basis of digitalization, a few of which are: the mathematical rules of programs, the algorithmization of processes, their manifest operationalism, the breakdown of the analog into discrete orders, the symmetrical configuration of networks through interconnected knots, and the binary formation of the whole constellation and its logic of either/or decisions. Of course, the World Wide Web does indeed enable everyone to easily connect with practically anyone anywhere anytime, so long as she or he has an address and is online, which is to say, so long as she or he holds the line and follows its dictates. But the relationalities of the Web do not constitute binding connections, nor do they constitute a community or a way of living, which is founded in the collective sharing of sense and "response-ability."[4] Jean-Luc Nancy in particular emphasized the "com" or "with" of communication, inquiring into its relation to community and the conditions of "being-in-common" (Nancy 2014: 2–3, 9 and 34). In contrast, connectibility does not lead to collectivity; it excludes alterity rather than including it. Its result is the ideology of a merely relational participation that tellingly fails to distinguish between "sharing," "taking part in" and "having part in" and that fetishizes the strict symmetry of interhuman relations rather than grappling with their fundamental asymmetry.

This literal "in-difference" of interhuman relations is brought into being by the ideology of the digital age, which once liked to think of itself as an all-inclusive, non-ideological era redefining the public sphere, transparency and democracy through ubiquitous involvement. But it has failed, because participation and the transparency of its structures alone cannot make good on the promises of the kind of democratic equality that the digital community and its utopia of "telematics" (Flusser 1996: 114) made into its primary ideologeme at the very outset. The public sphere, transparency, and democracy cannot be deduced from nor reduced to one another, but the ideology of the digital age seems to be convinced that the use of technology and the possibility of participation are alone sufficient for creating a corresponding political sensibility and a

---

[4] Response-ability is founded in responsivity. It is more than mere legal or duty-based responsibility because it foregrounds alterity. Response-ability responds to the primacy of the Other and thus always is in relation to an Other.

sense for equality and justice. Within the confines of connectibility, participation can produce nothing more than an endless proceduralism based in binary grammars that put either/or decisions above everything else. Thus, they allow neither for "taking part" in collective life nor "sharing" common things, just as they are incompatible with the old Platonic or Christian idea of methexis, the meta-hexis as the act of caring for the whole, whether it be kosmos, physis, or creation. What dominates is nothing but formal exchange and practices of transmitting, saving and repeating data and information.

Data and information are not even capable of revealing truth, not to speak of their inability to serve as guarantees of transparency. They cannot be reduced to knowledge, just as praxis cannot be reduced to operations (Mersch 2016b). The digital mode of "equal rights" and what might be called "connective" transparency as opposed to "responsible" transparency are matters of indexes and protocols, which is to say that what counts are the number of "clicks," "followers," and "friends" one has or the quantity of data one posts or downloads, rather than content and semantics. It is thus no wonder that we are constantly being forced to choose. When we are linked in, we are constantly selecting, a procedure that fortifies the association of participation with choice and transparency with selectivity, which are both based on the decision-making logic that can only count to "two": "for" or "against," "all" or "nothing," "zero" or "one," "on" or "off." It is the mathematical regime of binaries that determines technology, which, for its part, seems to only be open to the horizon of the decidable and repeatable. Just like technology itself, we choose programs, look for links, "like" and "dislike," and in particular those data through which we reveal ourselves, all with the end effect of freely surrendering ourselves to the algorithms of the global data industries. Today, there is no transparency without this dark side, which is, in essence, the bright side of economization. Those who do not choose, who are not on Facebook and other social media sites, do not take part, remain excluded, and are viewed with suspicion, so that the transparency produced today is reduced to the quantities of connections, their use and their exploitation.

The Future of Transparency

Thus, neither our intentions nor our actions are transparent, nor are the structures of publicity and the organizations that run them. The only thing that is transparent are the traces that we leave behind. Stored in huge data repositories, they can be retrieved at any time in the form of data profiles. Rationality is not the key parameter of social transparency, nor is that which is communicable. What shapes the limits of social transparency is the possibility to capitalize on data generated by network participants and the archives of data beyond our reach. "Connectible" transparency is not transparency for others, even if it sometimes seems so, but rather capitalization based on exploitation. In a word, it is transparency for the purposes of the valorization of value. It serves to predict what we will have wanted in the future, and its truly diabolical nature reveals itself in the fusion of its promise of freedom and this seizure of our desire. Whoever participates gives themselves over to technological infrastructures that at once exploit them or enable them to communicate with others. Participation thus means participating in the infrastructure. In the end, the only alternative is between participating or opting out. What is more, as long as we play along with the digital game, we accept its rules and revalidate its power. There is nothing outside ubiquitous and persuasive computing. The consequence is that the social is affected in a way that seems to have begun to transform it into a digital machine ruled by calculations of choice and mathematical logic (Mersch 2014). By being connected, we are subordinated to these logics: we are their "followers" before we even sign up on Twitter or Facebook. This means that although we can still change the language of our experience, lifestyles and habits, we cannot change the technologies: they force themselves upon us and compel us to affirm them.

The ubiquity of computer logic also tends to cancel out and cover over all nuance, gradation and "in-between," subordinating it to the inescapable binaries of "on" and "off," "zero" and "one," "all" or "none." Thus, the network as a kind of immanence or metasystem serves as the determining factor of participation, the possibility of openness, freedom and transparency and with them the future of democracy. Only the propagation of connections through links and knots count, because while there are passages, loops and limits, there are no *diastēmata*, no intervals, liminal spaces, moments of unclarity or open points. The networks follow a linear, binary logic based on intersection and expansion, not difference and differentiality (*différance*). As a persistent branching-out, the network's strands disperse in all kinds of directions, and yet they remain deterministic because we can only go where their trajectories have already paved a path. They thus seem to have ruled out the creativity of an Other, of indeterminacy, or anything unthought that might have fallen between the cracks. Within the network, we are subjected to its rules and regimes, as its subjects we actualize its graphematic structure. Finally, it is clear that there is an insurmountable incommensurability between the exclusively syntactic relations on the one hand and the always chaotic and unpredictable "knot" of interpersonal relations on the other. The things that networks can do and represent are qualitatively different from the loose weave of "knots" (Laing 1970) of inter-human relations, which can hardly be disentangled. Inter-human relations can only be adequately described as a form of originary responsivity, which involves an indeterminable oscillation between activity and passivity, intentionality and event. There is a similar disparity between the above-discussed distinctions between information and knowledge, freedom and choice, community and connectivity, communication and connection, and transparency and selection.

The ubiquitous application of technological concepts is rewriting an entire philosophical system, substituting subjectivity with actor-networks, sociality with participation, praxis with operativity, reflection with reference, and iterability with feedback. Our conclusion is that networks are incapable of constituting community, but can at best create diagrams, patterns and maps. In other words, they only offer us loose linkages and false bonds, an agglomeration or cluster of users that, using Nancy's expression, constitute a "struction" (Nancy 2013), but not sociality. Han called these clusters a "digital swarm" that are destined to dead end in a "gathering without assembly" (Han 2013: 11). This decay of sociality affects the possibility of transparency and freedom, which remain the perpetually unfulfilled promises of the digital age. They will be upheld as long as computers and networks continue to generate little more than a dispersion of choices. By producing nothing but either-or-decisions, they call the future of transparency into question by dispensing with a key element: trust. Trust, after all, is not a matter of choice, but the very condition of possibility of making decisions.

Works Cited

Alloa, Emmanuel. 2011. *Das durchscheinende Bild. Konturen einer medialen Phänomenologie.* Berlin: diaphanes.
Eco, Umberto. 1987 [2002]. *Art and Beauty in the Middle Ages.* Trans. Hugh Bredin. New Haven: Yale University Press.
Etzioni, Amitai. 2012. Is Transparency the Best Disinfectant? *Journal of Political Philosophy* 18 (4): 389–404.
Flusser, Vilém. 1996 [2011]. *Into the Universe of Technical Images.* Trans. Nancy Ann Roth. Minneapolis: University of Minnesota Press.
Habermas, Jürgen. 1978. Der Ansatz von Habermas. In *Transzendentalphilosophische Normenbegründungen*, ed. Willi Oelmüller, 123–159. Paderborn: Ferdinand Schöningh.
———. 1979. What Is Universal Pragmatics? In *Communication and the Evolution of Society*, trans. Thomas McCarthy, 1–68. Boston: Beacon Press.
———. 1981. *Theory of Communicative Action*, 2 vols, trans. Thomas A. McCarthy. Boston: Beacon Press.
Han, Byung-Chul. 2012 [2015]. *The Transparency Society.* Trans. Erik Butler. Stanford: Stanford University Press.
———. 2013 [2017]. *In the Swarm: Digital Prospects.* Trans. Erik Butler, Cambridge, MA: MIT Press.
Hegel, G.W.F. 1842 [1975]. *Aesthetics: Lectures on Fine Art.* Trans. T.M. Knox. Oxford: Clarendon Press.
Heidegger, Martin. 1927 [2010]. *Being and Time.* Trans. Joan Stambaugh. Albany: State University of New York Press.
———. 1949/50 [1971]. The Origin of the Work of Art. In *Poetry, Language, Thought*, trans. Albert Hofstadter, 15–86. New York: Harper Perennial.
Horkheimer, Max, and Theodor W. Adorno. 1947 [2002]. *Dialectic of Enlightenment: Philosophical Fragments.* Ed. Gunzelin Schmid Noerr, trans. Edmund Jephcott. Stanford: Stanford University Press, 1.

Kant, Immanuel. 1784a [1996]. An Answer to the Question: What Is Enlightenment? In *Practical Philosophy*, trans. and ed. Mary J. Gregor, 11–22. Cambridge: Cambridge University Press.

———. 1784b [2007]. Idea for a Universal History with a Cosmopolitan Aim. Trans. Allan W. Wood. In *Anthropology, History and Education*, ed. Günter Zöller and Robert B. Louden, 107–120. Cambridge: Cambridge University Press.

Kittler, Friedrich. 1986 [1999]. *Gramophone, Film, Typewriter*. Trans. Geoffrey Winthrop-Young and Michael Wutz. Stanford: Stanford University Press.

Laing, Ronald D. 1970. *Knots*. London: Penguin.

Mersch, Dieter. 2008. *Tertium datur*. Einleitung in eine negative Medientheorie. In *Was ist ein Medium*, ed. Stephan Münker and Alexander Roesler, 304–321. Suhrkamp: Frankfurt am Main.

———. 2013. *Ordo ab chao/Order from Noise*. Berlin: diaphanes.

———. 2014. Pro-Grammata. Einige Überlegungen zu einer Theorie der Programme. In *Programm(e). Medienwissenschaftliche Symposien der DFG Bd. 1*, ed. Dieter Mersch, and Joachim Paech (Hg), S. 461–486. Berlin: Diaphanes.

———. 2016a. Meta/Dia: Two Approaches to the Medial. In *Media Transatlantic: Developments in Media and Communication Studies between North American and German-speaking Europe*, ed. Norm Friesen, 153–182. Cham: Springer.

———. 2016b. Kritik der Operativität. Bemerkungen zu einem technologischen Imperativ. *Internationales Jahrbuch für Medienphilosophie* 2: 31–53.

Nancy, Jean-Luc. 1991. *The Inoperative Community*. Trans. Peter Connor, Lisa Garbus, Michael Holland, and Simona Sawhney. Minneapolis: University of Minnesota Press.

———. 2013. Of Struction. Trans. Travis Holloway and Flor Méchain, *Parrhesia*, Vol. 17: 1–10.

———. 2014 [2016]. *The Disavowed Community*. Trans. Philip Armstrong. New York: Fordham University Press.

Nietzsche, Friedrich. 1887 [2001]. *The Gay Science*. Trans. Josefine Nauckhoff. Ed. Bernard Williams. Cambridge: Cambridge University Press.

———. 1889 [2010]. *Twilight of the Idols*. In *The Anti-Christ and Other Writings*, trans. Judith Norman, ed. Aaron Ridley and Judith Norman. Cambridge: Cambridge University Press.

———. 1988. *Kritische Studienausgabe (KSA)*. Ed. Giorgio Colli and Mazzino Montinari. Munich: dtv/de Gruyter.

Rautzenberg, Markus, and Andreas Wolfsteiner. 2010. *Hide and Seek. Das Spiel von Transparenz und Opazität*. Wilhelm Fink: Paderborn.
Schnädelbach, Herbert. 2005. *Kant*. Reclam: Leipzig.
Tuchman, Barbara. 1978. *A Distant Mirror: The Calamitous 14th Century*. New York: Ballantine Books.
Turner, Fred. 2006. *From Counterculture to Cyberculture: Stewart Brand, the Whole Earth Network, and the Rise of Digital Utopianism*. Chicago: Chicago University Press.
Waldenfels, Bernhard. 2007. *The Question of the Other*. Albany: State University of New York Press.

The Privatization of Human Interests or, How Transparency Breeds Conformity

Thomas Docherty

Introduction

"I am really two people," said the double agent and spy, Kim Philby. "I am a private person and a political person. Of course, if there is a conflict, the political person comes first" (Tweedie 2013). Espionage works by exposure, by making transparent that which is secret; and it depends upon the spying agent being able to occlude their personal, private self behind a deceptive mask. It operates in an extreme form of critical scrutiny, like a hermeneutic exercise in semiotics. As Philby's statement shows, it also operates by regulating the claims of the political self with those of the private self; but in such a way as to ensure that politics trumps privacy.

Following from this, we might usefully probe some ethical issues basic to one of the most pressing issues of our time: in a transparent society, or in a society of surveillance, what are the limits (if any) of the "private

T. Docherty (✉)
University of Warwick, Coventry, UK
e-mail: T.Docherty@warwick.ac.uk

© The Author(s) 2018
E. Alloa, D. Thomä (eds.), *Transparency, Society and Subjectivity*,
https://Doi.org/10.1007/978-3-319-77161-8_14

person"? How do we regulate the claims of privacy with those of participation in a polity or with being a "political person"?

We tend to consider political persons as being those whose life conditions are essentially public: they exist in "public life." However, what constitutes "the public"? If we consider something as being revealed to or addressed to "the public," then it must, almost by definition, address *no one in particular* but *all in general*. In this state of affairs, "the public" is of indefinite identity (Westall and Gardiner 2015). "The public" becomes a purely abstract entity, with the consequence that the category of "politics" is in danger of becoming purely theoretical, with no substantive grip on the material conditions of everyday lives. Such everyday lives are intensely, viscerally experienced by clearly identified "private" individuals. However, an attention to such particularity drives us necessarily towards ethics as a sole determinant of our social conditions. It reverses the priorities that structured Philby's thinking, threatening thereby the very possibility of our understanding society as being "political" in any way. How can we regulate private and public so as to avoid the spy's unethical treachery while yet retaining the primacy of the political as the determinant of our social lives?

Transparency can be conceptualized as that which erases the boundary between private and public, but it can also be considered as that which eradicates the difference between the secret and the revealed. There may indeed be a relation between transparency as a condition of modernity (in modern "surveillance-society" with its "culture of ethical openness") on one hand, and espionage as the studied conduct of practical secrecy on the other. Here, I will relate these emerging questions to a very specific understanding of "modernity," in order to argue that transparency has become a fundamentally conservative mechanism through which the ethics of private "behaviors" that establish norms of social conformity replaces any possibility of political change in the world.

My claim is that modernity is characterized by a reduction of the political such that it collapses and becomes merely personal, as in the slogan "the personal is political." Further, the personal or private realm of *intimacy*, itself often shaped by a philosophy of "pity," now operates in direct opposition to the social, and to the sociality of norms and normative human behaviors (Boltanski 2007: 13–14). The consequent logic, I will show, is that *critique* itself becomes conditioned entirely by the question of transparency. The fundamental cultural questions of our time become: how transparent, how true, how authentic is the *subject* or *self* that proposes any specific criticism? In this, we end up looking for a self that is "beyond hypocrisy," a self that hides nothing, that reveals all and everything, in all and everything that it is and does. However, the conservative consequence is that the demand for such transparency thereby shifts attention away from the supposed object of criticism, away from the phenomena or conditions that require critique, leaving them untouched, secure—even endorsed.

This yields a subject, "I," characterized as the fragility of the self as an anorexic size zero. The self becomes identified as a "ground zero" against which everything that it judges is to be measured, qualified, and quantified. We used to call this "neutrality" and to associate it with "objectivity." However, I will show that such objectivity is, in fact, deeply and profoundly subjective. This neutral objectivity of the "degree zero" of criticism pretends to eliminate from view the "private" subject carrying out the criticism; yet, simultaneously, the act of criticism itself becomes the primary mode in which the subject asserts itself. In asserting itself, it subdues the object of the critique in order to identify the position from which the criticism arises: that is, it says, above all, "I am," "I am that I am" (Coleridge 1975: 173–174).

This is at the root of all identity politics in cultural criticism; and it eschews the political precisely when it claims to be acting in the most overtly political fashion possible. In this—fundamentally the problem regarding modernity as such—not only does the self become axiomatically transparent; but also, sadly, there is nothing left to see. We have obliterated the political agency of the self—and with that we also obliterate our personal responsibility for history or for any agency.

Intimacy as Privation

In her 1958 study of *The Human Condition*, Hannah Arendt offers a highly original definition of modernity. Modernity is characterized by the emergence of society itself, by the birth of "the social." Society as such has not always been with us, she argues; and its precise historical emergence yields a specific set of problems regarding politics. Essentially, "the social" emerges when the borders between the private and public realms become blurred, when "housekeeping" ("economics"—*oikos nomos*—the law of the household) emerges "from the shadowy interior of the household into the light of the public sphere" (Arendt 1998: 39). The existence of "society" is another way of describing what happens when matters pertinent primarily to the private realm enter the public domain.

Our characteristic contemporary version of this is to be found in the slogan "the personal is political," a slogan that was at one time deemed crucial to the advancing of radical feminist politics. Though originating in feminism, the phrase has also had a much wider purchase in our contemporary condition, which is increasingly shaped by criticism that is grounded in variant modes of identity politics. Far from being radically critical of social norms, this turn has in fact been instrumental in consolidating conservative and anti-critical norms, essentially because it empties our political life of meaningful content or substance, displacing politics into autobiography (Judt 2010: 202).

The further consequence of this emergent modernity, for Arendt, is that we start to prioritize, prize, and even systemically overdetermine the values of intimacy. She suggests that this can be dated fairly precisely: it can be seen in "[t]he astonishing flowering of poetry and music from the middle of the eighteenth century until almost the last third of the nineteenth, accompanied by the rise of the novel, the only entirely social art form" (Arendt 1998: 39).

Things were different in antiquity. Antiquity has no place for what Arendt calls "the social" at all. The ancient world draws a clear divide between the claims of the private realm, the household or *oikos*, and the public realm, the *agora* or shared public place where debate orders the way in which people organize their world. These are simply different orders of being: they do not constitute the inside and outside of some unified entity. It is not the case that the walls or boundary of the household signal the hinge that both separates and holds together one single entity that has its interiority and exteriority on either side of the walls. In terms more pertinent to my argument, this is a straightforward division between economics and ecology, between *oikos nomos*, as the law of the household, and *oikos logos*, or reasoned concern for our environment.

The ancient world's private realm is shaped by the struggle for biological survival. As such, it is governed by *necessity*, granting the head of the household the right to exercise violence—but only so that we can escape from the necessary struggle for survival into classical freedom, where we have the luxury of engaging choice as a realization of historical contingencies. As Arendt puts it, "force and violence are justified in this [private] sphere because they are the only means to master necessity … and to become free" (Arendt 1998: 31). By contrast, it is the public realm that is axiomatically the realm of freedom, characterized as the space or realm in which "free men" (i.e. men who have mastered the basic needs of survival) engage in dialogue to establish the polity. In this public realm, participants regulate conflict through its diversion from violence into dialogue, while "force or violence becomes the monopoly of government" (Arendt 1998: 31). This invites comparison with Hobbes, when he argued in 1651 that it is only through an appeal to some entity that transcends individual subjects that we can avoid a state of nature in which we would have only a "war of every man against every man," and in which justice would have no place (Hobbes 1994: 78).

Modernity, according to Arendt, blurs the distinction of private and public, bringing the two orders of being together, and thereby producing "the social." If we follow this logic, the consequence is that our very understanding of the private and the public must change. Once conjoined, and even though they are conjoined in a "blurred" fashion, they become distinct elements of the one phenomenon. The private sphere is elevated and magnified to encompass the greater *idea* of the political (or ideology as such); and in this, we also get a sudden prioritization of the *values* of the private realm, especially that of "intimacy."

A "blurring" of the distinction of private and public also introduces the idea and even the structural necessity of a concept of transparency as such. Prior to modernity, there is no relation at all between these two: we do not "look through" a wall that separates them: they are simply different orders of being. In modernity, however, they become intrinsically related to each other, integral to each other's definition and delineation.

They open themselves to deconstruction by establishing a structural relation that constitutes what we call, after Arendt, "society" itself.

Modernity establishes intimacy as a phenomenon conditioned by secrecy, as if intimacy can be found only in a place secreted away; yet it is also a phenomenon that, though occluded, can be looked into, however opaque the window may be. The task of modern criticism now becomes precisely one of hermeneutic—*kerygma*—seeing through the glass darkly, "spying," "unmasking," revealing that which remains occluded as the essence of interiority, be it the interior meaning of a text, the interior psyche of a writer or other individual, the interior structure of an ideology and so on. Criticism becomes the decryption of an enigma.

Transparency—as the structuring of this very specific kind of intimacy—becomes the primary cultural determinant of modernity. Transparency normalizes criticism as a form of hermeneutic grounded in the same kind of distrust that shapes both secrecy and espionage. In doing so, it incidentally but intrinsically characterizes the political as the normalization of social conformity, proposing thereby that any subversion of those norms can be initiated only in the realm of privacy. That is Winston Smith's logic, for example, in *Nineteen Eighty-Four*, where he and Julia envisage sex as a subversive political act designed to undermine totalitarianism.

We can test Arendt's dating of this phenomenon. In 1759, Voltaire published *Candide*. Famously, the tale's ostensible "message" is given at the end. Candide and his group, having submitted to terrible misfortunes, come across an old man. They ask him if he has any detailed news about the recent assassination of the Grand Mufti. He has none:

> J'ignore absolument l'aventure dont vous me parlez; je présume qu'en général ceux qui se mêlent des affaires publiques périssent quelquefois misérablement, et qu'ils le méritent; mais je ne m'informe jamais de ce qu'on fait à Constantinople; je me contente d'y envoyer les fruits du jardin que je cultive. [I know nothing at all about this story you're telling me; I presume that, in general, those who get mixed up in public matters sometimes die horribly, and deservedly so; but I don't seek to know what goes on in Constantinople; I'm happy just to send there the produce from the garden that I tend]. (Voltaire 1968: 148–149; my translation)

The "lesson" for Candide is that it is best to withdraw entirely from the public realm. Candide's *economic* existence is now to be fully governed by *ecology*: "il faut cultiver notre jardin" [we have to tend our garden]. The private realm takes precedence over the public, and even involves the abandonment of any public role. It also confirms the residual idea that the private realm is that where we struggle for bare life, tending a private garden for sustenance: this is how Candide will survive.

This mid-eighteenth-century text seemingly advocates a withdrawal from the world or public realm, and a concentration on the ecological: the management of the local concerns of a small household. It re-draws ecology—*oikos logos*—as the ground for an economy—*oikos nomos*. Crucially, however, it also does this by prioritizing the "privacy" of such ecology: it removes ecology from the worldly environment, and makes it an individual and private matter. The world, as such, is lost: Constantinople may as well not exist.

The withdrawal from the public realm is conditioned by a corresponding elevation of the values of intimacy. Candide, Cunégonde, Paquette, Martin, Friar Giroflée and even Pangloss exist in communal intimacy with each other, as the final paragraph of the tale makes clear. Better to find one's real self in private like this than to concern oneself with political and the public realm—which in *Candide*, in an inversion of Arendt's ancient world, is shaped by violence and tyrannical mayhem.

This returns us to an earlier sense of the private: Arendt's explanation of the root of the word in "privation." Arendt indicates the link between privacy and privation, which were intimate terms in the ancient world: "A man who lived only a private life, who like the slave was not permitted to enter the public realm, or like the barbarian had chosen not to establish such a realm, was not fully human" (Arendt 1998: 38). We have lost that sense of privation because of a kind of reversal: modern individualism has so enriched the private intimate sphere that we often prioritize it over the public. This, in fact, is Candide's own personal end-point; but it is very important to see that, in this emergent modernity, the political is being restricted, collapsed into the private sphere.

In short, "the political is personal"; or politics is a private matter. That is problematic, for it also means the end of politics as a matter of public concern or as something that structures the shared public sphere.

Communication as Betrayal

However, is it the unproblematic case that the private realm *can* be thus positively valorized? Arendt points out that, for Aristotle, "man's highest capacity ... [was] not *logos*, that is, not speech or reason, but *nous*, the capacity of contemplation, whose chief characteristic is that its content cannot be rendered in speech" (Arendt 1998: 27). In one way, this is the very extreme of the valorization of the private self: a self that is so intimate with itself that it cannot communicate.

Wittgenstein had considered the same issue, albeit in a very different political and cultural context. In his posthumously published *Philosophical Investigations*, the question takes the form of the "private language" problem: "can we ... imagine a language in which a person could write down or give vocal expression to his inner experiences—his feelings, moods, and the rest—for his private use?" (Wittgenstein 2009: §243).

Wittgenstein, as we know, answers this in the negative. Yet, in doing so, he also again reinstates our problem regarding the private realm and its relation to the public. He allows for the utter privacy of sensation—the limit- or test-case is the sensation and experience of pain—but although it may be true that that experience is utterly private, it is so in a philosophically trivial sense. It constitutes a test case of his closing proposition in the *Tractatus*: "Whereof we cannot speak"—Aristotle's *nous*, the utter intimacy of self-with-self that constitutes sensation—"thereof we must pass over in silence" (Wittgenstein 2001: §7). Therefore we cannot comprehend this privacy, this intimacy of self-with-self, nor can we communicate it. "Comprehension"—axiomatically, intrinsically, and by definition—requires a community of speakers or writers.

Otherwise put: that which constitutes our understanding of reality is not the sensation considered in its isolation from the world; rather, it is the communication of the sensation (even if only to oneself) and its understanding or agreement as to its meaning and/or significance. This is often referred to as the "community" solution of the question of a private language. How can we describe pain? We have a vocabulary for it; but we can never "know" each other's experience of it. What we may call the "logic of sensation" is what I describe as "intimacy."

Language is essentially a community event; and "the public" is where that event exists, and where it can be subjected to analysis, testing, verification, falsification—or simply to debate. Indeed, we can go so far as to say that these verifications, falsifications, and debates *constitute* the public sphere. Meanings are communally produced as elements in the constitution of "the public," the public realm as a space for language. This is why an address to "the public" is an address to a generality, a non-identifiable "community."

A "private language" is that address when made to a particular; and its only consequence is a confirmation of my identity with myself, a confirmation that this sensation of pain, say, constitutes "me," "now." However, this "I" exists within a community that gives a reality to the sensation of pain, and confirms is as a particular example of a general condition (even if the specifics of pain, or of "red," for each member of the community may be different). To subscribe to this radical intimacy—this collapsing of the political sphere into the private—is to confirm a radical identity politics: as I noted above, all it says, eventually, is "I am I." It intrinsically reduces all poetry, all writing, to autobiography. Arendt contests the radical atomization in this account of society more succinctly: No human life, not even the life of the hermit in nature's wilderness, is possible without a world which directly or indirectly testifies to the presence of other human beings" (Arendt 1998: 22).

In one way, this position seems to lead to an endorsement of the ethics of the spy. It suggests that it is only the political life—only that which is transparently available in the public space or *agora*—that constitutes the reality of a self or a life. The consequence of that, as with Philby, is that the private self must be subjugated to the priorities of the political. At that point, the private life has become colonized by the political, to such an extent that public resistance to whatever constitutes political norms becomes impossible, because resistance itself has been privatized. The autonomous acts of the individual agent become legitimate—speakable, readable, *legible*—only to the extent that they conform to social norms. A critique of those norms can then only be viewed and understood either as a folly or as an act conditioned by a kind of "criminality" that the public sphere regards as (literally) unspeakable.

The more productive way of looking at this disturbing condition is to say that language—the community of communication as such—becomes the site not only of community but also of a specific problem: the problem concerning transparency. Does our speech—*logos*—reveal, transparently, the sensation of the self—*oikos*? Is reason as such the transparent realization or manifestation of the empirical or experiential self?[1] In its crudest and most basic form: does the body itself—as and when it appears in the public sphere—reveal, transparently, the private person?

That is surely an uncomfortable proposition, for it opens the door to an unacceptable politics in which individuals can be discriminated against because of their biological or ethnic condition (race, gender, sexuality, physical condition as able-bodied or disabled and so on). Yet the alternative also seems awkward, because it makes language and communication the site of obfuscation and obscurity; and what follows from that would be an implicit endorsement of a mode of social life itself as espionage. Like Philby, betrayal and mistrust would become legitimized as a normative condition of social life or of politics.

Technologies of the Public

For Arendt, the key issues here are biopolitical. In Arendt's ancient public realm, the presence of the body—the speaking body—was important and central to political life. It was not possible to be political within the private realm, for there we were not freed from necessity, from the demand for biological survival. Modernity, in changing this, coincides also with technological change, especially with the change in technology and consumerism that produces what Habermas calls the "public sphere." Above all, these changes involve coffee and print.

As Markman Ellis points out, "coffee's eruption into daily life seems to coincide with the modern historical period," with the first coffee houses in London dating from the 1650s, in "a city gripped with revolutionary fervor." Johnson defined a coffee house as "A house of entertainment

---

[1] This is a different way of exploring Paul de Man's concerns in his "Rhetoric of Temporality" essay, in *Blindness and Insight* (1983). See my criticism of that work in my *After Theory* (1996: 119–125).

where coffee is sold, and the guests are supplied with newspapers." It becomes clear that "In the coffee-house, men learnt new ways of combinatorial friendship, turning their discussions there into commercial ventures, critical tribunals, scientific seminars and political clubs" (Ellis 2005: xi–xii). The drug of caffeine combined with the daily urgency of print helped to construct the specifically modern phenomenon of the public sphere itself.

We should note that the "public sphere" in Habermas is markedly different from the "public space" or public realm in Arendt. For Habermas, the technological innovations here—print and the institutional commerce of coffee—produced a less tangible, less physically material instance of the political. Language itself—texts—are constitutive of the political; and it is this condition of "communication" or of a "culture of conversation" that gives us a public *sphere*, which exists, for Habermas, both within *and beyond* the material space of coffee-houses, public squares and the like. Importantly, my body does not need to be "present" in the public sphere to exist or to exert an influence there. Politically, we inaugurate what will become a long historical process of "de-materialization."

This public sphere can be and often is largely characterized precisely by my personal absence, and the replacement of my physical speaking self with the virtual written or textual self. The *text* is now precisely the site of our issue regarding transparency: what does the *text* reveal or conceal? These are the questions that now shape the conversation that constitutes politics in/as the public sphere itself. Politics now becomes an issue regarding textual hermeneutics, regarding those various transparencies that I mentioned above (revelation of meaning, of self, of ideology).

The material force of body language (and its attendant potential for violence), we might say, gives way to the abstractions of reason itself, *logos*. However, this—the operation of logic/reason—is what now demands transparency. Further, it requires confidential trust, and this is something that does not depend upon the idea that reason is manifest in the physical body or in the physical force that can be exerted by the material body as such.

For Habermas, therefore, the public sphere is a somewhat nebulous affair, constituted by speeches, memories, films, literature, newspapers, symbolic forms—but only insofar as these are shared elements, only insofar as they are communicable. The public sphere is constructed by and constituted by acts of communication. Sensation is banished from this public sphere, for sensation is a "purely" personal matter, dependent upon the physical body itself. Habermas essentially rejects the political importance of intimate sensation as such. Controversially, one might even go so far as to say that he rejects the value of material experience, and prefers instead to prioritize the existence of communicative acts. At the very least, we can say that, in the shift from public space to public sphere, we have made private life more precarious, through that combination of technology (print) with a specific regulation of the material and physiological body (as affected by a drug, caffeine).

In our contemporary moment, there has been a further turn in technology. In an age of digitization and of the "virtual" self, private life can become more precarious still. The consequence of this further stage of technological development is that we are now well on the way towards the evacuation of content and substance from politics itself. In *Precarious Life*, Judith Butler comes close to describing what is at stake here. For her, the question focuses on how and under what conditions a subject must assume ethical responsibility: "Does anyone stand by the words they utter? Can we still trace those words to a speaker, or, indeed, a writer?" (Butler 2006: 129). She attempts to resolve the conundrum of "the structure of address" through an engagement with the "face-to-face" in Levinasian ethics; but in doing so, she blurs the distinction between the face as itself the immaterial condition of an ethical command and actual human faces (even if in mediated form in images and representations). However, she arrives still at the fundamental question regarding bio-political transparency when she wonders about the task of cultural criticism, and whether it might be "to return us to the human where we do not expect to find it" and "to interrogate the emergence and vanishing of the human at the limits of what we can know, what we can hear, what we can see, what we can sense" (Butler 2006: 151).

We can understand this better, in terms specifically of a politics of cultural transparency, if we turn to Peter Sloterdijk. Sloterdijk begins *Bubbles*, the first volume of his *Spheres* "Microspherology" trilogy, by giving us an image of a child blowing a soap bubble (an actual image, the mezzotint called *Bubbles*, by GH Every, 1887, after John Everett Millais). He describes what happens:

> ... a large oval balloon, filled with timid life, quivers off the loop and floats down to the street, carried along by the breeze. It is followed by the hopes of the delighted child, floating out into the space in its own magic bubble as if, for a few seconds, its fate depended on that of the nervous entity.... For the duration of the bubble's life the blower was outside himself, as if the little orb's survival depended on remaining encased in an attention that floated out with it. (Sloterdijk 2011: 17)

This is not just transparency; it is also a dramatization of a deconstruction. Our "spatial" understanding of the politics of transparency in terms of the interiority of privacy and the exteriority of politics is put under question in the figure of the bubble. This bubble yields an understanding of political life as such, in which the inside of the self can continue to exist *as an interiority of the body* while *simultaneously being externalized* in the bubble (perhaps even the cartoon "speech bubble" that figures and reveals thought). The image also demonstrates that this relation is structured by precariousness, in the extremely temporary and fragile condition of the bubble itself. As or when it bursts, what happens to the *psyche* that evaporates? Does that have a repercussive effect on the self that remains within the child's body?

Sloterdijk's bubble is a useful image for the new transparency that dominates contemporary culture. It describes the fragility of the self when it enters the public terrain, and it also maps a kind of disengagement of the self: the child's breath, *psyche* or soul may be "inside" the bubble, yet it also remains inside the material body of the child. What this reveals, yet again, is the necessity of a deconstruction of the interior/exterior structure that conditions modernity, precisely in the form of transparency. Transparent modernity is also now conditioned by this fundamentally fragile precariousness. The significant contemporary shift here is that this precariousness is not just the precariousness of the self, already so well documented in contemporary theory and sociology. It is also the precariousness of politics itself, which faces a structural demise or disappearance. In our contemporary predicament a "philosophy of transparency" shifts into a "culture of immateriality" that calls into question the very possibility of linking a speaker to a speech. The consequence, as far as cultural criticism is concerned, is that we produce a problem regarding the responsibilities—ethical *and* political—of the subject, and above all of the subject as cultural critic, in her or his own writings.

The dangerous issue that we face here is, in its most fundamental condition, the possible complete evisceration of the public sphere, and its replacement instead with a culture—even a cult—of intimacy. This, in turn, reduces politics to a populist celebration of celebrity, in which subjects and citizens are encouraged to believe in their own intimacy with public figures (populist UK newspapers calling the Royal Family by first or even pet-names: "Charlie," "Wills" and so on). It was surely only a matter of time before the whole political domain itself became dominated and shaped by celebrity, as in the figures of Donald Trump in the US, or various populist figures (Marine Le Pen, Geert Wilders, Nigel Farage) from the far right in Europe. When we reach this stage, "political" critique can be reduced to the attempt to spy through the keyhole and to catch people unawares at their most intimate moments. Hence we get arguments about the size of Trump's "hands" (metonymy for "penis"), or stories emerging about various scandals in private life (sexual, financial, and so on). In short: the political world collapses into the most intimate part of the human self.

This entails the demise of politics, and its replacement with gossipy prurience. Meanwhile, economic structures (of mass inequality, or the enshrining of financial privilege, of organizing all relations in terms of profit-making and rent-seeking) continue without being substantially subjected to question or to real and material change in the polity. We dignify all this, however, by the inauguration of newer forms of economics, and most specifically, the establishment of the new economics of well-being, the quantification of human happiness, the economic structures of the private intimate life.

This amounts to the perversion of intimacy into corruption. The corresponding politics is grounded in espionage: the mistrust that says we are being betrayed, and that demands transparency to reveal that betrayal.

This explains the general sense of *ressentiment* or resentment that shapes political movements in our time. "Everyone knows" that everyone is being cheated in some way; and everyone knows who is to blame: it is the figure of "the foreigner," the figure of anything that stands outside of whatever constitutes "my own" personal, private, intimate identity. In this way, politics has become fully personalized, as if we could solve political crises by sole reference to our own private desires and identity. The entire political realm disappears into the private.

Political action now becomes, at best, an action aimed at validating specific cultural identities (in which the self finds allegiance with other individuals with "protected" traits of race, gender, sexuality and so on); and, at worst, a matter of personal whim in which, like Trump, pathological lying becomes normative. This is not lying in the usual sense of occluding truth: it is rather a specific psycho-political condition in which statements can be made and rejected almost in the same sentence. Like the schizophrenic who lives in a continuous present tense, Trump represents the zenith of a specific "modernity" as such: it is the modernity of the "modern author" that we found in Swift's 1704 *Tale of a Tub*. This author, standing up for the moderns against the knowledge of the ancients, is *so* modern and consistently up-to-date that each new sentence is effectively a new departure, erasing the past even as he writes, such that, logically, his sentences themselves are out-of-date even as he tries to write them.

In this (like Trump and other celebrity-politicians), the modern individual—conditioned by that transparency that is seen in the alleged intimacy that we "ordinary" people can have with celebrities—erases the past, erases history, erases anything that might be called evidence and empirical reality, and forges forward into the constant invention of a new—but now radically unhinged—self. In the end, politics is reduced to personal faith—faith in a face, an individual—instead of reason. This is the ground of the new fundamentalism that grounds all judgment and all criticism in my own person, in "my" own personal whim. It says, "this is so," and when asked "why," it replies "because I am me." It is a gross perversion of the Lutheran principle caught in the phrasing of responsibility, "Here I take my stand."

Society as Coercive Conformity

Arendt's argument—that modernity is conditioned by the intrusion of the private into the public realm—offers us a new fundamental distinction: the private sphere is *not* the opposite of the political, but of the social:

> The decisive historical fact is that modern privacy in its most relevant function, to shelter the intimate, was discovered as the opposite not of the political sphere but of the social, to which it is therefore more closely and authentically related. (Arendt 1998: 38)

The triumph of "the social" produces the normative demand for social conformity, such that it is only in the intimate sphere that we can find distinctiveness.

At one level, of course, we have never had such a high degree of transparency in all things. A culture of transparency has led to the production of a huge amount of previously unrevealed information and data. This is so much the case that the analysis of "big data" has itself become almost a full academic discipline. It is as if there has been a clear correspondence between mass society, mass higher education, and mass data.[2] Yet this is not entirely new. Structurally, we have seen similar things before. With the development of what sociologists identified as "mass society" we had to find new ways of understanding how society worked. The harvesting of "big data" was preceded in the 1940s in the UK by the Mass Observation social research project. Mass Observation operated in the mode of espionage: investigators eavesdropped on private conversations, spied and reported on work colleagues and so on. "Big data" operates in exactly the same way, but with more advanced technology.

Behind this social development lies the elevation of economics as a kind of meta-discipline, as a kind of "code" that will somehow help us to understand all social, political, cultural—and, above all, interpersonal

---

[2] The harvesting of such "big data" has itself also become an important political weapon. See, for example, Carole Cadwalladr's (2017) exposé of Robert Mercer and the "Cambridge Analytica" organization. In this, Cadwalladr shows how "big data" is being used to manipulate behavior—and attitude or emotions—among voters. This is analyzed also in Thompson (2016: 21–22).

and private—relations. Capital economics colonizes the subject through the economics of intimacy. Economics, however, depends upon two things: a lot of information, and a tendency to abstraction; and it works on the basis of a presumed (abstract) equality of all individuals (for each is simply the node or nexus of abstract bits of information) in a society.

As Arendt argued, "mass society" is another way of describing a unified homogeneous social world. Mass society indicates that various social groups have been absorbed into one specific identity, precisely as a single identifiable mass. Further, "the social has finally ... reached the point where it embraces and controls all members of a given community equally and with equal strength" (Arendt 1998: 41). It follows that "society equalizes under all circumstances, and the victory of equality in the modern world is only the political and legal recognition of the fact that society has conquered the public realm, and that distinction and difference have become private matters of the individual" (Arendt 1998: 41).

The public realm had once been where individuals displayed their individuality and distinctiveness. Now, it is the space for conformity and an abstract equality, which we often mistake for "democracy." The only real distinctiveness to be found in that world, now, is financial: it is the distinction between the 1 percent and the rest. Meanwhile the interests of economics are diverted from the political constitution that endorses this, and are directed instead into the personal and private realm. Personal distinctiveness—the basic condition that demands democracy as a political structure—is now a private matter; democracy in the public sphere lapses into the merest populism. This makes the demand for "transparency" all the more pressing; but it also means that the demand for transparency has become determinedly complicit with the acceptance of a normative surveillance; and what surveillance is looking for is "deviant" behavior or conduct.

Arendt describes the resulting predicament well, writing that "It is decisive that society, on all its levels, excludes the possibility of action, which formerly was excluded from the household. Instead, society expects from each of its members a certain kind of behavior, imposing innumerable and various rules, all of which tend to 'normalize' its members, to make them behave, to exclude spontaneous action or outstanding achievement" (Arendt 1998: 40). To survive in the material world of the public sphere, in these conditions, is to refuse the very possibility of criticism or of dissidence: only conformity to predetermined social norms will be recognized as legitimate. The political is now emptied of content, or—at best—reduced to the status of personal character.

Worse, having driven critique and dissent into the private realm, society now becomes explicitly a surveillance society that demands transparency, a transparency in which our inmost and most intimate self must be spied on. Society looks into this most intimate selfhood for evidence of deviant behavior and deviant thought. The nightmare dystopia of Orwell's "Household Spies" is upon us at this point; and transparency becomes the instrument by which dissent will be eradicated and conformity established. Politics has given place to pious prurience, but a prurience that is coercive.

Precarious Subjectivity

This situation extends well beyond the domain of everyday politics. It infiltrates every social and cultural institution. The issue of "behaviors" has now become a key term in institutional and political management, and is subject to the monitoring of "human resources" departments, perhaps nowhere more so than in an institution that should be the most welcome host for dissent: the University. It is also important in the structural organization of society at large, an administered society that demands certain types of behavior, and dismisses criticism of its norms *precisely because* that criticism is mooted *as* "political." In this situation, it is as if being politically active in the public sphere (or even at work) is somehow intrinsically subversive of the existing (allegedly non-political, natural) order of things. This prioritization of "behavior" goes together with the demotion of "labor" in our contemporary transformation of material labor into the less material forms of "service." We no longer make or produce things, but engage simply in service industries. We don't make doors and windows, we just hold them open for each other to go through or look through.

Gorz points out that contemporary technology, and especially digitization of industries, has led to the position where work becomes "the management of a continuous information flow," in and through which it is not the specific knowledge or vocational skill of the worker that is important; rather it is her or his adaptability, her or his behavior that matters. The emphasis is on "behavioral skills, expressive and imaginative abilities and personal involvement in the task at hand" (Gorz 2010: 6–7). Performance is now measured in terms of the employee's personal commitment to specific forms of "acceptable behavior." Transparency in contemporary society is vital insofar as it strives to ensure that the citizen *really* commits to determined social conformity. In our behavior, we must *show* that we are the "shiny happy people" of the utopian polity. Transparency cultures are profoundly coercive; we must "really" love our Big Brothers.

In this state of affairs, it is the human subject herself whose Sloterdijkian bubble has now burst, and has become profoundly *immaterial*, insubstantial and of no consequence. We are now conditioned as immaterial subjects: transparent and precarious, like the child's balloon. Worse, however, the political sphere itself has also thus become immaterial. It is nothing more than a contemporary business, a series of transactional relations shaped not by material content but by normative processes, whose legitimacy is governed precisely by mass conformist behavior.

This—the contemporary triumph of a politics of transparency—leads us to politics as espionage. Political power has shifted from the boardroom to the bedroom; and political "participation," such as it is, is no more than peering pruriently through someone's window. The voyeur has replaced the voter; and this makes us all merely "onlookers" onto the political and public sphere.

Transparency as the Poor Substitute for Truth

We are witnessing here the culmination of a particular neoliberal political drive. Throughout the 1980s, many advanced economies succumbed to Chicago School economics (normalized for politics by Reaganomics and Thatcherism above all), an economics driven by the primacy of *private* gain, profit and greed. When Gordon Gekko in Oliver Stone's *Wall Street* sermonized that "greed is good," he was simply reiterating the frequent statements of Milton Friedman. Neoliberalism was underpinned by a logic of privatization: the systematic transfer of commonly shared wealth—as held in various utilities such as telecommunications, gas, electricity, water and the like—into a small number of private hands. This was "justified" by a determination to shrink the State, and to shrink also the public sphere in direct proportion to the minimization of government.

Simultaneously all values—ethical, social, cultural, political and so on—were monetized. The prevailing discourse of securing "value for money" instrumentalizes all human relations as mechanisms for profit. Yet how could one *measure* "value" if not in *quantitative* terms? Thus, "value for money" was actually the sleight-of-hand cover for the more venal determination to seek profit: "more money out to me, and less money invested by me." When all values can be commercialized in this way—reconstituted as commodities—then it becomes the whole of human interests that are subject to privatization. Nowhere is this more evident than in the University, as an institution that has become fully financialized: "knowledge" itself, reduced to "bits of information" that we manage economically, efficiently, has itself been privatized, as students find themselves privately indebted for the acquisition of their degrees. The position is general across the whole of society. In the contemporary age of digitization, we annihilate every possible opposition to the flow of capital. As Gorz puts it, "Everything becomes a commodity. Selling oneself extends to all aspects of life. Everything is measured in money" (Gorz 2010: 23).

It is not so much that we are barred from the public sphere or from participation in politics. It is the case, rather, that the public sphere is now so eviscerated of content that all we have are our own privatized interests. The philosophical position that follows from this yields an extremely serious problem. Transparency has become our poor substitute for truthful speaking; and truth itself has become a matter of whatever any individual private subject wishes to believe. Under the sign of transparency, we all have our own "alternative facts," for there is no shared common public sphere wherein we might test our "facts" against empirical and material realities that are commonly shared and acknowledged. While it remains imperative that we can discern covert political motives, covert significations, and corrupt but hidden activities, a culture of transparency will not solve the problems: it is simply the obverse of a culture of surveillance, in which our behaviors are restricted, controlled, and reduced to political insignificance.

Works Cited

Arendt, Hannah. 1998. *The Human Condition*. 2nd ed. Chicago: University of Chicago Press.
Boltanski, Luc. 2007. *La souffrance à distance*. Paris: Gallimard.
Butler, Judith. 2006. *Precarious Life*. London: Verso.
Cadwalladr, Carole. 2017. Robert Mercer. London, *Observer: New Review*, February 26.
Coleridge, Samuel Taylor. 1975. *Biographia Literaria*. Ed. George Watson. London: Dent.
De Man, Paul. 1983. *Blindness and Insight*. Minneapolis: University of Minnesota Press.
Docherty, Thomas. 1996. *After Theory*. 2nd ed. Edinburgh: Edinburgh University Press.
Ellis, Markman. 2005. *The Coffee-House: A Cultural History*. London: Phoenix.
Gorz, André. 2010. *The Immaterial*. Trans. Chris Turner. Kolkata: Seagull.
Hobbes, Thomas. 1994. *Leviathan*. Ed. Edwin Curley. Indianapolis: Hackett.
Judt, Tony. 2010. *The Memory Chalet*. London: Heinemann.
Sloterdijk, Peter. 2011. *Spheres: Vol. 1, Bubbles*. Trans. Wieland Hoban. Cambridge, MA: Semiotext(e).
Thompson, Mark. 2016. *Enough Said: What's Gone Wrong with the Language of Politics*. London: Bodley Head.
Tweedie, Neil. 2013. Kim Philby, Father, Husband, Traitor, Spy. *Telegraph*, January 23. http://www.telegraph.co.uk/history/9818727/Kim-Philby-Father-husband-traitor-spy.html.
Voltaire. 1968. *Candide*. Ed. J.H. Brumfitt. Oxford: Oxford University Press.
Westall, Claire, and Michael Gardiner. 2015. *The Public on the Public*. London: Palgrave.
Wittgenstein, Ludwig. 2001. *Tractatus Logico-Philosophicus*. 2nd ed. London: Routledge.
———. 2009. *Philosophical Investigations*. 4th ed. London: Wiley-Blackwell.

Part III

From the Panopticon to the Selfie and Back

Transparency and Subjectivity: Remembering Jennifer Ringley

Vincent Kaufmann

The Invention of Reality Television

Who does remember you, Jenni? In 1996, you were twenty years old, webcams had just been invented, they were relatively expensive and not as good as they are today. The Internet was still in its infancy, not yet interactive, not yet Web 2.0. But you were quick on the draw, you started in 1996 as one of the first "webcasters" or "web artists," as you used to describe yourself. You were a student, somewhere in Pennsylvania, and you had created a website called Jennicam, you had bought some of these webcams and you were visible 24/7 in your dorm room. Visibility was quite cheap and it was profitable so long as you were the only one to invest in webcams. Jennicam lasted seven years, from 1996 to 2003, and at its peak each day netted you around four million visitors, who were not yet called "followers," since the vocabulary of social media had not yet

---

V. Kaufmann (✉)
University of St. Gallen, St. Gallen, Switzerland
e-mail: vincent.kaufmann@unisg.ch

© The Author(s) 2018
E. Alloa, D. Thomä (eds.), *Transparency, Society and Subjectivity*,
https://doi.org/10.1007/978-3-319-77161-8_15

been created. Visitors are voyeurs, followers are improved, interactive voyeurs, and the history of humankind is one of endless progress.

Over the years, Jennicam improved and become sophisticated, with a differentiated structure of paywalls that gave access to further rooms of your now-larger apartment (as you were getting rich and had consequently moved to Washington). Depending on their interests and their revenue, the visitors could watch you in your living room, reading, talking, thinking, taking care of your laundry or doing nothing, in your kitchen, cooking, eating and maybe thinking, or in your bedroom, sleeping and sometimes masturbating a little bit or having a good time with your boyfriend. In the two first years, you also engaged in strip-tease, but this was a service you gave up after having apparently been hacked and threatened by some of your clients. Although no precise data are available, it is reasonable to assume that your bedroom was probably subject to more visits than your kitchen und subsequently also more expensive for site visitors to watch, at least if everything happened according to mainstream microeconomics.

Some experts claim you invented reality television (Pop17 2008), but this is a complicated issue and one more question for historians of media. Some TV formats from the eighties or the beginning of the nineties certainly could be considered the ancestors of modern reality television, and it is also unclear whether the creative employees of Endemol who apparently launched modern reality television with "Big Brother" in 1999 had any idea about Jennicam. Were they enthusiastic visitors of your bedroom, or did they just land on the same idea, more or less the same idea? Was Jennicam plagiarized by "Big Brother"? We might never really know, but if they were your fans, it would be an irony of history for reality television to have been invented by a future media, so to speak. For the internet to reprogram television, to make it invent reality television would be ironic. It would be ironic yet consistent with the whole history of media, which consists of complex series of actions, reactions and feedback loops, or of processes of cross-contamination (Debray 2004). And when we think about contamination, we could as well pretend, since you defined yourself as a web *artist*, that you were actually just doing with a few new technical devices what many "performers" already did live in art galleries and elsewhere in the sixties and seventies. That would also mean that you should be remembered not only as one of the first virtual exhibitionists but also as the manager of one of the first virtual art galleries, this one systematically devoted to yourself.

Whatever you have invented, Jenni, you have to admit that between Jennicam and the reality television formats invented around the turn of the millennium, quite a few differences come to mind. The quality of picture and sound of your website was obviously not the same as that offered by television. Today TV is playing catch-up to the quality of the Internet, which has dramatically improved; television screens now aim for high and higher definition to rival those of computer screens, but at the end of the nineties, this was not yet an issue. Moreover, Jennicam was probably too democratic a project to really last, although one might argue that with regard to the general time-frame of the Internet economy, seven years was not that bad. The main problem, in comparison with reality television, was that Jennicam was not *exclusive* enough. All you needed was a connection and some money to buy a few webcams and there you were, visible 24/7. That's not how the then-emerging economy of attention or visibility really worked. According to Georg Franck, attention is among the most desirable and precious things we wish for, it is even our new currency, but it only works this way as long as it remains exclusive, since that allows us to accord value to visibility (Franck 1998). As soon as visibility is accessible to everyone, it becomes meaninglessness or at least devoid of value. True visibility has to be exclusive, and therefore it is necessarily asymmetrical: you only get visibility when a lot of (invisible) people watch you (Heinich 2012). That was initially the case with Jenni, who seems to have had some first mover advantage there, but did her business remain sustainable once everybody can—and therefore did—jump in?

It is arguable that this change is why reality television might eventually turn out to be a better business plan than Jennicam, at least if the goal is to get visibility. You have of course to go through unpleasant castings with nasty juries and then, when you are in, you face even nastier competitors who are just as willing to do everything they can to survive the ritual weekly eliminations that are part of almost all reality television shows and amount to symbolic executions, as shown by their metaphorical version, *The Hunger Games* (Collins 2008–2010), in which the executions are made real. But if you get through, if you prevail, the benefits in terms of visibility are very high. You deserve to be watched because you have paid the price, because you have sacrificed a lot of yourself. You have given up your intimacy, you have accepted rivalry, violence, and humiliation for weeks, actively or passively, which is precisely what makes your life interesting or even exciting (Pörksen and Krischke 2012). By comparison, Jennicam is not only a low-definition show but also, compared to the sacrificial logic of reality television, a low-intensity show, with no exclusivity, no exclusions, no violence, no humiliation. Even Jenni's exhibition of intimacy seems not to have been up to the standards we are now used to, especially since we have free access to all imaginable and even some unimaginable forms of pornography.

.com or .net? From Animality to Perversion

Of course Jenni had nothing to do with pornography and prostitution—or did she? Wasn't she a *web artist*? There was a strange Freudian slip on CBS, when the popular Jenni was invited to David Letterman's late-night talk-show (Letterman 1998). Instead of displaying *jennicam.com* as her website address, CBS displayed the address *jennicam.net*, which even now leads to a website offering all kinds of paid casual as well as virtual sex. This confusion between art and prostitution seems laden with implication. Whatever the reason, the legend also has it that a few years later, Jenni had to close her website because of PayPal's anti-nudity policy. But of course the Internet as a whole allows for many kinds of paid access to nudity or pornography. At the end of the day, nobody knows for sure whether Jennicam has disappeared because to some extent it *was* falling into the category of adult websites or whether because Jenni wanted to avoid any assimilation with pornography and prostitution, since, as she claimed, she was just in the transparency business.

With regard to such an ambiguity, there was also the statement Jenni made when she was invited to the famous CBS show. Imagine the snickering Letterman asking the web artist what her parents or her boyfriend might think about her new job, as if he were shocked by her shamelessness. Would she lose her composure or at least blush a little bit at his questions? No, she wouldn't and had the following prepared answer: she was not trying to get visibility, she just did not care about being watched or not, the other's gaze was not her problem. And if families spend hours watching animals fucking and devouring each other without any modesty or shame on TV, that is, caring even less than herself whether they are watched or not, why would it be a problem if she showed herself doing nothing, eating, talking, thinking and having sexual intercourse here and there, but obviously not devouring any of her fellow students?

This interesting point in the Jennicam story provides us with a first definition of transparency. *Transparency is the way animals do it.* Animals are transparent, they don't know modesty or shame, most of the time they are naked anyways and they couldn't care less about their visibility, whatever they do. Animals don't blush, their transparency is not blurred by the stains of modesty or shame. Being transparent, showing everything but without trying to stage it, like Jenni pretends to do, therefore amounts to becoming (an) animal. This is not really new. Voltaire's famous answer to Rousseau's *De l'Origine de l'inégalité parmi les hommes*, one of the first manifestos for a transparent communication between the humans, is still relevant today: "On n'a jamais employé tant d'esprit à vouloir nous rendre bêtes. Il prend envie de marcher à quatre pattes quand on lit votre ouvrage" (Voltaire 1978). Your work, your dream of transparency makes me feel like I would walk on all fours and moreover it makes me stupid, *bête*, which in French refers again to animality: animals are *bêtes*, they think they have nothing to hide to the point that they probably do not even think something.

At this first step, and with regard to our friends the animals as well as to the almost innocent young Jenni who seems to be unable to feel something like shame or guiltiness, transparency seems quite close to innocence. Or maybe not? If transparency leads us to animality, the final destination could also be bestiality, since a lot of animals behave in a bestial way, that is, like the beasts they are. And therefore transparency might have something to do not only with innocence but also with perversion, since the perverts have this wonderful ability to behave like animals and sometimes like wild beasts, without any shame; an ability to cross the frontiers of civilization, to return to the savage "nature" in which everything is allowed—something like the lost "real" (Lacan) that the neurotic would only dream of (Freud 1953).

And if transparency concerns the perverts, it becomes a more complex notion, since it implies something like a "will to show": perverts are not only able to act, but also able to show that they act, to the point that the showing or the staging is even a basic dimension of perversion (Clavreul 1967). Which means that animals are to some extent perverts that families can watch on TV, paradoxically because they don't do it in order to be watched. Animals are PG-rated perverts or maybe metaphorical perverts, just as symmetrically, in many reality shows participants engage in metaphorical pornography, when they have to struggle with all kinds of disgusting stuff, when they have to immerse themselves in mud, like pigs, or when they are forced to suck animal penises, at least if they want to keep taking part in shows.

Of course there is a difference here. Animals do not care about being watched, whereas reality show participants always do, like the perverts, because to some extent they are perverts and therefore they never stop playing hide and seek with the other's gaze—or the Other's gaze, according to Lacan's terminology (Lacan 1977). Reality show participants would immediately protest or cease participating if the cameras were gone, while animals obviously pay no attention to whether they are on stage or not, or whether they are the objects of the Other's gaze (for there is actually no such thing as an Other in the realm of nature). Even when they walk around naked for weeks, as they did for instance on the *Adam and Eve* show, reality show participants remain on the side of perversion rather than animality. We are waiting for a Rousseauian (or Voltairean?) version of it in which the participants would go on all fours, but even that would not guarantee that they would be animals rather than perverts. It is certainly far too late for them to claim that they have no shame, as if they were truly in Paradise (and not on some Thai island), insisting like the biblical Adam and Eve that they were unaware of their being naked.

Where does this leave us regarding transparency and Jenni? Perhaps transparency could be defined as *a tightrope walk between perversion and animality, the latter consisting in hiding nothing, in showing everything without modesty or shame, in having no secrets.* This is precisely what Jenni stands for, not only when she puts herself on camera 24/7, but also by spending quite some time talking, explaining her feelings, her most private thoughts. The Jenni of the next (technological) generation will no longer need to talk, she will have a microchip implanted in her brain and we will be able to follow all her thoughts live, but for now we still depend on very primitive transparency devices and one has to concede that given the technological state of the art around the year 2000, Jenni has basically done her best.

Moreover though, Jenni represents the tightrope walk itself. She seems to oscillate between perversion (or pornography)—her exhibitionism was especially difficult to deny when she was stripping in her first years—and almost animal indifference to the other's gaze when she pretends not to care about being watched. Maybe this indifference is not only animal, but also cultural and even specifically American, since there is probably no other culture that goes so far in telling or training people not to care about the other's gaze or opinion, to rely on self-confidence rather than to trust others (Carroll 1988; Thomae 2000). And it is also typically American that this attitude does not lead to a systematic defense of privacy or intimacy but on the contrary to a nothing-to-hide-policy. Your gaze does not matter and therefore I will not hide, and even stage myself 24/7 on the Internet. I will let you into my bedroom even if—or *because*— I don't want to sleep with you. Transparency is defined here as *not only animal or perverse but American*. Jenni had to be American, just as Facebook or Google now have to be, as these companies are the main drivers of the dramatic shifts and changes currently underway with regard to privacy and therefore to transparency. It was after all Google's CEO, Eric Schmidt, who has declared that we have nothing to fear from big data if we have nothing to hide, a statement endorsed in many ways by Mark Zuckerberg, Facebook's CEO, who according to the lightly fictionalized biopic *The Network* started his brilliant career by breaking into the privacy of his female fellow-students of Harvard. The key to success is to have a good start in life.

Jenni oscillates between exhibitionism and indifference, although from a European perspective, the indifference is quite hard to believe. Can she really ignore that she is being watched, like an animal? Is she stupid enough—*bête* enough—to think that *jennicam.com* might not trigger any bad thoughts among her "followers"? And how exactly should the spectators react if they are not supposed to have bad thoughts as they would if they were watching *jennicam.net* rather than *jennicam.com*? Like perverts, or on the contrary like animals, seeing something without watching it, as if it were not a show, as if it were something natural? We will never really know, but we have now to finalize our definition of transparency: transparency consists in *disclosing everything without restriction, and choosing to do so because there is nothing to hide, because there is no secret of any relevance.*

What Jenni shows, in other terms, is that she has nothing to hide, but also, at the same time, nothing to *show*. As evidence—or at least as the symptom—for this situation, think about what remains at the heart of the Jennicam dispositive: that is, Jenni's body, which like her face is "average," not cute, not sexy, but on the other hand not ugly, although probably a bit too fat and maybe not quite tan enough. Unlike the faces of a porn star, professionals working for *jennicam.net* or carefully selected participants in reality shows, Jenni's face is the kind that would go unnoticed on the street, she would not turn heads, she would not be ogled or watched. Jenni's almost perfect transparency means that there is a point where her visibility coincides with its contrary, with invisibility. I have nothing to hide, therefore I make everything visible, I have nothing to hide, therefore I am invisible, I show you everything about me because there is nothing to be seen. "Transparency" as a concept works a little bit like Freud's *Unheimliche* (the Uncanny): there is a point where it capsizes and starts to mean its opposite, and this is indeed uncanny, turning a word deemed familiar into something suddenly alien. On the one hand, a transparent person showing everything is more or less an exhibitionist, but on the other hand a transparent person remains invisible, since she has nothing to show rather than nothing to hide. This is not an "either… or" definition: Jennifer Ringley is so to speak symbolic of both aspects of transparency.

If we keep drawing on psychoanalytical categories, we could say that transparency includes a double horizon: a perverse horizon that we have already discussed, but also a psychotic horizon where transparency as visibility reverts to invisibility. It does not mean that Jenni would be psychotic, just as she is probably not a pervert, but one cannot exclude some borderline position there, especially when we consider her (proclaimed?)

indifference to the other's gaze. After all, and although technically speaking everybody can create his or her own Jennicam, it is a matter of fact that most people don't do it, not only because they don't feel like exhibitionists, but more generally because the other's gaze is part of their subjective configuration. We know intuitively or unconsciously that it is there and we tend to protect ourselves against it, to negotiate with this gaze, unless we have the strange courage of the disconnected psychotic, a courage that might revert anytime to paranoia, to delusion of persecution. I don't know if Jenni's courage is something we should admire or feel sorry for.

Introducing Winston

Why would we link transparency with psychosis? Because the psychotic "subject" is an empty subject, a subject without subjectivity, a subject which has nothing to hide because it has no longer anything "personal" to show, and maybe never had. We can link psychosis to delusion, grandiloquent delirium, but we know that the more grandiloquent the psychotic discourse, the emptier it is in terms of subjectivity. And this is why most of the time the psychotic is doomed to silence rather than to grandiloquence. The psychotic remains silent, unable as it were to express himself as a subject while trying, for this very reason, to go unnoticed, which is precisely the reason why he might eventually get noticed. We see that there is no subject to be seen there, we see the lack of singularity and therefore his attempts to conform to the way the others behave (Lacan 1993). We see that there is nothing there but a conformist which reminds us of Woody Allen's Zelig, the famous chameleon character who behaves systematically in exactly the same way as his immediate entourage.

At least this is the way things work in a "normal" society that consists of subjects who are more or less happy or proud to be subjects. But let's switch from Jenni, the possible originator of a show akin to "Big Brother," to the actual inventor of Big Brother, that is, Eric Blair *alias* George Orwell, and more precisely to Winston Smith, the main character of Orwell's *1984*. In the world of *1984*, the rules applying to visibility and subjectivity are basically inverted. The novel starts with Winston in his flat, trying to hide from Big Brother, that is, from the intrusive screen allowing for total surveillance of the citizens of Oceania. He tries to hide for a while because he wants to write in his diary. From the beginning of the story, and not just later, when he meets Julia and falls in love with her, Winston is on the side of transgression, he breaks the most fundamental rule imposed by Big Brother which is the prohibition of subjectivity. He writes in his diary because he is a singular subject, because he claims his subjectivity, and he can do so only by hiding himself from Big Brother. Subjectivity is what Big Brother is not supposed to see (although he sees it, as we will learn in the second part of the novel, be it only because at some point, when he can no longer see Winston hiding in a corner, he will necessarily notice that Winston has something to hide). Subjectivity is the invisible part of himself, it is the part Big Brother should not be able to control and therefore tries immediately to destroy, since Big Brother represents total control and total visibility (Han 2015).

Like all other citizens of Oceania, Winston tries to go unnoticed, to remain invisible: he knows that he has to hide his difference, his singularity. But the world of *1984* is only a paradise for Zeligs and psychotics. Obviously Winston is not good enough at going unnoticed because the world of Oceania makes it impossible to ever be good enough at it. As soon as there is anything to be hidden, a diary with a few thoughts or remarks about oneself, Big Brother will notice and the hider will become an outlaw right away, as good as dead. Big Brother sees the invisible immediately, the hidden, the subjectivity which is, again like a stain or a blind spot that blurs transparency. To some extent this is actually the only thing Big Brother truly sees: the stain, the little difference, the ephemeral blushing, the few minutes spent writing in a diary in the corner, the little lack of enthusiasm during compulsory gymnastics in front of the screen or the little deferral in yelling with the crowd against Goldstein, *the* enemy. Big Brother sees only the stains, he is obsessed with cleanness, and cleanness works here as another possible definition of transparency that implies that subjectivity is dirty, resists cleanness and transparency. It is the dirty part of each of us, the part we want to hide because after all we are not animals. The dirty part of ourselves, our souls.

1984 tells the tragedy of transparency and therefore the tragedy of the destruction of subjectivity, which starts with Winston's diary and unfolds with his affair with Julia, since there is an obvious connection between love and subjectivity. There is no such thing as love to turn anyone into a subject, no such thing as being chosen as a singular individual by another singular individual. Love is the nightmare of Big Brother because you can't imagine something dirtier. As a matter of fact, you can only imagine it, since all lovers hide from all Big Brothers of the world, from all intrusive Others. "Secret lovers" is almost a pleonasm because in the world of *1984*, love is always secret, something that dismisses the gaze of the Other, that makes it powerless or useless. It is perfectly logical that Winston stops being tortured when he gives up Julia, when he betrays their love and asks his executioners to torture Julia instead of himself. Immediately the torture stops and it does not really matter whether Winston will really be executed later or not because as a subject he is dead anyway (as well as Julia). *1984* is one of the most tragic and true love stories ever written.

In Lacanian terms, subjectivity could be defined as the way we relate to the real, that is, to this dirty part of ourselves that we have to give up in order to become human and social beings, the dirty part the lovers are doomed to rediscover when they are really alone, when they go to the countryside and maybe to the animals, like Winston and Julia. When we can no longer relate to the real, when we are disconnected from it, we become psychotics or "robots" performing the programs somebody wants us to perform, unable to negotiate ourselves with the real, unable to constitute ourselves in subjects through this negotiation. Big Brother takes aim at this disconnect, he wants to cut us from our dirty part, he wants stainless subjects that lack subjectivity and are therefore entirely submitted to him, easily programmed, leaving him alone in charge of the real, of the dirt. He deprives us of our subjectivity, of our opacity, and when we claim it back, as Winston does, he sends in his rats, as if the abject real would return, bite itself through our asshole and kill ourselves and our stains from inside, just as the same rats—Winston's nightmare—have bitten themselves through his beloved mother when he was a child. The rats are the real when it has been confiscated by Big Brother. The return of the real triggers panic.

From Big Brother to "Big Brother"

How do we switch back again from Winston to Jenni, from Big Brother, the invisible principle of surveillance that forces the subject into transparency and invisibility, to Jennicam? And how do we take that further step to "Big Brother," to reality shows in which (almost) everybody is ready to show everything and more in order to remain visible as long as possible? What would Orwell think of the contemporary forms of transparency and surveillance? What would he think of the era of voluntary servitude (*servitude volontaire*) we seem to have entered?

In Orwell's *1984*, visibility is almost a damnation, a death sentence that can only be escaped by remaining or becoming transparent, that is, by giving up or at least not showing any kind of subjectivity. This was the Fascist or the Stalinist nightmare. In the contemporary world, as already mentioned above, visibility has become the most desirable thing, and those who want a little piece of it have to be as transparent as possible, that is, to display as much as they can of themselves. *The ambiguity of transparency comes from the fact that it is about having nothing to hide as well as about showing everything, about psychosis as well as wild exhibitionism and more generally perversion.* Henceforth Big Brother seems no longer to stand and to work for a stainless humankind. As if he had convinced himself that he would never get rid of all the stains, it seems that he—that is, the current media ecosystem and the economy of attention it favors—has decided to make all the stains as visible as possible, or more exactly, since visible stains are no longer stains of the same kind, by dissolving the stains of subjectivity in their own visibility, as well as authenticity or singularity in staged authenticity and singularity.

Between these two apparently contradictory faces of transparency, there is actually a common denominator: the absence or the destruction of subjectivity. We have already discussed what that means on the side of psychosis. Let's therefore complete the description on the side of perversion. Whereas the psychotic is disconnected from the real (and therefore from his own subjectivity), the pervert relates without any taboo or obstacle to it: rather than being a principle of negotiation, his subjectivity disappears in his ability to be at the service of the real, to make himself the instrument of the real, a situation that can be described to some extent as an addiction to the real, as many psychoanalysts have noticed, sometimes not without some *schadenfreude*. These perverts think they are free to behave like animals, and moreover they think they don't need a psychoanalytical cure, but actually they can't stop fucking around, they are just poor addicts (André 1993).

Although there are clearly some (psychoanalytical) biases here that we will not discuss further, let's note that the price paid by the pervert in order to live out his fantasies (or more exactly: to live out what remains a fantasy for the neurotic and what disappears as a fantasy when lived out by the pervert) is something like a de-subjectification, a loss of subjectivity conceived as the "place" determining his singularity as well as the place of a moral instance, that is, an ability to distinguish, for example, between good and evil. There is no need to further discuss the obvious immoral dimension of perversion as well as the relation between morality and subjectivity, but the other aspect, the "de-singularization," is at least as relevant here. Perversion de-personalizes the subject, makes him or her a piece of a machinic dispositive (as Deleuze would have put it). In courts, perverts often defend themselves by invoking "compelling impulses," as if no subject were there to stop them.

This is probably best shown in many of the sexual orgies staged in Sade's novels, which combine bodies (or body parts) into sexual machines to which the perverts submit themselves more or less voluntarily, therefore becoming the subjects of the sexual machine and nothing else (Dufour 2009). And as far as subjectivity is concerned, Sade's representations are echoed by testimonies such as the one by Catherine Millet, for instance, who seems to have been rather gifted for perverse sexuality, especially for countless swinger-parties, and who has described quite clearly her participation in orgies as the pleasure to be knocked-out or destroyed as a subject: I am not there, actually, and this is probably why I am able to stage myself and my swinger parties in such a transparent or *impassive* way, as often noticed in the comments on her famous account *The Sexual Life of Catherine M*. No subject there, and no shame, no blushing, no stains: Catherine Millet has been replaced by an "abject," has reached the abjection of "herself,"[1] has worked towards her becoming

---

[1] In her account Catherine Millet writes "avilissement maximum" (*maximum degradation*). Cf. Millet (2001: 118).

animal, with no other stains to show us than the natural ones: her shit, her menstrual periods, that is, all kinds of things she does not fail to mention as not preventing her from taking part in orgies. Transparency means *to show the shit that comes out of you*, literally or not, and since we are talking about one of the most common things that might happen to human beings, so common actually that we even share it with all other species, we can reasonably assume that the shit coming out of us is not what constitutes us as singular subjects and does actually not even constitute us as human beings—on the contrary.[2]

I don't want to imply that the participants in reality shows are necessarily immoral criminals, sexual addicts, disgusting perverts, or machinic zombies performing a program designed by some other being or from elsewhere. But it is possible to assume that extreme practices such as those described by Sade or Millet are the escape horizon of reality television or its horizon, since many—if not all—reality shows include obviously perverse dimensions. And what further matters with this comparison is the issue of de-subjectification that obviously takes place in most reality shows, on the one hand because Big Brother does never stop watching you, leaving you with no space for yourself, with no privacy and on the other hand because, as we know very well, reality shows always consist of scripted reality—ex-post as well as ex-ante: you are there in order to perform a script, a program, not in order to be yourself. One might argue that this is banal and certainly not a problem, aren't we all playing roles and haven't we read George Lakoff? But are we sure that reality television leaves the subject lured into it safe? From what we can read in the tabloids devoted to the economy of visibility, it seems that the rate of suicides (and attempts) of former participants in reality shows is relatively high, as if they had been alienated, destroyed by this strange experience of "reality."

---

[2] Let's zoom back to the Stalinist Big Brother as incarnated in one of its most terrifying versions in the Cambodia of the Khmers Rouges : it seems that in some "villages" (or death camps ?), the inhabitants were forced to hand over their excrements to the "organization" and were punished when there was not enough. Transparency (and at the same time de-subjectification, dehumanization) happen when Big Brother not only forbids the use of the pronoun "I," as it was the case in Cambodia, but also controls your excrements. When human excrements become manure, humans become animals, that is, transparent (cf. Wolton 2015: 985–1042).

De-subjectification is the common denominator of the "psychotic" and the "perverse" perspective on transparency. Whether you want to escape Big Brother, surveillance or attention or whether you do whatever you can to get as much visibility as possible, the solution is called transparency and the price to pay for it is de-subjectification. The more you give up your subjectivity and your singularity, the more you fit the current economy of attention, which extends from its audiovisual dimension favoring exhibitionism to the conformist logic of the social media allowing for total surveillance. The economy of attention, which can also be defined, in Guy Debord's terms, as the spectacle (Debord 1995), wants transparency and requires therefore de-subjectification. Whenever we enter the spectacle, we face alienation, not only in the Marxist sense of the term, as implied by Debord's theory of the spectacle, but also in the psychological sense, which means literally that the spectacle forces us to give up our identities, that is, ourselves or our selves, for the benefit of those who try to program us as actors in the competition for visibility or perhaps as users of social media. The spectacle wants us to execute its various programs and it can only achieve its goal if we abide by transparency. Which is probably a reason to do exactly the opposite.

Works Cited

André, Serge. 1993. *L'Imposture Perverse*. Paris: Seuil.
Carroll, Raymonde. 1988. *Cultural Misunderstandings. The French-American Experience*. Trans Carol Volk. Chicago and London: The University of Chicago Press.
Clavreul, Jean. 1967. Le Couple Pervers. In *Le Désir et la Perversion*, ed. Piera Aulagnier, Jean Clavreul, François Perrier, Guy Rosolato, and Jean-Paul Valabrega. Paris: Seuil.
Collins, Suzanne. 2008–2010. *Hunger Games* (3 vol.). New York: Scholastic Books.
Debord, Guy. 1995. *The Society of Spectacle*. Trans. Donald Nicholson-Smith. New York: Zone Books.
Debray, Régis. 2004. *Transmitting Culture*. Trans. Eric Rauth, New York: Columbia University Press.

Dufour, Dany-Robert. 2009. *La Cité Perverse. Libéralisme et Pornographie*. Paris: Denoël.
Franck, Georg. 1998. *Ökonomie der Aufmerksamkeit*. Munich: Carl Hanser.
Freud, Sigmund. 1953. The Sexual Aberrations. In *Three Essays on the Theory of Sexuality. The Standard Edition of the Complete Psychological Works of Sigmund Freud*, Vol. VII, trans. James Strachey. London: Hogarth Press and the Institute of Psycho-Analysis
Han, Byung-Chul. 2015. *The Transparency Society*. Stanford: Stanford University Press.
Heinich, Nathalie. 2012. *De la Visibilité. Excellence et singularité en régime médiatique*. Paris: Gallimard.
Lacan, Jacques. 1977. *The Seminar, Book XI: The Four Fundamental Concepts of Psychoanalysis*. Trans, A. Sheridan. London: Hogarth.
———. 1993. *The Seminar, Book III: The Psychoses*. Translation R. Grigg. New York: Routledge/Norton.
Letterman, David. 1998. *The CBS Late Night Show*. https://www.youtube.com/watch?v=0AmIntaD5VE.
Millet, Catherine. 2001. *La Vie sexuelle de Catherine M*. Paris: Seuil.
Pop 17. 2008. JenniCAM Invented RealityTV. https://www.youtube.com/watch?v=4ii0gLK3meM. Accessed 30 May 2017.
Pörksen, Bernhard, and Wolfgang Krischke. 2012. *Die Casting-Gesellschaft. Die Sucht nach Aufmerksamkeit und das Tribunal der Medien*. Köln: Halem.
Thomä, Dieter. 2000. *Unter Amerikanern. Eine Lebensart wird besichtigt*. Munich: C.H. Beck.
Voltaire. 1978. Letter from August 30, 1755. *Correspondance*, vol. IV. Paris: Gallimard-Pléiade.
Wolton, Thierry. 2015. *Histoire Mondiale du Communisme, Tome 1: Les Bourreaux*. Paris: Grasset.

Putting Oneself Out There: The "Selfie" and the Alter-Rithmic Transformations of Subjectivity

Jörg Metelmann and Thomas Telios

I. What Is a Selfie?

Venice, Santa Lucia, Terminal Station. Crossing the train station concourse and entering the forecourt, a world opens up: the Canale, the vaporetti, the gondolas, churches and palazzi. So much uniqueness, so much culture, so many stories. If one wants to slip—on the way to the major sights—into the narrow alleys, it's just a matter of turning left, then right, crossing the Ponte degli Scalzi, keeping the Burger King to your left, entering the Calle Lunga and turning left again a few meters later and following the trail toward Rialto. And finally, here, at the Ponte de la Bergama, tourist traffic halts because it's selfie time. A smile for the world captured in my hands, in the background can finally be seen the "real" Venice as a bit of flair, the little channels (in Venice called "rio"), the small bridges, and the narrow route along the Fondamenta del Rio Marin. Everyone poses—mostly alone, but also with others for an "ussie."

J. Metelmann (✉) • T. Telios
University of St. Gallen, St. Gallen, Switzerland
e-mail: joerg.metelmann@unisg.ch; thomas.telios@unisg.ch

© The Author(s) 2018
E. Alloa, D. Thomä (eds.), *Transparency, Society and Subjectivity*,
https://doi.org/10.1007/978-3-319-77161-8_16

Some show off their muscles, some their décolletage; some wear sunglasses, some not; some hold their dogs and pose with one arm extended to hold the camera and some—the experts—carry a selfie stick bought at the Ponte degli Scalzi. Picture taken, okay—what's next?

It is no understatement to suggest that most of the 150,000 tourists strolling through "la Serenissima" on peak days could be plopped down right here, and after the selfie was taken, led right back to their trains, cars, buses, or cruise liners—the Venice selfie is taken and shared, the "little self" was here, *ergo sum*. And the magnificent world? It disappeared, it was reduced to scenery, and as such: it became replaceable. Canale Grande, Rialto, San Marco square—none of them matter. Had that not been the case, the Dutch "fakebooking" student Zilla van den Born wouldn't have had such great success sending vacation selfies to her family, allegedly from Laos, Cambodia, and Thailand, when in reality they were taken and altered in her student flat. No need to have *been* to a place, only to have a photo of oneself there. And what argument could anyone muster against photographic proof, after all?

Pathological Narcissism?

Such critical impressions—which even one of this chapter's authors experienced during a stay in the Laguna—have been part of the selfie discourse ever since the selfie was made mainstream by the release of the iPhone in January 2007. For many, photographing endlessly the ego is the perfect expression of a culture that is not only narcissistically formed but socially malformed: LOOK! AT! ME! I'm here, I'm there, I'm in the picture therefore I am. In scanning a space like a location scout, who has time to take in the space itself, to look at the people passing by? The critique has practically become a truism.

In order to attempt a diagnosis, an obvious question serves as a starting point: How does the selfie, this mobile self-portrait, relate to the long tradition of the artistic self-portraiture that has undergirded the Western cultures of individualism and individualization from the Renaissance to the present day? It's true that, unlike the self-portrait, the selfie is not taken for private enjoyment, but for public display. It's typically shared via social media immediately after being taken. But how has this particular digital practice changed the status of the photographs? And from whose point of view, exactly, are they taken?

Tradition of the Self-Portrait?

The world recedes, the "little self" comes to the fore—but what exactly is expressed? Looking back at the art history for an answer, one finds (at least) two positions. A more affirmative reading stemming from the art critic Jerry Saltz aligns the selfie to the longer history of self-portraits represented, for example, by Parmigianino's "Self-Portrait in a Convex Mirror" (1523/24): "All the attributes of the selfie are here" in Parmigianino's painting, writes Saltz: "[T]he subject's face from a bizarre angle, the elongated arm, foreshortening, compositional distortion, the close-in intimacy" (Saltz 2014).

Saltz pays little attention to the mirror that, especially in early modern times, combined attributes of both truth and lie. Interpreting another famous self-portrait, Johannes Gumpp's "Self-Portrait" (1646), the French philosopher Jean-Luc Nancy points out the difference between two sorts of similarity: the mechanical-optical similarity of the mirror-image and the imaginary-reflexive similarity of the self-portrait (cf. Nancy 2015). On the left side of the painting Gumpp swaps what he sees (and is invisible for us) with the image in the mirror (that we can see). On the right side of the canvas he shows the face as a handmade mask looking at us. Gumpp's preference between the two kinds of truth established by those two depictions is being clarified beyond any doubt by two allegorical figures: To the left he positions the cat as symbol of shrewd deceit, to the right we see the dog as symbol of blunt truth.

Nancy subscribes to this allegorical representation because he perceives the mirror reflection ("le reflet") as impregnated with narcissism. In the absence of the mirror-image, however, the portrait presents an opportunity to become similar to someone else. For Nancy, this production of a non-mirror-similarity is the *conditio sine qua non* to form a self that goes beyond mere re-presentation, deceit and narcissism in order to unveil something that is not known and not yet shown, a not-yet-visible part of the self.

From this perspective, selfies are wholly illusory masks of the ego, since the person is always present in the narcissistic mirror of the double camera that the iPhone 4 introduced in order to photograph in both directions, front and back. The person in the image may look at us, may show us her face, but we remain caught in the similarity between the specular reflection and the face as a mask: We cannot find a different, more genuine self.

This would also hold true for Jerry Saltz who—despite the parallel lines he drew—could not find classical self-portrait's claims for eternity in the selfie. The traditional self-portrait lives by "the tension between an external interest in the extraordinary person (or at least imagined to be extraordinary) and her programmatic self-staging" as the art historians Ulrich Pfisterer and Valeska von Rosen point out (Pfisterer and von Rosen 2005: 23). The latter would qualify only for VIP selfies such as those in Kim Kardashian West's notorious 2015 volume *Selfish* to stand in this tradition. For the normal smartphone user, the following rule applies: I am not special, therefore I must programmatically follow and copy extravagant self-stagings for reasons of the economy of attention.

Forgetting the "Weariness of the Self"?

If selfies, as mass phenomenon, do not represent a self in the sense of the "extraordinary person," then what *do* they represent?

Shortly after gaining notoriety for the clip "Super Cool" (*Supergeil*) produced for the supermarket chain Edeka, the performance artist Friedrich Liechtenstein published a small book, "Selfie Man" (2014), which opens with a remarkable thesis: "Selfies are escapism as response to self-oblivion" (*Selfies sind Eskapismus als Antwort auf das Sichvergessen*). Liechtenstein's *aperçu* calls forth the classic relation between self, authenticity and truth, yet he denies its relevance for the emerging selfie culture. For him the selfie does not enact any work on the self, it does not inform identity politics, but rather is a technique that does not deal with the self as a determined entity or essence—although the citation glosses over whether the forgetfulness is individual or collective. Is the "little self" an affirmative subversion of the claim to be someone, to be oneself, a self?

This fits perfectly into Alain Ehrenberg's proposal of Western cultures as agglomerations of "wearied selves" (Ehrenberg 2010) who have exceeded all motivation and power to subject to the highly normative practice of constant self-modeling. Instead, according to Liechtenstein, they prefer to take tiny little pictures of their "little selves" as a form of self-management—yet these pictures do insist on being published, even in book form. Liechtenstein's thesis, however escapistic, confirms the urge to manage one's own post-identity in highly performative ways.

One preliminary conclusion might be worded thus: The world has disappeared, the selfies as "little selves" are there, but as mirror reflections they do not (and cannot) show a self, because the self as a unique position has been replaced by "selfing" as an endless process and a media spectacle. But: For whom? From whom? And for what reason?

The Desire of Pictures

As already stated, the selfie is not taken for the purpose of analysis, but for the purpose of sharing. Looking at the selfie is not about content such as a six-pack or the boobs of a star like Kardashian West. What is shared in and with the selfie is the difference itself that becomes visible in the huge archive of self-similar selfies. For this reason, the British art historian Daniel Rubinstein, like many other theorists, emphasizes on the fact that it is difficult, if not impossible, to apply the established semiotic toolbox for its interpretation. The right question is not "What does the selfie show?" but "Where is it?" (Rubinstein 2015: 176). It's only this second question that opens the horizon for understanding selfie culture as a virtual field of self-similarities that constantly both mutate and replicate the original image.

Putting aside the question whether selfies can be analyzed semiotically or not, Rubinstein's plea for a perspective beyond clear subject-object-relation is valid; at least more valid than fears of selfie-induced cultural decline. In this sense, selfies seem to exemplify the approach of W.J.T. Mitchell, who claimed that we should stop trying to interpret images and start asking: "What do pictures want?" No longer should we attempt, according to Mitchell, to make sense of the interpreter's deepest wishes so as to understand the pictures' content or message. In order to investigate the relation to the picture beyond clear roles and patterns, Mitchell tries to make them less transparent and comprehensible, and insists that we ought to withdraw from the temptation to conceptualize them as a transparent medium that makes something visible (Mitchell 2008: 69). Methodologically, he sets up two basic premises: first, that pictures enjoy a special status as animated beings, quasi-actors and pseudo-persons; second, that any interpretation of pictures views them as "subalterns" carrying the stigma of difference and ambiguity in serving both as mediators and as scapegoats in the field of human visuality (Mitchell 2008: 66).

Framing selfies in this non-transparent way Mitchell has proposed, beyond the search for a fixed self, we can begin to see selfies as subaltern and as contrasted to a self that—seen this way—becomes only allegedly fixed. This impulse also underlies Liechtenstein's "Selfie Man," which proposes a radically subjective immersion in the world of the selfie, thus leaving behind imperatives of coherent and authentic self-modeling in order to embrace contingency that—paradoxically enough—can provide for a new feeling of safety. Ultimately, he reminds us, there certainly are billions of other users who are both unique and distinct in doing this same thing.

"I" Is the Others

From this perspective, selfies are viewed and liked not by friends in the common and old-fashioned sense of the word (friends at home, in school, at work etc.), but by friends in the sense of other social-media users: It is one of the consequences of globalism, writes culture critic Nadja Geer (2016: 133), that the world around us (*Mitwelt*) demands attention, rather than the individual human beings around us (*Mitmensch*). On social-media platforms, responsibilization (the responsibility for one's personal appearance on social media) meets interconnected machines, networks, and platforms. The result are visual codes that might have had an emancipative, Do-It-Yourself premise, but due to the general connectivity of the internet have always been "positioned in digital media cultures and, via economies of networking (clicks, likes, tags and comments) linked to cultural techniques of naming, collecting, sorting and counting" (Reichert 2015: 89). Being so embedded in public forums creates a normative form of transparency: The most-liked selfies—the prominent, "exceptional" people—are taken as normative standards and drive "normal" users to contort themselves just to project themselves into these famous pictures. Social pressures to conform, which had formerly been a local phenomenon that went hand in hand with retreat rooms and sites of escape, have now become ubiquitous.

II. The Selfie, Selfing, and Subjectivation

To sum up our phenomenology and theoretical framing of the selfie, we could settle on four central features of our discussion: The selfie is *oblivious*, as Liechtenstein discussed; it's *shared*, per Rubinstein; it's *serial*, as Mitchell explained, and above all it's *determined by others*. These four features correlate with salient points of contemporary theories of subjectivity and can serve to inscribe the selfie, as cultural practice, into current modes that regard the subject as a product of the Social. In this part we will slightly change the order in which we presented the aforementioned elements and begin by presenting aspects of Nancy's "com-munication" (*shared*), Butler's "iterability" (*serial*), Gambetti's "void" (*oblivious*) and (post-)Marxist alienation (*determined by others*). Fundamentally, we are working from the assumption that we are entitled to understand "selfing"—*this repetitive taking and archiving of selfies in order to be shared*—as a process of subjectification, that is, as a way of determining an individual and his or her psyche vis-à-vis social instances, norms, and behavioral patterns. At the same time, there needs to be differentiation between general types and processes of such determination and the concrete production of a certain singularized self. In order to do that we operate according to Bührmannn and Schneider's semantical distinction between (general) "subjectivation" and (concrete) "subjectification" (Bührmann and Schneider 2008: 100, Foucault 1978). The main question is: Does the self that takes selfies of itself insert, attach, or suppress itself vis-à-vis a certain way of production by (re-)producing itself through the active proliferation of pictures of itself that it actuates? Our aim in this discussion is to prepare the ground for our thesis of the selfie's blank space as a new form of *alter-rithmic* transparency that we will lay down here and conclude at the third part of the paper.

Shared: Com-munication

In "Being Singular Plural" (1996), Jean-Luc Nancy lays down a concept of communication according to which communication neither connects, nor conveys meaning, but on the contrary—through *sharing*—a being, a subject, is induced that realizes itself as being from the very beginning an in-common, because it has been brought forth through this common sharing (Nancy 1996: 94). By revisiting, in this conceptual framework, the Aristotelian notion of "pollachôs legomenon," Nancy asserts that "Being is said in many ways," that "the singularity of Being is its plural," that "[t]he multiplicity of the said (that is, of the sayings) belongs to Being as its constitution" (Nancy 1996: 38). Mediation, that is, how the plurality and the singularity are related one to the other, remains constitutive for subjectivation also in this post-Hegelian context, but it is neither something external that gets embodied, nor a historical-philosophical necessary step towards the subject's fulfilled manifestation. Mediation is the point of departure of every attempt to grasp the being in its common/plural character and as such an intermediary point of departure through which every understanding of the subject in its plurality has to go though. The latter makes it possible for Nancy to extract the notion of mediation in the form of a "mediation without an instrument," since this mediation is causally necessary in order to grasp the subject in its plurality, but not necessarily existent in an individual form.

From this perspective, selfie's selfing would coincide with a sharing, with a com-munication, and could indeed be the result of a dialogue with the community of all the separately collected pictures. Moreover, regarding every picture as a "mediation without an instrument" illustrates the necessity that the mediation can neither be exhausted in one sole picture/medium, nor that this picture/medium is a finite one. Furthermore, the pictures taken are not to be counted additively so as to be thought of as being accumulated in order to let a sedimentary multiple picture arise. The pictures taken one after the other do not add to the subject in order to be summed up as the subject, but constitute the Being as a holistic being-in-common where all the pictures co-exist parallel to one another.

Yet something feels awkward when retrospectively looking at the pictures accumulated throughout the selfie's selfing: Though the subject is depicted in all of them and all of them could be regarded as partial expressions of this subject-in-common that is common to all of them, there seems to be no consciousness of the subject selfing itself. The pictures do reveal a process, they do reveal a common process, and they even do reveal the subject as a common process. At the same time though, the subject encapsulated in those pictures *is* no longer, but it has found its way out, it became a fugitive in those pictures and the subject judging the subject in the picture is no longer the subject captured in those pictures.

The subject is constituted by all the pictures taken, but it is also impossible for it to identify with them because they illustrate a subject in the past: The subject is all of them together, but it has no consciousness of itself as discernible entity, no matter how meticulously transparent it has shaped itself. Framing the selfie's selfing with Nancy thus provides for a preliminary aspect of what might be called the selfie's blank space, that is, a subjectivation process without concrete subjectification.

Serial: Iterability

The same argument can be found when taking Judith Butler's "iterability" into account, understood as modus operandi of subjectivation processes. Butler does not understand iterability solely as "the operation [...] by which the subject who 'cites' the performative is temporarily produced as the belated and fictive origin of the performative itself" (Butler 1997: 49), but also as a "logic" "that governs the possibility of social transformation" (ibid.: 147).

Could we read selfie's selfing as such an iterative process? The self's pictures are taken incessantly, successively, and they keep reiterating rather than just repeating themselves since the subject keeps effacing through/on them contingently differently every time. The problem is that through those reiterations not the structures among which the subject will emerge are being perturbed and subverted. Rather, this process brings about the different potentialities as which the subject might prospectively arise. Repetition is the appearance of something new in the orthodox Derridean sense, but those repetitions do not allow for the subject to come to terms with its being different from its outside, as Butler indicates. Nor can these reiterations abort power structures before congealing as subject.

Seen this way, it is rather the collective, the amalgam, of all its yet opaque potentialities that selfing renders transparently possible and visible. The selfie's selfing reiterates not what the subject really and unalterably is, but rather the virtual and actual prospect of its becoming a subject and of the different manifestations the subject can take on. As such, selfing renders present and visible the logic of subjectivation processes, not the concrete subjectified substantialization of a certain subject. The latter is taken further in Zeynep Gambetti's theory of the void.

Oblivious: The Void

Taking Hannah Arendt's conceptualization of the subject as a starting point, Gambetti claims that the "self is an entity that is always more than the sum of its social identities. Social identities operate through an articulating principle whose locus is the self, but the self is always something in excess of identity, in excess of language and therefore of conceptualization or symbolization" (Gambetti 2005: 431). According to her, the benefit of Arendt's understanding of singularity as "ontological human condition" (ibid.) lies in the fact that "no identity can be so fixed that an actor's actions will be fully explained through general discursive causalities" (ibid.) since these processes generate a certain force of negativity that ultimately allows for the subject to overcome its complete determination. This negativity is what Gambetti frames as the "void": "Arendt's notion of plurality is her version of the negativity—the void—that enables the queering of social determinations" (ibid.). Combining the void with another Arendtian notion, that of natality, Gambetti will go a step forward and assert that the subject as worldly existence is an insertion of "something new into the world" (Gambetti 2005: 432) that needs to be observed and classified or categorized as such by the others.

The latter seems to adjoin what we deemed from the very beginning as important in order to decipher selfing as subjectivation process. In order for the subject to acquire visibility and—well noted, visibility is not a quality inherent to the subject, but it has to be asserted as possessed or obtained by the context in which the subject acts—it needs to emerge. This genesis of the subject through the selfies it produces is nonetheless at the same time a structuration process, because as long as the subject emerges it gets conformed to the structure it effaces. Every picture accumulated is a new structure that necessitates the subject to conform itself with by remaining loyal to the picture taken. The self emerges in this framework at the intersection of all its selfies. Nevertheless, as soon as those picture-structures and the subject at their intersection emerge, a set of negational relationships arise between those structures. If every picture is a different structure, then the subject has to conform itself to every one of them. From this, different processes of structuration and confirmation unravel out of those pictures that result in an overdeterminating struggle over the subject.

In this sense, the subject is ultimately a thick, opaque network of negativity pictures/structures that proliferate through the subject's structuration as plain void. Again, what we see is how selfing resolves in a subjectivation process out of which a subject emerges that this time is an indeterminable negational relation. Neither void nor content, but the impossibility—caused by the opacity of the pictures collected—of attaching itself to a certain picture-structure is the subject that selfing enables.

Determined (by Others): Alienation

This kind of negational relation argued for with Gambetti can be completed by our fourth aspect, the almost classical negation of the subject in processes of self-alienation or self-reification—broadly, its determination by others. In their long paths as notions enabling a radical critique of social structuration, "alienation" and "reification" inevitably have to start from a pivotal point: That there is a subject at hand either as point of departure (alienation) or as point of arrival (reification). By both alienation and reification, the subject functions as the necessary focal point in order to determine the beginning of its estrangement (alienation) or the state of affairs from which its disentanglement will commence (reification).

The necessity of a subject possessing a minimal core of subjectivity is indicative of the subject as the ultimate horizon framing classic or Western-Marxist subjectivation discourses. The political normativity of the subject's emancipation underlying the post-Marxist discourse is also not redeemed of any residues of subjectivity. The grounding line of the subject's production alongside biopolitical frameworks—immanent as these frameworks may traverse—is to foreclose this very subject's emancipation as a real possibility. By forestalling it they reinstitute—this time in form of an external normative promise—the subject as a prospectively necessarily emancipated one, resettling it thus once more as the necessary pivotal point of their analytics. For this reason, even more elaborate concepts such as those of communicative capitalism (brought forth by Jodie Dean 2005), or neo-liberal flexibility (as laid down by a series of theorists like Luc Boltanski and Eve Chiapello 1999 or Alain Ehrenberg 1998) can be asserted as inadequate in order to address selfing as a certain process of capitalist self-alienating socialization.

Selfing, as seen in the three previous theories, neither precludes or presupposes, nor envisages a sovereign, integral, and qualitative subject. It does not connect the subject-to-be to a community of subjects while proclaiming the latter as the promised land of fulfilled politicization that has reached its outer goal. Nor does selfing convey a hierarchical norm that the subject embodies. From this perspective, selfing does not stand for a "relation of relationlessnes," as Rahel Jaeggi's recent, most advanced, reinterpretation of alienation would demand (Jaeggi 2014). The subject itself has to keep sustaining its sets of pictures with new data, because, should this relation come to a standstill, that would also mean the death of the subject. By generating incessant pictures of itself, the self-selfing-itself eludes its self-alienating concretization by rendering any self-determination process impossible. Through the proliferation of the pictures that the subject collects of itself, it creates an opaque net of appearances that undermines its own fixation. With no kernel of subjectivity laying at hand, the concepts of self-alienation or reification are rendered obsolete. The subject becomes one without being subjectified, since no concrete content arises at the end.

Transfer: Relation as Form

Summarizing this second chapter we can conclude that—from the background of poststructuralist theories of subjectivity—framing "selfing" as the cultivation of a visual ego provides us with insights according to which we could understand selfing as a vector of subject's production, yet—as shown—selfing at the same time possesses a force and carries many diverse elements that resist clear classification. As observed in the four theories cited above, the selfie's selfing (a) is com-municated in Nancy's sense, but remains opaque since it cannot rewind its component parts from the past. It cannot be understood as (b) an iteration leading to a concrete subjectification, but only as a process that manifests the making of a subject, since its reiterative processes do not exert a change upon their context. It can be seen as organized (c) around Gambetti's void of negative relations to other selfies, but this also does not allow for a positive or affirmative understanding of the self, but only for a negativist understanding of it. Finally, the selfies are not (d) an expression of digital alienation (understood, very basically, as the mismatch between external picture and internal image of the self), since during or through the selfing no substantial self is to be found or produced in order for it to be alienated.

Through the cartography we offered, a paradox has become clear, namely that none of the subjectivation processes accounted for managed to engender or subordinate selfing completely under their own accounts of subjectification. In each and every one of them selfing seemed only upon a first glance to qualify as application and exemplification of the subjectification processes that the consulted theories promulgate, but at the very same time selfing proved itself to be a process that subverts, drives *ad absurdum*, renders impossible and undermines each and every one of those subjectification processes. In this regard, selfing seems to question the necessary presumption that subjectification follows upon subjectivation. This paradoxical constellation breaks with every theory of subjectivity that we have discussed in our paper and ultimately, according to the thin assumption, it problematizes processes of subjectivation, or else, according to the thick assumption, it questions the possibility of any theory of subjectivation as such. Our hunch is that selfies, as a phenomenon of opaque visibility, position selfing in the age of algorithms not as a process of substantializing a subject that was created in relation to its outside, but as a process of *substantializing (this) relation as form* (on this topic, see also Thomas Berns' analyses of the algorithmic management of relations included in this volume).

There is no political space that the selfie impedes, and no structure that the selfie subverts. There is also no dialogue that takes place through the selfie, and no surplus that is created. No place of negotiation is brought forth through this process as there are no concrete entities struggling for political participation or visibility that the selfie makes visible. There are no contents conveyed, nor any aspirations forged. The subjectivation does not lead to concrete positions of desires, wills, or interests, but keeps the subjects in their non-existence. If essentialist notions of subjectivity presupposed agency and therefore emancipation and should the constructivist notions of subjectivity have enriched our understanding of the powers-to-be at work, the selfies leave the subject naked in its form and dependent on being shared. This subject position can be that of a *tabula rasa*, a "blank slate", or a "blank space", as we would like to call it, that holds the potential to display a hundred potential stories despite never becoming the history of the concrete self as it is always determined by the form of relations to abstract numerical others in vast quantities.

To capture this important aspect which makes the phenomenon so new in the history of subjectivity, we might talk of *alter-rithmic* subjectivity, from Latin "alter" for "the other/s" (Metelmann 2017). Determined by algorithms, having to be shared on sharing platforms and in need of *quantified others* instead of "qualitative" others characterized by co-presence, inter-subjectivity and dialogue, being oneself boils down to being a content-free, relational form. It is, as already mentioned, not something, but anything; it is the constellation of a purely formal relation.

Both elements for themselves are strictly speaking not new: We've learned from the works of Friedrich Kittler (1992, 1999) about the media *a priori* of any kind of subjectivity and we all live from birth onward under the pressure to adapt to social environments (family, friends, groups, colleagues etc.). The only new component is these two forces' technical connection through social-media platforms, enabling them to conquer the "return channel" as the Internet activist Jaron Lanier put it: The new power of platforms is to determine the way people see and feel themselves, a technology of power that was unknown till today (Lanier 2015). The individual is thereby configured as a big-data effect and appears as a "mass original" (Metelmann 2016) both highly individualized and totally collectivized.

III. Conclusions: Towards the End of the Modern Dream of Transparency

In conclusion, we might ask: What do these observations mean for the transparency discourse? What's the story behind the reconfiguration of subjectivity as alter-rithmic in form of the selfie? And how does selfing precipitate or decelerate the emergence of a transparent self?

Our claim would be that our observations hint at a paradigm shift that makes the traditional inside-outside distinction, as the basis of the modern transparency discourse, obsolete (cf. Chul-Han 2015). As shown, the selfie as subjectivation process without subjectification does not produce contextualized, socially embedded, individually meaningful selves: We neither have a subject that delegates its own production to technology (subjectivation) nor does technology fully subjectify (subjectification). As a result, we cannot speak of an "outsourcing" of the self to media and machines, because this would assume either an already constituted self (which is not the case) or a successful creation (which is not the case either). As such, there is no point in differentiating between interiority and exteriority or privileging the one over the other. From this perspective, the specific form of subjectivity that the selfie demonstrates leads us to something beyond the classic transparency discourse. This discourse, like Wittgenstein's famous ladder, is something you have to use and climb in order to see that there is no subject at the bottom of it, that is, after the selfing process: Its semantics simply do not apply to this anymore.

According to Manfred Schneider's seminal study on the "dream of transparency," the semantics of this dream consists of an undistorted access to the truth, moving from the observing outside to a meaningful inside. And this dream is, as Schneider frames it, "the impossible" (2013: 302). Going through the history of this dream, Schneider sees a movement away from its life in "books, heads, utopia, plans, pictures, programs" (Schneider 2013: 22) to more concrete social players. Formerly prominent in and owned by literature, film and the arts, this movement has now been taken over by the "machinery" of politics, science and technology (ibid.). In considering the selfie, we might specify his thesis by marking the distinction between on the one hand a "quantified self" (Lupton 2016, cf. also Bernard 2017) that could be seen as a striking example of this expropriation and on the other hand the selfie as a still more "qualified" phenomenon of subjectivity that seems to stand in the long tradition of modern subjectivity but already moves beyond its frontiers.

This tradition, starting with Descartes' "cogito," became culturally relevant as soon as Jean-Jacques Rousseau urged himself to "say all" about himself. As we have interpreted it throughout this paper, this "tout dire" should not be understood in terms of extensive enunciations, that is, as expression of a concealed inner self awaiting to be expressed, but rather in terms of a visualization of the interior, as a real possibility of a perspectivization that has to come from the outside (cf. Brooks 1995: 16). Since this "incipit" (ibid.), the modern subject had to become fully transparent, authentic, and responsible for the unique kernel it carries. Tragically enough, this "tout dire" coincided with the opaqueness of societal communication, namely with the fact that there is no direct access from the outside to the inside (Starobinski 1988). Nevertheless, this claim provided for a very strong narrative in the culture of the Western self: It sufficed in providing the idea that becoming oneself has to go through the full expression and visualization of the singularity, depth, and truth of the proper self. The fact that there is no direct access from the outside to the inside not only did not dull the claim's intensity, but actually aggravated it. Becoming transparent by expressing oneself and exteriorizing one's innermost world became henceforth a normative ideal, the impossible dream of self-realization, self-understanding and self-determination. It became the presupposition of every communication and the condition of political participation. Which better vector in order for this norm to be realized than the selfie that supposedly hides nothing, that allegedly is executed by the subject itself and that purportedly results in the (self-) revelation of the subject as it really is?

As we've argued, the selfie can be positioned in this genealogy of the modern self, but the very premises of the game have been altered as the basic distinction between exteriority and interiority no longer make sense. It might still be applied to forms of *quantified selves* in a stricter sense, but the selfie remains erratic in its processuality as a substantialized form, referring back to traditions (of the self-portrait) and genealogies (of the modern subject) without being subsumable to them. In our reading, the selfie indicates, pushes forward, and conditions not transparency, but the end of transparency as a dream. It thus opens up the path for new paradoxical forms of becoming: The new dream is to be fully visible, but not recognizable—transparent, yet opaque (Saltz 2013). In this way, selfing renders the subject visible, and makes it transparent. At the same time though, selfing undermines the subject's transparency, by making it opaque, annihilating thusly any chances for transparency the subject might have ever possessed. At the end, it seems as if not only theory still has to learn a lot about the new fabric of the social imaginary. It also seems that artists such as the ever-controversial Kanye West might be able to inspire these debates, and this premise might not be so far-fetched as we might have originally thought, as he has declared, commenting on his controversial video "Bound 2," that he wants to be "clearing a path for people to dream properly."

Works Cited

Bernard, Andreas. 2017. *Komplizen des Erkennungsdienstes. Das Selbst in der digitalen Kultur*. Frankfurt am Main: Fischer Verlag.
Boltanski, Luc, and Eve Chiapello. 1999 [2005]. *The New Spirit of Capitalism*. Trans. Gregory Elliott. London: Verso.

Brooks, Peter. 1976 [1995]. *The Melodramatic Imagination. Balzac, Henry James, Melodrama, and the Mode of Excess.* New Haven: Yale University Press.
Bührmann, Andrea D., and Werner Schneider. 2008. *Vom Diskurs zum Dispositiv. Eine Einführung in die Dispositivanalyse.* Bielefeld: transcript.
Butler, Judith. 1997. *Excitable Speech. A Politics of the Performative.* New York and London: Routledge.
Chul-Han, Byung. 2015. *The Transparency Society.* Stanford: Stanford University Press.
Dean, Jodi. 2005. Communicative Capitalism: Circulation and the Foreclosure of Politics. *Cultural Politics* 1 (1): 51–74.
Ehrenberg, Alain. 1998 [2010]. *The Weariness of the Self: Diagnosing the History of Depression in the Contemporary Age—Depression and Society.* Montreal and Kingston: MacGill-Queen's University Press.
Foucault, Michel. 1978 [1990]. *The History of Sexuality. An Introduction.* Trans. Robert Hurley. London: Penguin Books.
Gambetti, Zeynep. 2005. The Agent Is the Void! From the Subjected Subject to the Subject of Action. *Rethinking Marxism* 1 (3): 425–437.
Geer, Nadja. 2016. Selfing versus Posing. *POP. Kultur und Kritik* 8: 124–134.
Jaeggi, Rahel. 2005 [2014]. *Alienation.* Trans. Frederick Neuhouser and Alan E. Smith, New York: Columbia University Press.
Kardashian West, Kim. 2015. *Selfish.* New York: Rizzoli.
Kittler, Friedrich A. 1992. *Discourse Networks, 1800/1900.* Trans. Michael Metteer. Stanford: Stanford University Press.
———. 1999. *Gramophone, Film, Typewriter*, Trans. Geoffrey Winthrop-Young and Michael Wutz. Stanford: Stanford University Press.
Lanier, Jaron. 2015. Jaron Lanier im Gespräch: Warum wollt ihr unseren Quatsch? *Frankfurter Allgemeine Zeitung*, 2 (7). http://www.faz.net/aktuell/feuilleton/debatten/die-digital-debatte/internet-vordenker-jaron-lanier-im-gespraech-13679623-p4.html. Accessed 28 Jun 2017.
Liechtenstein, F. 2014. *SELFIE MAN. #DerTagIstDein-Freund.* München: Blumenbar.
Lupton, Deborah. 2016. *The Quantified Self.* London: Wiley.
Metelmann, Jörg. 2016. Pop und die Ökonomie des Massenoriginals. Zur symbolischen Form der Globalisierung. *POP. Kultur und Kritik* 8: 135–149.
———. 2017. Selfies. In *Nach der Revolution. Brevier digitaler Kulturen*, ed. Timon Beyes, Jörg Metelmann, and Claus Pias, 26–37. Hamburg: Edition Speersort.
Mitchell, W.J.T. 2008. *Das Leben der Bilder. Eine Theorie der visuellen Kultur.* München: Beck.

Nancy, Jean-Luc. 1996 [2000]. *Being Singular Plural*. Trans. Robert D. Richardson and Anne E. O'Byrne. Stanford: Stanford University Press.
———. 2013 [2015]. *Das andere Porträt*. Trans. Thomas Laugstien. Zürich: diaphanes.
Pfisterer, Ulrich, and von Rosen Valeska. 2005. Vorwort: Der Künstler als Kunstwerk. In *Der Künstler als Kunstwerk. Selbstporträts vom Mittelalter bis zur Gegenwart*, ed. Ulrich Pfisterer, 11–23. Stuttgart: Reclam.
Reichert, Ramon. 2015. Selfie Culture. Kollektives Bildhandeln 2.0. *POP. Kultur und Kritik 7*: 86–96.
Rubinstein, Daniel. 2015. The Gift of the Selfie. In *Ego Update—Zukunft der digitalen Identität*, ed. Alain Bieber, 162–176. Düsseldorf: Walther König.
Saltz, Jerry. 2013. Kanye, Kim, and 'The New Uncanny'. http://www.vulture.com/2013/11/jerry-saltz-on-kanye-west-kim-kardashian-bound-2.html#. Accessed 16 Jul 2017.
———. 2014. Art at Arm's Length: A History of the Selfie. http://www.vulture.com/2014/01/history-of-the-selfie.html. Accessed 12 Jun 2017.
Schneider, Manfred. 2013. *Transparenztraum*. Berlin: Matthes & Seitz.
Starobinski, Jean. 1988. *Jean-Jacques Rousseau: Transparency and Obstruction*. Trans. Arthur Goldhammer. Chicago: University of Chicago Press.

Interrupting Transparency

Clare Birchall

Certain aspects of Donald Trump's presidential campaign and the early days of his administration challenge a binary visual code that pits opacity against openness, as well as a teleological narrative that establishes transparency as the logical incarnation of Enlightenment ideals and an administrative norm today. This chapter will begin by outlining the way in which the story of American government transparency is commonly told in order to contextualize the challenge Trump's political style poses to that narrative arc and its underlying logic. Because of the ideological nature of contemporary transparency tools, the way in which, for example, open government data shifts responsibility to netizens by outsourcing auditing activity, an interruption of technocratic transparency in its data-driven form might not in all circumstances be a regressive move. We face great risks if populist authoritarianism is allowed to govern without

---

I would like to thank Emmanuel Alloa and Dieter Thomä for their invitation to the University of St. Gallen and for their astute comments on a draft of this chapter.

C. Birchall (✉)
King's College London, London, UK
e-mail: clare.birchall@kcl.ac.uk

© The Author(s) 2018
E. Alloa, D. Thomä (eds.), *Transparency, Society and Subjectivity*,
https://doi.org/10.1007/978-3-319-77161-8_17

adequate oversight or accountability, and transparency tools may have an important part to play in this. But it is highly likely that a technocratic transparency heavily reliant upon open data and third party applications would not, in any case, be robust enough to contend with the multiple elisions and performances Trump and others in his administration employ. Rather than bemoaning the displacement of technocratic transparency, it might be more productive to utilize the unsettled conditions of visibility in which openness and obfuscation merge to recalibrate and radicalize the politics of transparency.

The Trajectory of Transparency

Writing this chapter in the early stages of the Trump administration, there are signs that received wisdom about the tenor and trajectory of American political transparency need to be revised. Before identifying these new conditions, it is worth recounting the way in which the story of American government transparency thus far is commonly understood. It would be erroneous to suggest that this story is easily translatable to other contexts, but my remarks about the state, as well as the stakes and fate of transparency in the face of right-wing populism are certainly pertinent to other national arenas.

While there is a history of secrecy in government that troubles the coherence of any story we can relate concerning US transparency, in broad terms the latter is often related as follows. Influenced by ideals of the Enlightenment desire to demolish the "unlit chambers where arbitrary political acts, monarchical caprice, religious superstitions, tyrannical and priestly plots, epidemics and the illusions of ignorance were fomented" (Foucault 1980: 153), the founding fathers instituted a principle of publicity in civic life whenever conditions allowed. For example, article 1, section 5 of the Constitution, states, "Each House shall keep a journal of its proceedings, and from time to time publish the same, excepting such parts as may in their judgment require secrecy." Section 9 of the same article makes it clear that financial openness was also a concern: "a regular statement and account of receipts and expenditures of all public money shall be published from time to time." While Mark Fenster reads the qualifier "from time to time" as an indicator of "limited disclosure practices" (2010: 638), and considers the separation of powers to block "the creation of a uniform, comprehensive approach to public access" (637); such provisions do, no matter how tentatively, acknowledge the place and power of public oversight and open government. "Transparency" in relation to an organization set on making its actions and outputs available to public scrutiny might be a modern term, only coming into common parlance in the 1990s, but the hesitant overture to openness and accountable governing in the US Constitution predates this by approximately 200 years.[1]

Debates around publicity in the early twentieth century were instrumental in establishing the character that transparency assumes within the US political scene today. In 1913, Woodrow Wilson and his ally, Louis Brandeis, put forth political policies that offered arguments against, and alternatives to opaque quarters of government and finance. In support of Wilson's series of reforms proposed in his "New Freedom," Brandeis published a series of articles in *Harper's Magazine* in which he advocated publicity as an anti-trust measure and to curb excessive commission for bankers. Through both men, the desire to "open the doors and let in the light on all affairs which the people have a right to know about" (Wilson 2008 [1913]: 69) was legitimized and given life.

This impetus assumed legislative form in the guise of the Federal Register, established in 1935 (a process in which Brandeis played a central role) ensuring daily publication of presidential documents and executive agency rule and notice documents. Due to digital technology, the register is now online and the archives are also being digitized. Supplementing the Federal Register in a show of commitment to open government came a series of measures throughout the twentieth century. None gave a clearer signal of in principle transparency (even while classification would in practice impede the fantasy of access) than the Freedom of Information Act (FOIA), implemented in 1966 and strengthened in the wake of the Watergate scandal and the fall of Nixon. On the

---

[1] In terms of European history, many histories of transparencies cite Anders Chydenius's "Ordinance on Freedom of Writing and of the Press" (1766), instituting *offentlighetsprincipen*, the principle of publicity, into Swedish civic life, as the earliest example of a modern government committed to publicity.

back of FOIA, the Government in the Sunshine Act (1976) drew its name from Brandeis' assertion that "sunlight is said to be the best of disinfectants" (1913) by ensuring that executive branch agencies hold open meetings. Also of note is the Presidential Records Act (1978), which instituted public ownership of the official records of Presidents and Vice Presidents.

Drawing on this history, particularly the way in which the health of democracy becomes entwined with the quality and extent of citizen oversight and access, government transparency in the twenty-first century has reached new heights. Recent years have seen a shift in thinking about the role of citizens in democratic states and their relationship to those that govern. Representative democracy has been outmoded as an ideal in favor of participatory democracy. Transparency provided meaning to the former and energy for the latter (see Meijer 2015). In the process, transparency changes from a mechanism that improves the view citizens have of the state and the politicians representing their interests to an apparatus that stages a call to action—a demand upon us to not only keep the state and politicians in our purview, but to engage with the data on display in meaningful ways. Today, transparency is positioned by open government advocates and lobbyists as a quasi-religious, universal good or, as Patrick Birkinshaw suggests, a human right (2006) that reaches beyond partisan politics. Regardless of whether the dominant party happens to be Republican or Democrat, transparency is seen to bolster democratic accountability *and* participation. It is bi-partisan; post-ideological even.

Though civil liberties and citizen oversight were clear casualties of President Bush's "war on terror" after the attacks on the World Trade Center on September 11, 2001, the transparency baton was picked up with renewed energy by Barack Obama as a presidential candidate. Obama campaigned on the ticket of government transparency in 2008 as a way to differentiate his vision and offering from the investment in covert and opaque government that seemed to characterize the Bush administration (see Birchall 2011a). In practice, once in office, Obama made extensive use of the state architecture of secrecy and covert securitization (including the State Secret Privilege; the practice of extraordinary rendition; the use of drone strikes and covert cyber weapons; a punitive approach to whistleblowers; and the mining of worldwide communications metadata). Yet, Obama also set in motion various initiatives that would bolster his claim to be "the most transparent administration in history" (Obama quoted in Easley 2013).

Obama's initiatives included technological solutions like the open government data portal, data.gov, intended to "increase public access to high value, machine readable datasets generated by the Executive Branch of the Federal Government," as the website claims; the Open Government Directive (issued on December 8, 2009), intended to "institutionalize a culture of open government" (White House 2009b: 4); an intra-agency review of classification procedures long seen as overly complex and restrictive, set on restoring "the presumption against classification" (White House 2009a) that had been suspended during the Bush administration; and (somewhat reluctantly) the instigation of the White House visitor's log.

The way in which open data became a touchstone of US government transparency during the Obama administration constitutes a significant shift in transparency's history. The scale of storage and speed of search capacities inherent to new media pushes this story in two directions. In one direction, we can see that such affordances make the dream of real-time government transparency, and a form of participatory democracy, possible in a way that older technologies could never realize. In another, less utopian direction, government transparency that relies on open data becomes articulated to the market logic and profit motives of the new data economy. Such an articulation muddies the claim that democratic accountability rather than economic growth is the driving force behind government commitments to open data.

The data economy is based on the economic activity to be generated by the reuse and repurposing of open data. In light of this, data sets regarding health, the environment, crime statistics and so forth, freely available in usable formats on government sites, can provide the content for various applications and web tools produced by the private sector. Democratic and economic gains become intertwined to the point where government accountability might be made possible only by the intervention of tech-savvy mediators and translators who will always be selective in both the data they choose to make available and the kinds of questions their apps allow consumer citizens to ask of that data. Such applications, and the developers that make them, therefore delimit and determine the scope of state transparency and the relationship citizens can have with the state. Technocratic transparency has to be considered not as a passive medium that makes the workings of the state visible, then, but as a series of *dispositifs* that are themselves far from transparent.

The arrival of Trump in the White House in 2017 has altered the stakes of transparency once again. Mark Fenster writes: "The United States, whose 50-year-old Freedom of Information Act (FOIA) has served as a model for much of the activism that the age of transparency called forth, might be departing from the long arc of transparency's ascent under a Trump administration" (2017: 173). At the time of writing, it is early days for this relatively inexperienced administration and so any observations are necessarily provisional and subject to revision in the coming months and years. Nevertheless, I want to consider three recurring scenes in the current conjuncture that offer insight into how transparency has been interrupted; the way in which its narrative arc has been derailed and its role as a counterweight to secrecy dislodged.

The first scene of note is the concern over the preservation and continued commitment to open data expressed by open data activists, educators, environmentalists, and librarians during the winter of 2016 and first few months of 2017 as the transition between administrations took place. The second is the invocation of conspiracy theories evident during Trump's campaign and early presidency. The third recurring scene, very much connected to the second, is any occasion where what has been labeled "post-truth," and related terms like "alternative facts," "post-fact," and "fake news," have come into play. Such terms are important to the current enquiry because they represent a new distortion of transparency and authenticity claims.

Trumping Transparency

Disappearing Data and "Memory Holes"

The transition period between the Obama and Trump administrations and the early days of the Trump administration prompted many concerns regarding the continued availability of open data generated by government agencies. It was, and remains, uncertain whether the production of new data and preservation of existing data will be a priority. In response, there was a flurry of interventions that involved transparency advocates, political historians, archivists, and environmental activists backing up federal datasets and web pages for fear that a Trump administration would remove what is available (Gerstein 2016). For example, the "End of Term Web Archive" (http://eotarchive.cdlib.org/index.html) and the call for assistance with its "End of Term Presidential Harvest" (http://digital2.library.unt.edu/nomination/eth2016/about/) is a collaboration between a group of university, nonprofit and government libraries. It calls on technologically competent researchers to identify federal web pages and data sets in need of preservation for the record. Because of the technological restrictions sometimes placed on downloading data even while that data can be searched in multiple ways online, data sets present a particular problem for archivists; much open data is therefore still vulnerable despite web archiving.

Concern about loss of data extends beyond the library community. This has prompted Abbie Grotke of the Library of Congress to comment, "This year, we've seen a lot of these activities just sprout up. We are losing control a little bit" (quoted in Gerstein 2016). She could be referring to events such as the University of Toronto's "Guerrilla Archiving Event: Saving Environmental Data from Trump" that took place on December 17, 2016: an organized "hackathon" intended to assist the efforts of the End of Term Web Archive to preserve information and data from the Environmental Protection Agency, especially that relating to climate change, water, air, and toxics programs (https://ischool.utoronto.ca/content/guerrilla-archiving-event-saving-environmental-data-trump). Grotke's comments also speak to the work carried out by organizations such as DataRefuge.org a group similarly motivated by a desire to preserve climate and environmental federal data in the face of an administration that denies the validity of climate change science.

We could extend Grotke's comments to lone operators like Maxwell Ogden, a programmer for the open data sharing project Dat Project, who decided to archive all nine gigabits of the data on the Obama administration's Open.Whitehouse.com pages on Inauguration Day (see Lynch

2017); or Russ Kick who established "The Memory Hole," which archives deleted web-pages and social media feeds relating to Trump (http://thememoryhole2.org/blog/trump-deletions). Kick's endeavor is obviously concerned with preserving a different form of content to that contained by datasets, but is nevertheless prompted by concerns regarding accountability and the public record that also shape a desire to preserve statistical data.

Once Trump came into office, any indication that data was going missing or being displaced was met with concern. For example, Meritalk, a public-private news outlet focused on government information technology, ran an article reflecting the unease in transparency quarters that data on open.whitehouse.gov had been badly archived to https://open.obamawhitehouse.archives.gov in formats that meant data was compromised in terms of usability (Lynch 2017). In fact, deleting federal records is against the law, and because of the multiple copies made of key data such as that recorded by NASA's Lunar Reconnaissance Orbiter, it is almost impossible for some datasets to disappear. Consequently, science journalist Megan Molteni comments that citizens should be less worried about archiving existing data and more concerned about making sure that datasets are renewed. "Archiving is inherently static … Datasets, on the other hand, are dynamic. And keeping open data pipelines, and the funding that makes them possible, is what scientists and concerned citizens should really be worried about" (Molteni 2017). A commitment to feeding datasets with new content was bolstered when the Open Government Data Act passed into law in late 2017, but it remains to be seen how much agencies will be encouraged and given resources to adhere to this law.

Conspiracy Theory Redux

The appearance of conspiracy theories in American political discourse is nothing new. Historians including Bernard Bailyn (1967), David Brion Davies (1971), Gordon Wood (1982), and more recently Michael Butter (2014) have tirelessly charted the influence and proliferation of conspiracist thinking at various points in American history, whether it be the belief in a systematic enslaving conspiracy against the American colonists conducted by the English that fueled the War for Independence, or the conspiracist rhetoric that followed in the wake of the 1820 Missouri Compromise and fed into the Civil War. In neither example were conspiracy theories the prerogative of the fringe. Rather, "they were obviously considered," Michael Butter convincingly demonstrates, "a legitimate form of knowledge and not the kind of popular counter-knowledge, ridiculed by experts, as which they are usually regarded today" (2014: 35).

While there may be nothing new about conspiracy theories being espoused from positions of power in American life, then, the latter part of Butter's comment makes all the difference. Mainstream liberal political rationality (see Bratich 2008) and scientific rationality (see Fiske 1993) have stigmatized and delegitimized conspiracy theorizing in the contemporary era. When Trump expresses or repeats conspiracy theories, then, he speaks into an epistemological conjuncture that has expertise in place to disavow conspiracist thinking. To contend with this, Trump's conspiracy theories have to not only arrive into that knowledge-scape, but intervene and shape it. Accompanying conspiracy theories, therefore, is a populist anti-intellectualism that marginalizes expertise and questions facts, and the oft-repeated accusation that the liberal media produces "fake news." I will suspend a discussion of these until the next section to briefly outline some of the conspiracy theories for which Trump has secured airtime.

Conspiracy theories, obviously, come in a variety of shapes and sizes depending on the geopolitical site of production and scope of circulation. There are many sub-genres to this by-now well-developed discourse— those that imagine alien involvement in earthly affairs; ironic and playful conspiracy theories that configure paranoia as a performance rather than pathology; conspiracy theories that fear government collusion with other powerful agencies against its populace; conspiracy theories about anti-government conspiracies that seek to undermine national values; conspiracy theories that chart a long historical trajectory for omniscient secret organizations; and localized conspiracy theories about one particular event. These are not necessarily mutually exclusive categories.

The conspiracy theories espoused and repeated by Trump steer clear of extra-terrestrials, though he has at one time or another made statements that could be described by the other categories listed above. His warning that a Clinton victory would be proof that "a small handful of global special interests [are] rigging the system" (Trump 2016) has much in common with macro conspiracy theories that reach for enigmatic societies like the Bilderberg Group or Illuminati to link a global elite and explain concentrations of power. Often, however, Trump and his team introduce conspiracist skepticism not as the sustained narrative that Richard Hofstadter charts in his classic study of "the paranoid style in American politics," coherent until the "characteristic paranoid leap into fantasy" (1964: 78), but simply as a series of fragments that highlight gaps, doubts, inconsistencies that dispense with the necessity of evidence and seem to arrive in the middle of a "leap" and never land.

Trump repeats conspiracist fragments he has encountered, as though he is a conduit only, never quite taking responsibility in order to clear the way for future deniability. Sometimes, he uses the phrases "some people say" and "many people think" to repeat an unfounded conspiracy theory. Other times, he repeats an accusation from one specific source. For example, Trump's claim that GCHQ assisted the Obama Administration in wiretapping Trump Tower during the presidential campaign was gleaned from Andrew Napolitano, a retired New Jersey Judge, who had made the claim in his role as an analyst on Fox News (see Patel-Carstairs, 2017). Crucially, the volume of conspiracist statements and variety of channels through which the Trump camp have used to disseminate them leaves little chance for fact/reality checks to have equal traction. Besides, "The virtual world far prefers the outrageous, the new, the controversial to the normal routine of reason and verification," which is why Trump's unverified claims were reposted and reported more than factual claims (Scherer 2017).

Trump's preferred conspiracy fragments/theories are those that feature and seek to delegitimize particular political opponents (Obama wasn't born in the US; Ted Cruz's father was associated with JFK's assassin, and, by implication, the assassination itself; "Hillary Clinton [met] in secret with international banks to plot the destruction of US sovereignty in order to enrich these global financial powers, her special interest friends and her donors" [Trump 2016]); institutions (the "liberal media" isn't reporting Islamic terrorism and misrepresents Trump's achievements; the Federal Reserve artificially propped up the economy during Obama's time in office); or knowledge that threatens his interests (climate change science is a money-making hoax). Trump does this by utilizing the language and narrative tropes of conspiracy thinking to represent power relations. In Fredric Jameson's oft-quoted terms, this is best thought of as a degraded form of "cognitive mapping" (1988); degraded because it cannot adequately link "the most intimately local—our particular path through the world—and the most global—the crucial features of our political planet" (MacCabe 1995: xivf).

Elsewhere I have questioned delegitimizing gestures like Jameson's, arguing that conspiracy theories (as one example of "popular knowledge") are best understood not as symptoms of a crippled epistemology, but as discursive phenomena that stage a confrontation with the undecideability of knowledge (Birchall 2006). Rather than leading us into the abyss of relativism, conspiracy theories thought in this way force ethical decisions about the nature of veracity and knowledge upon us. This won't necessarily be a simple task, of course, not least because the concepts and criteria we usually depend upon to assist us in assessing knowledge are also under attack.

Post-truth Phenomena

Accompanying conspiracy theories are a range of epistemologically disorientating phenomena that displace the rationalist consensus that Butter sees as providing the ground from which conspiracy theories are judged as irrational. These "post-truth" phenomena, which take a variety of forms and are ascribed particular names ("fake news," "alternative facts"), are produced at such a rate it is highly likely that, by the time this chapter comes into print, there will be others. These phenomena have also been the subject of many an op-ed; so much so that it may seem redundant to recount common knowledge here. Nevertheless, I will briefly chart this ground in order to consolidate the connections between the different phenomena and the way in which they all disrupt the epistemological assumptions and binary logic of visuality that have shaped the story of transparency, and its implicit faith in revelation, to date.

Hannah Arendt, over fifty years ago, remarked that "No one has ever doubted that truth and politics are on rather bad terms with each other, and no one, as far as I know, has ever counted truthfulness among the political virtues" (2000: 545). While truth, then, may always have had a weak hold on political discourse, christening the current moment as "post-truth" speaks to the lack of common or firm ground from which judgments about statements in the public sphere can be evaluated. Vertigo-inducing layers of untruths, half-truths, lies, exaggerations, decontextualized facts, and propaganda have all allowed Trump to shape public opinion through "appeals to emotion and personal belief" rather than "objective facts" (see Oxford Living Dictionaries). For example, Trump's claim on Twitter on November 27, 2016, that he "won the popular vote if you deduct the millions of people who voted illegally" (https://twitter.com/realDonaldTrump/status/802972944532209664), landed well with Republican voters—one poll suggested 52 percent of Republicans believed Trump on this point because it chimed with their partisan beliefs (see Oliver and Wood 2016) and spoke to floating fears concerning legitimate citizenship and the subversion of democracy. Of course, belief in the veracity of Trump's claims might even be irrelevant for some supporters as lying confirms Trump's self-professed anti-establishment status. Under extreme forms of individualist ideology, lying and cheating are wholly acceptable as part of the struggle for survival and supremacy. This is true even while Trump denounces the political system for being corrupt. Following this logic, the lone maverick can lie to beat a deceitful system. What is key here is that supporters offer allegiance to Trump because of what his claims, soundbites and theories license them to *feel* rather than enable them to *know*.

In a similar fashion to the way in which Trump repeats and circulates conspiracy theories without fully owning those statements, he also uses quotation marks to place a claim in the public sphere while creating some distance from it. For example, on March 4, 2017, Trump tweeted the following: "Terrible! Just found out that Obama had my 'wires tapped' in Trump Tower just before the victory." (https://twitter.com/realDonaldTrump/status/837989835818287106). Afterwards, press secretary

Sean Spicer claimed that the use of the phrase "wires tapped" was not meant literally and that "The President used the word wiretaps in quotes to mean, broadly, surveillance and other activities" (quoted in Diamond 2017). It is highly likely that Spicer is not just employing sophistry here, but is also acknowledging a fundamental feature of how Trump's communications are received by supporters. During the Presidential campaign, Salena Zito, writing in *The Atlantic*, suggested that Trump's supporters take him "seriously but not literally" (2016). For supporters, the liminal state between the figural and the literal, between something *like* wiretapping taking place in Trump Tower under Obama's watch and *actual* wiretapping taking place, challenges a consensus reality from which they might have felt excluded. Eschewing normal procedures of knowledge production and verification, the liminal ground corroborates suspicions without necessitating facts.

Much has been written about the rise of "fake news"—an umbrella term that encompasses humorous stories that are circulated online and then consumed as "news"; political propaganda and smear stories; and latterly any news item that does not support Trump's agenda. Trump and his team began to appropriate the term "fake news" as a way of defusing accusations of lying, questioning the neutrality of facts, and taking command of the public stage. In using the term to refer to stories in the mainstream press and television media that do not favorably represent his administration's goals, Trump shifts the parameters of truth from content to tenor. Indeed, in a press conference on February 16, 2017, Trump remarked "the news is fake because so much of the news is fake." He went on to explain this tautology: it is not the facts that he has a problem with, but "the tone." "Fake," here, designates the critical tone rather than a forgery. It becomes shorthand for any news that Trump would like to be dismissed. Placed within the wider conjuncture, "'fake news' is but a single symptom of a far more massive destabilization, as people on every possible side of every possible political spectrum re-orient themselves to what feels like the new political realities of 2017" (Cohen 2017).

In "Truth in Politics," Arendt distinguishes between pre-modern and modern lying. Pre-modern lying constitutes the obfuscation of a known truth. Modern lying destabilizes the terms by which truth can be ascertained and instills its own "reality." She puts it thus: "the difference between the traditional lie and the modern lie will more often than not amount to the difference between hiding and destroying" (2000: 565). Writing primarily about totalitarian regimes, her comments still speak to the violence of simulation at work in Trump's strategies. While theorists such as Jean Baudrillard (1983) have long diagnosed these shifts, Trump harnesses this simulacral regime in which the "real" is obscured in favor of the image/performance, and truth supplanted by rhetoric; or as Jodi Dean puts it, consensus reality is supplanted by virtual reality (1998: 8). The journalist Peter Pomerantsev argues that Trump is one of a number of politicians, including Vladimir Putin, who subvert "the idea that there is any knowable objective truth at all"; an operation that earns Trump the label "the postmodern president" (Pomerantsev 2017).

Despite its capacity for sharing knowledge, the techno-economic environment provides few checks on the ascendance of post-truth phenomena. In fact, the networked affordances of new, and especially social media have supported the circulation of post-truth's empty signifiers. Jodi Dean coined the phrase "communicative capitalism" in 2005 to capture the way in which communications technologies have harnessed and emptied out ideals of liberal democracy (such as access, inclusion, discussion and participation) so that political opportunity is obscured by "a deluge of screens and spectacles" (Dean 2005: 55). In the place of politics, citizens are offered access to a network that will never allow for strong oppositional voices to be registered in a meaningful way. Since Trump's election, Dean has updated the concept to reflect the current conjuncture:

> In the affective networks of communicative capitalism, each communicative utterance or contribution is "communicatively equivalent" in that it adds something to the communicative flow. Whether a post is a lie doesn't matter; in fact, lies often circulate more quickly and easily than facts. Whether an article is ill-conceived is unimportant, especially since a significant portion of what passes as an "article" online was generated by an algorithm in order to improve its rank in search engine results. What matters is simply that something was expressed, that a comment was made, that an image was liked and shared. (2017: 38)

In communicative capitalism, and perhaps even more so in communicative capitalism under Trump, revelations (of facts, proof, malfeasance, etc.) are depoliticized and rendered ineffective by the volume of rival content that can be circulated without commitment (whether the process is automated or not). If communicative capitalism offers a poor substitute for political engagement, post-truth phenomena produce a ghostly incarnation of a public sphere, demanding attention, affective investments even, without conferring agency.

All of which has serious implications for a discussion of transparency. The story of transparency in the US, in which transparency is intimately tied to the teleological trajectory of the democratic (and scientific) project of America, must now be revised. The link between the provision of information and accountability has always been fragile due to the possibility of misdirection and deception, but is now under enormous strain. Not only has the White House become a prime source of conspiracy theories and "alternative facts," it has also failed to make a commitment to open government and scientific data and practices.

Mark Fenster explains the break in the story of transparency imposed by Trump as a turning away not from transparency altogether, but from a particular meaning of transparency. Whereas government transparency understood as a technocratic tool "focuses on the information a government must disclose—certain kinds of documents and certain types of meetings most prominently," when the case for transparency is articulated in moral terms, it "holds that the state must refrain from hiding itself and the truth from the public" (2017: 173). Given Trump's track record of showing disrespect (to women, the disabled, Mexicans, Muslims, etc.) any reference to morals in relation to him will grate for many. Nevertheless, I want to work with the two tendencies Fenster has identified, including a moral meaning of transparency, as it helps us to focus on the way in which Trump has hijacked and derailed this discourse:

> Trump's candidacy deployed populist rhetoric to criticize existing political institutions for their distance from and invisibility to the public [...] Trumpland would be a visible, legible government with which his voters [...] could identify. Trump promised to be morally transparent, if not technocratically so. (Fenster 2017: 174)

Trump's self-stylization as a plain talking, anti-establishment, anti-intellectual, jargon-free figure invokes moral transparency in Fenster's terms, "suggesting that [Trump] hides nothing" regardless of whether he speaks the truth or not (173).

Of course, both strains of transparency often coexist. Woodrow Wilson won his presidential campaign on a "sunshine" platform. He wrote, "Government ought to be all outside and no inside. I, for my part, believe there ought to be no place where anything can be done that everybody does not know about … Secrecy means impropriety" (1913/2008: 70), thus presenting government transparency as a moral imperative. But he also helped to implement technocratic transparency—establishing, for example, the Federal Trade Commission in 1914, which imposed government oversight and open information on businesses with the aim of breaking monopolies, promoting competition, and protecting consumers. Obama, too, instilled a moralistic transparency alongside his procedural systems. On the campaign trail in 2008, he wanted voters to register the difference between his open politics and the secret machinations of post 9/11 securitization under George W. Bush. "For a long time now," Obama remarked at a 2009 swearing-in ceremony for senior officials in Washington DC, "there's been too much secrecy in this city" (quoted in Stolberg 2009).

As outlined above, this approach went hand in hand with Obama's vision of open government data. Moral transparency has historically served as the rationale and fuel for technocratic transparency; a point Fenster himself acknowledges (2017). Trump has broken this relationship between transparency's meanings.

Both understandings of transparency—technocratic and moralistic—place suspicion on "everything that does not submit to visibility" (Han 2015: 13). With respect to technocratic transparency, suspicion is cast on data and information that is left off the public record. In the terms set up by Trump's moral transparency, intangibles that cannot easily be brought into the limited conditions of visibility as dictated by communicative capitalism become fashioned as sources of suspicion. Consider Trump's hints that Ted Cruz's father was an acquaintance of Lee Harvey Oswald and may, therefore, be linked to the assassination of JFK. Rafael Cruz's denial brought nothing forth—no Twitter-friendly counter-story or proof—and was therefore less visible than the photograph and original story in the *National Enquirer* on which Trump's claim was based. Trump even bemoaned the lack of a denial when Rafael, Ted and a communications director had each issued one in the mainstream press (see Farley 2016). This is a two-stage process. First, Trump ignores a certain visibility, claiming a void where there is in fact content (the denial). Second, he uses the self-produced void as proof of the veracity of that which he has made visible (the accusation). The issue becomes undecideable within a public realm that affords more weight to the criterion of circulation than truth and exploits the instability of the category of the visible to full effect.

Trump therefore casts suspicion on events and actions, but he also has more nebulous targets. Fenster writes, "Trump and his compatriots among right-wing populists have found political purchase and electoral success by decrying a lack of transparency. They claim that political and cultural elites have ignored the democratic will by secretly abandoning national traditions" (2017: 173). Suspicion is also cast, then, on the intangible ideology of progressive multicultural liberalism itself, presenting change as a force that obfuscates "true" American values. Transparency in this scenario would be a mechanism that punctures ideology by exposing the way it presents cultural norms and values as natural. The revelation of progressive tenets as ideological, of course, is itself a deeply ideological maneuver in the way that it naturalizes a link between conservative values and Americanism. Just as American as conservative values, of course, are the notions of freedom and equality that have been repurposed and reinvigorated to enable subjugated identities and rights to gain visibility and legitimacy since the 1960s. Transparency, when called for from the edge of right-wing populism, then, is simply a call for a new regime of visibility built on different criteria and values. It calls for more visibility for hitherto "forgotten" non-elite, lower-middle-class white voters.

To summarize my argument so far: Trump has derailed transparency in three main ways. First, by invoking moralistic transparency in lieu of, rather than alongside, technocratic transparency, Trump's administration has perverted the former and placed the ascendance of the latter in jeopardy and, therefore, changed the course of the story of American transparency thus far.[2] Second, in severing any residual links between visibility and truth, Trump places in doubt claims made about transparency's efficacy. Third, by muddying the opposition between openness and occlusion, Trump's post-truth arsenal unsettles the binary logic on which transparency's legitimacy partly resides. Of note in this regard is the way in which Trump distances himself from the traditional mechanisms of government secrecy as much as he does government technocratic transparency. He has repeatedly been at odds with the intelligence agencies (see Visser 2017) and seems to give Fox News reports as much weight as secret intelligence when shaping policy.

Appropriating the Interruption: Towards Radical Transparency

In considering these three scenes, then, we can see an interruption to the trajectory of, and story we have told ourselves about government transparency in America. Elsewhere, I have called for such an interruption (2011b, 2015), though never in the form of Trump's post-truth politics. I have done so because technocratic transparency in the US became largely reliant upon the provision of open data under Obama through the federally funded data.gov (the gateway to agency datasets). While there is nothing *ipso facto* problematic about open data provision, and is in many ways highly desirable, it tends to provide data in place of accountable and responsible political decisions and meaningful public engagement. It also encourages a subjectivity conducive to, and accepting of, neoliberalism as the burden of monitoring, regulating, and translating the transactions of the state shifts from the state to the citizen. Moreover, the open data provided is the raw material of the data economy in which data entrepreneurs re-purpose open government information to commercial ends. This reliance upon mediated and commercialized open government data

---

[2] Mark Fenster elaborates: "[Trump's] hostility to criticism and apparent distaste for the First Amendment, his penchant for controlling information about himself, and his never having been subject to public transparency laws in his business career suggest that his administration will not be more compliant with the spirit or letter of open government laws than those that came before and may well be less so" (2017: 173).

to navigate the state produces a certain relationship between government and governed, representatives and represented that is highly delimited and delimiting in its political scope.

I do not want to downplay the risks posed by an administration that abuses moralist transparency to play ocular games and pays little heed to technocratic transparency. If Obama era open data-driven transparency reinforced a certain form of neoliberal subjectivity by bestowing responsibility to relatively disempowered citizen auditors, Trump's vertiginous obfuscating maneuvers in plain sight almost certainly leave citizens more unsettled and disenfranchised. Nevertheless, it may be that this disruption to the story of transparency can be used as an opportunity to rethink what kind of transparency best creates accountable and ethical government and offers real political scope for citizens, rather than a formation that seriously delimits participation.

While I will leave questions of practical implementation to others, I want to speculate on what could constitute this "radical transparency." In organizational theory, "radical transparency" signifies an organization that implements total openness at all levels of operation, but we could rework "radical" in terms of politics rather than scale. "Radical transparency" might then be envisaged as a mechanism able to subvert dominant attitudes towards disclosure's limited and prescribed role in the political sphere. Radical transparency would allow citizens to position themselves in relation to data (rather than be positioned by it). It would allow for explicitly political rather than technical solutions to social problems. It would have to be worthy of democracy—envisaged not as "an ambient milieu, as the natural habitat of postmodern individuality" but as an arena of "struggles and sacrifices" (Rancière 1992: 22) as well as decisions. A radical transparency would be a mode of revelation that avoids the reinforcement of neoliberal subjects and relations. It would need to understand the mediated nature of, and ascribe alternative cultural values to, data and transparency. It would need to politicize data, transparency, and openness in general—to ask what role revelation should play in democratic representation and participation.

Radical transparency would understand that certain forms of openness might only make structurally inequitable systems work more efficiently (see Lefebvre 1974: 28-9) or reinforce the social stratification behind digital access. This would not necessarily involve a move away from data technologies—neither data as such nor the technologies that make the storage and circulation of it are the problem here. Rather it is the delimitation of their position and role within a network by political, technological and economic protocols with which we can take issue. It might involve platforms that are programmed to explicitly state the value of open data (to whom or what). It might require, as Felix Stalder suggests, communications technologies that enable large-scale sociality to ensure that transparency is horizontal rather than top-down (2011: 22). It would obviously entail a commitment to the kind of structural shifts that would enable equal access to technology and the skills to navigate it rather than just an in principle democratization of data.

In addition, radical transparency would commit not to ever more data, but data that is radically contextualized: that is, accompanied by an account of the conditions, assumptions and politics that informed the production and gathering of the data in the first place rather than the provision of metadata (which merely makes data searchable) or the packaging of data within apps (which might decontextualize as much as contextualize). After all, a dataset provided to us through transparency tools is not itself transparent: not only has it been gathered with a particular agenda in mind and a certain methodology, statistics that show a success story can belie other goals or values that have been sacrificed in the process (see Morozov 2013: 85).

Crucially, radical transparency would not fuse moralistic and technocratic transparency, but would be ethical in nature. If, as Wendy Brown has shown, moralism knows in advance what it thinks and feels and knows about a situation (for example, that transparency is inherently democratic and progressive, that it always and in every circumstance promotes accountability), ethics is an encounter with the other that necessitates a responsible decision to be made in an undecideable field (see Brown 2001: 18-44). For Derrida, there is an aporia at work in the role of knowledge in the ethical decision:

> Saying that a responsible decision must be taken on the basis of knowledge seems to define the condition of possibility of responsibility (one can't make a responsible decision without science or conscience, without

knowing what one is doing, for what reasons, in view of what and under what conditions), at the same time as it defines the condition of impossibility of this same responsibility (if decision-making is relegated to a knowledge that it is content to flow or to develop, then it is no more a responsible decision, it is the technical deployment of a cognitive apparatus, the simple mechanistic deployment of a theorem). (Derrida 1995: 24)

A programmatic decision, made as an affirmation of one's own subjectivity and knowledge, revokes and devolves responsibility to an already known, calculable way of deciding. I am not making a "free" decision if I make it according to moral (or ideological) terms already set. Ethical transparency, then, wouldn't be a transaction offered in lieu of making responsible decisions. Rather, it would stage an encounter with otherness and prompt those decisions.

"Radical transparency" would not be an adjunct to politics, added after the fact to make the state visible. Instead, it would constitute the conditions of possibility and impossibility of politics. It might be best, then, to think of "radical transparency" as a holding space for something yet to come. "Radical" indicates not more (of the same) transparency, whether moralistic populist transparency or technocratic data driven transparency, but a transparency robust enough to contend with "post-truth" figures, strategies and politics.

Works Cited

Arendt, Hannah. 2000. Truth in Politics. In *The Portable Hannah Arendt*, ed. Peter Baehr, 574–575. New York: Penguin.
Bailyn, Bernard. 1967. *The Ideological Origins of the American Revolution.* Cambridge, MA: Belknap.
Baudrillard, Jean. 1983. *Simulations.* Los Angeles: Semiotext(e).
Birchall, Clare. 2006. *Knowledge Goes Pop: From Conspiracy Theory to Gossip.* Oxford: Berg.
———. 2011a. "'There's Been too Much Secrecy in this City": The False Choice between Secrecy and Transparency in U.S. Politics. *Cultural Politics* 7 (1): 133–156.

———. 2011b. Transparency, Interrupted: Secrets of the Left. *Theory, Culture & Society* 28 (7–8): 60–84.

———. 2015. Data.gov-in-a-Box: Delimiting Transparency. *European Journal of Social Theory* 18 (2): 185–202.

Birkinshaw, Patrick. 2006. Transparency as a Human Right. In *Transparency: The Key to Better Governance*, ed. Christopher Hood and David Heald. Oxford: Oxford University Press.

Brandeis, Louis. 1913. Other People's Money. *Harper's Weekly*, November 29. http://www.law.louisville.edu/library/collections/brandeis/node/191. Accessed 19 Mar 2017.

Bratich, Jack. 2008. *Conspiracy Panics: Political Rationality and Popular Culture*. Albany: State University of New York Press.

Brown, Wendy. 2001. Moralism as Anti-Politics. In *Politics Out of History*, 18–44. Princeton, NJ: Princeton.

Butter, Michael. 2014. *Plots, Designs, and Schemes: American Conspiracy Theories from the Puritans to the Present*. Berlin and Boston: De Gruyter.

Chydenius, Anders. 1766. His Majesty's Gracious Ordinance Relating to Freedom of Writing and of the Press. Trans. Peter Hogg. In Juha Mustonen (ed.), (2006). *The World's First Freedom of Information Act: Anders Chydenius' Legacy Today*, 8–17. Kokkola, Finland: Anders Chydenius Foundation.

Cohen, Kris. 2017. Fake News Isn't a Truth Problem, It's a Personhood Problem. *Chapati Mystery*, January 22. http://www.chapatimystery.com/archives/imperial_watch/fake_news_isnt_a_truth_problem_its_a_personhood_problem.html. Accessed 21 Feb 2017.

Davis, David Brion. 1971. *The Fear of Conspiracy: Images of Un-American Subversion from Revolution to the Present*. New York: Cornell University Press.

Dean, Jodi. 1998. *Aliens in America*. New York: Cornell University Press.

———. 2005. Communicative Capitalism: Circulation and the Foreclosure of Politics. *Cultural Politics* 1 (1): 51–74.

———. 2017. Not Him, Us (and We Aren't Populists). *Theory and Event* 20 (1): 38–44.

Derrida, Jacques. 1995. *The Gift of Death*. Trans. D. Wills, Chicago and London: University of Chicago Press.

Diamond, Jeremy. 2017. Spicer: Trump Didn't Mean Wiretapping When He Tweeted About Wiretapping. *CNN*, March 14. http://edition.cnn.com/2017/03/13/politics/sean-spicer-donald-trump-wiretapping/. Accessed 21 Mar 2017.

Easley, Jonathan. 2013. Obama Says His Is 'The Most Transparent Administration' Ever. *The Hill*, February 14. http://thehill.com/blogs/blog-briefing-room/news/283335-obama-this-is-the-most-transparent-administration-in-history. Accessed 5 Apr 2017.

Farley, Robert. 2016. Fact Check: Trump Defends Claim on Oswald and Cruz's Father," *USA Today*, July 23. https://www.usatoday.com/story/news/politics/elections/2016/07/23/fact-check-trump-lee-harvey-oswald-rafael-cruz/87475714/. Accessed 5 Apr 2017.

Fenster, Mark. 2010. Seeing the State: Transparency as Metaphor. 62 Admin L. Rev 617. http://scholarship.law.ufl.edu/cgi/viewcontent.cgi?article=1571&context=facultypub. Accessed 12 Dec 2016.

———. 2017. Transparency in Trump's America. *Governance*, January: 173–175. http://onlinelibrary.wiley.com/doi/10.1111/gove.12272/full. Accessed 21 Feb 2017.

Fiske, John. 1993. *Power Plays, Power Works*, London and. New York: Verso.

Foucault, Michel. 1980. The Eye of Power. In *Power-Knowledge: Selected Interviews and Other Writings 1972–1977*, ed. Colin Gordon, 146–165. New York: Pantheon Books.

Gerstein, Josh. 2016. Fears Rise of Trump-era 'Memory Hole' in Federal Data. *Politico*, December 13. http://www.politico.com/story/2016/12/trump-federal-data-fears-232591. Accessed 7 Jan 2017.

Han, Byung-Chul. 2015. *The Transparency Society*. California: Stanford University Press.

Hofstadter, Richard. 1964. The Paranoid Style in American Politics. *Harpers Magazine*, November, 77–86.

Jameson, Fredric. 1988. Cognitive Mapping. In *Marxism and the Interpretation of Culture*, ed. Cary Nelson and Lawrence Grossberg. London: Macmillan.

Lefebvre, Henri. 1974. *The Production of Space*. Trans. D. Nicholson-Smith, Oxford: Blackwell.

Lynch, Morgan. 2017. White House Open Data Disappears, Raising Transparency Questions. *Merital*, February 16. https://www.meritalk.com/articles/white-house-open-data-disappears-transparency-donald-trump-sunlight-foundation/. Accessed 21 Feb 2017.

MacCabe, Colin. 1995. Preface. In *The Geopolitical Aesthetic: Cinema and Space in the World System*, ed. Fredric Jameson. Bloomington: Indiana University Press.

Meijer, Albert. 2015. Government Transparency in Historical Perspective: From the Ancient Regime to Open Data in The Netherlands. *International Journal of Public Administration* 38 (3): 189–199.

Molteni, Megan. 2017. Old-Guard Archivists Keep Federal Data Safer Than You Think. *Wired*, February 19. https://www.wired.com/2017/02/army-old-guard-archivers-federal-data-safer-think/. Accessed 21 Feb 2017.

Morozov, Eugene. 2013. *To Save Everything, Click Here: Technology, Solutionism and the Urge to Fix Problems that Don't Exist*. London and New York: Allen Lane.

Oliver, Eric, and Thomas Wood. 2016. A New Poll Shows 52% of Republicans Actually Think Trump Won the Popular Vote. *Washington Post*, December 18. https://www.washingtonpost.com/news/monkey-cage/wp/2016/12/18/a-new-poll-shows-an-astonishing-52-of-republicans-think-trump-won-the-popular-vote/?utm_term=.4b2165462aea. Accessed 12 Mar 2017.

Oxford Living Dictionaries. Post-Truth. https://en.oxforddictionaries.com/definition/post-truth. Accessed 21 Feb 2017.

Patel-Carstairs, Sunita. 2017. Fox Pulls Andrew Napolitano off Air After GCHQ Trump Wiretap Claim. *Sky News*, March 21. http://news.sky.com/story/fox-pulls-andrew-napolitano-off-air-after-gchq-trump-wiretap-claim-10809396. Accessed 27 Mar 2017.

Pomerantsev, Peter. 2017. The Rise of the Postmodern President. *Newsnight*, March 16. http://www.bbc.co.uk/programmes/p04x293b. Accessed 25 Mar 2017.

Rancière, Jacques. 1992. *On the Shores of Politics*. Trans. L. Heron. London: Verso.

Scherer, Michael. 2017. Can President Trump Handle the Truth? *Time Magazine*, March 23. http://time.com/4710614/donald-trump-fbi-surveillance-house-intelligence-committee/. Accessed 15 Mar 2017.

Stalder, Felix. 2011. The Fight over Transparency. *Open* 22: 8–22.

Stolberg, Sheryl Gay. 2009. Obama Finds that Washington's Habits of Secrecy Die Hard. *New York Times*, April 4. http://www.nytimes.com/2009/04/05/us/politics/05transparency.html. Accessed 1 Jun 2017.

The White House. 2009a. Memorandum for the Heads of Executive Departments and Agencies: Classified Information and Controlled Unclassified Information. May 27. http://www.whitehouse.gov/the_press_office/Presidential-Memorandum-Classified-Information-and-Controlled-Unclassified-Information/. Accessed Nov 2016.

———. 2009b. Open Government Directive. December 8. http://www.whitehouse.gov/open/documents/open-government-directive. Accessed Nov 2016.

Trump, Donald. 2016. Campaign Rally Speech. *West Palm Beach*, Florida, October 13. Full transcript at *PBS* http://www.npr.org/2016/10/13/497857068/transcript-donald-trumps-speech-responding-to-assault-accusations. Accessed 15 Mar 2017.

Visser, Nick. 2017. Trump Administration Increasingly at Odds With US Intelligence Community. *The Huffington Post*, February 16. http://www.huffingtonpost.com/entry/donald-trump-intelligence-agencies_us_58a52530e4b045cd34be99aa. Accessed 6 April 2017.

Wilson, Woodrow. 1913/2008. *The New Freedom*. Charleston, SC: BiblioBazaar LLC..

Wood, Gordon. 1982. Conspiracy and the Paranoid Style: Causality and Deceit in the Eighteenth Century. *The William and Mary Quarterly* 39 (3): 401–441.

Zito, Salena. 2016. Taking Trump Seriously, Not Literally. *The Atlantic*, September 23. https://www.theatlantic.com/politics/archive/2016/09/trump-makes-his-case-in-pittsburgh/501335/. Accessed 23 Mar 2017.

Virtual Transparency: From the Panopticon to the Expository Society and Beyond

Bernard E. Harcourt

Winter 1973. Michel Foucault is struggling to reconceptualize power in the wake of May '68, of the failures of the student uprising, of the authoritarianism of the French state. How is it, Foucault tries to comprehend, how is it that we tolerate, so easily and so comfortably, *the intolerable*? The French government of Georges Pompidou has outlawed non-parliamentary leftist political parties and arrested and imprisoned hundreds of leftist militants. Prison riots have erupted across France in 1971 and '72, leaving the country in a state of turmoil. Not enough, though, to bring about any substantive political change. Despite the protests and riots, and all the political agitation, there's generalized apathy among French citizens.

In Paris, Foucault delivers his third annual lecture series at the Collège de France: a deeply historical and theoretical analysis of eighteenth- and nineteenth-century forms of social conflict (Foucault 2013). His analysis resonates with current events and directly challenges, *sub silencio* as is his way, the dominant Marxist theories of state apparatuses, repression, and

---

B. E. Harcourt (✉)
Columbia University, New York, NY, USA
e-mail: bernard.harcourt@columbia.edu

© The Author(s) 2018
E. Alloa, D. Thomä (eds.), *Transparency, Society and Subjectivity*,
https://doi.org/10.1007/978-3-319-77161-8_18

superstructural power—especially Althusser (Balibar 2015: 285–289). By no accident, Foucault titles his lectures *The Punitive Society*—with the emphasis on "society," on relations of power *throughout society*: the problem of power is not just a question of the Pompidou government, it is far more dispersed and capillary. In Rio de Janeiro, in May 1973, Foucault elaborates these themes into five conferences on "Truth and Juridical Form"—with the emphasis, now, on the way in which various legal devices produce truth differently. One of those devices, we know well, will emerge with prominence in his thought: penitential exclusion, or the prison as a juridical form.

Both in Paris and in Rio, Foucault directs his audience to a certain Nicolaus Heinrich Julius, doctor in medicine, prison reformer, professor at the University of Berlin, and colleague of Hegel.[1] "This man," declares Foucault, "this man named Julius, whom I highly recommend that you read, and who delivered for several years in Berlin a course on prisons, is an extraordinary personality who had, at times, an almost Hegelian wisp [*un souffle presque hégélien*]" (Foucault 1994: 607). The reason is that Professor Julius had discerned, during the 1820s, a remarkable disruption in our technologies of knowing and our strategies of power. An architectural mutation that reflected a profound transformation of power relations across society.

Antiquity, Julius observed, had discovered the architectural form of the "spectacle." The spectacle became, in ancient times, the way to know and to control. As Julius elaborates in his "Lectures on Prisons" in 1827,[2] in a passage that would become a keystone for Foucault in 1973—I am quoting Julius here: "It is a fact worthy of the highest interest, not only in the history of architecture, but in that of the human mind in general: that in the earliest times, not only in classical antiquity, but even in the Orient, the genius mind conceived and then pleased itself to decorate—with all the treasures of human magnificence—buildings that were designed to make accessible to a large multitude of men the spectacle and inspection of a small number of objects, such as in temples, theaters, amphitheaters,

---

[1] As a physician, Julius "worked on the staff of poorhouses and in the military" (Johnston 2000: 180 n.47). Julius was also a noted prison reformer (Singer and Adler 1916: 392).

[2] Julius lectured in Berlin in 1827 "under the auspices of the newly formed Verein für die Besserung der Stafgefangen, a prisoners' aid society" (Johnston 2000: 180 n.47).

where they would watch the blood of humans and animals flow" (Julius 1831: 384–385). And although the ancients invented the form of the spectacle, and would instantiate it in those arenas and amphitheaters filled with blood, at no time did they think or imagine of inverting the architecture. "All the while," Julius notes, "the human imagination never seems to have applied itself to provide a small number of men, or even a single man, the simultaneous view of a great multitude of men or objects" (384–385).

Julius then adds—moving forward, to his own times—that there would be a fundamental transformation in modernity, away from the architectural model of the spectacle, toward its very opposite: "It would be a task reserved to modern times (and I intend to develop this idea later), to a period marked by the growing influence of the state and of its many interventions—deeper, day by day, into every detail and every relation of social life—to ensure and perfect the grand goal of constructing and distributing edifices intended to simultaneously surveil [*surveiller*] at one and the same time a great multitude of men" (385).

It is here that Foucault picks up the thread. Lecturing in Paris on *The Punitive Society* in 1973, Foucault remarks:

> [T]his is precisely what happens in the modern era: the reversal of the spectacle into surveillance. We are in the process of inventing, says Julius, not only an architecture, an urbanism, but an entire disposition of the mind in general, such that, from now on, it will be men who will be offered in spectacle to a small number of people, at the limit to only one man destined to surveil them all. The spectacle turned into surveillance, the circle that citizens formed around the spectacle—all that is reversed. We have here a completely different structure where men who are placed next to each other on a flat surface will be surveilled from above by someone who will become a kind of universal eye. (Foucault 2013: 25)

Foucault would return to this remarkable passage on Julius and develop it further in 1975, in his chapter in *Discipline and Punish* on "Panopticism," where, again speaking of Julius, Foucault would declare: "A few years after Bentham, Julius wrote the birth certificate of this [disciplinary] society" (Foucault 2015: 499).

Foucault had originally come across the idea of panoptic surveillance during his research into the origins of clinical medicine and the medical gaze (Foucault 1977). The architect Bruno Fortier had shared with Foucault plans for a circular hospital at the *Hôtel-Dieu* from 1770—a design, based on the shape of a radiant star, that would become the central object of study in the seminar that Foucault conducted at the Collège de France during 1973–1974 on "The History of the Institution and Architecture of the Hospital in the Eighteenth Century" (Foucault 2003: 352), a seminar that would result in the publication of a collected volume, *Les Machines à guérir. Aux origines de l'hôpital moderne* (Barret-Kriegel et al. 1979). As evidenced by the mid-eighteenth-century plans that Fortier had dug up, the design of a "huge radiant hospital" that would make possible "a constant and absolute surveillance," in other words the model of panoptic surveillance, far predated Bentham's *Panopticon* (see ibid: 48; Bentham 1995). In fact, Foucault traced the origins of the first model of "this isolating visibility" to the dormitories of the Military Academy of Paris in 1751, noting that "all the major projects for the redevelopment of prisons … would take up the same theme [of the complete visibility of bodies], but, this time, under the mantra almost always reminded of Bentham. There was hardly any text, or project concerning prisons where one did not find that 'trick' of Bentham—namely, the 'Panopticon'" (Foucault 1977: 191).

With his repeated emphasis on the reversal of spectacle into surveillance, Foucault was undoubtedly gesturing to Guy Debord, who had placed the spectacle at the center of his conception of modernity (Debord 1967). In contrast to Debord, and as Julius had stressed over a century earlier, the spectacle had originated in antiquity—not modernity—and would centrally characterize those far earlier periods. What defines modernity, then—or at least the nineteenth century—was not the appearance of the spectacle, but rather its eclipse and reversal into surveillance. Or, even more strikingly, the creation of a whole panoptic society, of a punitive society.

Foucault appropriated as metaphor Bentham's term "Panopticon" in order to capture the ethos of disciplinary power in nineteenth-century French society. And a key element of that ethos was a form of *unilateral transparency*. Foucault articulated the central traits and techniques of disciplinary power through carefully crafted notions of *transparency*: a spatial organization that ensures the exact observation of human subjects so that "the techniques that make it possible to see induce effects of power" (Foucault 1979: 170–171); an architecture that permits the confinement of the individuals who are watched and have the knowledge of constant surveillance (172–173); a perfect control over time, a normalizing form of judgment, a generalized form of truth-production that constantly evaluates and judges those who are being watched, and that ultimately hides the gaze of the watcher, so that those watched begin to internalize the discipline themselves (184–192).

On this last point, Foucault emphasized, "*The examination transformed the economy of visibility into the exercise of power*. Traditionally, power was what was seen, what was shown and what was manifested," Foucault elaborated. "Disciplinary power, on the other hand, is exercised through its invisibility…. In discipline, it is the subjects who have to be seen. Their visibility assures the hold of the power that is exercised over them" (187). And in addition to the visibility, these architects of power also played with acoustic transparency. Foucault would note that "Bentham in his first version of the Panopticon had also imagined an acoustic surveillance, through pipes leading from the cells to the central tower" (Foucault 2015: 482 n.2; Foucault 1973: 607–609). And Julius, with his Hegelian wisp, Foucault adds, "himself had tried to develop an asymmetric listening system" (Ibid.).

The central features of disciplinary power were refracted in the Panopticon, with its constant visibility, and so Foucault appropriated the metaphor in homage to Bentham. In an unpublished draft of *Discipline and Punish*, Foucault jotted down his reasoning:

> If we characterize as "disciplinary" the apparatuses of spatial distribution, of extraction and accumulation of time, of individualization and subjection of bodies through a game of watching and recording, then let's honor Bentham and call "panoptic" a society in which the exercise of power is ensured on the model of generalized discipline. And let's say that, at the turn of the eighteenth and nineteenth centuries, we saw clearly emerge "panoptic" societies of which Bentham could be considered, depending on your view, the prophet, the witness, the analyst or the programmer. (Foucault 2015: 1467)

"Let's honor Bentham": Foucault named nineteenth-century French society "panoptic" as a metaphor to capture the central features of discipline. "The Panopticon," Foucault emphasized in *Discipline and Punish*, "must be understood as a generalizable model of functioning; a way of defining power relations in terms of the everyday life of men" (Foucault 1979: 205). And it captured the transparency features of discipline extremely well: how the Panopticon preserves the enclosure of the dungeon, but offers "full lighting" and enables the trap of visibility (200); how it produces the internalization of power so that "the perfection of power should tend to render its actual exercise unnecessary" (201); and the experimental, laboratory nature of the edifice—"a privileged place for experiments on men" (204). "We are much less Greeks than we believe," Foucault declared. "We are neither in the amphitheater, nor on the stage, but in the panoptic machine, invested by its effects of power, which we bring to ourselves since we are part of its mechanism" (217).

Foucault's reference to *un souffle presque hégélien*—that Hegelian wisp—may have been a clue of things to come, though. "Only when the dusk starts to fall does the owl of Minerva spread its wings and fly," as Hegel would notoriously write (Hegel 1952: 13). Within a couple of years, perhaps even by 1976 with his discussion of biopower in *La Volonté de savoir* and his lectures *"Il faut défendre la société,"* Foucault had already begun to move away from the idea that panoptic surveillance could serve as a model of power relations in contemporary society. Turning his attention more intensely to the rise of a neoliberal paradigm of biopower, Foucault began to articulate during the latter part of the 1970s a different form—or rather a supplemental form of power relations, namely, "security."[3] He would elaborate this in his lectures at the Collège de France on *Security, Territory, Population* in 1978 and *The Birth of Biopolitics* in 1979.

The form "security" was tied to the arts of maximizing and minimizing—to the competence of economists: reaching an equilibrium point for populations as a whole, not focused on the event in a spectacular way,

---

[3] I will use *sécurité* to refer to the term Foucault originally coined and later renamed *gouvernementalité*, and will reserve the term "governmentality" to refer to later work that is generally referred to as his "governmentality studies."

nor on the individual in a disciplinary manner. Security differed markedly from surveillance. Discipline is centripetal, it focuses on minor disorders and seeks to eradicate them. Security, by contrast, is centrifugal. It is tolerant of minor deviations and seeks to optimize, to minimize or maximize, rather than to eliminate (Foucault 2004: 46, 7). And both, of course, differ from the juridical model, the form of law, which divides in a binary way between the permissible and the prohibited, and then penalizes the latter (7).

Foucault, however, did not provide as powerful an architectural schematic to visualize biopower. There was, to be sure, the tripartite series that Foucault presented in his lecture on January 11, 1978, in *Security, Territory, Population*: the juridical exclusion of lepers in the Middle Ages; the grid-like regulation and disciplinary quarantine of entire cities during the plague in the sixteenth and seventeenth centuries; and the medical campaign of security against smallpox in the eighteenth century (11–12). Or, even closer to architecture, the tripartite series that Foucault discussed, also on January 11, 1978: the text by Alexandre Le Maître on *La Métropolitée* in the seventeenth century; the construction of artificial cities under Louis XIII and XIV; and the redevelopment of Nantes at the end of the eighteenth century (15–19). All the same, we still lacked a precise schema—akin to the arena for the spectacle, or the Panopticon for surveillance—to properly visualize security in a neoliberal age, as a means to better understand, first, how contemporary neoliberalism distributes power, and, secondly, more punctually, how the digitization of neoliberalism affects those distributions.

But although Foucault would never experience our digital age, he would imagine a time of total awareness and monitoring. Presciently, Foucault drew the outline of a possible future where all our personal data would be recorded and mined. In an interview Foucault gave in Stockholm in March 1968, after the publication of *The Order of Things*, he hypothesized a society of "universal notation," a possible world of big data (Foucault 1968).[4] The passage may be productive to reread in light of our experiences in the new digital age:

---

[4] Special thanks to François Ewald who pointed me to this passage from the interview in April 2013 (e-mail on file with author).

Question: If the man, whom you discern at the end of *The Order of Things*, is in the process of disappearing from our knowledge, the new historical *a priori* implies, then, a transformation of unprecedented importance—namely, the emergence of a vision of knowledge structured in a new way. Can we say anything about its new guiding principles?

Foucault: That is a bit difficult. But I think we could nevertheless say that we wanted for the first time, not to know everything, not to make ourselves master of the universe in the manner of Descartes, not to achieve absolute knowledge in the sense of the nineteenth century, but to say everything. Everything is noted, the unconscious of man, his sexuality, his daily life, his dreams, his wishes and his impulses, etc. We write down his behavior, social phenomena, people's opinions and their dispositions, their acts and their political attitudes, etc. All this becomes the subject of a discourse. And it is this passage to a universal notation, this transcription into a language of all the world's problems, which seems to characterize contemporary culture.

Question: Does this implicate a change of historical *a prioris*?

Foucault: That is difficult to answer. But it does seem to me that this universal transcription necessarily implies a form of science of another type than what marked the nineteenth century, when the task was not to say everything, but to explain it all.

Question: And this cannot remain within the confines of our current system?

Foucault: I do not know. Our impression of a rupture, of a transformation may be quite illusory. This may be the last or a new manifestation of a system that imprisons us, and makes us believe that we will soon find ourselves in another world. Maybe it's an illusion? We always have the impression that the sun has risen for the first time (Foucault 1968: 661–662).

"Everything is noted, the unconscious of man, his sexuality, his daily life, his dreams, his wishes and his impulses, etc.": Remarkably, this is not an illusion today, but our digital condition. And it differs markedly from

Virtual Transparency: From the Panopticon to the Expository... 377

prior architectural models of power. Neither the spectacle, nor surveillance are entirely fitted to the present digital age. Instead, we need to develop new concepts about our own exposure and about the overarching principle of *virtual transparency*.

Today, a new digital way of life dominates in most advanced-capitalist liberal democracies and in many other places around the globe. It is a digitized, cosmopolitan condition that is captured, almost entirely, by electronic communications—a rich social, professional, personal and political circuit of text messages and e-mails, digital photos and scans, PDFs, Skype calls, Facebook, and Twitter, a world of Google and Bing searches, and pings, and Snapchats, of digital subscriptions, Flickr photos, Vimeos, and Vines, of Instagrams, YouTube videos, and webcams. And with it, embedded within it, there is a whole technology of *virtual transparency* that allows for pervasive data-mining, digital profiling, facial-recognition, Amazon recommendations, eBay offers, Google algorithms, and NSA surveillance. It is a new world in which we expose ourselves and our most intimate desires and every activity, inescapably, to the technological capabilities of the market and the state.

This new world thrives on invasive digital technology. Google collects and mines our g-mails, attachments, contacts, and calendars. Netflix and Amazon recommend films and books that we want to read next. Twitter tracks our Internet activity on all the websites that carry its icon. Facebook's smartphone app collects information from our other phone apps, and pushes advertisements onto them. Instagram verifies ad impressions, measures their success, and provides feedback to the advertisers as to which are most effective. Neighbors use packet sniffers or free Mac software, like Eavesdrop, to tap into our unsecured networks. Google's street view cars capture and record our usernames, passwords, and personal emails on unencrypted WiFi traffic.

And, thanks to the stunning Snowden revelations, we now know that the NSA has practically free access to all of this information. With its PRISM program, launched in 2007, the agency has access to the data from Google, Facebook, Microsoft, Yahoo, PalTalk, YouTube, Skype, AOL, Apple, and more. Bart Gellman of the *Washington Post*, after fully reinvestigating the PRISM program, affirms that this is *direct* access: "From their workstations anywhere in the world, government employees cleared for PRISM access may 'task' the system and receive results from an Internet company without further interaction with the company's staff" (Bart Gellman quoted in Greenwald 2004: 109). Glenn Greenwald meticulously documents the awesome scope of surveillance (Greenwald and MacAskill 2013). The possibilities, reach, and amounts of data are simply staggering.

Many describe this new age as giving access to truth. Data mining and artificial intelligence, we are told, will allow us to know when epidemics arise, where crime will occur, what we will want to consume. But these forms of data collection and mining do not so much give us access to truth, as they constitute a new form of power. They are less a means to truth, than an exercise of power. Today, power circulates differently in society because of the digitization of our information.

In my last book, *Exposed: Desire and Disobedience in the Digital Age* (Harvard, 2015), I tried to offer a way to understand our willing exposure to the surveillance of the NSA, Google, Facebook, Amazon, Netflix, and the other tentacular arms of our intelligence-security complex. I described what I called "the expository society." Today, I suggested there, both of the classic forms—spectacle and surveillance—are no longer adequate. With digital technology, they have been surpassed—or need to be complemented—by a third: *exposition*. We are not forced into an arena, nor are we forced to be seen or to reveal our most intimate desires. There is no single amphitheater, nor is there a telescreen forcibly anchored into our homes. We are not being surveilled or monitored, so much as we are *exposing* ourselves knowingly, willingly, happily, with all our passion, desire, and love. The relation is now inversed, a second time: we, digital subjects, we *expose* ourselves in a frenzy.

If one had to identify a single architectural structure to capture the exposure of our digital age, it would no longer be an arena, nor a Panopticon, but instead the crystal palace, the mirrored-glass pavilion: part pleasure palace, part high-tech construction, partly aesthetic and partly efficient, these glass and steel constructs allow us to see ourselves and others through mirrored, reflecting, and somewhat translucent surfaces (Bennett 1988). They are spaces in which we play and explore, take selfies and photograph others. They reflect and incorporate our surroundings, near and far, including distant buildings and the skyline. At times, they resemble a fun house, at other moments they make us anxious. They intrigue and amuse us. And they hide pockets of obscurity.

The mirrored-glass structures of the artist Dan Graham serve as an excellent illustration of the expository nature of our digital age. Made of reflective glass and steel beams, open-topped, these sculptures invite us in and capture our imagination. Graham's *Hedge Two-Way Mirror Walkabout*, the Metropolitan Museum's 2014 Roof Garden Commission, which he designed with Günther Vogt (Fig. 1), is precisely a space of seeing, mirroring transparency and opacity. It is a glass-mirrored space that reflects the surrounding buildings and the people walking around the garden and terrace. It thrives on the same pleasure principles as our digital exposure, as people gaze and make faces, bend and stare to see how the glassed-mirror reflects their image. It functions by means of participation and produces, through the transparencies, reflections, and mirroring, a new virtual space.

Fig. 1 Dan Graham, Günther Vogt *Hedge Two-Way Mirror Walkabout*, Installation Metropolitan Museum, New York, (2014). Photographs copyright © Tod Seelie, reproduced by permission

Dan Graham's glass pavilions somehow epitomize the virtual transparency and exhibition of our digital lives. It is a space in which we play and make ourselves at home, where we can try to orchestrate our identities, digital selves, and traces, create a space for our pleasure, entertainment, and productivity, while we render ourselves exposed to the gaze of others and, of course, to ourselves. We embrace digital exposure with a wild cacophony of emotions, ranging from fetishism and exhibitionism for some, to discomfort, hesitation, and phobia for others—and including, along the way, curiosity, experimentation, play, lust, some distance, resistance, uncertainty, and even disgust or loathing. Regardless of our emotions and desires, though, we can be seen. We are exposed.

A new form of digital power circulates through society. It has several distinctive features, but I will focus on two here: virtual transparency and phenomenal opacity.

1. Virtual Transparency

Neither literal, nor entirely phenomenal, there is a new kind of transparency that characterizes our digital age—*virtual* transparency. It is not, predominantly, literal in the sense that we are not facing a perfectly clear or see-through glass surface or a translucent object.[5] We are not faced with transparency as "a physical fact" (Rowe and Slutzky 1963: 49). The digital medium distorts the presentation of ourselves and of others, allowing us to emphasize certain traits or desires, to see some things better than others. We can create new profiles and change them, experiment, twist them, disfigure them to a certain degree. Not entirely, of course, because all of our clicks and keystrokes are collected, meaning that all our habits and impulses, even the least thought through, form part of our digital selves. But there is sufficient room for distortion to believe that we are not seeing through the self.

In this sense, Philip Johnson's glass house is almost too modern a symbol for our postmodern times—as is Mies van der Rohe's Farnsworth

---

[5] For the conventional definition of literal transparency and the contrast with phenomenal transparency, (see Rowe and Slutzky 1963), and (see Rowe and Slutzky 1971). For a contextualization of these texts, see (Mertins 1996; Krauss 1980; and Somol 1994). Special thanks to Jonah Rowen.

House, the "Miesian glass box" (Riley 1995: 11). Though an intriguing metaphor—useful in many ways, as we will see, more ways than we might first think—Johnson's glass house, completed in 1949, is almost too literally transparent. It reveals more the modern ambition of genuine transparency rather than our current digital condition, where we are able to see more reflections and overlapping spaces, behind as well as in front of us, but where these figures are more often distorted, elongated, somewhat manipulated.

"Modernity has been haunted," Anthony Vidler writes, "by a myth of transparency: transparency of the self to nature, of the self to the other, of all selves to society, and all this represented, if not constructed, from Jeremy Bentham to Le Corbusier, by a universal transparency of building materials, spatial penetration, and the ubiquitous flow of air, light, and physical movement" (Vidler 1992: 217). But the modern ideal is "notoriously difficult to attain" and "quickly turns into obscurity (its apparent opposite) and reflectivity (its reversal)" (220). Johnson's glass house is almost too literal.

Virtual transparency is somewhat more phenomenal, insofar as it reflects an organization or a design or structure that is intended to communicate the notion of a transparent space (Rowe and Slutzky 1963: 48; Rowe and Slutzky 1971: 288). It produces a perceptual effect from the superposition of overlapping planes. But it also does more than that.[6] In part, it incorporates phenomenal opacity, a term that Vidler proposes (Vidler 1992: 219), because it playfully engages with distortions in order to seduce us to look, to take selfies, to expose ourselves. There are the mirroring effects of the fun house that draw us all in. We experiment with new engineered glass products that create certain odd reflections, new materials that affect what we see and how. We add colors, we insert new technology within the sheets of glass, we double and curve the mirror.

The ambition of virtual transparency magnifies the disciplinary ambition of visibility within enclosed structures. Recall that there was, importantly, a gradual evolution from rendering visible to transparency during

---

[6] That is, for those who do not simply debunk the idea of phenomenal transparency as merely a hermeneutic phantom or as a ghost, see Krauss 1980; Martin 2010: 55–57; Martin 2003 (discussing the shallowness and thinness of the transparency metaphor).

the disciplinary turn. "The old simple schema of confinement and enclosure," Foucault wrote, "began to be replaced by the calculation of openings, of filled and empty spaces, passages and transparencies" (Foucault 1979: 172). Rendering visible would develop into internal transparency, to the point that the Panopticon itself would "become a transparent building in which the exercise of power may be supervised by society as a whole" (207). Foucault refers to Bentham's Panopticon as his "celebrated, *transparent*, circular cage," and places the element of transparency at the center of the *panoptic* principle: it is what made "architecture transparent to the administration of power" (emphasis added, 208; see also 249). The element of transparency played an important role in the internal structure of the disciplinary edifices. "The perfect disciplinary apparatus would make it possible for a single gaze to see everything constantly," Foucault emphasized (173).

But in our digital age, we have moved beyond the internality of transparency. Our ambition is to see through brick walls and physical barriers, to turn internal structures inside out, to break down entirely the internal-external differentiation, in order to see into devices and to decipher the invisible. The mirrored-glass structure allows us to do that by using reflections to open spaces and break down walls. The digital technology allows us to do that by transcending the physical obstacles and barriers. It is not by accident that Admiral Poindexter named his program "total information awareness." Neither is it an accident that the NSA's "Treasure Map" seeks to know every single device connected to the web. There is an exhaustivity, internal *and* external, to this drive to know that is unparalleled—throughout the commercial and intelligence/security sectors.

2. *Phenomenal Opacity*

While so many expose themselves on social media, many of the most voyeuristic among us try to dissimulate our gaze and shield our own information. Truth is, expository power functions best when those who are seen are not entirely conscious of it, or do not always remember. The marketing works best when the targets do not know they are being watched. Information is more accessible when the subject forgets that she is being stalked (Duhigg 2012). The retail giant, Target, which excels at data-mining and targeting customers, has this down to an art form and has developed "best practices" to make sure that the targeted consumers are not aware they are being targeted. As a marketing analyst at Target explains: "as long as a pregnant woman thinks she hasn't been spied on, she'll use the coupons. She just assumes that everyone else on her block got the same mailer for diapers and cribs. As long as we don't spook her, it works" (Duhigg 2012). And so, Target will mix in ads for lawn mowers or wine glasses next to diapers and infant clothing. And as long as it looks or feels like the items are chosen by chance, the targeting pays dividends. But they depend on creating pockets of opacity.

Frank Pasquale explores this in *The Black Box Society*, where he ably demonstrates how "[f]irms seek out intimate details of potential customers' and employees' lives, but give regulators as little information as they possibly can about their own statistics and procedures. Internet companies collect more and more data on their users but fight regulations that would let those same users exercise some control over the resulting digital dossiers" (Pasquale 2015: 3–4; see also 156–160). This is the central recurring problem, in Pasquale's words, of "transparent citizens vs. an opaque government/corporate apparatus" (156).

This is where the modernity of Philip Johnson's glass house, the literal transparency of the structure, offers unexpected insight. You will recall, at its innermost core, the glass house contains a closed opaque cylindrical shape made of solid bricks—dark brown, rock-solid blocks, from floor to ceiling, even protruding out of the top of the structure. Indeed, at the heart of literal transparency, it turns out, there needs to be, there must be a closed cell.[7] Without the dissimulation and distortions of mirrored-glass, it turns out that we always revert to the enclosed cell—the locked trunk, the safe, the closet, the iron cage—and reproduce its epistemology (see Sedwick 1990; Zerilli 2005). No one can see in, and from within, no one can see out, supposedly.

These pockets of opacity represent, in effect, the opposite of the Panopticon: there is no ambition here for ordinary citizens to *internalize* the surveillance, since that would render them less legible and it would reduce their consumption. This is certainly true for advertisers. As Vaidhyanathan

---

[7] In Johnson's glass house, it serves as the fireplace/chimney and the bathroom.

suggests, in *The Googlization of Everything*, "ChoicePoint, Facebook, Google, and Amazon want us to relax and be ourselves" (Vaidhyanathan 2011: 112). This is also true for the NSA, which has entire units devoted to surreptitiously planting surveillance devices in sealed, packaged routers, servers, and other computer network devices—technologies of surveillance that only work through deception and opacity (Greenwald 2004: 148). Just like the Stasi used steam to unseal and reseal envelopes so that the recipients never knew their mail had been opened, the NSA magically undoes factory seals and carefully reseals them so that the buyers do not know that backdoor surveillance has been inserted into the machinery (149).

The crystal palace is the place of virtual transparency, but also phenomenal opacity. This is what expository power looks like. To be sure, there remains an element of spectacle. We stand in front of the mirror, often if only virtually. We are in the space of agonistic struggle par excellence. We live in a globalized virtual gaze—among millions of viewers, all sharing and tweeting around the country, perhaps even around the globe. It is not only the physical spectacle that matters, not the singular location, since we are scattered across the city, in front of the Plasma, with our iPhones and tablets. We are not together, we are separated, segregated but everywhere in this digital age.

There is also a large dose of surveillance. There may be, at the entrance to the museum, facial recognition technology to identify suspects. There are surveillance cameras fixed throughout and at every corner. There must be, to ensure the security of the viewers. Space is controlled. But more than that, there is all the monitoring and surveillance, ranging from Google to Target to the NSA—that captures all our Tweets and our texts, our posts on Facebook, the photos that we share, the apps we download, our internet surfing, how we spend, what we read, with whom we speak—in short, all our activities are recorded, captured, analyzed in this big consumer fair, to better target us, to better punish us when appropriate. Bentham's prison is not entirely removed from the present digital condition.

But to those we must add the element of exhibition: to make visible, to be seen, to be filmed. This little theater of personal exposure, well managed and hopefully properly disseminated. A wily post on Facebook that might go viral, a clever Tweet that might get retweeted. You have to look in the camera to be seen, or post a selfie to be broadcasted around the world. While others watch, simply, to look, to observe, to examine, to contemplate those who are willing to expose themselves. Seeking someone they know, maybe their son or daughter, or just for fun. And then we all meet, again, in front of the screen, spectators of the surveillance and the exhibition, viewers monitoring the performances and expositions, watched by means of our texts, our mobile apps, our photos, our Facebook posts, our Tweets, all our communications. This is a circuit which turns on itself in an infinite loop of spectacle, surveillance, and exhibition, with information analyzed, dissected, labeled, mined, marketed, datafied, resold. For consumption. To sell more goods, to increase viewership, to stimulate more consumption. To control as well, and punish at times.

Power circulates differently in our digital society. It does so because of our desire. For many of us, we are drawn in, even hesitantly, through our lust: this digital space seduces us into buying the most recent smart phone, downloading an irresistible application, clicking on a tantalizing image, giving free rein to our curiosity, addictions, fetishes, and ambitions. It recommends things to us we did not even know we wanted—but do, it turns out. We live today in a new political and social condition that is radically transforming our relations to each other, our political community, and ourselves: A new virtual transparency that is dramatically reconfiguring relations of power throughout society, that is redrawing our social landscape and political possibilities, that is producing a dramatically new circulation of power in society. It is a new form of power tied to our own exposure and exhibition, and to our own and others' voyeurism. It is an *expository power*.

Most often, it is the product of our seemingly simplest desires, the pleasures of curiosity, the stimulus of a quick distraction—it is those trifling gratifications that fuel and feed this expository power. The iPhone is a slick and seductive object, designed to please us. The sound of the "click" that the iPhone "shutter" makes is perfectly satisfying. The "swoosh" of a sent e-mail is a sensual pleasure. That, and the convenience, the efficiency, the ease, and the apparent costlessness with which we can shop online, renew a subscription with a click, deposit a check on our mobile phone, read a book electronically. And for those of us who hesitate at first or proceed reluctantly, still, the allure of free Gmail, of costless storage on Google Drive, of gratis transfers of megabytes of our data on Wetransfer.com, of free calendaring—these have made exposure practically irresistible. We know, of course, that none of it is "free" and that we pay for it by giving complete access to our personal data (Vaidhyanathan 2011: 9 and 26). We also pay for it, as Jodi Dean suggests, in our time and focus (Dean 2012). But those costs do not feel prohibitive, or sufficiently so, at the moment—which is, ultimately, what makes our digital surrender so ambivalently irresistible.

No, we are not so much being coerced, *surveilled*, or secured today, as we are *exposing* or *exhibiting* ourselves knowingly, many of us willingly, with all our love, lust, passion, and politics, others anxiously, ambivalently, even perhaps despite ourselves—but still, knowingly exposing ourselves. The relation of power is inverted: we, digital subjects—we, "digital persons" (Solove 2006), "digital selves" (Zhao 2005), "data doubles" (Ericson and Haggerty 2000: 611)—we give ourselves up in a mad frenzy of disclosure. Many of us exhibit our most intimate details in play, in love, in desire, in consumption, in the social and in the political, throughout our rich digital lives—through our appetites, in our work, for our political convictions, to become ourselves.

And as these digital technologies develop, they increasingly feed into a security regime of policing and military interventions—of drone warfare, of NYPD surveillance, of digital propaganda. It is difficult to imagine overcoming the contrast and tension between the virtuality of our digital surveillance and the physicality of our military interventions and policing. But that is happening on a daily basis. Every new technology seems to feed magically into the security apparatus.

It turns out that the expository society fits within a larger coherent form of governing. Total information awareness is just one piece of a new politics of how we govern ourselves at home and abroad (Harcourt 2018). An important chapter, to be sure. But only a piece of the larger picture.

The perfect illustration is a government program launched in the final year of the Obama administration. It was called the Center for Global Engagement, and it was created through an executive order dated March 14, 2016, funded to the tune of about $20 million.

The Center would target susceptible, vulnerable or influenceable persons suspected of easy radicalization, and would send them enhanced third-party content intended to dissuade them from joining ISIS. In the words of Kimberly Dozier at the *Daily Beast*, "The Obama administration is launching a stealth anti-Islamic State messaging campaign, delivered by proxies and targeted to individual would-be extremists, the same way Amazon or Google sends you shopping suggestions based on your online browsing history" (Dozier 2016).

There are several steps here, all of them modeled on the Amazon and Google recommendation techniques. First, targets need to be identified, and will be using their digital traces on social media and other digital venues. The idea here is to narrow in on persons who are susceptible to being radicalized. Second, content has to be enhanced and improved, so that it is more effective. Here, the new Center will provide assistance, through financial support, consultancies, and other aid, to third-parties who make content. The idea here is to "give local nonprofits, regional leaders, or activists invisible financial support and technical expertise to make their videos or websites or radio programs look and sound professional—and let them own and distribute the message." In these efforts, the Center will be following the lead of the private sector, and using best practices of the advertising industry. So, "Facebook spokesman Jodi Seth said they'd shared research with [Center director Michael] Lumpkin and other administration officials showing 'factors that help make counter-speech more successful,' including the format of the content (i.e., generally it is better to share photos and video instead of text) and tone of the content (the most successful forms of counter-speech were constructive, and satire and humor worked better than attacks)." Third, the Center will then direct the enhanced third-party content to the targets. This is "the delivery of the content" and it is "where the big data analysts come in. Lumpkin will be contracting private companies that crunch the public trail of information Internet users leave behind, just like they do for large retailers looking for new buyers." Lumpkin explains that he "wants to focus on those who are vulnerable to ISIS's message and emulate how ISIS goes after its followers" (Dozier 2016).

In all this, the new Center will, naturally, efface all "Made in USA" labels. There will be no U.S. messaging, and no indication of U.S.

participation. Everything will be dissimulated for easier reception. "The new center 'is not going to be focused on U.S. messages with a government stamp on them, but rather amplifying moderate credible voices in the region and throughout civil society,' said Lisa Monaco, speaking at the Council on Foreign Relations. 'Recognizing who is going to have the most legitimate voice and doing everything we can to lift that up and not have it be a U.S. message'" (Dozier 2016).

Increasingly, our models of governing will operate on these digital advertising methods—the most up-to-date, private for-profit technology. The methods can be summarized as follows: First, dissimulate: do not let the target know you are targeting them. Second, predict and target: identify based on digital traces likely suspects. Third, enhance the message: use photos and videos, rather than text only, create clickbait. Fourth: bury it and feed it. This is increasingly sophisticated propaganda. It assumes and exploits the fact that our subjectivities are shaped, malleable. It is, of course, a direct response to the new contagious nature of social media indoctrination. And what it depends on is us sharing our information. Willingly. With all our pleasure. It depends on us using social media.

How many governments are doing the same? Where is the information that we read on the web coming from? How does this feed into larger structures of foreign affairs and military intervention?

Beyond the expository society is a far darker place where all our friendly hedonistic exposure feeds directly into a new governing paradigm abroad and at home. A governmental approach with far more sophisticated methods of propaganda, identification, and punishment. It is to those new forms of governing that we now need to attend—beyond the expository society.

Works Cited

Balibar, Étienne. 2015. Lettre d'Étienne Balibar à l'éditeur du cours. In M. Foucault, *Théories et institutions pénales. Cours au Collège de France, 1971–1972*, ed. Bernard E. Harcourt, 285–289. Paris: Gallimard/Le Seuil.

Barret-Kriegel, B., A. Thalamy, F. Beguin, and B. Fortier. 1979. *Les Machines à guérir. Aux origines de l'hôpital moderne*. Pierre Mardaga: Bruxelles.

Bennett, Tony. 1988. The Exhibitionary Complex. *New Formation* 4 (Spring): 73–102.
Bentham, Jeremy. 1995. *The Panopticon Writings*, ed. Miran Božovič, London: Verso.
Dean, Jodi. 2012. *The Communist Horizon.* New York: Verso.
Debord, Guy. 1967. *La Société du spectacle.* Paris: Buchet/Chastel.
Dozier, Kimberly. 2016. Anti-ISIS-Propaganda Czar's Ninja War Plan: We Were Never Here. *The Daily Beast*, March 15, http://www.thedailybeast.com/articles/2016/03/15/obama-s-new-anti-isis-czar-wants-to-use-algorithms-to-target-jihadis.html.
Duhigg, Charles. 2012. How Companies Learn Your Secrets. *New York Times*, February 16, http://www.nytimes.com/2012/02/19/magazine/shopping-habits.html.
Ericson, Richard V., and Kevin D. Haggerty. 2000. The Surveillant Assemblage. *British Journal of Sociology* 51 (4): 605–622.
Foucault, Michel. 1968. Interview avec Michel Foucault. In M. Foucault, *Dits et Écrits*, ed. Daniel Defert, François Ewald and Jacques Lagrange, Paris: Gallimard, 1994, vol. I, no. 54: 651–662.
———. 1973. La vérité et les formes juridiques. In M. Foucault, *Dits et Écrits*, Vol. II, no 139, ed. 1994: 538–623 [ed. 2001, vol. I: 1406–1491].
———. 1977. L'oeil du pouvoir. Entretien avec J.-P. Barou et M. Perrot. In *Le Panoptique*, éd. par J.-P Barou, Paris, Pierre Belfond, 1977; reproduced in *Dits et Écrits*, vol. III, no. 195, 1994: 190–207.
———. 1979. *Discipline and Punish: The Birth of the Prison*, trans. Alan Sheridan, New York: Vintage.
———. 1994. *Dits et Écrits.* Ed. Daniel Defert, François Ewald, and Jacques Lagrange. Paris: Gallimard.
———. 2003. *Le Pouvoir psychiatrique. Cours au Collège de France, 1973–1974*, éd. J. Lagrange, Paris, Gallimard/Le Seuil.
———. 2004. *Sécurité, Territoire, Population. Cours au Collège de France. 1977–1978.* Paris: Gallimard/Le Seuil.
———. 2013. *La Société Punitive. Cours au Collège de France, 1972–1973*, ed. Bernard E. Harcourt, Paris: Gallimard/Le Seuil.
———. 2015. *Surveiller et Punir. Naissance de la prison*, ed. Bernard E. Harcourt, Paris: Gallimard, *La Pléiade*, Vol. II.
Greenwald, Glenn. 2004. *No Place to Hide: Edward Snowden, the NSA, and the U.S. Surveillance State.* New York: Henry Holt.

Greenwald, Glenn, and Ewen MacAskill 2013. NSA Prism Program Taps in to User Data of Apple, Google and Others. *The Guardian*, June 6, https://www.theguardian.com/world/2013/jun/06/us-tech-giants-nsa-data.
Harcourt, Bernard E. 2018. *The Counterrevolution: How our Government Went to War Against its Own Citizens*. New York: Basic Books.
Hegel, G.W.F. 1952. Author's Preface. In *Hegel's Philosophy of Right*, trans. T.M. Knox, London: Oxford University Press.
Johnston, Norman. 2000. *Forms of Constraint: A History of Prison Architecture*. Chicago: University of Illinois Press.
Julius, N.H. 1831. *Vorlesungen über die Gefängniskunde*, Berlin: Stuhr, 1828, 2 vol., *Leçons sur les prisons, présentées en forme de cours au public de Berlin, en l'année 1827*, trans. (vol. I) H. Lagarmitte, Paris: F. G. Levrault.
Krauss, Rosalind. 1980. Death of a Hermeneutic Phantom. *Architecture + Urbanism* 112 (January): 189–219.
Martin, Reinhold. 2003. *The Organizational Complex: Architecture, Media, and Corporate Space*. Cambridge, MA: MIT Press.
———. 2010. *Utopia's Ghost: Architecture and Postmodernism, Again*. Minneapolis, MN: University of Minnesota Press.
Mertins, Detlef. 1996. Transparency: Autonomy & Relationality. *AA Files* 32 (Autumn): 3–11.
Pasquale, Frank. 2015. *The Black Box Society: The Secret Algorithms that Control Money and Information*. Cambridge, MA: Harvard University Press.
Riley, Terence. 1995. *Light Construction*. New York: Harry N. Abrams.
Rowe, Colin, and Robert Slutzky. 1963. Transparency: Literal and Phenomenal. *Perspecta* 8: 45–54.
———. 1971. Transparency: Literal and Phenomenal... Part II. *Perspecta* 13/14: 287–301.
Sedwick, Eve Kosofsky. 1990. *Epistemology of the Closet*. Berkeley, CA: University of California Press.
Singer, Isidore, and Cyrus Adler. 1916. *The Jewish Encyclopedia: A Descriptive Record of the History, Religion, Literature, and Customs of the Jewish People from the Earliest Times to the Present Day*. Vol. 7. New York: Funk and Wagnalls.
Solove, Daniel J. 2006. *The Digital Person: Technology and Privacy in the Information Age*. New York: New York University Press.
Somol, Robert. 1994. Oublier Rowe. *Formwork: Colin Rowe*, ANY 7/8, 8–15.

Vaidhyanathan, Siva (2011) *The Googlization of Everything: (And Why We Should Worry)*, Berkeley, CA: University of California Press.

Vidler, Anthony. 1992. *The Architectural Uncanny: Essays in the Modern Unhomely.* Cambridge, MA: MIT Press.

Zerilli, Linda M.G. 2005. "Philosophy's Gaudy Dress": Rhetoric and Fantasy in the Lockean Social Contract. *European Journal of Political Theory* 4: 146–163.

Zhao, Shanyang. 2005. The Digital Self: Through the Looking Glass of Telecopresent Others. *Symbolic Interaction* 28 (3): 387–405.

Author Index[1]

A
Adler, Cyrus, 370n1
Adorno, Theodor W., 45, 262
Akhabbar, Amanar, 208n8
Ala'i, Padideh, 30
Alembert, Jean-Baptiste Le Rond d', 92, 136, 142, 150
Alexander, Herbert, 184
Alighieri, 90, 91, 91n6
Allen, Woody, 315
Alloa, Emmanuel, 4, 25, 31, 35, 88n4, 266
Althusser, Louis, 157, 171, 370
André, Serge, 319
Aquinas, Thomas, 5, 85–102
Arendt, Hannah, 9, 79, 285–293, 298, 299, 332, 354, 355
Aristotle, 35, 36, 59, 88, 107, 266, 290
Artaud, Antonin, 165
Assange, Julian, 2, 45, 45n1
Augustine, 122–124, 127
Austin, J. Matthew, 194
Austin, John L., 254, 254n11, 255

B
Babrius, 86
Bachelard, Gaston, 161
Bacon, Francis, 63, 64, 86, 87, 140, 141
Bailyn, Bernard, 350
Balibar, Étienne, 370
Barber, Benjamin R., 195
Barret-Kriegel, Blandine, 372
Barth, Karl, 117, 118, 119n8, 121
Bastedo, Michael N., 193
Bataille, Georges, 157, 160

---

[1] Note: Page numbers followed by 'n' refer to notes.

Baudelaire, Charles, 61, 99
Baudrillard, Jean, 356
Baume, Sandrine, 7, 44, 205–207, 209n9, 214, 215, 216n21
Beam, Christopher, 182
Beethoven, Ludwig van, 108
Belavusau, Uladzislau, 63
Benjamin, Walter, 25, 26
Bennett, Tony, 378
Bentham, Jeremy, 4, 6, 7, 39, 40, 57, 61, 66–72, 74, 133–153, 155, 156, 180, 203, 206, 209, 209n9, 210, 215, 216n22, 371–374, 381, 382, 384
Berlusconi, Silvio, 15–17
Bernal, John Desmond, 167
Bernard, Andreas, 338
Berns, Thomas, 8, 27, 243, 245n3, 336
Bertot, John Carlo, 181
Besley, Timothy, 195
Birchall, Clare, 11, 30, 346, 353
Birkinshaw, Patrick, 346
Bismarck, Otto von, 47
Blake, William, 61
Blanchot, Maurice, 162
Boethius, 35
Boltanski, Luc, 284, 334
Bopp, Franz, 164
Borry, Erin, 180
Bossy, John, 111, 111n4
Bovens, Mark, 214, 216n21, 220
Bowman, Nicholas A., 193
Božovič, Miran, 6, 40, 70, 140n5
Brandeis, Louis, 2, 45, 180, 345, 346
Braque, Georges, 49
Bratich, Jack, 351
Brecht, Bertolt, 25, 60n3
Bredin, Jean-Denis, 217n23, 219

Brenner, Joel, 23
Brito, Jerry, 180, 189
Brooks, Peter, 338
Brown, Wendy, 362
Brunschvicg, Léon, 160
Buchanan, James M., 195, 196
Buchheim, Thomas, 60
Bührmann, Andrea D., 329
Buijze, Anoeska, 212, 212n11
Burgundio of Pisa, 34, 36
Bush, George W., 346, 347, 358
Butler, Judith, 254–256, 294, 329, 331, 332
Butter, Michael, 350, 351, 353

C

Cadwalladr, Carole, 298n2
Calderón de la Barca, Pedro, 108
Calvin, Jean, 110, 112, 116, 120
Camus, Albert, 162
Canguilhem, Georges, 160, 161
Canus, Julius, 137, 138
Carroll, Raymonde, 313
Carter, Angela, 152
Carter, Jimmy, 183
Cavell, Stanley, 68n4
Cervantes, Miguel de, 106
Chambers, Simone, 46
Chaplin, Charlie, 73
Chardin, Pierre Teilhard de, 167
Chiapello, Eve, 334
Chion, Michel, 141
Christensen, Lars Thøger, 28
Chydenius, Anders, 345n1
Cillizza, Chris, 185
Clarke, Paul A. B., 195, 196
Clastres, Pierre, 172
Claveul, Jean, 312

Author Index

Clinton, Hillary, 17, 75, 352
Coate, Stephen, 195
Coetzee, John Maxwell, 122, 124, 125n12, 128
Coglianese, Cary, 188
Cohen, Kris, 355
Colclough, David, 63
Coleridge, Samuel Taylor, 285
Collins, Suzanne, 309
Colman, Andrew M., 196
Combes, Muriel, 251n9
Constant, Benjamin, 7, 203, 206–207, 207n4, 215, 215n19, 215n20
Conti, Brooke, 116n7
Cornelissen, Joep, 28
Cruz, Ted, 352, 358
Cutler, Fred, 215

D

Davies, David Brion, 350
Dawes, Sharon S., 180, 181
De Boer, Wietse, 110
De Man, Paul, 122, 124, 124n11, 125, 125n12, 128, 292n1
Dean, Jodi, 334, 356, 386
Debaise, Didier, 253
Debord, Guy, 171, 321, 372
Debray, Régis, 308
Deleuze, Gilles, 158, 170, 273, 319
Den Boer, Monica, 212, 212n12, 212n13
Dennett, Daniel C., 21–24, 47
Derrida, Jacques, 6, 42, 122, 122–123n10, 157, 158, 162, 166–170, 172–174, 243, 254–256, 254n11, 362, 363

Descartes, René, 4, 66–72, 74, 75, 77, 80, 164, 168, 259, 338, 376
Desrosières, Alain, 249
Diderot, Denis, 4–6, 62–66, 133–137, 135n1, 136n2, 139, 139n4, 141–153
Diogenes Laertius, 62
Docherty, Thomas, 9, 48
Dozier, Kimberly, 387, 388
Dufour, Dany-Robert, 319
Duhigg, Charles, 382, 383
Dürrenmatt, Friedrich, 138n3

E

Eco, Umberto, 12, 263n1
Eggers, Dave, 1, 76, 77
Ehrenberg, Alain, 327, 334
Eigeldinger, Frédéric, 207
Ellis, Markman, 292, 293
Elster, Jon, 7, 40, 203, 205, 210, 211, 220, 221, 221n30
Emerson, Ralph Waldo, 68n4, 80
Erasmus of Rotterdam, 63
Ericson, Richard V., 386
Erkkilä, Tero, 7, 203, 205, 208, 208n6, 210, 211, 220
Etzioni, Amitai, 7, 273
Euripides, 4, 62–66
Evans, Jocelyn A. J., 191
Ewald, François, 375n4

F

Fanon, Frantz, 162
Farel, Guillaume, 116–118
Farley, Robert, 359

Fenster, Mark, 28, 31, 180, 207, 220, 221, 344, 348, 357–359, 360n2
Ferraris, Maurizio, 158
Fichte, Johann Gottlieb, 68
Finel, Bernard I., 180
Fiske, John, 351
Fleming, Joseph Z., 182n3
Flusser, Vilém, 276
Fortier, Bruno, 372
Foucault, Michel, 6, 12, 40, 46, 62, 63, 65–67, 70, 155, 156, 159, 162–168, 163n3, 170, 172–174, 207, 217–219, 219n29, 329, 344, 369–376, 374n3, 382
Fox, Jonathan, 31
Franck, Georg, 309
Freud, Sigmund, 312, 314
Friedman, Milton, 302
Frye, Northrop, 112
Fung, Archon, 190, 192
Furet, François, 158, 158n2, 172
Furnas, Alexander, 192, 193

G

Galison, Peter, 233n10
Gambetti, Zeynep, 329, 332, 333, 335
Gardiner, Michael, 284
Garrett, R. Sam, 184
Gauchet, Marcel, 172
Gay, Peter, 107
Geer, Nadja, 328
Gellman, Bart, 377, 378
Genet, Jean, 99–101, 100n20
Geroulanos, Stefanos, 6, 28, 157n1, 172

Gerstein, Josh, 349
Giedion, Siegfried, 49
Gilbert, Elizabeth, 186
Gilbert, Michael D., 185
Ginsberg, Wendy R., 183
Glissant, Édouard, 158
Goethe, Johann Wolfgang von, 5, 61, 105–108, 106n1, 118, 121, 270
Gorbachev, Mikhail, 30
Gorz, André, 300–302
Gosseries, Axel, 204, 207, 208n7
Götz, Norbert, 30
Goya, Francisco de, 108
Graham, Dan, 379, 380
Greenspan, Alan, 183
Greenwald, Glenn, 378, 384
Gregory the Great, 89
Griffis, Carson, 184n9
Grimaldi, James V., 190
Grimes, Justin M., 181
Grimmelikhuijsen, Stephan G., 47
Gris, Juan, 49
Gropius, Walter, 52
Grotke, Abbie, 349
Guindani, Sara, 31
Gumpp, Johannes, 325

H

Habermas, Jürgen, 42, 213, 216, 227n3, 229, 264, 292–294
Haggerty, Brian, 184
Haggerty, Kevin D., 386
Haldane, John Burdon Sanderson, 167
Hale, Thomas N., 181
Hammann, Christine, 207n5

Author Index 397

Han, Byung-Chul, 44, 270–273, 279, 316, 358
Hansen, Hans Krause, 30
Harcourt, Bernard E., 11, 12, 48, 386
Harper, Jim, 182, 190
Hasen, Richard L., 185n12, 193n18
Hau, Harald, 193n19
Haupt, Friederike, 77
Haydn, Joseph, 108
Heald, David, 180
Heerwig, Jennifer, 191, 194
Hegel, Georg Wilhelm Friedrich, 65, 266, 330, 370, 373, 374
Heidegger, Martin, 74, 262, 267n2, 271–273
Heinich, Nathalie, 309
Helvétius, Claude Adrien, 71
Hesiod, 5, 86, 86n2
Hintikka, Jaakko, 68
Hirschi, Caspar, 8, 47, 226n1, 238
Hobbes, Thomas, 287
Hofstadter, Richard, 352
Holbein, Hans, 108
Hölderlin, Friedrich, 60, 60n3, 101, 275
Homer, 58n1
Honig, Bonnie, 59
Hood, Christopher, 31, 180, 212, 219
Hooke, Robert, 33
Horkheimer, Max, 45, 262
Horwitz, Sari, 190
Howells, Christina, 100
Hülsewiesche, Reinhold, 63, 64
Hupe, Peter, 28, 29
Huxley, Julian, 167

I
Islam, Roumeen, 194, 195
Isocrates, 62

J
Jaeger, Paul T., 181
Jaeggi, Rahel, 334
Jameson, Fredric, 353
Jeanmart, Gaëlle, 245n3
Jevons, William Stanley, 208, 208n8, 220
Johnson, Philip, 183, 292, 380, 381, 383, 383n7
Johnston, Norman, 370n1, 370n2
Jones, Jeffrey M., 182n2
Judt, Tony, 286
Julius, Nikolaus Heinrich, 137, 370–373, 370n1, 370n2

K
Kahn, Alfred, 183
Kahneman, Daniel, 192
Kant, Immanuel, 7, 30, 45, 164, 180, 203, 206, 207, 207n3, 213, 213n16, 216, 260, 261, 263–265
Kaufmann, Daniel, 195
Kaufmann, Vincent, 10, 48
Kelly, Erin, 7, 203, 205, 211, 220
Kennedy, John F., 183
Kepes, György, 49, 51
Khawaja, Noreen, 5, 39
Kick, Russ, 350
Kierkegaard, Søren, 109, 121, 128
Kittler, Friedrich, 267n3, 337
Klueting, Harm, 114n6

Korte, Gregory, 185
Koselleck, Reinhart, 213, 213n17
Koyré, Alexandre, 161
Krauss, Rosalind, 380n5, 381n6
Krischke, Wolfgang, 310
Kubrick, Stanley, 167
Kuhne, Cecil C., 184

L

Lacan, Jacques, 160, 173, 312, 315
Laing, Ronald D., 279
Lakoff, George, 320
Lanier, Jaron, 337
Latour, Bruno, 25
Lea, Henry Charles, 110, 110n3
Lefebvre, Henri, 361
Lefort, Claude, 158, 159, 171
Leibniz, Gottfried Wilhelm, 164, 168
Leiris, Michel, 157
Lejeune, Philippe, 123n10
Leon, Joes I., 182n3
Leroi-Gourhan, André, 6, 160, 162, 166–169, 166n4, 172–174
Letterman, David, 310
Levinas, Emmanuel, 160, 294
Lévi-Strauss, Claude, 157, 159, 160, 162, 168, 169, 173
Levy, Lili, 185
Libaert, Thierry, 28
Liechtenstein, Friedrich, 326–329
Linzey, Andrew, 195, 196
Liptak, Adam, 193n18
Lissitzky, El, 49
Lithbau, Eric, 183n7
Locke, John, 64, 66, 180
Lord, Kristin M., 106n1, 109, 123, 180, 206

Luhmann, Niklas, 8, 43, 225–240
Lupia, Arthur, 209n10
Lupton, Deborah, 80, 338
Luther, Martin, 105, 110–114, 118
Lynch, Morgan, 349, 350
Lyon, David, 72
Lyotard, Jean-François, 157, 158, 173, 173n6

M

MacAskill, Ewen, 378
MacCabe, Colin, 353
McDevitt, Ryan C., 191
Macey, Jonathan, 235n11, 236, 237n12
McNealy, Scott, 1
Madison, James, 39, 180, 195, 196
Manin, Bernard, 195
Mansick, Mike, 182n4, 190
Mantegazza, Paolo, 85, 86, 86n1
Maravall, Jose Maria, 195
Marker, Chris, 167
Marklund, Carl, 30
Martin, Reinhold, 381n6
Maupertuis, Pierre-Louis Moreau de, 136n2
Mauss, Marcel, 166
May, Albert L., 194
Meijer, Albert, 47, 180, 186, 212, 212n12, 212n15, 346
Melone, Matthew A., 184
Merleau-Ponty, Maurice, 68, 69, 157, 159–162, 171
Mersch, Dieter, 9, 36, 267, 268, 274, 277, 278
Mertins, Detlef, 380n5
Metelmann, Jörg, 10, 48, 336, 337
Michelangelo, 152

Mill, John Stuart, 39, 127, 180
Miller, Jacques-Alain, 140
Millet, Catherine, 319, 319n1, 320
Mitchell, William John Thomas, 327–329
Moati, Raoul, 254n11
Moholy-Nagy, László, 49–51
Molteni, Megan, 350
Morgenstern, Christian, 58
Morgenstern, Oskar, 42, 43
Morozov, Eugene, 362
Moser, Cornelia, 212, 212n14
Moss, Michael, 192
Mücke, Dorothea E. von, 122n9
Myers, W. David, 111

N

Nadeau, Christina, 213, 214, 214n18
Nancy, Jean-Luc, 272, 275, 276, 279, 325, 329–331, 335
Naurin, Daniel, 7, 203, 205–207, 211, 212n11, 217, 220
Neu, Tim, 237
Neumann, John von, 42
Newton, Isaac, 33, 40
Nietzsche, Friedrich, 36, 78, 262, 267n3, 270, 271, 273
Nixon, Richard, 183, 345

O

Obama, Barack, 2, 17, 156, 157, 182, 183, 183n7, 186, 187, 346–349, 352–355, 358, 360, 361, 386, 387
Oliver, Eric, 354
Oliver, Richard W., 212n15

O'Neill, Onora, 194, 195
Orwell, George, 1, 10, 17, 73, 300, 315, 318
Owen, Robert, 61

P

Parain, Brice, 101, 101n21
Parmigianino, 325
Parsons, Talcott, 43
Pasquale, Frank, 383
Patel-Carstairs, Sunita, 352
Perloff, Marjorie G., 107
Perrault, Drew, 181, 189
Pfisterer, Ulrich, 326
Phaedrus, 86
Picasso, Pablo, 49
Pingeot, Mazarine, 57
Piotrowski, Suzanne J., 30, 180, 181
Pitkin, Hannah, 40
Plato, 34, 35, 62, 63, 169, 261, 273, 277
Plutarch, 62, 63
Poindexter, John Marlan, 382
Pollitt, Christopher, 28, 29
Pomerantsev, Peter, 356
Pörksen, Bernhard, 310
Pozen, David, 44
Prat, Andrea, 190, 212, 212n12, 212n15
Przeworski, Adam, 195
Pucci, Pietro, 58n1
Putin, Vladimir, 356
Pythagoras, 107n2, 142, 143

R

Rabelais, François, 59n1
Rancière, Jacques, 361

Author Index

Raphael, 108
Rasmusen, Eric, 209n10
Rautzenberg, Markus, 267n2
Reichert, Ramon, 329
Reinbold, Fabian, 78
Reinhart, Carmen, 213, 248n6
Rembrandt, 108
Richir, Marc, 217n24
Riley, Terence, 381
Rilliet, Albert, 117
Ringley, Jennifer, 10, 307–321
Robinson, David G., 193n18
Rodchenko, Alexander Michailowitsch, 49
Rogoff, Kenneth S., 248n6
Rosanvallon, Pierre, 75, 158, 158n2, 172
Rose, Hajo, 26, 52
Rosen, Valeska von, 326
Rosendorff, Peter B., 181
Rousseau, Jean-Jacques, 4, 5, 7, 38, 39, 60, 85–102, 107, 121–128, 122n9, 123n10, 125n12, 128n14, 155, 156, 168, 169, 171, 180, 207, 207n5, 216–219, 217n23, 218n26, 218n27, 219n28, 311, 312, 338
Roussel, Raymond, 165
Rouvroy, Antoinette, 8, 243, 246
Rowe, Colin, 49, 380, 380n5, 381
Roy, Deb, 21–24, 47
Rubinstein, Daniel, 327, 329

S

Sade, Donatien Alphonse François de, 163, 319, 320
Saltz, Jerry, 325, 326
Sartre, Jean-Paul, 5, 39, 85–102, 124n11, 157, 157n1, 160–162
Scherer, Michael, 352
Schlegel, Friedrich, 126n13
Schmidt, Eric, 244, 313
Schnädelbach, Herbert, 263
Schneider, Manfred, 5, 37, 69, 86, 157n1, 338
Schneider, Werner, 329
Sedwick, Eve Kosofsky, 383
Semple, Janet, 140
Sen, Amartya, 195
Seneca, Lucius Annaeus, 137
Shakespeare, William, 71
Shaw, Katherine, 191, 194
Shea, Louisa, 65
Shelley, Percy Bysshe, 58–62
Simmel, Georg, 12, 17
Simon, Herbert A., 192
Simondon, Gilbert, 8, 243, 250–253, 251n9, 252n10
Singer, Isidore, 370n1
Sloterdijk, Peter, 294, 295
Slutzky, Robert, 49, 380n5, 381
Snowden, Edward, 2, 23, 182, 377
Socrates, 34, 87, 87n3
Solove, Daniel J., 386
Somol, Robert, 380n5
Sophocles, 4, 57–62
Spengler, Oswald, 107, 107–108n2, 108, 112
Stalder, Felix, 362
Starobinski, Jean, 38, 92, 122, 125–128, 126n13, 128n14, 156, 207, 207n5, 217, 217n23, 218, 338
Steiner, George, 59, 60
Stiglitz, Joseph E., 194, 195
Stokes, Susan C., 195

Author Index 401

Stollberg-Rilinger, Barbara, 232n8, 234
Stone, Oliver, 301
Sunstein, Cass, 186, 187, 187n14, 192
Swift, Jonathan, 297
Szper, Rebecca, 194

T

Taylor, Charles, 69
Telios, Thomas, 10, 48
Tentler, Thomas N., 110n3
Thatcher, Margaret, 238, 301
Theimer, Sharon, 183n7
Thomä, Dieter, 4, 41, 65
Thompson, Mark, 298n2
Thoreau, Henry David, 60
Thurneysen, Eduard, 118–121, 119n8, 127
Titian, 108
Torres-Spelliscy, Ciara, 185n12
Trilling, Lionel, 122
Trousson, Raymond, 207
Trump, Donald, 11, 74, 157, 174, 296, 297, 343, 344, 348–361, 360n2
Tuchman, Barbara, 263n1
Tullock, Gordon, 195, 196
Turner, Fred, 268
Tweedie, Neil, 283

V

Vaidhyanathan, Siva, 383, 384, 386
Van Ryzin, Gregg G., 181
Vandeul, Angélique de, 136
Vasiliu, Anca, 34, 35, 88, 88n4
Vaughn, Robert G., 30

Vico, Giambattista, 101
Vidler, Anthony, 381
Vishwanath, Tara, 195
Visser, Nick, 360
Vitruvius, Marcus, 87
Vogt, Günther, 379
Voltaire, 9, 288, 311
Voss, Heinrich, 105, 106, 108

W

Wahnich, Sophie, 218, 218n25
Wald, Matthew L., 190
Waldenfels, Bernhard, 263
Warner, Michael, 111n5
Weil, David, 190
West, Kanye, 339
Westall, Claire, 284
Williams, Bernard, 68
Wilson, Woodrow, 345, 358
Wittgenstein, Ludwig, 32, 290, 338
Wolfsteiner, Andreas, 267n2
Wolton, Thierry, 320n2
Wood, Gordon, 350
Wood, Thomas, 354

X

Xenophon, 34

Z

Zerilli, Linda M.G., 383
Zhao, Shanyang, 386
Zito, Salena, 355
Zuckerberg, Mark, 2, 76, 313
Zweig, Jason, 190
Zwingli, Huldrych, 110, 119–121, 119n8, 127

Subject Index[1]

A

Access/accessibility, 31, 41, 45, 53, 57, 58, 60, 66, 69, 70, 73, 74, 80, 128, 134, 153, 164, 180, 181, 189, 190, 204, 204n2, 205, 208, 211, 212, 212n11, 217, 220, 238, 264, 265, 268, 273, 275, 308–310, 338, 345–347, 356, 362, 370, 377, 378, 382, 386

Accountable/accountability, 2, 7, 32, 64, 75, 79, 156, 184, 187, 187n14, 214–216, 220, 344–347, 350, 357, 360–362

Algorithmic/algorithmization, 8, 27, 243–256, 276, 336

Anonymity, 25, 77

Asymmetry, 28, 32, 44, 118, 276, 309, 373

Authenticity, 32, 39, 67, 99, 120, 121, 125, 126n13, 127, 168, 169, 285, 318, 326, 328, 338, 348

Autobiography, 92, 99, 106, 107, 116n7, 121, 138, 286, 291

Auto-Icon, 92, 98, 106, 107, 116n7, 121, 122n10, 135, 136, 138, 139

B

Big data, 245, 247, 253, 298, 298n2, 313, 337, 375, 387

Blind spot, 46, 81, 270, 272, 316

C

Commercial, 27, 73, 74, 78, 158, 193n18, 293, 302, 360, 382

---

[1] Note: Page numbers followed by 'n' refer to notes.

© The Author(s) 2018
E. Alloa, D. Thomä (eds.), *Transparency, Society and Subjectivity*,
https://doi.org/10.1007/978-3-319-77161-8

Subject Index

Communicability/communication/
communicative, 5, 9, 12, 15,
18, 28, 38, 43, 76, 79, 91,
93–98, 100–102, 108n2, 151,
158, 181, 189, 255, 263, 264,
268, 269, 272, 274–276, 278,
279, 290, 292–294, 311, 330,
334, 338, 339, 346, 355–358,
362, 377, 385
Community, 30, 62, 76, 113–118,
121, 157, 159, 161, 168, 169,
196, 263, 264, 268, 274, 276,
279, 290–292, 299, 330, 334,
349, 385
Concealment, 44, 70, 78,
270–272
Confession, 5, 38, 39, 47, 92,
105–129, 245n3
Consciousness, 39, 108, 147, 148,
150, 151, 157, 174, 227n3,
331
Conspiracy theory, 348, 350–354,
357
Control, 5, 7, 29, 64, 71, 72, 74,
110, 122, 157, 172, 181,
186, 187, 189, 195, 214,
215, 226, 227, 236, 237,
256n13, 272–275, 299, 316,
320n2, 349, 370, 373, 383,
385
Counter-surveillance, 24
Critical Transparency studies, 3, 4,
28, 30
Critique, 6, 46, 106, 110n3, 158n2,
159, 160, 171–174, 254, 255,
269, 273, 285, 291, 296, 300,
324, 333
Cybernetic, 166, 268

D
Data, 2, 9, 11, 13, 24, 27, 30, 73,
75, 80, 188, 191, 193–195,
193n18, 244, 245, 247, 249,
250, 250n8, 253, 255, 256,
269, 274, 277, 278, 298, 308,
334, 343, 344, 346–350, 357,
358, 360–363, 375, 377, 378,
383, 386
Data mining, 247, 377, 378, 382
Data sets, 27, 347, 349
Democracy/democratic, 2, 7, 9, 30,
42, 46, 156, 158–160, 172,
180–182, 187, 188, 194–196,
208, 208n6, 220, 236, 240,
268, 276, 278, 299, 309, 346,
347, 354, 356, 357, 359, 361,
362, 377
Deterrence, 72, 136
Diaphane/diaphaneity/diaphanous,
4, 33–38, 52, 88, 89n5, 266
Digital/digitization, 9, 11–13, 18,
27, 30, 77, 78, 80, 264, 268,
269, 273–279, 294, 300, 302,
325, 328, 335, 345, 362,
375–388
Disciplinary/discipline, 13, 145,
146, 184, 236, 260, 273,
371–375, 381, 382
Disclosure, 2, 32, 47, 107, 180, 181,
184–190, 184n9, 185n12,
193n18, 194, 212, 219, 345,
361, 386

E
Emancipation, 9, 60, 61, 75, 112,
260–262, 268, 328, 334, 336

Subject Index 405

Enlightenment, 5, 6, 9, 11, 31, 37, 38, 41, 44–47, 87, 133–153, 155, 156, 174, 239, 259–270, 272, 273, 343, 344
Equality, 9, 162, 218n26, 260, 273, 276, 277, 299, 359
Exhibition/exhibitionism/exhibitionist, 10, 124, 125, 273, 309, 310, 313–315, 318, 321, 380, 384, 385
Expository society, 11, 12, 369–379
Exposure, 11, 23, 26, 28, 32, 48, 52, 72, 151, 157, 216n22, 283, 377–380, 384–386, 388

F

Freedom, 1, 46, 62, 64, 112, 114, 124, 156, 186, 204, 211, 215, 215n20, 250, 260, 267, 268, 271, 278, 279, 287, 345, 359
Free speech, 4, 7, 62–64, 79, 81

G

Gaze, 2, 23, 33–35, 41, 49, 70, 80, 119–121, 126, 140, 140n5, 140n6, 145, 147, 152, 156, 311–313, 315, 317, 372, 373, 379, 380, 382, 384
God, 5, 86, 91, 109, 110, 114, 121, 123, 127, 128, 134, 140, 140n5, 142, 144, 145, 147–152, 263
Governance, 24, 29, 30, 156, 209, 260
Governmentality, 8, 27, 243–256, 374n3

I

Immediacy, 36, 38, 53, 68, 128, 217
Information, 3, 7, 9, 17, 22, 23, 41, 44, 74, 75, 80, 81, 87, 156, 157, 159, 174, 179–182, 184–192, 185n12, 187n14, 193n18, 194–196, 204–206, 208–212, 209n9, 209n10, 212n11, 212n15, 215–217, 220, 227, 249, 250, 264, 268, 269, 277, 279, 298, 299, 301, 302, 349, 350, 357, 358, 360, 360n2, 377, 378, 382, 383, 385–388
Interaction, 27, 43, 47, 48, 70, 190, 246, 250, 308, 378
Internalization, 40, 72, 73, 80–81, 146, 374
Internet, 10, 18, 27, 184, 264, 307–310, 313, 328, 337, 377, 378, 383, 384, 387
Intimacy, 115, 122, 262, 284, 286–291, 296, 297, 299, 310, 313, 325
Invisibility, 8, 10, 37, 73, 74, 77, 109, 110, 121, 126, 134, 141, 143, 145, 150, 151, 246, 309, 314, 316, 318, 325, 357, 373, 382

L

Legitimacy/legitimation, 8, 40, 75, 117, 160, 161, 214, 229–237, 239, 240, 248, 249, 291, 300, 301, 359, 360

406   Subject Index

M

Mediation, 36, 161, 169, 267, 272, 274, 294, 330, 361
Medium, 5, 9, 33–38, 49, 88, 89, 91, 94, 95, 116, 158, 259, 260, 264–267, 328, 330, 348, 380

N

Narcissism/narcissistic, 10, 11, 47, 48, 273, 274, 324–326
Neoliberal, 157, 173, 301, 302, 334, 360, 361, 374, 375
Network, 9, 29, 174, 264, 268, 274–276, 278–280, 328, 329, 333, 356, 362, 377, 384
Neutrality, 9, 30, 36, 38, 47, 52, 163, 259, 266, 268, 285, 355

O

Obfuscation, 9, 11, 28, 263, 292, 344, 355
Objectivity, 38, 247–249, 285
Opacity/opaque, 1–13, 28, 80, 100, 102, 121, 126, 140n6, 157–159, 170, 172, 174, 175, 216–218, 262, 266–271, 288, 317, 332–336, 339, 343, 345, 346, 379–383

P

Panopticon, 3, 6, 10, 12, 40, 61, 69–74, 76, 77, 80, 133–153, 155, 159, 369–379
Parrhesia, 4, 62–67, 71, 72, 74, 79, 81

Participation, 29, 41, 44, 156, 181, 183, 187, 187n14, 211, 215n20, 260, 264, 265, 268, 269, 271, 274–279, 284, 301, 302, 319, 336, 339, 346, 356, 361, 379, 388
Perversion, 10, 78, 79, 296, 297, 310–315, 318, 319
Plurality, 47–53, 57, 330, 332
Power, 2, 4, 12, 17, 32, 40, 46, 48, 59, 61, 64, 71, 77, 95, 112, 113, 124, 134, 141–143, 155, 156, 158, 161, 169, 172, 174, 180, 182, 210, 214, 215, 215n20, 217, 218n27, 235, 249, 250, 255, 256, 260, 263, 267, 268, 278, 301, 327, 332, 336, 337, 345, 351–353, 369, 370, 372–375, 377, 378, 380, 382, 384–386
Prison, 6, 72, 134, 140, 145, 146, 152, 155, 369, 370, 372, 384
Privacy, 1, 7, 10, 47, 48, 110, 111n4, 118, 159, 188, 190, 204, 244, 250, 262–264, 283–302, 313, 320
Privatization, 9, 53, 111, 283–303
Public, 2, 16, 21, 63, 92, 110, 156, 180, 203, 225, 244, 260, 284, 324, 344, 387
Publication, 6, 30, 31, 162, 208, 231, 263–265, 269, 345, 372, 375
Public eye, 2, 24, 139, 216n22
Publicity, 7, 8, 39–41, 44, 122n9, 129, 180, 203–221, 244, 246, 278, 344, 345, 345n1

Subject Index

Public life, 9, 29, 209, 210, 225, 269, 284
Public realm, 286, 287, 289, 291–293, 298, 299, 359
Public sphere, 9, 41, 63, 66, 79, 239, 260, 276, 286, 289, 291–294, 296, 299–302, 354, 357

R

Reality, 8, 10, 24, 45, 47, 49, 92, 99, 100n19, 100n20, 101, 122, 172, 213, 238, 240, 244–246, 251–253, 252n10, 275, 290, 291, 297, 302, 307–310, 312, 314, 318, 320, 324, 352, 355, 356
Regulation, 2, 7, 8, 44, 156, 179, 181–187, 189–192, 196, 220, 225–240, 294, 360, 375, 383
Representation/representative, 65, 78, 93, 96, 107, 122, 159, 161, 163–165, 163n3, 171–174, 194–196, 210, 214, 215n20, 218, 232, 234, 235, 267, 294, 319, 325, 346, 361
Ritual, 8, 42, 111, 225–240, 309

S

Secrecy/secret, 1, 12, 13, 15–18, 23, 24, 32, 39, 74, 75, 90, 97, 97n14, 111, 124, 144, 158, 180, 188, 204, 206, 208, 214, 216, 217, 218n27, 261, 283, 284, 288, 312, 314, 317, 344, 346, 348, 351, 352, 358, 360

Security, 12, 23, 27, 73, 188, 227, 346, 358, 374, 375, 378, 382, 384, 386
Selfie, 3, 10, 11, 48, 323–339, 378, 381, 385
Self-knowledge, 4, 41, 69, 80, 128
Self-transparency, 12, 13, 80, 158, 172
Social media, 13, 47, 73, 76, 79–81, 274, 277, 307, 321, 325, 328, 337, 350, 356, 382, 387, 388
Spectacle, 37, 92, 93n7, 95, 171, 218n26, 238, 321, 327, 356, 370–372, 375, 377, 378, 384, 385
Subjectivation/subjectivity, 10, 12, 30, 40, 48, 57–81, 128, 162, 173, 174, 245, 247–250, 252–254, 256, 260, 279, 285, 294, 296, 300–302, 307–321, 323–339, 360, 361, 363, 373, 378, 386, 388
Surveillance, 1, 2, 9–13, 17, 23, 24, 26, 40, 48, 52, 71–75, 111, 134, 141, 147, 153, 182, 185, 212, 214, 218, 236, 270, 283, 299, 300, 303, 316, 318, 321, 355, 371–375, 377, 378, 383–386

T

Technocracy/technocratic, 11, 226, 343, 344, 348, 357–363
Transparency International, 74
Trust, 8, 9, 28, 46, 47, 156, 181, 183, 193, 193n18, 225–234, 239, 264, 271, 275, 280, 293, 313

V

Visibility, 10, 11, 48, 68, 70, 72, 77, 126, 142, 155, 214, 215, 218, 219, 219n29, 244, 271, 274, 307, 309–311, 314–316, 318, 320, 321, 333, 336, 344, 358–360, 372–374, 381

W

Wikileaks, 2, 12, 15, 17, 18, 23, 45, 74